GILBERT



# Estate and Gift Taxation

**VADA WATERS LINDSEY**
*Professor of Law*
*Marquette University Law School*

Seventeenth Edition

GILBERT

860 Blue Gentian Road, Suite 350
Eagan, MN 55121
1-877-888-1330



Printed in the United States of America

**ISBN:** 978-1-62810-553-7

# Summary of Contents

# Capsule Summary

## I. INTRODUCTION

### A. THE ESTATE TAX

The present estate tax was enacted in 1916 for the purpose of limiting the dynastic accumulation of wealth and is a tax upon the ***transfer of property***, not upon the property itself.

### B. THE GIFT TAX

Enacted in 1932, the present gift tax acts ***to prevent estate tax avoidance*** and is also imposed on the transfer of property.

### C. COORDINATION OF THE FEDERAL ESTATE AND GIFT TAXES

The Tax Reform Act of 1976 ***unified*** the computational, although not the substantive, aspects of the two transfer taxes so that generally the tax will be the same whether property is transferred during life or upon death.

### D. THE GENERATION-SKIPPING TRANSFER TAX

First introduced in 1976, this separate transfer tax was intended ***to prevent tax avoidance*** by giving successive life estates. Because of its complexity, application of the tax was continuously deferred and eventually repealed retroactively by provisions of the Tax Reform Act of 1986, which substituted a new generation-skipping tax currently in force. The tax is computed at a ***flat rate of 40%***.

### E. TAXING JURISDICTION

Jurisdictional bases for the taxes are citizenship, residence, and location of the property. As to ***citizens and residents***, taxes reach ***all property*** transferred without regard to location. In the case of ***nonresident aliens***, however, tax exposure is ***dependent upon location*** of the property within the United States.

### F. PORTABILITY OF THE DECEASED SPOUSAL EXCLUSION AMOUNT ("PORTABILITY)"

In 2010, Congress temporarily permitted a ***decedent's executor*** to make an ***election*** which allowed a surviving spouse to use the ***decedent's unused applicable exclusion*** *amount* of the ***last deceased spouse***. This is known as portability. The portability election was ***made permanent*** in 2012.

### G. THE TAX CUTS AND JOBS ACT

Congress enacted the Tax Cuts and Jobs Act in 2017. The Act ***temporarily doubled the basic exclusion amount*** to $10,000,000 for the estate and gift taxes and the generation-skipping transfer tax. This amount is adjusted for inflation. The Act sunsets after December 31, 2025. Hence, the basic exclusion amount will revert to $5,000,000 on January 1, 2026.

## II. SUBSTANTIVE ASPECTS OF THE ESTATE TAX

### A. GROSS ESTATE

#### 1. Inclusions in Gross Estate

I.R.C. §§ 2033–2046 set forth the types of property and property transfers includible in the gross estate.

#### 2. Section 2033—Property Owned by Decedent

***All property owned*** by the decedent at death that is transferred to another on account of the decedent's death is ***included*** in the decedent's gross estate.

##### a. Transfers Taxed

Taxable transfers include not only transfers by will or intestacy, but also by some other arrangement whereby decedent has effectively directed property that he owns to another as a result of his death.

###### (1) Limitations—"Ownership" Interest "Transferred" to Another

The decedent must own property at death, and it must be transferred to another. The fact that death is merely the occasion by which a property right arises in another is not enough (e.g., a posthumous, discretionary bonus paid by a decedent's employer to the decedent's family is not included in the decedent's estate because the decedent had no right to the bonus at death).

##### b. Types of Property Subject to Tax

All types of property are subject to the tax—real and personal, tangible and intangible, including:

**(1)** Debts cancelled by will;

**(2)** Choses in action that survive the decedent;

**(3)** Income from income-producing property up to the date of decedent's death;

**(4)** Present value of rights to future income;

**(5)** Post-death payment from decedent's business if made in liquidation of his interest in the business (but not post-death profits); and

**(6)** Employment benefits payable upon death pursuant to a bargained for employment contract.

##### c. Types of Interests Subject to Tax

All types of interests are subject to tax—present, future, vested, and contingent. However, the interest ***must be devisable or inheritable***, and it must be transferred from the decedent to another.

###### (1) Life Estates and Analogous Interests

Interests that terminate on decedent's death, such as a life estate granted to a decedent by another or a remainder contingent upon the decedent's survival, are not "devisable or inheritable" and thus not taxable.

##### d. Nature of Ownership Required for Tax

A decedent must have beneficial ownership. The estate tax does not reach bare legal title.

(1) "Substantial Ownership" Doctrine

This doctrine has not been applied to the estate tax. But those situations where it might be used have been accounted for by specific estate tax provisions.

e. **Relationship Between Section 2033 and Other Taxing Provisions**

Although not taxable as property owned by the decedent, the gross estate includes certain lifetime transfers by a decedent that have a "testamentary" character and certain types of property interests that "pass" from the decedent to a beneficiary at the decedent's death even though there may not be a "transfer" by decedent under technical property law. [I.R.C. §§ 2035–2042] As a general rule, the ***specific taxing provisions take precedence over section 2033*** (the general taxing provision). However, specific taxing provisions take precedence only to the extent that the type of transfer or type of property they address is the one intended to be covered by the specific provision.

f. **Impact of State Law**

State property law affects the federal estate tax law insofar as it defines the interests and rights a decedent has with respect to property. However, federal estate tax law determines whether the type of interest or right owned and transferred by decedent is taxable.

(1) **Determination of State Law**

In determining the nature of a decedent's interest in property under state property law, federal courts are ***bound only by state statutes or the decisions of the highest court of the state***.

3. **Section 2034—Dower or Curtesy Interests**

The interest of a decedent's surviving spouse in the decedent's property arising from state dower, curtesy, or statutory "forced share" rights is subject to the estate tax.

a. **No Deduction for Marital Interests**

Property owned at death by a decedent is included at its full value, without a reduction for the surviving spouse's marital interests therein.

b. **Distinguish—Community Property Rights**

The vested one-half interest of a surviving spouse in community property is not included in a decedent's gross estate.

c. **Effect of Marital Deduction**

The marital deduction [I.R.C. §2056] operates to remove from the taxable estate most of the property included under section 2034.

4. **Section 2035—Gifts Made Within Three Years of Death**

a. **Background**

(1) **Former Tax on Transfers in Contemplation of Death**

Prior to 1977, transfers within three years of death were included in a decedent's gross estate only if made ***"in contemplation of death"*** (i.e., operative element of the tax was the decedent's subjective intent).

(2) **1976 Tax Reform Act**

The effect of the 1976 Act was to reduce substantially the need to include deathbed gifts in a decedent's gross estate, since such gifts would be taxed when made and added to the estate tax base to determine the estate tax.

(3) **1981 Tax Act**

The Act eliminates most outright gifts from inclusion in the decedent's gross estate.

(a) **Continued Major Impact of Section 2035**

Any gift taxes paid or payable with respect to gifts made within three years of a decedent's death are included in the gross estate. Also, as noted below, section 2035 interacts with sections 2036, 2037, 2038, and 2042 so as to include property in a decedent's gross estate under its express language. Section 2041 continues to interact with section 2035 by virtue of section 2041(a)(1)(B) and (a)(2).

b. **Relation Between Section 2035 and Other Taxing Sections**

Section 2035 interacts with other specific taxing sections to produce a tax under those sections if a taxable interest or incident of ownership is transferred, released, or relinquished ***within three years of death***. In such cases, there is ordinarily included in the gross estate the same amount that would have been included had the transfer or relinquishment not taken place.

(1) **Limitation—Coextensive Interaction**

The substantive provisions of both section 2035 and the specific taxing section must apply.

(2) **Exception to Interaction**

There is no interaction with section 2040. If joint tenancy property is transferred or severed within three years of death, only the value of any interest retained by the decedent is taxed.

(3) **Exception—Grantor Trusts Under Section 676**

Any transfer from a portion of a trust that is revocable and taxed to the grantor of the trust under section 676 is treated as being transferred by the grantor and not from the trust, thereby making section 2035 inapplicable.

5. **Section 2036—Transfers with Retained Life Interests**

If decedent makes an inter vivos transfer but retains either a life interest in the property or a power to designate enjoyment of the property during life, the full value of the property transferred is included in the gross estate. Section 2036 is ***inapplicable where there is a bona fide sale for an adequate and full consideration in money or money's worth***. Substance over form principles apply in determining whether there is an actual bona fide sale.

a. **Requirement of a transfer**

Property in which decedent has a life estate or power to affect enjoyment must have been "transferred" by the decedent during the decedent's life in order to be taxable under section 2036. "Transfer" includes indirect as well as direct transfers.

(1) **Reciprocal Trust Doctrine**

If A and B transfer equal amounts on separate irrevocable trusts and A provides that B should enjoy the income for life with remainder to B's issue, and B provides for income to A for life, remainder to A's issue, A is treated as the actual settlor of the B trust, and B is treated as the actual settlor of the A trust. Consequently, on A's death, the value of the B trust is included in A's gross estate (a transfer with a retained life interest).

(2) **Time of Transfer**

Section 2036 is limited to transfers made on or after March 3, 1931.

(a) **Outright Gifts and Gifts on Irrevocable Trust**

A transfer ordinarily occurs when title passes from the transferor.

(b) **Gifts on Revocable Trusts**

Courts are split as to the creation of a revocable trust. Some hold the transfer occurs when property is transferred to the trustee; others hold there is no transfer until the power to revoke lapses or is released.

(c) **Additions to Trust**

Additions to a trust created prior to March 3, 1931, may result in proportionate taxation.

b. **Requirement That Interest or Power Be Retained**

Section 2036 tax attaches ***only*** if the transferor retained a requisite interest or power.

(1) **Subsequent Reconveyance**

Ordinarily, section 2036 does not apply where the decedent reacquires an interest after the transfer. However, the interest is treated as having been retained if the donee's subsequent reconveyance was prearranged.

(2) **Limitation**

A retained interest or power must be in the very property transferred. Thus, transfers in return for the transferee's promise to pay an annuity to the transferor are treated as the purchase of an annuity (not a reservation of a life estate).

c. **Time Periods**

The retained interest or power must be retained for the decedent's life, for a period that cannot be determined without reference to the decedent's death, or for a period that does not end before the decedent's death.

d. **Nature of Interest Retained Under Section 2036(a)(1)**

The requisite interest for taxation is defined as either ***"possession or enjoyment of the property"*** or the ***"right to income from the property."***

(1) **Possession or Enjoyment**

A legally enforceable right to "possession and enjoyment" or "right to income" is not required, but the mere fact of possession is not enough; there ***must be an understanding or agreement*** (can be inferred from possession in certain cases).

(2) **Right to Income**

Similarly, receipt of income must be pursuant to an "understanding," but such an understanding need not be a legally enforceable obligation as long as it has been performed. An understanding can be inferred from the fact of continued receipt.

(a) **Indirect Beneficial Interests**

"Right to income" may be found whenever income is to be used for the benefit of the transferor during life (e.g., to discharge the transferor's legal obligations).

(b) **Discretionary Trusts**

The trustee's discretionary power to use trust income for the transferor's benefit will not invoke the tax, as long as the transferor is not a trustee and cannot otherwise compel use of trust property or income for his benefit.

d. **Nature of the Power Retained Under Section 2036(a)(2)**

The requisite power is defined as "the right, ***either alone or in conjunction*** with any person, to designate the persons who shall possess or enjoy the property or the income therefrom."

(1) **Power Must Affect Beneficial Enjoyment or Possession**

Section 2036(a)(2) applies ***only*** where the power affects the enjoyment of the income or possession of the property. It ***does not apply*** where the decedent retains only the power to change the beneficiary of the remainder.

(2) **Beneficial Power Not Required**

The power need not be exercisable in the transferor's favor. But nonbeneficial ***powers must be discretionary***; nonbeneficial powers governed by an ***"ascertainable standard"*** are mandatory and thus outside the scope of this section.

(3) **Form of the Power**

Any power that has the effect of designating or shifting enjoyment during the transferor's lifetime qualifies (e.g., transferor's power to direct accumulation of trust income or to invade corpus for the benefit of the income beneficiary).

(4) **Power to Affect Possession or Enjoyment**

Property is includible under section 2036(a)(2) where the decedent retained the power to affect the time and manner of a beneficiary's possession and enjoyment. But a power to affect only post-death enjoyment (e.g., power is exercisable only by will) is not taxable under section 2036 (but will be included under section 2038).

(5) **Administrative Powers**

Purely administrative powers are generally ***not taxable*** because not dispositive or distributive.

(a) **Former Rule—Section 2036 Inapplicable**

Prior to the 1976 Tax Reform Act, mere retention of voting control over shares of a closely held corporation transferred on trust was not considered a "power to designate," and hence did not result in taxation of the shares in the transferor's estate. [**United States v. Byrum**]

(b) **"Anti-*Byrum*" Amendment**

An "anti-*Byrum*" amendment was added to the Code in 1978. Under section 2036(b), a person will be considered to have retained the "enjoyment" of stock transferred during life, and the stock will be included in her estate, if the donor ***retains the right to vote the transferred shares*** and, if at any time within three years of her death, the donor ***"controls" the corporation*** whose shares were given away.

(6) **In Whom Power Vested?**

If the power is a beneficial one, it will usually result in taxation whether possessed by the decedent or by another. However, if the power is (i) ***purely discretionary***, (ii) ***exercisable solely*** by another person, and (iii) the decedent had ***no right or power to compel*** its exercise in his favor, there will be no tax under section 2036.

e. **Amount Includible**

The amount included in the gross estate is the ***full value of the property*** subject to the retained interest or power, determined as of the date of decedent's death (or at the alternate valuation date). Where the retained right relates only to a portion of the property, only that portion is taxed.

(1) **Intervening Estate**

If the retained right is subject to an intervening life estate that cannot be affected by the interest or power, the amount taxable is reduced by the value of the intervening estate.

(2) **Power to Accumulate Income**

If decedent retained the power to direct the accumulation of income, both the property and the accumulated income it produces are taxed.

f. **Relinquishment or Transfer of Retained Interest or Power Within Three Years of Death**

The entire property will be included in the decedent's gross estate under section 2035 if the decedent relinquishes a retained interest or power will within three years of death.

6. **Section 2037—Transfers Taking Effect at Death**

A lifetime gift is included in the donor's gross estate if (i) the transferee's possession and enjoyment of the property is ***contingent upon surviving the transferor***, and (ii) the transferor retained a ***reversionary interest*** in the property valued at ***more than 5% of the value*** of the property (at the time of the transferor's death). Section 2037 is inapplicable to "a bona fide sale for an adequate and full consideration in money or money's worth."

a. **Lifetime Transfer**

The transferor must transfer property during life.

b. **Survivorship Requirement**

A transferee's possession and enjoyment (not "title") must be contingent ***solely*** on surviving the transferor.

(1) **Effect of Alternative Event**

Section 2037 is inapplicable if the beneficiary can take upon the happening of some alternative event (unless that event is so extreme as to be "unreal").

c. **Reversionary Interest Requirement**

The reversionary interest requirement is met where there is any possibility that the property transferred may return to the transferor, or the transferor's estate, or be subject to a power of disposition by the transferor.

(1) **Exceptions**

A mere expectancy is not a "reversionary interest," nor is a right to receive or dispose of only the income from the transferred property. And a third party's purely discretionary power to distribute all or a part of the property to the transferor will not give rise to the tax.

(2) **Joint Powers**

Such powers are outside the scope of section 2037.

(3) **Express Terms vs. Operation of Law**

For post-October 7, 1949, transfers, it is sufficient if the reversionary interest arises either by express terms of the instrument of transfer or by operation of law, but with respect to pre-October 8, 1949, transfers, the reversionary interest must arise by the express terms of the instrument.

d. **De Minimis Rule**

The reversionary interest must exceed 5% of the value of the property transferred. Value is determined as of the time immediately before the decedent-transferor's death, utilizing standard actuarial and mortality tables.

e. **The "Negative" Requirement—Power of Appointment in Another**

Section 2037 will not apply if, at the time of decedent's death, some other person possesses a taxable power to appoint the property away from decedent to a beneficiary of the present transfer.

(1) **Must be a taxable power**

A "taxable power" means one that would result in taxation of the property in the holder's estate under this section.

f. **Amount Taxable**

Only the value of the interest that is dependent on survivorship is included in decedent's gross estate.

7. **Section 2038—Revocable Transfers**

Transfers wherein the decedent possesses, at death, a ***power to alter, amend, revoke, or terminate, either alone or in conjunction with any other person***, are includible under section 2038. Section 2038 is inapplicable to "a bona fide sale for an adequate and full consideration in money or money's worth."

a. **Requirement of a Transfer**

The property must have been transferred by the decedent during the decedent's lifetime.

### b. Power Must Be Exercisable at Death

The requisite power must be exercisable by the decedent, or by the decedent and another, at the time of the decedent's death.

#### (1) Contingent Powers

A contingent power will not result in inclusion under section 2038 where the ***contingency is outside the decedent's control*** and has not occurred at the time of the decedent's death. But such a power may support taxation under section 2036.

#### (2) By Whom Is the Power Exercisable?

Joint as well as individual powers are taxable under section 2038, and it is ***irrelevant that the co-holder of the power is an adverse party***.

#### (3) Indirect Access to Power Sufficient

Although a decedent may not technically possess a power, section 2038 is applicable if the decedent can compel the exercise of a taxable power by another.

#### (4) Source of the Power

As to transfers made after June 22, 1936, it is immaterial whether the decedent retains the power as long as it is exercisable at death.

### c. Nature of the Taxable Power

Taxable powers under section 2038 include not only powers to revoke a transfer but also powers to alter beneficial enjoyment and to affect the time and manner of a beneficiary's enjoyment. The power must be discretionary because ***purely administrative powers are not taxable***.

#### (1) Power to Revoke

This includes any power under which the decedent had the right to repossess the property transferred, directly or indirectly (e.g., a spouse's right under community property law to set aside improper gift).

#### (2) Power to Terminate

This covers any power to end a trust and cause a distribution of trust property before expiration of the specified term. A power to accelerate the time of enjoyment of the trust property is also a taxable power of termination.

#### (3) Power to Alter or Amend

This refers to ***any discretionary power***, the exercise of which will affect beneficial enjoyment of the transferred property (e.g., power to direct accumulation or distribution of income to substitute or add new beneficiaries).

### d. Amount Taxable

Only the value of the interest subject to the taxable power is includible under section 2038.

### e. Relationship to Section 2036(a)(2)

There is considerable overlap in the taxing scope of sections 2036 and 2038; but there are also a number of differences. Principal differences concern the time the transfer is made, the source of the taxable power, powers to control enjoyment of the property after the decedent's death, contingent powers, and the amount includible.

**f. Relationship to Section 2035**

Sections 2035 and 2038 specifically provide for taxation when a power to alter, amend, revoke, or terminate is relinquished during the three-year period ending on the decedent's death. Furthermore, any transfer from a portion of a trust that is revocable and taxed to the grantor of the trust under section 676 is treated as being transferred by the grantor and not from the trust, thereby making section 2035 inapplicable.

**g. Relationship to Section 2037**

Section 2038 also overlaps with the tax on transfers "taking effect at death" under section 2037.

**8. Section 2039—Annuities**

A surviving beneficiary's interest in an annuity contract or analogous type of arrangement entered into after March 3, 1931, is taxable to the estate of the decedent if (i) the ***beneficiary's interest is receivable by reason of surviving the decedent,*** and (ii) the ***decedent was receiving***, or had a right to receive, payments under the contract or arrangement.

**a. Nature of Survivor's Interest**

A beneficiary's interest is not limited to typical annuity-type payments, but benefits in the nature of life insurance proceeds are not taxable under section 2039. However, they may be taxable under section 2042. Whether a benefit is life insurance turns on whether a "life insurance risk" exists at the date of the decedent's death.

**(1) Survival of Decedent Requirement**

Benefits must be payable "by reason of surviving the decedent" but need not be conditioned solely on survivorship.

**(2) Nature of Contract**

The contract or arrangement is not limited to a typical annuity-type contract.

**b. Nature of Decedent's Interest**

The decedent must have been receiving, or have had a right to receive, payments under the arrangement, either alone or in conjunction with another, for life or for any period not ascertainable without reference to death or for any period which does not in fact end before death.

**(1) Decedent's Interest in the Contract**

Payments under a plan that is technically separate from the survivor's benefits plan will qualify if the separate arrangements form an integrated plan.

**(2) Annuity or Other Payment**

Although the decedent's interest does not need to be in the form of an annuity, compensation that the decedent was receiving, or was entitled to receive, at the time of death is excluded because section 2039 is limited to post-employment benefits.

(3) **Right to Receive**

If the decedent has received everything the decedent is entitled to receive under the plan, survivor benefits pursuant thereto are not taxed under this section.

c. **Amount Includible**

The amount included in the decedent's gross estate is the value of the survivor's benefit that is ***proportionate to contributions*** made by the decedent or the decedent's employer.

9. **Section 2040—Joint Interests**

In general, co-tenancies with right of survivorship are included in the gross estate of the first joint tenant to die. Tenancies in common and community property are not taxable under section 2040; rather, they are included under section 2033.

a. **General Rule of Inclusion**

Section 2040 includes the ***full value of the property except the amount proportionate to the surviving joint tenant's original contribution*** to the acquisition of the property.

b. **Required Nature of Survivor's Contribution**

Only those amounts that did not originally belong to the decedent and that were not transferred from the decedent to the survivor for less than full and adequate consideration in money or money's worth (e.g., gifts) may be attributed to the survivor as an "original contribution."

(1) **Income from Donated Property**

Income derived from donated property is treated as originating with the donee-survivor.

(2) **Post-Gift Appreciation**

Profits attributable to post-gift appreciation in value of the donated property may constitute an original contribution by the donee-survivor.

(a) **Exceptions**

There is no exclusion from the decedent's estate where the same property is reconveyed in joint tenancy or where there is a reinvestment of joint tenancy property.

(3) **Assumption of Mortgage**

If the survivor jointly assumed a mortgage with the decedent in connection with the acquisition of the joint tenancy property, the ***survivor's proportionate obligation under the mortgage is treated as an original contribution***.

(4) **Burden of Proof**

The decedent's estate has the burden of proving what part of the property was contributed by the survivor.

c. **Relationship to Other Taxing Sections**

Section 2040 generally does not interact with other specific estate tax sections; rather, it ordinarily supersedes those sections.

(1) **Severance of Joint Tenancy**

Section 2040 tax does not apply where the joint tenancy is severed prior to death. However, if the decedent retains an interest as a tenant in common, that interest will be included in the gross estate under section 2033.

(2) **No Interaction with Section 2035**

If a decedent transfers joint tenancy property within three years of a joint tenant's death, the property will not be included under section 2035.

d. **Qualified Joint Interests**

Under section 2040(b), if a ***qualified joint interest*** exists (i.e., property held by the decedent and the decedent's spouse as tenants by the entirety or joint tenants with right of survivorship), ***only one-half of the value of the property is includible*** in the gross estate of the first to die, without regard as to which co-tenant furnished the consideration at the time of the joint tenancy's creation. If the spouses own the property as joint tenants with another person, it is not a qualified joint interest.

e. **Distinguish—Community Property**

Although community property represents a form of concurrent ownership, section 2040 is inapplicable. Because each spouse owns a vested interest in one-half of the community property, one-half of the community property is included in the estate of each spouse under section 2033.

10. **Section 2041—Powers of Appointment**

Property subject to a general power of appointment created on or before October 21, 1942, is included in the gross estate of the holder of the power if the power is exercised. And, where the general power was created after October 21, 1942, the property subject to the power is included in the holder's gross estate, whether the power is exercised or not.

a. **Nature of the Taxable Power of Appointment**

Section 2041 is limited to general powers of appointment.

(1) **Definition of "General Power of Appointment"**

A general power is a power that is exercisable during life or by will in favor of ***the holder, the holder's estate, the holder's creditors, or the creditors of the holder's estate***. However, an ***exception*** is made for powers to invade or appropriate property for the benefit of the holder that are limited by an ***ascertainable standard relating to health, education, support, or maintenance***.

(2) **Form of the Power**

The power need not be in any particular form, and the capacity in which it is exercisable is immaterial. Similarly, the power need not technically lie with the decedent (e.g., the decedent is deemed to possess a general power if the decedent can compel exercise for the decedent's benefit).

(3) **Limited to Donated Powers**

The tax only applies to donated powers from a third party. However, reserved powers are taxable, if at all, under sections 2036 through 2038.

(4) **Direct or Indirect Benefit**

A general power exists where property may be appointed directly or indirectly for the decedent's benefit. For example, a decedent has a general power where the decedent can appoint property to a trust in which the decedent is beneficiary.

(5) **Special (Nongeneral) Powers Distinguished**

All powers which are not general are "special" or "nongeneral" and are outside the scope of section 2041.

b. **Preexisting Powers—Special Rules**

Powers ***created on or before October 21, 1942***, are includible under section 2041 ***only if exercised***. This would include powers exercised by will or powers exercised during life if the property subject to the power would have been included in the holder's gross estate under sections 2035 through 2038 had that property been transferred by the decedent.

(1) **Lapse or Release**

Lapse or release of the power is not an exercise and will not support the tax under section 2041.

(2) **Joint Powers**

A preexisting power granted jointly to the decedent and another person is not taxable.

c. **Post-1942 Powers—Special Rules**

General powers created ***after October 21, 1942***, are includible under section 2041 ***whether or not exercised***. However, the power must be exercisable at the date of the holder's death; thus, a power that is subject to a contingency beyond the holder's control and that has not occurred at date of death is not a taxable power of appointment.

(1) **Lapse or Release**

A release of a post-1942 power is subject to tax under section 2041. A ***"lapse"*** during a calendar year is ***treated as a release*** to the extent that the property that the holder can appoint exceeds of the ***greater of $5,000 or 5%*** of the value of the property subject to the power.

(2) **Joint Powers**

Post-1942 joint powers are taxable unless the co-holder is the donor of the power or an adverse party. A permissible appointee is not considered an adverse party. However, if a joint holder is a permissible appointee, only a proportionate amount of the value of the property subject to the power is included in the decedent's gross estate.

11. **Section 2042—Life Insurance**

Proceeds of life insurance on decedent's life are included in the gross estate if: (i) ***payable to, or for the benefit of, the estate***, or (ii) payable to some other beneficiary and the decedent possessed ***"incidents of ownership"*** in the policy at the time of death.

### a. What Constitutes Life Insurance?

For insurance contracts written after December 31, 1984, the contract must be a life insurance contract under applicable state law, and it must meet three additional tests: (i) the ***cash value*** cannot exceed the net single premium cost for the coverage provided; (ii) the ***premiums paid*** cannot exceed a "guideline premium limitation"; and (iii) the ***death benefit*** must fall within the "cash value corridor." If the contract meets the applicable state law definition but does not meet all of the three additional requirements, the excess of the death benefit over the cash surrender value is deemed to be life insurance for purposes of the estate and gift tax.

### b. Proceeds Payable to Insured's Estate

This includes all proceeds payable to the decedent's estate or executor and proceeds payable to some other beneficiary if that beneficiary is legally bound to use the proceeds to discharge obligations of the insured's estate.

### c. Proceeds Payable to Other Beneficiaries

Proceeds not payable to, or for the benefit of, the insured's estate are taxable only if the decedent-insured possessed incidents of ownership in the policy at the time of death.

#### (1) "Incidents of Ownership"

This includes any right or interest in the policy, whereby the insured has the power to control the existence of the policy, to rearrange the economic interests therein, or to affect the benefits payable thereunder.

##### (a) Examples

Incidents of ownership include the right to cancel the policy, borrow against the policy, change the beneficiary designations (including contingent beneficiaries), and affect the time and manner of enjoyment by the selection of settlement options.

##### (b) Reversionary Interests

The Code specifically provides that a reversionary interest is an incident of ownership if the value of the interest exceeds 5% of the value of the policy immediately prior to the insured's death.

#### (2) "Possession" of Incidents of Ownership

The decedent-insured need not have retained incidents of ownership; it is sufficient if these incidents are possessed and exercisable by the decedent at the time of death (but inability to exercise is immaterial unless the court considers economic interest).

##### (a) Joint Powers Taxable

Taxation is not affected by the fact that concurrence of an adverse party may be required for exercise.

##### (b) Indirect Possession

The decedent will be deemed to "possess" incidents of ownership where the incidents are exercisable indirectly as trustee, by virtue of a controlling interest in a closely held corporation, or as a partner.

(c) **Buy-Sell Agreements**

Owners of closely held businesses frequently enter into buy-sell agreements and fund these agreements with life insurance. With an entity purchase agreement, the business holds the incidents of ownership. With a cross purchase agreement, co-owners take out insurance on the other co-owners' lives. The co-owner who takes out the policy owns the incidents of ownership.

d. **Assignment of Incidents of Ownership**

Proceeds remain taxable to the decedent if the transfer was made under circumstances that would result in inclusion under sections 2035 through 2038.

e. **Amount Includible**

In general, the entire value of the proceeds is included under section 2042.

f. **Life Insurance and Community Property States**

An insurance policy is a community asset if purchased with community property.

(1) **Insured Dies First**

If the insured dies first, one-half the proceeds is taxable in the insured's estate.

(2) **Spouse Dies First**

If the spouse dies first, that spouse's one-half interest in the present value of the insurance is includible under section 2033. Upon the insured's death, all proceeds attributable to premiums paid by the insured with separate property are included in the insured's gross estate.

12. **Section 2043—Consideration**

The estate tax is imposed only upon gratuitous transfers; transfers for ***"full and adequate consideration in money or money's worth"*** are not taxed.

a. **Partial Consideration**

Where property is transferred for less than adequate consideration, the amount by which the value of the property exceeds the value of the consideration is included in the gross estate.

b. **Measure of consideration**

Consideration that will support a binding contract will not necessarily preclude estate taxation. The consideration must constitute the economic equivalent of the transferred property.

c. **Consideration Must Move to Decedent**

Additionally, the consideration must move to the decedent; an economic detriment suffered by the transferee in consideration of a transfer will not prevent estate tax exposure.

d. **"Business Transaction Exception"**

Even though consideration received for the transfer is not the economic equivalent of the property, if there is a bona fide business reason for such a transfer and ***no intent to make a donative transfer***, the transfer is not subject to tax. Note that donative intent, or lack thereof, is not ordinarily determinative.

e. **Release of Marital Rights**

The statute specifically provides that the release of dower or curtesy, or of similar marital rights, is ***not sufficient consideration*** to preclude estate taxation.

13. **Section 2044—Certain Marital Deduction Property**

Property that qualifies for a marital deduction as ***"qualified terminable interest property" is included in the surviving spouse's estate*** upon the spouse's death unless the spouse disposed of the life estate before death under circumstances where a gift tax would attach.

14. **Section 2045—Prior Interests**

An interest in property, or powers with respect to property, that will produce estate tax exposure will do so without regard to when the particular transfer, interest, right or power was made, created, exercised, etc., unless otherwise specifically provided.

15. **Section 2046—Disclaimers**

Section 2046 incorporates the gift tax rule under section 2518 as to when a disclaimer or renunciation will be effective for estate tax purposes.

## B. ESTATE TAX DEDUCTIONS

### 1. Introductory Analysis

Five deductions are allowed under the estate tax: (i) certain expenses of and claims against the estate; (ii) certain losses; (iii) the charitable deduction; (iv) the marital deduction; and (v) state death taxes.

### 2. Section 2053—Expenses, Indebtedness, and Taxes

A deduction is allowed for expenses of the estate and for various claims against the estate, including debts and taxes owed by decedent.

#### a. Funeral and Administrative Expenses

Deductible expenses include funeral expenses and expenses of administration, including executor's commissions, attorneys' fees, and other necessary expenses such as court costs, accountant's fees, etc.

#### b. Claims Against the Estate

Debts and other claims assertable against the estate are deductible if they are the decedent's legally enforceable obligations that existed at the time of death. Thus, income taxes and gift taxes that accrue prior to death are deductible, but death taxes which arise at or after death are not deductible.

##### (1) Contractual Claims

Claims against the estate that are founded upon a promise or agreement are deductible only if the consideration for the agreement was "full and adequate consideration in money or money's worth."

#### c. Unpaid Mortgages

The amount of any unpaid mortgage is deductible if the full value of the property (undiminished by the mortgage liability) is included in the gross estate.

d. **Limitations**

(1) **Must Be Allowable Under Local Law**

Claims and expenses are deductible only if "allowable by the laws of the jurisdiction under which the estate is being administered."

(2) **No Double Deductions**

If an item of expense could be allowed either as an income tax or estate tax deduction, the executor must make an election—both deductions cannot be taken (except for estate expenses attributable to "deductions in respect of decedent").

3. **Section 2054—Losses**

Deduction for losses is limited to casualty or theft losses that are not compensated by insurance or otherwise.

a. **No Double Deductions**

A loss that might be deductible for income tax and estate tax purposes may be claimed against one or the other tax, but not both.

4. **Section 2055—the Charitable Deduction**

A deduction is allowed for the value of all property transferred by a decedent to certain organizations operated exclusively for religious, scientific, literary, educational, or other charitable purposes.

a. **Limitations on Deductible Amount**

The deduction is limited to the value of the property that passes to the charitable object and that was included in the decedent's gross estate. If the property is burdened with an obligation to pay any death taxes, the deduction is reduced by that amount.

b. **Split Interest Gifts**

Charitable remainder gifts or charitable "lead" gifts must be in the form of a statutorily defined "annuity trust," "unitrust," or "pooled income fund" for the interest of the charitable object to be deductible.

(1) **Limitations**

No deduction is allowed if another noncharitable remainder precedes the charitable remainder or the income interest is for a term of years that exceeds 20 years.

5. **Section 2056—the Marital Deduction**

A deduction is allowed for the value of property passing to the decedent's surviving spouse.

a. **General Scope of Deduction**

(1) **Value of Property Passing to Surviving Spouse**

The deductible amount is limited to the net value of the property that passes to the surviving spouse (i.e., the value of the property reduced by any mortgages or other debts, expenses, and taxes that burden or encumber the property).

(2) **Maximum Allowed**

The value of all property passing to the surviving spouse is deductible as long as it meets the substantive requirements.

(3) **Effect of Community Property**

A bequest of decedent's one-half interest in community property to the surviving spouse qualifies for the marital deduction to the same extent as a bequest of separate property.

b. **Requirements for Marital Deduction**

There are ***five basic requirements*** for the allowance of the marital deduction.

(1) The surviving spouse must have been a ***United States citizen or resident***.

(a) The underlying rationale is to prevent property from escaping estate taxation as a nonresident alien is subject to the tax for property located in the United States.

(b) An exception is allowed for a "qualified domestic trust." The exception requires that at least one trustee to be a citizen or domestic citizen, the trustee withholds tax on a distribution, the executor makes an election to have the trust qualify as a qualified domestic trust, and meet all requirements established by the Treasury Department. Upon the death of the surviving spouse, a tax is imposed on the value of any property remaining in the trust.

(2) The ***property must "pass"*** from the decedent to the surviving spouse.

The passing requirement is met where the surviving spouse receives property from the decedent or the decedent's estate under circumstances where the property transferred is included in the decedent's gross estate.

(3) The property passing to the surviving spouse must have been ***included in the decedent's gross estate***.

(4) Decedent must have been married at the time of death and the spouse must survive the decedent. A decedent spouse in a ***same-sex marriage is entitled to claim the marital deduction*** for transfers made to a surviving spouse.

(5) The interest must be a ***"deductible interest."***

All interests in property passing to the surviving spouse are deductible interests except:

(a) Interests not included in decedent's gross estate;

(b) Interests that would be deductible under section 2053;

(c) Interests in property for which a deduction for losses is allowable; and

(d) Nondeductible terminable interests.

c. **The "Nondeductible Terminable Interest" Rule**

As noted, no deduction is allowed for certain "terminable interests."

(1) **Definition**

A "terminable interest" is an interest in property that will ***terminate or fail upon lapse of time or the happening of some event or contingency***.

(2) **Examples of Terminable Interests**

Examples of terminable interests include life estates, terms for years, and defeasible fees.

(3) **Distinguish—Deductible Terminable Interests**

The marital deduction is allowed for other interests, although they are technically terminable. These include patents, bonds and notes, and estate trusts.

d. **Five Exceptions to "Terminable Interest" Rule**

(1) **Survivorship Exception**

A marital deduction will be allowed even though the surviving spouse's interest is conditioned upon the spouse surviving the decedent for a period of up to six months, or not dying from a common disaster, as long as the spouse does, in fact, survive the conditional period or does not die as a result of a common disaster.

(2) **Life Estate with Power of Appointment Exception**

The marital deduction is allowed if the surviving spouse is entitled to all income from the property (or a specific portion thereof) for life, payable at least annually, and if the surviving spouse is granted a power to appoint the property (or a specific portion thereof) to the surviving spouse or to the surviving spouse's estate, and if this power is exercisable by the surviving spouse alone and in all events.

(3) **Qualified Terminable Interest Property ("QTIP")**

This is property that passes from a decedent, in which the surviving spouse has a qualifying income interest for life, and with respect to which the decedent's executor ***makes an election*** to have the property qualify as a QTIP interest.

(a) **Qualifying Income Interest**

The surviving spouse has a qualifying income interest for life if the surviving spouse is entitled to all of the income from the property (or a specific portion thereof) payable at least annually and no person has a power to appoint any part of the property to anyone other than the surviving spouse (except that the surviving spouse or some other person may be granted a power of appointment if this power is exercisable at or after the surviving spouse's death).

(b) **Effects of Election**

If the QTIP interest qualifies for the marital deduction, the QTIP property is included in the surviving spouse's gross estate. Also, the gift tax will apply if the surviving spouse makes a lifetime transfer of the income interest in QTIP property.

(c) **Partial Elections Permitted**

The executor may elect to qualify all or any portion of the QTIP property for purposes of the marital deduction.

(4) **Insurance Settlement Exception**

The marital deduction is allowed for certain interests passing to the surviving spouse in the proceeds of life insurance, endowment, and annuity contracts where conditions similar to the life estate with power of appointment exception are satisfied.

**(5) Charitable Remainder Trusts**

A marital deduction will be allowed for the value of the income interest passing to a decedent's surviving spouse if the surviving spouse is the only noncharitable beneficiary of a trust that qualifies as a charitable remainder annuity trust or unitrust.

**6. Deduction for State Death Taxes**

Under section 2058, a deduction is allowed for inheritance, legacy, estate, and succession taxes actually paid to any state of the United States, territory, or the District of Columbia.

**a. Limitations**

The state death tax deduction is subject to two principal limitations: (i) a deduction is limited to property subject to both federal and state death taxes; and (ii) the deduction is allowed if the state death taxes are actually paid within a period of four years following the filing of the estate tax return, and the deduction from the gross estate must be claimed within the same four-year period.

# III. SUBSTANTIVE ASPECTS OF THE GIFT TAX

## A. TAXABLE GIFTS

### 1. Four Basic Elements of a Taxable Gift

- **a.** The identity and capacity of donor and donee;
- **b.** Subject matter of the gift;
- **c.** Sufficiency of the transfer that will attract the tax; and
- **d.** Lack of adequate consideration.

### 2. Donor and Donee

**a. Donor**

**(1) Beneficial Owner**

The transfer is taxable to the person or persons who owned a beneficial interest in the property transferred.

**(2) Nonresident Aliens**

Nonresident aliens are only taxed on gifts of property located in the United States, and transfers of intangible property by nonresident aliens are generally not subject to a gift tax at all.

**(3) Identity of Donor**

The tax is imposed on the actual owner and transferor (not simply the nominal transferor).

**b. Donee**

The donee need not be identified or ascertained. A gift to an entity is treated as a gift to persons who own beneficial interests in the entity.

### 3. Subject Matter of the Gift

The gift tax is imposed upon transfers of property.

a. **Property—in General**

The term "property," for gift tax purposes, generally includes any type of interest in property, real or personal, tangible or intangible, and encompasses equitable, future, and contingent interests.

b. **Types of Property Subject to Tax**

(1) **Foreign Real Estate**

If a United States citizen or resident makes a gift of real property located outside of the United States, it is a taxable gift.

(2) **Tax-Exempt Securities**

A gift of tax-exempt government bonds or securities is subject to gift taxation even though these bonds or securities are exempt from income taxation.

(3) **Debts**

Forgiveness of a debt and payment of the debts of another are taxable as gifts. A gratuitous transfer of the donor's own note or check is not taxable until the donee cashes the check or collects the note.

(4) **Promise to Transfer Property in the Future**

Assumption of a legal obligation to transfer property in the future is a taxable gift.

(5) **Gifts of Income**

A gratuitous transfer of a right to receive income from property is a taxable gift.

(6) **Annuities**

In general, the transfer of an annuity or the irrevocable designation of the beneficiary of an annuity is a taxable gift of the value of the contract or benefits.

(7) **Disposition of Life Estate in QTIP Property**

If the spouse disposes of the life interest during the spouse's lifetime, the spouse will be treated as having made a gift of the full value of the property to which the interest relates, not just the life interest itself.

c. **Performance of Personal Services**

The gratuitous performance of services for another is not subject to the gift tax.

d. **Right to Use Property**

Most authorities had held that allowing another to use money or property without paying interest or rent does not result in a taxable gift. However, the Supreme Court has held that an interest-free loan can be a taxable gift of the reasonable value of the use of the money lent.

4. **Sufficiency of Transfer**

While no specific form of transfer is required, property owned by the donor must be irrevocably transferred to the donee for the gift tax to attach.

a. **Form of Transfer**

(1) **Direct and Indirect Gifts**

Taxable gifts may be made directly or indirectly. Thus, if A transfers property worth $20,000 to B on condition that B transfer property worth $5,000 to C, A has made two taxable gifts: a gift of $15,000 to B and a gift of $5,000 to C.

(2) **Delivery and Donative Intent**

Neither delivery nor donative intent are necessary elements for federal gift tax purposes.

b. **Complete vs. Incomplete Transfers**

Only complete transfers are subject to the gift tax.

(1) **Categories of Incomplete Transfers**

(a) **Retained Interests**

To the extent that the donor retains an interest in the property, the transfer is incomplete.

(b) **Revocable Transfers**

If the donor can revoke the transfer without the consent of an adverse party, the gift is incomplete.

(c) **Power to Alter or Amend**

Even though the donor retains no interest or power to revoke, a retained power to change beneficiaries (alter or amend the transfer) renders the gift incomplete.

(2) **Payments Made Under an Incomplete Trust**

Even though a gift is incomplete, if the income is paid over to a beneficiary, there is a completed gift of that income.

(3) **Relinquishment of Powers**

An incomplete transfer is completed and subject to gift taxation when, and if, the donor relinquishes the interest or power that rendered the gift incomplete in the first instance.

c. **Nature of the Retained Powers**

(1) **Power Must Affect Beneficial Enjoyment**

(a) **Power that Affects Time or Manner of Enjoyment**

A gift is complete for gift tax purposes (although not for estate tax purposes) even though the donor has retained power to affect the beneficiaries' time and manner of enjoyment of the property.

(b) **Administrative Powers**

Purely administrative powers retained by the donor that do not affect beneficial enjoyment will not render a gift incomplete.

(c) **Capacity of Power Held is Irrelevant**

The capacity in which the power is held is immaterial. A gift is incomplete if the donor is the trustee, and the trustee has the power to control beneficial enjoyment of the property.

(d) **Discretionary vs. Nondiscretionary Powers**

In order for a gift to be incomplete, the power must be discretionary. A gift is complete if the donor's power that is governed by an ascertained standard.

(e) **Power to Remove Trustee**

Power to compel exercise of the power by the trustee or to remove the trustee and appoint a successor trustee, including the donor, is an incomplete gift.

(2) **Contingent Powers**

For purposes of the gift tax, the fact that exercise of the reserved power is contingent upon the happening of an event beyond the grantor's control will not render the gift incomplete.

(3) **Joint Powers**

Unlike the result under sections 2036 and 2038 of the estate tax, a transfer that can be altered or revoked by the settlor only with the consent of a person possessing a ***"substantial adverse interest"*** is a complete transfer and a taxable gift.

(a) **Persons with a "Substantial Adverse Interest"**

Ordinarily, the beneficiaries of the trust, as well as their successors in interest, are deemed to have the requisite adverse interest. The trustee, on the other hand, does not have a substantial adverse interest.

(b) **Amount Taxable**

Only the value of the adverse party's interest is subject is complete and subject to the gift tax.

### 5. Treatment of Concurrent Interests in Property

#### a. Creation of Concurrent Interests

If property is acquired in co-tenancy, there is a taxable gift to the extent that the value of the undivided interest acquired by one co-tenant exceeds what that co-tenant contributed to the purchase price.

(1) **Exception for Certain Joint Interests**

If a donor transfers money to a joint bank account or joint brokerage or purchases United States Savings Bonds registered in a form of joint ownership, the gift is incomplete the donee actually withdraws funds.

#### b. Termination of Concurrent Interests

If the creation of a concurrent interest was a taxable gift, a later severance will not produce a second taxable gift, provided each co-tenant receives his or her share of the property. A transfer of a concurrent interest by the co-tenants to a third party is treated as a gift by each co-tenant.

### 6. Adequate and Full Consideration

For purposes of the gift tax, a gift is a transfer for less than adequate and full consideration in money or money's worth.

a. **"Money or Money's Worth"**

As with estate tax provisions, consideration must be measurable in monetary terms and must move to the transferor; and release of dower, curtesy, or similar marital rights is not sufficient consideration to prevent gift tax exposure.

b. **Ordinary Course of Business Exception**

Business motivated transfers that proceed from arm's length negotiation and are ***free from donative intent*** are not taxed as gifts even though not supported by sufficient consideration.

c. **Divorce Settlements**

I.R.C. § 2516 provides that transfers pursuant to a written agreement between spouses in settlement of marital property rights or to provide a reasonable allowance for support of minor children are not taxable gifts, provided a divorce actually occurs within a three-year period beginning one year prior to the execution of the agreement.

## B. EXCLUSIONS

### 1. The Annual Exclusion (Section 2503(b))

A donor is allowed an annual exclusion for certain gifts. It is allowed on a ***per donee*** basis. The identity and number of the donees must be ascertainable. Moreover, there must be no condition or power that could operate to impair or destroy the gift. The distribution of income to beneficiaries cannot be discretionary.

a. **Amount of Exclusion**

The first $10,000 of gifts (indexed for inflation) given by a donor to any single donee in any calendar year is excluded in computing the donor's taxable gifts.

**(1)** Beginning in 1998, the $10,000 figure is indexed for inflation in increments of $1,000 and stands at $16,000 for 2022.

**(2)** For gifts to a spouse who is not a citizen, an annual exclusion of $100,000 is allowed (adjusted for inflation). For 2022, the inflationary amount is $164,000.

b. **Present Interest Requirement**

The annual exclusion is ***not allowed for a gift of a future interest in property***. For this purpose, a future interest is any interest, whether vested or contingent, that is limited to commence in use, possession, or enjoyment at a future date, or is subject to the will of some other person (e.g., the interest of a discretionary distributee).

**(1) Gifts to Minors**

**a) Outright Gifts to Minors**

An outright gift to a minor, whether it is with or without the appointment of a guardian, is not a future interest and qualifies for the annual exclusion. Similarly, an outright gift to a custodian under the Uniform Transfers to Minors Act is a gift of a present interest.

**b) Exception for Minor's Trusts under section 2503(c)**

Even though technically a "future interest," the annual exclusion is allowed for gifts on trust for the benefit of a minor if the property and the income must be used for the minor's benefit until age 21 (the excess may be accumulated), and the minor must have the right to require distribution of the property, and any accumulated income, upon attaining age 21.

(2) ***Crummey* Trusts**

A transfer will qualify for the annual exclusion even though income is accumulated as long as the beneficiary has the ***right to demand withdrawals*** for a designated period of time. This applies where the beneficiary is a minor child even though a guardian has not been appointed. The annual exclusion is also allowed for contingent beneficiaries who have demand rights.

**c. Annual Exclusion for 529 Accounts**

The annual exclusion is allowed for contributions to a 529 saving plan. An account owner can transfer an amount exceeding the annual exclusion and spread the contribution over five years for purposes of the annual exclusion. For example, an owner contributes $50,000 to a 529 account for a child in 2022. On the gift tax return, the owner can elect to use $10,000 of the annual exclusion each year for 2022 through 2026 for gifts to that child.

### 3. Exclusion for Certain Transfers for Educational or Medical Expenses

Section 2503(e) allows an unlimited exclusion for payments that a payer makes a payment directly to an institution or person furnishing education or medical services to another person.

## C. GIFT TAX DEDUCTIONS

### 1. Introduction

Two deductions are allowed under the gift tax: (i) the charitable deduction; and (ii) the marital deduction.

### 2. The Charitable Deduction (Section 2522)

The gift tax charitable deduction is virtually identical to the estate tax charitable deduction.

**a. Requirements**

The charitable deduction is allowed for the net value of property transferred to a qualified charitable organization. However, the deduction is limited to the amount of the "taxable gift" (i.e., the gross amount of the gift less the annual exclusion).

**b. Split-Interest Gifts**

As with the estate tax, charitable remainder gifts or charitable lead gifts must be made in the form of qualified "annuity trusts," "unitrusts," or "pooled income funds."

### 3. The Marital Deduction (Section 2523)

In computing "net gifts," a deduction is allowed for the value of any property transferred by the donor to the spouse.

**a. Requirements**

The basic rules are virtually identical to those governing estate tax marital deduction. It is allowed only for gifts to the donor's spouse, and only if the interest given to the spouse is a deductible interest.

**(1) Citizenship**

The donee must be a citizen of the United States. The marital deduction is denied if the spouse is not a citizen. If the donee spouse is not a U.S. citizen, the donor spouse is entitled to claim an annual exclusion of $100,000 (adjusted for inflation). The inflationary amount for 2022 is $164,000.

**(2) Community Property**

Community property qualifies as a "deductible interest" to the same extent as separate property.

**(3) Same-Sex Marriages**

As of 2013, the ***marital deduction is allowed*** for legally married same-sex couples.

**(4) Nondeductible Terminable Interest Rule**

Under section 2523(b), a terminable interest (defined the same as under the estate tax) is defined as one where "on the lapse of time, on the occurrence of an event or contingency, or on the failure of an event or contingency to occur, such interest transferred to the spouse will terminate or fail…" and third party may possess and enjoy the property after the interest of the spouse terminates.

**(a) Donor Retains an Interest or Has Power to Appoint an Interest**

A terminable interest is also nondeductible under the gift tax if the donor retains an interest in the property that would allow the donor to possess or enjoy the property after the donee-spouse's interest terminates or the donor has the power to appoint an interest in the property that he can exercise in such a manner that the appointee may possess or enjoy the property after the termination of the spouse's interest.

**(b) Joint Interests**

The fact that the donor-spouse has an interest in the property as a co-tenant with right of survivorship will not prevent allowance of the deduction for the undivided interest transferred to the spouse.

**(c) Interest in Unidentified Assets**

Like the estate tax, the nondeductible terminable interest rule under the gift tax is extended to situations where a nondeductible interest in an unidentified group of assets could be distributed to the spouse.

**(3) Exceptions to the Terminable Interest Rule**

Unlike the estate tax, the gift tax does not contain an exception for survivorship nor for insurance proceeds.

**(a) Life Estate with Power of Appointment**

The life estate with ***general*** power of appointment exception also applies to the gift tax marital deduction, and the requirements are identical to those under the estate tax.

(b) **"QTIP" Interests**

The gift tax allows a deduction for "qualified terminable interest property" given to one's spouse after making the required election. This exception tracks the QTIP rules under the estate tax.

(c) **Charitable Remainder Trusts**

The gift tax allows a deduction, like that allowed under the estate tax, for the value of the income interest given to one's spouse in a qualified charitable remainder annuity trust or unitrust.

**b. Maximum Allowed**

The gift tax marital deduction is based on the ***full value (100%)*** of the property transferred to the donee-spouse, subject to two limitations.

**(1) Net Value**

If the property is subject to an encumbrance, or if the donee incurs some obligation as a condition of receiving the gift, the deduction is limited to the net value of the property.

**(2) Annual Exclusion**

The allowable marital deduction must be reduced by the amount of any allowable annual exclusion.

**(3) Note—Prior Law**

Prior law will govern gifts made before 1982.

## IV. MISCELLANEOUS GIFT TAX RULES

### A. POWERS OF APPOINTMENT

Section 2514 specifically provides that the exercise of a general power of appointment or, in the case of post-1942 powers, the exercise or release of a general power of appointment, is treated as a transfer of the property subject to the power and is taxable as a gift.

**1. Meaning of General Power of Appointment**

A general power of appointment is a power in favor of the powerholder, the powerholder's creditors, the powerholder's estate, or creditors of the powerholder's estate

**2. A Power Limited by an Ascertainable Standard**

A power is not considered to be general if it is limited by an ascertainable standard relating to the powerholder's health, education, support, or maintenance.

**3. A Power Exercisable in Conjunction with Another Person**

If a powerholder holds a power created on or before October 21, 1942 that is exercisable in conjunction with any other person, it is not a general power of appointment. If a powerholder holds a power created after October 21, 1942 that is exercisable in conjunction with the creator of the power or someone with a substantial adverse interest, it is not a general power of appointment.

**4. Exercise or Release of a General Power of Appointment**

If a powerholder of a general power of appointment exercises or releases a general power of appointment created after October 21, 1942, it is subject to gift taxation under section 2514. For a power created before October 21, 1942, the powerholder must exercise the power for it to be a taxable gift.

### 5. Lapse of a General Power of Appointment

A lapse of a general power of appointment created after October 21, 1942 is considered to be a release of the power provided it meets the so-called ***"5 and 5"*** power. Under this rule, a lapse is considered to be a release to the extent that the property that can be appointed exceeds the greater of $5,000 or five percent of the aggregate value of the property subject to the power.

### 6. Nongeneral Powers of Appointment

A nongeneral power of appointment (also known as limited or special power) does not subject the powerholder to gift taxation irrespective of whether it is exercised or released. However, the Internal Revenue Service and the Tax Court take the position that the powerholder's exercise of such power over the trust corpus in which the powerholder has an unqualified income interest is a taxable gift of the income interest to the donee.

## B. DISCLAIMERS

An effective disclaimer (unqualified refusal to accept property) is not a transfer for purposes of the gift tax.

### 1. Requirements

Under section 2518, a disclaimer is effective for federal gift and estate tax purposes if:

- **a.** The disclaimer is in writing;
- **b.** The disclaimer is received by donor (or the estate) within nine months of the date of transfer (or within nine months of the day donee reaches age 21);
- **c.** The donee has not accepted the interest or any of its benefits; and
- **d.** As a result, the interest passes to someone other than the disclaimant, or the donor's or the decedent's spouse, without any direction on the disclaimant's or spouse's part.

### 2. Partial Disclaimers

Subject to certain limitations, partial disclaimers are valid for federal tax purposes.

## C. GIFT SPLITTING

Section 2513 provides that a gift made by one spouse to a third party may be treated as being made ***one-half by each spouse*** if the nondonor spouse consents to "split" the gift. If a spouse makes a gift of community property to another person, gift splitting is automatic because each spouse is considered to own 50 percent of all community property.

### 1. Requirements

The spouses must be married at the time of the gift and cannot remarry if one of the spouses dies or they get divorced during the year, and the spouses must be residents or citizens of the United States.

### 2. Limitation

Consent ***must extend to all gifts*** made by the spouses during that calendar year.

3. **Exception when donor spouse gives power of appointment to the spouse**

Gift splitting is not allowed where the donor grants the spouse a general power of appointment with respect to the property transferred.

4. **Joint and Several Liability**

When spouses split gifts, they are subject to joint and several liability that year for any gift tax liability related to the gifts that year.

# V. VALUATION

## A. INTRODUCTORY COMMENTS

Estate and gift taxes are both measured by the "fair market value" of property transferred. However, different rules concerning the valuation date and property subject to tax may apply for estate and gift tax purposes.

## B. RULES OF LAW RELATING TO VALUATION

### 1. Valuation Date

#### a. Gift Tax

Taxable gifts are valued as of the ***date the gift*** is made.

#### b. Estate Tax

Property included in the gross estate is valued immediately after the **date of the decedent's death**, or the executor may elect the **"*alternate valuation date*"** (six months after the date of the decedent's death). However, valuation changed solely by lapse of time is disregarded if the alternate valuation date is elected, and no election is allowed unless the election decreases both the gross estate and the estate tax payable.

##### (1) Application of Sections 2033 Through 2044

Assets included in the decedent's estate under sections 2033 through 2044 are valued at the date of the decedent's death (or alternate valuation date) instead of the value of the assets at the time of transfer.

##### (2) Procedure for Alternate Valuation Election

The executor's election to value the assets at the alternate valuation date is made on the estate tax return. The ***election is irrevocable***, and it affects all assets (except for those assets where value changes solely by lapse of time).

### 2. Fair Market Value

The standard for valuation is "fair market value," generally defined as the price that a willing buyer would pay a willing seller after arm's length bargaining where there is no compulsion to buy or sell and where both parties are aware of all relevant facts. The burden of proof as to valuation is upon the donor or estate.

#### a. Special Use Valuation for Estate Tax Purposes

Under section 2032A, in certain circumstances, farmland or real property used in a closely held trade or business may be valued for estate tax purposes at less than "fair market value."

#### b. Special Valuation Rules

Chapter 14 represents a legislative attempt to address the problem of "freezing" the value of property that is expected to appreciate and giving away the anticipated appreciation free of gift or estate tax liability. The problem is treated essentially as a gift tax valuation issue.

### (1) Transactions Affected

Chapter 14 affects four types of situations:

#### (a) Transfer of Interests in Corporations or Partnerships

Section 2701 generally applies where a person transfers an interest in a corporation or partnership to, or for the benefit of, a family member, and the transferor or an "applicable family member" retains an interest in the same corporation or partnership. Exceptions include situations in which: (i) market quotations are readily available for the transferred stock or retained interest; (ii) there is only one class of interest (or if two classes, they differ only as to voting rights); or (iii) there is a proportionate transfer of all classes of interest.

##### 1) Zero Value Rule for Retained Interests

The transferred interest is valued by subtracting the value of the retained interest from the proportionate fair market value of the entire enterprise. If the retained interest is an "applicable retained interest" (i.e., a distribution right, or a liquidation, put, call, or conversion right), it is assigned a value of zero.

###### a) Exceptions to Zero Value Rule

The zero value rule does not apply to the following:

i. Where the transferor (or applicable family member) does not hold at least 50% of the value or voting power of the entity immediately before the transfer;

ii. Distribution rights in the form of qualified payments;

iii. Distribution rights with respect to a retained junior equity interest; and

iv. A right that must be exercised at a specific time and in a specific manner.

###### b) Minimum Value Rule

If there is a transfer of a junior equity interest, the proportionate value of such interest is determined by valuing all junior equity interests at not less than 10% of the total value of all equity interests in the entity, plus the total amount of any indebtedness of the entity to the transferor (or to an applicable family member).

#### (b) Transfers of Interests in Trusts

A grantor retained income trust ("GRIT") is valued at zero for purposes of determining the value of the taxable gift of the remainder. However, a value is assigned if the retained interest is a qualified interest (i.e., a grantor retained annuity trust ("GRAT") or a grantor retained unitrust ("GRUT")).

##### 1) Applies to Term Interests Also

If a transferor gives a term interest but retains a remainder, the remainder is valued at zero unless the remainder is noncontingent, and the term interests are either GRATs or GRUTs.

2) **Exceptions**

The zero value rule of this section does not apply to the following:

a) Transfers to nonfamily members;

b) Incomplete gifts; and

c) Transfer of an interest in property that is to be used as a personal residence by the persons holding the term interests.

### (c) Property Subject to Restrictions

Various burdens on property (e.g., restrictions on its transfer) might be used to reduce its fair market value. To remedy this, section 2703 mandates that such restrictions be disregarded for purposes of estate, gift, and generation-skipping taxes.

1) **Exception—Bona Fide Business Agreements**

The rule of section 2703 does not apply to an option, agreement, right, or restriction that meets the following requirements:

a) There is a bona fide business arrangement;

b) The agreement is not a device to transfer property to members of the decedent's family for less than full and adequate consideration in money or money's worth; and

c) The terms are comparable to similar arrangements entered into by persons in an arm's length transaction.

### (d) Lapsing Rights and Restrictions

Prior to 1990, the gift and estate tax did not apply to situations in which someone transferred an interest in property by gift, while retaining valuable rights with respect to the property, and then permitted or caused these rights to lapse. In general, property is valued without regard for lapsing restrictions.

1) **Taxable Transfer**

The lapse of a voting or liquidation right in a corporation or partnership is treated as a transfer by gift or as a transfer includible in the decedent's gross estate.

a) **Limitation—Control**

The lapse is treated as a transfer only if the person holding the right immediately before the lapse and members of that person's family (both before and after the lapse) control the corporation or partnership.

b) **Amount of Transfer**

The taxable amount is the difference between the value of the interest retained immediately prior to the lapse and its value immediately after the lapse.

c) **Exception for Certain Restrictions on Liquidation**

Commercially reasonable restrictions imposed by an unrelated party in connection with a financing transaction and restrictions imposed by any federal or state law are not considered to be restrictions disregarded in valuing any interest.

c. **Estate Tax Value of Land Subject to Conservation Easement**

A decedent's executor may elect to exclude a portion of the value of land included in the gross estate if the land is subject to a "qualified conservation easement"—a perpetual restriction limiting the use of property exclusively for certain designated conservation purposes (except certain historic preservation purposes) that is granted to a "qualified organization."

## C. VALUATION METHODS

There are, essentially, three general methods of valuation commonly used.

### 1. Market Price Method

Where market prices for identical property are known (e.g., in the case of listed securities regularly traded on an exchange), these prices may be used to value the same property included in the gross estate. Similarly, appraisal may be based on "comparable sales."

### 2. Life Estates, Annuities, Remainders, Reversionary Interests, Etc.

Annuities issued by a company that regularly sells annuity contracts are valued by reference to the present cost of purchasing a similar contract from the company. All other annuities, life estates, reversions, and other future interests are valued under actuarial tables ("present worth tables)" These tables are found in IRS Publication 1457. Two of the most important tables are Table B (applies to a term certain, such as 10 years) and Table S (life table).

### 3. Unascertainable Values

For property that cannot be valued under the actuarial tables, the taxpayer has the burden of establishing the value of the property.

### 4. Capitalization of Earnings Method

Market value may be estimated by capitalizing the known earnings derived from the property.

## D. VALUATION OF SOME SPECIFIC ITEMS

### 1. Real Property

This is usually valued on the basis of comparable sales. Generally, an appraisal must take into account the property's "highest end best use." Section 2032A is intended to provide some relief from that standard for real property used in a trade or business.

### 2. Stocks and Bonds

a. **Listed Securities**

Fair market value is the mean between the highest and lowest selling price on the valuation date. If there are no sales on the valuation date, fair market value is the weighted average of the mean between the highest and lowest selling price on the nearest trading date before and after the valuation date.

b. **Unlisted Securities or Closely-Held Businesses**

Valuation must take into account all recent sales, corporate net worth, earning capacity, etc.

(1) **Control Premium**

Where stock owned represents effective control of a corporation, it may be valued at an amount greater than the market price because a willing buyer may be willing to pay more for such control.

(2) **Minority Interest Discounts**

A willing buyer of a minority interest in a business may not be willing to paying the market price because of the lack of control.

(3) **Effect of Buy-Sell Agreement**

The price established in a buy-sell agreement has been accepted as the value of the decedent's interest as long as the agreement was bona fide and binding on the decedent both during life and at death.

c. **Mutual Fund Shares**

This is valued at "net asset value" (i.e., asking price less any sales commission or "load").

d. **Bonds, Notes, Evidence of Indebtedness**

These are valued at face value plus accrued interest, unless evidence is introduced justifying a discount.

3. **Blockage**

Securities that constitute a large block of stock or bonds of a particular corporation may be valued at less than market value on the theory that the sale of such a large block will depress the market price obtainable.

# VI. COMPUTATION OF TAX

## A. GIFT TAX COMPUTATIONS

1. **Computational Procedure**

The gift tax is computed by applying the ***unified tax rates*** to the total of current and prior taxable gifts made by a donor, and then subtracting a figure obtained by applying the same rates of tax to the sum of all prior taxable gifts. Effective for transfers made after December 31, 1976, the same tax rate schedule is applied to both lifetime and testamentary transfers.

2. **Cumulative Nature of Tax**

The gift tax is imposed on a cumulative basis to all gratuitous transfers made by an individual during life. The effect is to expose current taxable gifts to higher marginal rates.

3. **Applicable Gift Tax Credit Amount**

The 1976 Tax Reform Act introduced a gift tax credit, applied directly against tax liability. This gift tax credit operates in tandem with the unified estate tax credit to provide, in effect, a single credit against transfer taxes, whether the transfers were made during life or upon death.

a. **Amount of Credit**

The credit is determined by computing the tax on the applicable exclusion amount. Under the Tax Cuts and Jobs Act of 2017, the basic exclusion amount was increased to $10 million (adjusted for inflation annually). During 2022, the applicable exclusion amount is $12,060,000, and the tax is computed at a flat rate of 40 percent. The tax on that amount is $4,769,800 ($345,800 + [11,060,000 times .40]). Hence, the applicable credit amount for 2022 is $4,769,800. The applicable credit amount effectively eliminates any transfer taxes upon taxable transfers under the gift tax up to that amount.

b. **Limitation**

The credit must be claimed against gifts in the order of time they are made, or it is forfeited.

c. **"Clawback" Regulations**

The 2017 Act is set to sunset after December 31, 2025 when the basic exclusion amount will revert to $5 million. The Treasury Department issued "clawback" regulations to ensure that who died after 2025 but made gifts totaling more than $5 million between 2018 and 2025 will not be subject to estate tax for those gifts.

d. **Relationship to Estate Tax**

Given that the unified applicable gift and estate tax credits are set forth under separate sections of the Code, it may appear that they operate consecutively. However, the computational mechanics of the estate tax ensure that only a single, unified credit will be allowed against lifetime and testamentary transfers.

## B. ESTATE TAX COMPUTATIONS

### 1. Computational Procedure

Under present law, the estate tax is computed by applying the unified rates of tax to the total of taxable estate and all "adjusted taxable gifts," and then subtracting "taxes payable," an amount obtained by applying the same rates of tax to the total of the taxable gifts that were included in the first computation. "Adjusted taxable gifts" means all taxable gifts made after December 31, 1976, that are not included in the taxable estate. "Taxes payable" includes gift taxes with respect to "adjusted taxable gifts" and any taxable gifts that were included in the gross estate.

### 2. Estate Tax Applicable Credit Amount

From the tax thus determined, the "applicable credit" may be subtracted. The result is the tax liability. Consistent with the gift tax, the tax on this liability is computed on a flat rate of 40 percent.

### 3. Other Credits Allowed Against Estate Tax

In addition to the unified estate tax credit, four other credits are allowed:

(i) Credit for certain pre-1977 gift taxes paid;

(ii) Credit for taxes paid on a prior estate (property previously taxed to another); and

(iii) Credit for certain foreign death taxes paid to another country that relate to property also included in the gross estate of a citizen-decedent.

*Note:* The credit for state death taxes paid has been repealed effective for the 2005 tax year.

## C. DECEASED SPOUSAL UNUSED EXCLUSION AMOUNT ("PORTABILITY")

### 1. Meaning and History

Section 2010(c) allows for ***portability of the unified credit between spouses*** for gift and estate tax purposes. This allows a surviving spouse to use the unused exclusion amount from the deceased spouse.

### 2. How to Elect Portability

The deceased spouse's ***executor must make an election*** on the estate tax return to allow the surviving spouse to use the deceased spousal unused amount (DSUE), and the tax return must be filed timely. The ***election is irrevocable***.

### 3. Use of the Last Deceased Spouse Applicable Exclusion Amount

#### a. Who Is a Last Deceased Spouse?

Only the DSUE of the last deceased spouse may be used. If the surviving spouse remaining and the second spouse dies, the second spouse is the last deceased spouse. That rule applies even if the second spouse's executor did not elect portability.

#### b. Examination of the Deceased Spouse's Tax Return

The IRS may examine a deceased spouse's return to determine the DSUE. This examination may take place even if the statute of limitation has expired. However, this authority does not permit the IRS to assess a deficiency against the deceased spouse's estate if the statute of limitations has already expired.

# VII. TAX ON GENERATION-SKIPPING TRANSFERS

## A. BACKGROUND AND INTRODUCTION

### 1. Definition

A generation-skipping transfer is, generally, a gift or bequest of an interest in property (in trust or otherwise) to persons who are assigned to a generation more than one generation younger than that of the donor or decedent ("skip person").

### 2. Repeal and Replacement in 1986

Originally enacted in 1976, this tax was never applied because of its complexity. Congress retroactively repealed the 1976 provision and, in 1986, replaced it with a new generation-skipping transfer tax. The new tax is substantively the same tax with simplified computations except that it also applies to "direct skips."

## B. TRANSFERS TO WHICH THE TAX APPLIES

The tax applies to "every generation-skipping transfer," including taxable distributions, taxable terminations, and direct skips.

### 1. Definitions

#### a. Taxable Distribution

This is any distribution from a trust (or any arrangement having a trust effect) to a "skip person," except for distributions considered taxable terminations or a direct skip.

b. **Taxable Termination**

This involves any termination (e.g., by death) of an interest in trust property except where a non-skip person has an interest in the property immediately following termination or if no distribution may afterwards be made to a skip person.

c. **Direct Skip**

This involves a transfer that is subject to gift or estate taxes but is made to a skip person.

d. **Interest in Property**

A person has an interest if she either (i) has a right to receive income or corpus from the trust or (ii) is a permissible recipient of income or corpus. A trust is treated as a skip person if all trust interests are held by skip persons or if no person holds a present interest, but all future distributions must be made to skip persons.

e. **Family Generations**

Generations are generally determined along family lines. The grantor, grantor's spouse and grantor's siblings would be one generation, their children (including adopted children) would be assigned to the first younger generation, and grandchildren would be assigned to the next younger generation, etc. Nonfamily generations are assigned on the basis of the difference in age between the beneficiaries and the grantor: a person born more than 12-$^1/_2$ years after the grantor would be in the first younger generation, and thereafter generations are determined on the basis of 25 years.

2. **General Exceptions**

The generation-skipping tax does not apply to a transfer to the extent that: (i) the property was subject to a prior generation-skipping tax; (ii) the prior taxable transfer was to a transferee assigned to a generation the same as or lower than that of the present transferee; and (iii) the transfer does not have the effect of avoiding the generation-skipping tax. Transfers for educational or medical expenses are also not taxable.

3. **Special Exception for Descendants with Deceased Parent**

A transfer to a grandchild of the transfer or (direct skip) is not taxable if the grandchild's parent (i.e., transferor's child) is dead.

## C. AMOUNT TAXABLE

1. **Taxable Distributions**

The taxable base is the value of the property received by the transferee minus any related expenses incurred by the transferee. If the tax is paid by a trust for the recipient of a taxable distribution, that tax is considered a taxable distribution.

2. **Taxable Terminations**

The taxable amount is the value of all property subject to the taxable termination minus certain expenses allowable as estate tax deductions.

3. **Direct Skips**

Tax is imposed on the value of the property received by the transferee.

#### 4. Valuation Rules

The property is valued at its fair market value at the time of the transfer minus any consideration furnished by the transferee.

##### a. Time of Transfer

Taxable distributions or a lifetime direct skip occurs on the date of the distribution or gift. The transfer date of a direct skip by bequest is the date of decedent's death. A taxable termination occurs on the date of termination.

#### 5. GST Exemption

There is an exemption that is equal to the applicable exclusion amount that may be allocated by the transferor among her transferred property. The exemption is not an exclusion; rather, it is used in the tax computation to determine the effective rate at which a generation-skipping transfer will be taxed. Under the Tax Cuts and Jobs Act, the applicable exclusion amount is $10 million (indexed for inflation). The applicable exclusion amount for 2022 after factoring in the inflationary adjustment is $12.06. ***Portability does not apply to the generation-skipping transfer tax.***

#### 6. Reverse QTIP Election

If a donee or surviving spouse makes a reverse QTIP election, the donor or deceased spouse will be entitled to the marital deduction but still claim the GST exemption for GST purposes as if a QTIP election had not been made. The donor or deceased spouse had to have made a QTIP election under section 2056(b)(7) or 2523(f). The ***reverse QTIP election is beneficial where the donor spouse has used up the basic exclusion amount but has not used up the GST exemption***.

### D. COMPUTATION OF TAX

The taxable amount of the generation-skipping transfer is multiplied by the applicable rate (i.e., the maximum federal estate tax rate in effect on the transfer date, multiplied by the inclusion ratio). The federal estate tax rate in 2022 is 40 percent.

### E. PAYMENT OF TAX

For taxable distributions, the transferee pays the tax. For taxable terminations, the trustee is liable for the tax; if there is no formal trust, "trustee" is the person in actual or constructive possession of the property. The transferor pays the tax in cases of direct skips.

## VIII. RETURNS AND PAYMENT OF TAX

### A. GIFT TAX

#### 1. Returns

A donor must file a gift tax return for any calendar year in which a gift is made. A gift tax return need not be filed if the only transfers made during the year are fully excludable from the tax or are nontaxable because of the 100% marital deduction. The donor is required to file a return and is primarily liable for the payment of the tax. The tax is due at the time that the donor must file the gift tax return.

##### a. Transferee Liability

If the donor fails to pay the tax, the government has a lien on the property to the extent of the tax due and also a right to hold the donee liable for the unpaid gift tax to the extent of the value of the property received.

### 2. Special Rules for Spilt Gifts

If a gift of future interest is split, both spouses must file a return, reporting one-half the property's value. If a present interest gift is split, the actual donor must file if the gift exceeds the annual exclusion (currently $16,000). The other spouse need not file unless the one-half value attributed to that spouse exceeds the annual exclusion. Both spouses are jointly and severally liable for payment of the tax.

## B. ESTATE TAX

### 1. Returns

The decedent's executor must file the estate tax return. It is due within nine months of the date of the decedent's death.

#### a. Limitation—Filing Amount

No return need be filed if the gross estate does not exceed the applicable exclusion amount.

#### b. Nonresident Aliens

A return is required only for estates of nonresident aliens if the part of the gross estate situated in the United States exceeds $60,000.

### 2. Payment of Estate Tax

The executor is primarily responsible for payment of tax. It is due at the same time the return must be filed.

#### a. Transferee Liability

If the executor fails to pay, persons holding legal or beneficial interests in the property included in the gross estate are liable for the payment of the tax to the extent of the value of their interest.

#### b. Time for Payment

Payment of the estate tax is due nine months after the decedent's death. Extensions are available at the executor's election for certain reversionary or remainder interests that are included in the decedent's gross estate. They may also be granted upon showing of cause.

##### (1) Installment Payments

In certain circumstances where an estate is substantially comprised of an interest in a "closely held business," the executor may elect to pay the estate tax related to the business interest in installments.

#### c. Apportionment

The burden of estate taxation generally follows the order of abatement prescribed by state law.

# Approach to Exams

In dealing with exam questions concerning federal estate, gift, or generation-skipping transfer tax issues, you must first recognize that a problem in the area exists, then focus on and analyze the specific tax issues presented, and, finally, apply the relevant rules of law to resolve the issues in the specific context in which they are presented.

## A. Recognizing a Problem

In every area of law, there are certain types of events, transactions that "flag" the existence of a relevant legal issue. The three taxes that are the subject of this Summary are all transfer taxes imposed upon the transfer of property. The "flag" for you to watch for is a ***transfer***.

### 1. What Kind of Transfer?

Only ***gratuitous transfers*** are taxed. Thus, when money, property, or services of equivalent value are received by the transferor in exchange for the property transferred, an income tax issue may arise, but a transfer tax issue is ordinarily ***not*** present.

### 2. Scope of the Transfer Concept

Taxable transfers can be quite subtle. Be alert for a transfer tax issue whenever ***beneficial enjoyment of property***, or some ***power to control beneficial enjoyment***, ***shifts*** from one person to another.

### 3. Lifetime vs. Testamentary Gifts

Generally, the subject of the gift tax is lifetime transfers, while the subject of the estate tax is transfers that occur as a result of a person's death. However, some lifetime gifts are exposed to the estate tax, either because the transfer is effectively completed by the transferor's death (e.g., a lifetime gift of a remainder following a reserved life estate).

### 4. Correlation of the Transfer Taxes

The three taxes are designed to assure that gratuitous transfers, whenever or however made, will be subject to tax and, with the introduction of the unified tax scheme in 1976, that they will be exposed to the same graduated rates of tax—whenever or however made. For the most part, the taxes are ***mutually inclusive*** (i.e., a transfer that is not exposed to the estate tax will be exposed to the gift tax). But, as will be seen, the taxes are ***not mutually exclusive***. Some taxable gifts may also be exposed to the estate tax, necessitating adjustments in the form of tax credits to relieve double taxation.

## B. Analyzing the Transfer Tax Issue

A detailed understanding of the pertinent provisions of the Internal Revenue Code is, of course, essential for identification and analysis of the particular issue or issues. Sometimes, the issues may be highlighted for you (e.g., Did A make a taxable gift? Is A entitled to any deduction in connection with the bequest to the surviving spouse). Frequently, however, you will be required to identify issues in addition to presenting reasoned conclusions (e.g., Discuss the estate and gift tax consequences, if any). In general, transfer tax issues fall into the following six general categories (the first four of which are the most common).

### 1. Is the Transfer Taxable at All?

a. Is the apparent shifting of beneficial ownership or enjoyment of a type that is subject to one or more of the general or specific provisions of the transfer taxes?

b. Is the transfer gratuitous, in whole or in part, or is it for a full consideration that is recognized as "adequate" for transfer tax purposes?

2. **Under Which Tax Does the Transfer Fall?**

a. If made during the donor's lifetime, does it fall within the definition of a "taxable gift" for gift tax purposes?

b. Even though made during the donor's lifetime, is it the kind of lifetime gift that is deemed "testamentary" in nature so that it may also be taxable for estate tax purposes?

c. If the transfer occurs at the time of death, did the decedent have a sufficient "interest" in the property so that it should be taxed in the estate forestate tax purposes?

d. If the decedent held only a lifetime interest, is there "generation skipping" involved so as to subject the property to the generation-skipping transfer tax?

3. **What Is the Value of the Property Transferred?**

4. **Are Any Exemptions or Deductions Allowable with Respect to the Transfer?**

5. **How Is the Tax to Be Computed?**

a. Should any prior transfers be taken into account in applying the graduated rates of tax?

b. Are any credits against tax allowable in computing the ultimate tax liability?

c. Is a surviving spouse able to use a deceased spouse's unused exclusion amount?

6. **Who Is Liable for Payment of the Transfer Taxes?**

## C. Apply Relevant Rules to Specific Situations

Ordinarily, it is not enough that you simply identify the issues and state the rules of law; you must also apply the issues and rules in the context of the specific factual situations presented by the problem. Keep in mind the following:

### 1. Do Not Fight the Facts

Accept the facts as given. For example, if you are told that "A gave property to B," do not dwell on the adequacy of consideration for the transfer unless other facts raise the issue of consideration.

### 2. Multiple Theories

Sometimes (particularly under the estate tax) a tax might attach under more than one section of the Code. Be alert to this and discuss ***all relevant theories*** under which the transfer might be taxed. At the same time, do ***not*** discuss theories of taxation that are not raised by the problem; a proper answer should not be a summary of the course.

### 3. Alternative Positions

Sometimes there is no clear-cut "answer" to a particular issue raised (i.e., an argument can be made either for or against imposition of the tax). If so, discuss both positions fully. At the same time, do not manufacture alternative positions.

# Estate and Gift Taxation

Seventeenth Edition

# Chapter One
# Introduction

| CONTENTS | PAGE |
|---|---|

# Chapter Approach

Questions involving the history, nature, and constitutionality of the federal transfer taxes (the estate tax, gift tax, and generation-skipping transfer tax) rarely appear on examinations. However, the ***purpose*** and ***interrelationship*** of the three transfer taxes are important to know as they are frequently relevant to questions relating to whether one or more of the taxes may be applicable to a particular transfer.

# A. The Estate Tax

## 1. Brief History

The federal government began imposing transfer taxes of various sorts prior to the beginning of the twentieth century. However, these early federal transfer taxes were only temporary expedients designed to meet some emergency need for federal revenue (e.g., prosecution of the Civil War) and were repealed when the emergency need ceased.

### a. Origin of Present Estate Tax—Revenue Act of 1916

Similarly, the need for revenue to wage World War I prompted a federal estate tax imposed by the Revenue Act of 1916. But here, the termination of hostilities did not produce a termination of the tax. Although its provisions have been refined by amendment over the years, the essential scope and thrust of that estate taxing scheme persist today in sections 2001 through 2209 of the 1986 Code.

## 2. Purpose

Although the federal estate tax raises a substantial amount in terms of absolute dollars, the percentage of federal revenue it produces is relatively insignificant. Proponents of the first federal estate tax were more concerned with socio-economic matters than fiscal effects. They saw the federal estate tax as a means of limiting and reducing the accumulation of wealth by American family "dynasties." Interestingly enough, this result has been achieved more through the income tax than the estate tax. However, the estate tax remains as an "ultimate" tax which adds the final element of progressivity to the federal revenue system (i.e., where a taxpayer has been able to accumulate substantial wealth in spite of the income taxes, the estate tax exacts a final levy). In addition, the increase in the applicable exclusion amount in recent years has made it less likely that decedents with moderate wealth will be subject to the federal estate tax.

## 3. Types of Transfer Taxes

State and federal transfer taxes are of two types: estate taxes and inheritance taxes. Simply stated, an estate tax is a tax upon the value of all property owned by a decedent that ***is transferred or transmitted*** to the decedent's heirs or beneficiaries upon the decedent's death. On the other hand, an inheritance tax is a tax upon the value of property ***received*** by an heir or beneficiary on account of a decedent's death.

## 4. Computation of the Tax

### a. Estate Tax Computation

In the case of an estate tax, a ***single set*** of deductions and exemptions are applied to the decedent's estate. With few exceptions, it does not matter how many heirs or beneficiaries share in the estate, or who they are. The federal estate tax is based on a flat 40% tax rate.

### b. Inheritance Tax Computation

In the case of an inheritance tax, however, ***separate*** exemptions and rates are applied to the share received by each beneficiary and, typically, the rates of tax and allowable exemptions vary according to the relationship of the beneficiaries to the decedent.

## 5. Overview of State Transfer Taxes

Many states impose transfer taxes, some under an estate tax system, others under an inheritance tax system or a combined inheritance/estate tax system. Some states impose neither an estate tax nor an inheritance tax. In the past, the estate tax in several states was equal to the repealed maximum federal credit. When Congress repealed the credit for decedents dying after December 31, 2004, it resulted in a repeal of an estate tax in many states. For states with an estate tax, the scope of state tax is generally very similar to that of the federal estate tax in terms of what types of property and what types of transfers are subject to the tax. Thus, a thorough understanding of the federal estate tax will facilitate an understanding of the relevant state death tax. Moreover, tax planning with a view to the federal estate tax will, in general, achieve satisfactory tax results under the state death tax as well.

## 6. Nature of the Federal Estate Tax

Although the federal estate tax is measured by the value of the property transferred, it is not deemed to be a property tax, but rather an excise or privilege tax. That is, the tax is imposed upon the transfer of the property, not on the property itself. Stated another way, the tax is not upon the ownership of property but upon the ***privilege of transferring property*** by devise, bequest, or inheritance.

### a. Constitutionality

This distinction between a tax on property and on a transfer of property has important legal significance. Under Article I, Section 9, Clause 4 of the United States Constitution, direct (property) taxes must be apportioned among the several states according to population, whereas indirect (transfer) taxes are subject only to the constitutional requirement of uniformity. Thus, by finding that the federal estate tax was imposed upon the ***transfer*** of property at death, not on the property itself, the United States Supreme Court was able to uphold the validity of the tax against the assertion that it was unconstitutional because not apportioned. [**New York Trust Co. v. Eisner,** 256 U.S. 345 (1921)]

## 7. Nonretroactive Application of Federal Estate Tax

It is well settled that the federal estate tax "should not be construed to apply to transactions already completed." [**Nichols v. Coolidge,** 274 U.S. 531 (1926)] Hence, even where it might be constitutionally permissible to apply estate tax amendments retroactively, Congress has, as a matter of ***policy,*** limited amendments to prospective application only. As a consequence, the estate tax law in effect at the date of the transaction in question governs—even though the law may subsequently have changed. Accordingly, throughout this Summary, references are made to prior law wherever significant distinctions exist in the present law.

# B. The Gift Tax

## 1. Brief History

The first federal gift tax was enacted in 1924. [Revenue Act of 1924] However, this tax was generally ineffective and was repealed in 1926. The flaw in the 1924 tax was traceable not only to the substantial exemptions it allowed, but also to the fact that it operated annually (like the income tax) rather than cumulatively, thereby failing to take the donor's previous gifts into account. The present gift tax has its origins in the Revenue Act of 1932. Its provisions have been refined by amendment over the years, but its essential thrust and scope persist today in sections 2501 through 2524 of the 1986 Code.

## 2. Purpose

The federal gift tax serves several purposes, one of which is to discourage avoidance of the federal income tax by the device of giving away income-producing property to those in lower income tax brackets. The gift tax exacts a "price" for this opportunity at the time the transfer is made. It is for this reason that any legislation repealing the federal estate tax has retained the federal gift tax.

### a. Curtailing Estate Tax Avoidance

However, the principal purpose of the gift tax is to limit avoidance of the ***estate tax*** by the device of lifetime gifts which would remove the transferred property from estate tax exposure on the donor's death. This is important to bear in mind since the scope of the gift tax and the interpretation of what transfers constitute taxable gifts are frequently based on consideration of the essential purpose of the tax.

## 3. State Gift Taxes

Although a number of states impose taxes upon lifetime gifts in addition to estate or inheritance taxes, many do not. However, in those states that have adopted a gift tax, the scope is generally similar to that of the federal gift tax.

## 4. Nature and Constitutionality of Federal Gift Tax

The federal gift tax, like the federal estate tax, has been interpreted to be a type of excise tax (i.e., a tax upon the ***transfer*** of property rather than upon the property itself). Thus, just as in the case of the estate tax, the gift tax has been held to be an indirect tax and hence not subject to the constitutional provision requiring apportionment of direct taxes. [**Bromley v. McCaughn,** 280 U.S. 124 (1929)]

# C. Coordination of the Federal Estate and Gift Taxes

## 1. Background

Although the federal estate and gift taxes are related in purpose and the separate provisions are frequently read "in pari materia" (i.e., construed together), differences do exist in the substantive scope of the taxes. Generally, the estate and gift taxes are ***mutually inclusive***—so that a transfer not taxed under one of the tax schemes will be taxed under the other. On the other hand, the two taxes are ***not mutually exclusive.*** Hence, some transfers may be taxed under ***both*** taxing schemes (although adjustments in the form of credits serve to eliminate double taxation).

#### a. Former Dual Tax Schemes

Prior to 1977, a true dual system of estate and gift taxation existed:

(1) ***Separate graduated rates*** were applied under the estate tax and gift tax; the gift tax rates being fixed at three-fourths of those of the estate tax within the same tax bracket.

(2) ***Separate exemptions*** applied to the two taxing schemes. This allowed for an optimum level of tax-free transfers. A person could make lifetime gifts which would utilize the gift tax specific exemption ($30,000) without any reduction in the estate tax exemption ($60,000).

(3) ***Most importantly, the estate taxes were applied only to property taxable under the estate tax***—not cumulatively to all gratuitous transfers. Thus, even though a person might have made substantial lifetime gifts, upon death the decedent's estate got a "new start" through the graduated estate tax rates.

### 2. The "Unified Tax" of the 1976 Tax Reform Act

The Tax Reform Act of 1976 did ***not*** unify the substantive aspects of the federal estate and gift taxes—numerous substantive differences in thrust and scope still remain. However, it ***did*** unify the ***computational*** aspects of the two transfer taxes and eliminated the dual system of rates and exemptions described above.

#### a. General Operation

Under the Tax Reform Act, a ***single set of graduated rates*** was applied to both lifetime and deathtime transfers. Further, the separate gift and estate tax exemptions (above) were repealed, and a ***single "unified credit"*** was enacted which, in effect, operates cumulatively to both lifetime and deathtime transfers. Moreover, the unified tax computation requires the estate tax to take into account lifetime gratuitous transfers, so that ***all*** gratuitous transfers are now taxed ***cumulatively.***

## D. The Generation-Skipping Transfer Tax

### 1. Background

Prior to 1976, there was opportunity for considerable estate tax avoidance through the use of so-called generation-skipping transfers. This was made possible by the fact that the estate tax does not apply to property in which the decedent possessed only a life interest or special power of appointment. Therefore, by granting successive life estates and special powers of appointment, estate tax exposure could be avoided through succeeding generations (limited only by the common law Rule Against Perpetuities, which has now been repealed in most states), even though each succeeding generation enjoyed the use of the property and considerable power with respect to its disposition. This potential for tax avoidance was long recognized as a significant flaw in the scheme of estate and gift taxation.

## 2. The Tax Reform Act of 1976

The 1976 Tax Reform Act introduced a completely new transfer tax—the "Generation-Skipping Transfer Tax." This tax was intended to eliminate the above-mentioned opportunity for tax avoidance.

### a. Separate Tax

The generation-skipping transfer tax was not an amendment to, or modification of, the estate or gift tax. Rather, it was an entirely ***separate system*** of transfer taxation (i.e., a tax is imposed upon the value of property at the time an interest therein shifts from one generation to a succeeding generation).

### b. Correlation with Estate and Gift Taxes

Nonetheless, the generation-skipping transfer tax was directly related to the estate and gift taxes insofar as it was designed to produce essentially the same tax result in the case of generation-skipping transfers as would have occurred had the property passed through successive generations by way of straightforward gifts or bequests. The tax was computed with reference to related estate or gift tax exposure.

## 3. The Tax Reform Act of 1986

The generation-skipping transfer tax provisions of the 1976 Act were perceived as "unduly complicated." As a result, Congress continually deferred the effective date for application. In 1986, Congress repealed the 1976 tax, but replaced it with a new generation-skipping tax.

### a. Essential Difference

The substantive provisions of the generation-skipping tax, as originally enacted in 1976, remain intact in the 1986 Code. The essential differences are:

(1) ***The tax is computed by applying a flat rate*** of tax to the actual amount of the generation-skipping transfer. Today, the flat rate is 40%. Under the 1976 Act, the estate and gift tax ***graduated*** rates were applied to the amount of the generation-skipping transfer ***as cumulated with*** the "deemed" transferor's taxable gifts and taxable estate.

(2) ***The circumstances in which the tax will apply have been expanded.***

### b. Pre-1986 Generation-Skipping Transfers

Recognizing the confusion that was caused by the continued deferral of the 1976 tax, this tax was repealed retroactively. Thus, generation-skipping transfers occurring after the 1976 Act but before the 1986 Act are ***exempt*** from generation-skipping taxes.

# E. Taxing Jurisdiction

## 1. Jurisdictional Bases for Estate and Gift Taxation

A number of bases for taxing jurisdiction are accepted under the Constitution as well as under conventional international law. But for estate and gift tax purposes, the jurisdictional bases are citizenship or residence and the location of property.

#### a. Citizens and Residents

The estate tax reaches all property owned by a citizen or resident of the United States ***without regard to its location.*** [I.R.C. § 2031] Prior to 1962, the statute excepted real property located outside the United States, but this exception was repealed. Similarly, the gift tax reaches all property transferred by a citizen or resident. [I.R.C. § 2501]

#### b. Nonresident Aliens

However, in the case of nonresident aliens, only property ***located in the United States*** is subject to the federal estate tax. [I.R.C. § 2501(a)(1)] ***Rationale:*** Since no "personal" relationship exists between the decedent and the United States, taxing jurisdiction must be based upon the property's presence within the United States. Gift tax exposure likewise depends upon location of the property within the United States. In addition, section 2501(a)(2) generally exempts from the gift tax transfers of ***intangible*** property by nonresident aliens.

# F. Portability of the Deceased Spousal Exclusion Amount ("Portability")

## 1. Brief History

Congress enacted portability in 2010 to temporarily permit a decedent's executor to make an election on the decedent's estate tax return to allow the surviving spouse to use the decedent's unused exemption amount for estate and gift tax purposes. [*See* I.R.C. § 2010(c)] The election was made permanent under the American Taxpayer Relief Act of 2012. Portability does not apply to the generation-skipping transfer tax.

## 2. Meaning of Deceased Spousal Unused Exclusion Amount

With respect to a surviving spouse, the deceased spousal unused exclusion amount is the lesser of the basic exclusion amount or the excess of the "applicable exclusion amount" of the ***last deceased spouse*** of the surviving spouse minus the tentative tax on the estate of the deceased spouse. [I.R.C. § 2010(c)(4)] The applicable exclusion equals the basic exclusion amount plus the deceased spousal unused amount. [I.R.C. § 2010(c)(2)]

# G. The Tax Cuts and Jobs Act

## 1. In General

Prior to the enactment of the Tax Cuts and Jobs Act (TCJA), the basic exclusion amount for estate and gift taxes and the generation-skipping transfer tax was $5,000,000 adjusted for inflation. Under the TCJA, the basic exclusion amount was doubled. The inflationary basic exclusion amount for 2022 is $12,060,000. The TCJA is subject to sunset after December 31, 2025. Hence, unless Congress repeals the sunset, the basic exclusion amount will revert to $5,000,000 (adjusted for inflation) on January 1, 2026.

# Chapter Two

# Substantive Aspects of the Estate Tax

| CONTENTS | PAGE |
|---|---|

# Chapter Approach

The estate tax is imposed upon the "taxable estate." [I.R.C. § 2001] This is defined as the "gross estate" less any allowable deductions. [I.R.C. § 2051] To determine the taxable estate, you need to determine:

## 1. The Gross Estate

What transfers or property are subject to the estate tax, or, as it is usually expressed, what transfers are "included in the gross estate"?

## 2. Any Allowable Deductions

After you have determined the total value of the gross estate, you need to identify any and all allowable deductions. To determine estate tax liability from the taxable estate, you need to make the computations discussed in Chapter Six.

These functional aspects of computing estate tax liability also define the two basic substantive areas of the estate tax law: the gross estate and allowable deductions.

# A. Gross Estate

## 1. Inclusions in Gross Estate—General Overview

Sections 2033 through 2046 of the Internal Revenue Code set forth the types of property and property transfers that are included in the gross estate. These provisions may be divided into five categories:

### a. Property Owned by Decedent

By virtue of sections 2033 and 2034, the value of all property owned by the decedent at death is included in the gross estate.

### b. Property Not Owned by Decedent

Moreover, property that the decedent gave away during life and thus not "owned" at death, may, under certain circumstances, be included in the gross estate. Sections 2035 through 2038 detail the situations in which the estate tax reaches inter vivos transfers.

### c. Special Types of Property and Transfers

Certain property interests, rights, or powers give rise to a type of transfer upon the death of the decedent and have a "testamentary" flavor, and yet might fall outside the scope of the above taxing sections because of technical, property law notions of "ownership" or "transfer." Sections 2039 through 2042 and 2044 address the possible estate tax exposure of four such special types of property: annuities [I.R.C. § 2039]; joint tenancies [I.R.C. § 2040]; powers of appointment [I.R.C. § 2041]; and life insurance [I.R.C. § 2042].

### d. Transfers Not for Consideration

Only ***gratuitous*** transfers are subject to the estate tax, not bargained-for sales or exchanges for consideration. Section 2043 outlines the nature and adequacy of consideration that will, for federal estate tax purposes, prevent a transfer (in whole or in part) from being considered gratuitous and thus insulate the transfer from the estate tax.

### e. Miscellaneous Provisions Related to the Gross Estate

These include the following:

#### (1) Certain Marital Deduction Property

Under the Revenue Act of 1981, certain property may qualify for the marital deduction even though the surviving (or donee) spouse is granted a limited interest which would not be taxable to the spouse under general rules of the estate tax. Section 2044 requires that this property be included in the spouse's gross estate.

#### (2) General Rule of Inclusion

Section 2045 sets forth a general rule of comprehensive inclusion. The substantive inclusion provisions of sections 2034 through 2042 operate without regard to when a transfer was made or when a property interest arose, except as otherwise specifically provided by law.

#### (3) Disclaimer or Renunciation

As will be seen, a valid disclaimer or renunciation of property is not a "transfer" for estate tax purposes (disclaimers are discussed in Chapter 4). Section 2046 incorporates the gift tax rules of section 2518 relating to the circumstances in which disclaimers or renunciations will be effective and thus outside the purview of the estate tax.

| CALCULATION OF GROSS ESTATE | | GILBERT |
|---|---|---|
| STEP 1: | | Take Property Owned by Decedent at Death |
| STEP 2: | + | Certain Property Given Away During Decedent's Life |
| STEP 3: | + | Special Types of Property and Transfers (e.g., annuities, joint tenancies, powers of appointment, life insurance) |
| STEP 4: | + | Transfers Not for Consideration |
| STEP 5: | + | Miscellaneous Provisions (e.g., certain marital property) |
| | = | Gross Estate |

## 2. Section 2033—Property Owned by Decedent

Section 2033 is the basic provision of the Code dealing with the gross estate. It is deceptively simple: "The value of the gross estate shall include the value of all property to the extent of the interest therein of the decedent at the time of [the decedent's] death."

### a. Introductory Analysis

For purposes of analysis, issues raised by section 2033 are typically divided into the following three categories and will be treated accordingly herein:

(1) ***The fundamental issues***—i.e., the types of ***transfers, property,*** and ***interests*** subject to section 2033, as well as the nature of ownership within its scope;

(2) ***The relationship of section 2033*** (the general taxing provision) ***to the more specific taxing sections*** which follow; and

(3) ***The impact of state law*** upon the federal taxing scheme.

### b. Transfers Taxed

Clearly, section 2033 reaches property transferred by will or intestacy. However, it is not limited to such transfers. As long as the decedent ***owns*** an interest in property ***at death,*** which is ***transmitted*** to another on account of the decedent's death, the property is included in the decedent's gross estate.

**Example:** Under Diane's contract of employment, Diane's employer agreed that if Diane should die while in its employ, it would pay to a person designated by Diane the sum of $5,000. Diane died while employed and her employer paid $5,000 to Diane's designee, Sam. Although the amount transmitted to Sam "passed" by contract, rather than by will or intestate succession, it is includible in Diane's gross estate under section 2033. ***Rationale*:** Diane's unqualified contractual right to designate the recipient of the payment gave her an "interest in property" which passed to another by reason of her death.

#### (1) Limitations—"Ownership" Interest "Transferred" to Another

For a tax to attach under section 2033, the property must be ***"owned" by the decedent at death,*** and it must be ***"transferred" from the decedent to another.***

##### (a) Property "Owned"

The mere fact that a decedent's death is instrumental in someone acquiring an interest in property is not enough to support imposition of the tax. The decedent must have had an ***interest*** in the property at death.

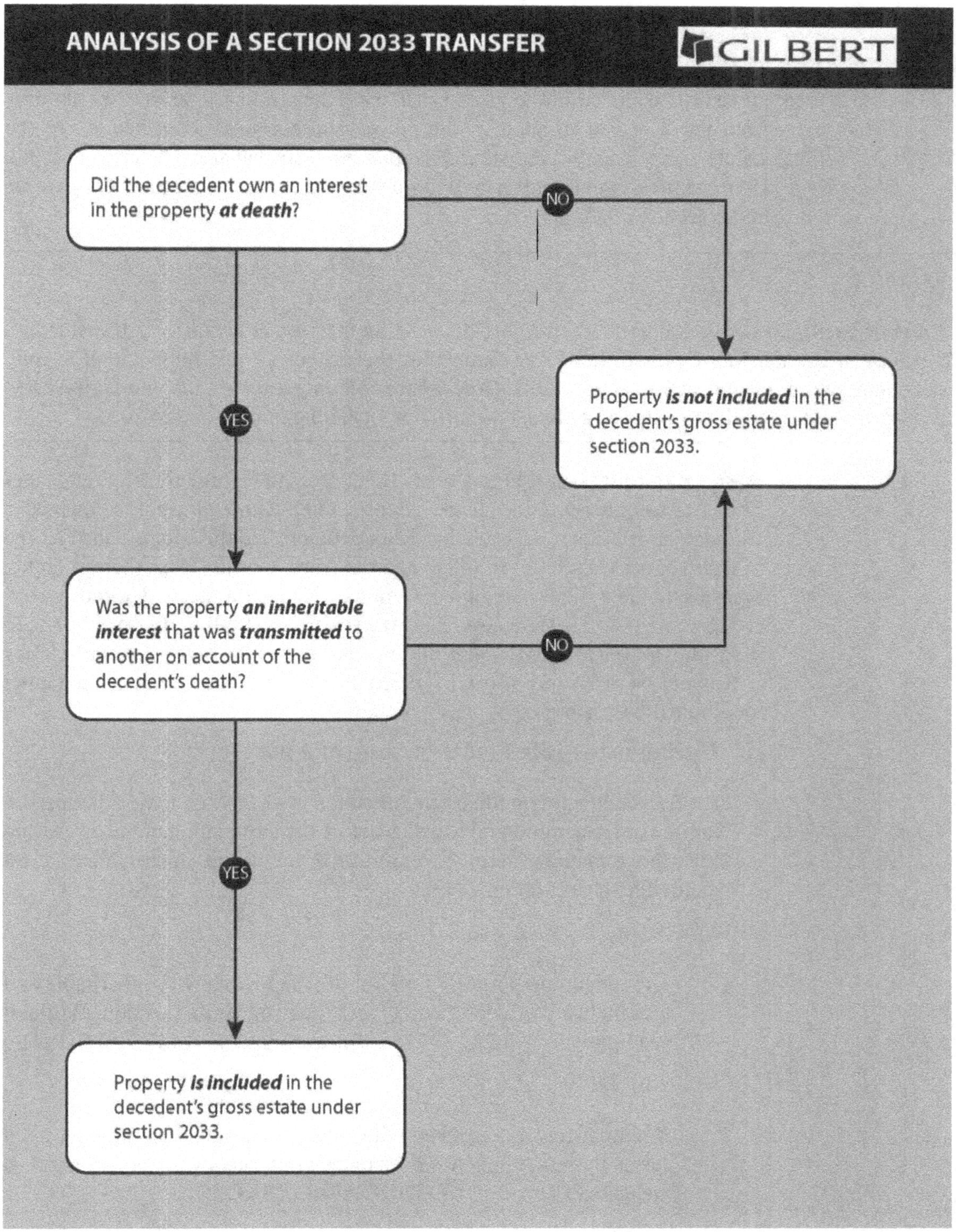


e.g. **Example:** A ***discretionary*** bonus awarded an employee ***after*** the employee's death and paid over to the employee's executor is not taxable in the employee's gross estate. Since the payment was a matter of discretion only, the decedent neither had a right to, nor interest in, the bonus; it is therefore immaterial that the decedent's death may have occasioned the transfer. [Rev. Rul. 65–217, 1965–2 C.B. 214]

### (b) "Transfer by Decedent"—Interests Terminating at Death

Although a literal reading of section 2033 might suggest that an interest owned at death is included in the gross estate even though that interest does not pass from the decedent to another, the proper and accepted interpretation of the statute is that it applies only to ***inheritable interests*** that are transferred at death. Hence, interests that terminate upon death (e.g., a life estate) are ***not taxable*** under section 2033.

**EXAM TIP** GILBERT

On your exam, be sure to remember that just because an interest in property is transferred because of the decedent's death ***does not mean*** that the property must be included in the decedent's gross estate under section 2033. Only ***inheritable interests*** are included. Interests that terminate upon death, such as a life estate, are not includible under section 2033.

e.g. **Example:** Ronald transferred Blackacre "to George for life, remainder to George Jr. and his heirs." George died. Although George "owned" a life estate in Blackacre at death, his death extinguished this interest and George Jr.'s remainder passed not from George but from Ronald. Thus, there is no tax exposure to George's estate under section 2033. [**Williams v. United States,** 41 F.2d 895 (Ct. Cl. 1930); *see also* **Helvering v. Rhodes' Estate,** 117 F.2d 509 (8th Cir. 1941) (involving a life income interest in trust); **Commissioner v. Rosser,** 64 F.2d 631 (3d Cir. 1933) (addressing a contingent remainder conditioned upon survival)]

#### 1) Distinguish—Life Estate for Life of Another

If a decedent enjoys a life estate measured by the life of some other person (a life estate pur autre vie) and dies before the termination of the measuring life, the remaining term of that life estate is an inheritable interest includible under section 2033.

##### a) Note

The remaining portion of a term of years is likewise inheritable and thus included in a decedent's gross estate under this section. [**Millard v. Malony,** 121 F.2d 257 (3d Cir.), *cert. denied,* 314 U.S. 636 (1941)]

##### b) And Note

A similar result is reached with future interests not contingent upon survival; the contingency goes to the question of valuation rather than inclusion. [Rev. Rul. 67–370, 1967–2 C.B. 325]

#### 2) Distinguish—Transfer by Decedent Subject to Retained Life Estate

The rule that interests terminating on death are not includible in the gross estate applies only to interests conveyed to the decedent by another. Transfers ***by*** the decedent with a ***retained*** life estate are included in the decedent's gross estate under section 2036 (discussed later in this chapter).

#### 3) Joint Tenancies

Although joint tenants have ownership interests in property and the death of one is instrumental in the transmission of the decedent's interest to the survivor(s), there is ***no "transfer"*** from a deceased joint tenant to the survivor(s). Rather, upon the decedent's death the interest is extinguished, and it passes to the surviving joint tenant(s) by "right of survivorship." Thus, there is no tax exposure under section 2033.

##### a) Section 2040

As discussed later in this chapter, section 2040 specifically addresses whether joint tenancy property is included in a joint tenant's gross estate upon death.

##### b) Distinguish—Tenancies in Common

A tenancy in common does not carry survivorship rights. Hence, an interest owned as a tenant in common is included in the gross estate under section 2033 since the undivided interest of a deceased co-tenant is devisable and inheritable. [**Harvey v. United States,** 185 F.2d 463 (7th Cir. 1950)]

### c. Types of Property Included Under Section 2033

Under the Regulations, all types of property—real or personal, tangible or intangible—are included in a decedent's gross estate under section 2033, including notes or other claims owned by the decedent, choses in action that survived the decedent's death, and accrued salary, rent, interest, dividends, or other accrued rights to income owned by the decedent. [Treas. Reg. § 20.2033–1]

#### (1) Future Interests

Interests in property that have not yet vested in possession (i.e., future interests, such as reversions and vested remainders) generally ***are included*** under section 2033 just like possessory interests. Thus, the present value of such interests is included in the gross estate. [**Frazier v. United States,** 322 F.2d 221 (5th Cir. 1963)—valuation being made by use of actuarial tables prescribed by the Regulations; Treas. Reg. § 20.2031–7]

##### (a) Contingent Interests

The fact that a future interest is contingent (either subject to a condition precedent or vested subject to divestment upon the happening of a condition subsequent) does not prevent its inclusion in the gross estate. The contingency, however, will affect the ***value*** of the interest. [Rev. Rul. 67–370, 1967–2 C.B. 3251]

##### 1) Computing Value

Some contingent interests can be valued by use of standard actuarial tables, while others are not susceptible of valuation by standard methods. If the value of an interest is not ascertainable (e.g., because it is highly speculative), it is includible in the gross estate and should be included on the estate tax return (since it is an interest in property owned at death), but the reduction in value on account of the contingency will be zero. [**Robinette v. Helvering,** 318 U.S. 184 (1943)]

### (2) Debts Cancelled by Will

If a decedent holds a note or otherwise has a claim against another, the amount thereof is includible under section 2033 even though the obligation is cancelled under the terms of the decedent's will. In other words, the cancellation is treated as if the decedent had bequeathed the amount of the debt to the creditor. [Treas. Reg. § 20.2033–1(b)]

#### (a) Distinguish—Self-Cancelling Installment Notes

With self-cancelling installment notes ("SCINs"), the result is different. For example, in **Moss v. Commissioner,** 74 T.C. 1239 (1980), the decedent sold stock during his life, taking back an installment note that recited that "[u]nless sooner paid, all sums, whether principal or interest, shall be deemed cancelled and extinguished as though paid as of the death of [the seller/decedent]." The Tax Court held that the installment buyer's obligation and hence any right to payments on the part of the decedent or his estate was thus extinguished by the decedent's death. Therefore, the unpaid balance on the note was ***not includible*** in the decedent's estate.

### (3) "Tax Exempt" Bonds, Etc.

According to the Regulations, statutory provisions exempting bonds, notes, bills, and certificates of indebtedness, as well as the interest thereon, from taxation are generally ***not subject*** to the estate tax. ***Rationale:*** Such tax is an excise tax on the transfer of property at death, not a tax on the property transferred. [Treas. Reg. § 20.2033–1(a)]

### (4) Injury and Death Claims

#### (a) Causes of Action for Wrongful Death

For many years, the Service insisted that wrongful death claims were includible in the decedent's gross estate under section 2033 if they accrued to the decedent's estate. However, the Service has reversed itself, conceding that the value of wrongful death claims (or the proceeds) is not included in the decedent's gross estate. [Rev. Rul. 75–127, 1975–1 C.B. 297]

##### 1) Rationale

"Simple logic mandates the conclusion that an action for wrongful death cannot exist until the decedent has died, at which point he is no longer a person capable of owning any property interests." [**Connecticut Bank & Trust Co. v. United States,** 465 F.2d 760 (2d Cir. 1972)]

#### (b) Distinguish—Actions That Survive Plaintiff's Death

On the other hand, any claims or causes of action owned by the decedent at the time of death and which survive the decedent's death are includible in the gross estate under section 2033. [**Maxwell Trust v. Commissioner,** 58 T.C. 444 (1972)]

**EXAM TIP** GILBERT

During your exam, don't be fooled by the fact that some personal injury claims are highly speculative. Under section 2033, ***even speculative claims must be included*** in the decedent's gross estate if the claim survives the plaintiff's death, although they may be valued very low or even at "zero."

### (5) Life Insurance

Section 2033 does bring the ***proceeds*** of insurance into the policy owner's gross estate if the owner is a person other than the insured (e.g., where a spouse owns an insurance policy on the life of the other spouse). However, the life insurance proceeds may be included in the insured's gross estate under section 2042 discussed later in this chapter.

#### (a) Life Insurance Owned by Someone Other than the Insured

If the insured is alive at the time of the policy owner's death, the value of the policy is included in the policy owner's gross estate under section 2033—measured by its replacement cost. [**DuPont's Estate v. Commissioner,** 233 F.2d 210 (3d Cir. 1956)]

### (6) Income-Producing Property

If a decedent owned income-producing property at death (e.g., rental real estate, stocks, or bonds that pay interest), the value of that property ***and*** the income therefrom that has accrued at the date of the decedent's death are included under section 2033. [Treas. Reg. § 20.2033–1(b)] On the other hand, income accruing ***after*** death ***is not*** included in the gross estate (although it is taxable to the recipient estate or beneficiary under the income tax).

### (7) Rights to Future Income

If the decedent owned at death a right to receive income in the future, the ***present value*** of that right is included in the gross estate. The present value is computed by reducing the amount of the expected payments to reflect the fact that money that will not be received until some future date is "worth" less than money presently in hand (since one will not enjoy the earning power of the future payments until they are received). This process, called "discounting," is accomplished by using actuarial tables specified by the Regulations. [Treas. Reg. § 20.2031–7]

e.g. **Example:** Gale agreed to play ball for a professional football team. His contract obligated the team to pay him, in addition to an annually negotiated salary, $300,000 per year for 10 years irrespective of whether he was able to play; and if Gale died during the 10-year period, payments would continue to be made to his estate. Gale was killed in the first year's spring training, before collecting any of the deferred "bonus" payments. The present value of the payments is taxable to his estate under section 2033.

#### (a) Income Derived from Property vs. Rights to Future Income

It is important to distinguish "rights" to future income that derive from the ownership of income-producing property (e.g., rental real estate) from rights to future income where the right itself is the property "owned" (such as Gale's bonus payments). In the former case, unearned income is not included under section 2033; however, this anticipated income does affect the valuation of the underlying property. In the latter case, the right to income has been "earned" and the right itself is the property included under section 2033.

**EXAM TIP** GILBERT

On your exam, be sure you distinguish between rights to ***future income that derive from the ownership of income-producing property*** (e.g., rental property, stocks) and ***rights to future income when the right itself is the property owned*** (e.g., right to receive rental payments). When "transferred" with the property, the right to future income is ***not includible*** under section 2033, but it most likely affects the ***valuation*** of the property transferred. However, if the only "property" transferred is the right to the income, post-death income would be included under section 2033.

### (8) Post-Death Payments from Decedent's Business

Whether payments made from a decedent's business subsequent to death are includible in the gross estate depends upon the nature of those payments.

#### (a) Liquidation Payments

Payments made in liquidation of a decedent's interest in the business are a "substitute" for that interest—i.e., property owned by the decedent at death—and are includible under section 2033.

#### (b) Post-Death Profits

However, where payments represent business profits accruing after the decedent's death and are paid to the estate or beneficiary because the decedent's successor continues to own the business interest, only the ***business interest*** is included in the decedent's gross estate, ***not the future profits.***

##### 1) Survivor's Benefits

Where business profits are paid to the decedent's beneficiary pursuant to a contract entered into by the decedent and business entity prior to the decedent's death, under the better view the value of these survivor's benefits is included in the decedent's gross estate. ***Rationale***: The decedent owned ***a contractual right*** at death (i.e., the amounts to be paid to the beneficiary are pursuant to a contract which is distinct from the ownership of the business interest itself). [**McClennen v. Commissioner,** 131 F.2d 165 (1st Cir. 1942); Rev. Rul. 66–20, 1966–1 C.B. 214. *But see* **Bull v. United States,** 295 U.S. 247 (1935) (benefits belong to survivor, hence not taxable in decedent's estate)]

##### 2) Partnership Liquidation Agreements

Many partnership agreements provide that, upon the death of a partner, the partnership will not be dissolved with its assets distributed to the partners. Rather, in lieu of any distribution of a deceased partner's interest in specific partnership property, the partnership agrees to pay that partner's estate or designated beneficiary a percentage of partnership earnings for a specified period of time. The better view is that such rights to future payments are included under section 2033 where the substance of the arrangement is that the partner's death extinguishes the partner's partnership interest. The partner's estate is left with the contractual right to future payments in lieu of any claim against the partnership for a distribution of the deceased partner's capital; it is only this contract right that the decedent owns at death. [**Estate of Riegelman v. Commissioner,** 253 F.2d 315 (2d Cir. 1958). Also, agreements among family members are subject to heightened scrutiny to avoid disguised bequests and gifts.

### (9) Employment Benefits

#### (a) Voluntary Payments

It is clear enough that ***voluntary*** payments made by an employer to a deceased employee's surviving spouse or family are ***not included*** under section 2033. Even though the death may have prompted the payments, the employee had no right to or interest in such payments before or at death.

#### (b) Benefits Pursuant to Contract

On the other hand, if death benefits are paid to specified beneficiaries as part of the bargained-for employment ***contract,*** they are included in the deceased employee's gross estate. Even though the employee did not receive the payment, the employee possessed at death a contractual right that such payments would be made to the employee's designated beneficiaries.

#### (c) Survivor's Benefits Under Employment Plans

Section 2039 (entitled "Annuities") was added to the Code in 1954 to clarify the estate tax exposure of survivor's benefits under employment plans and, since its enactment, has been the principal focus for the taxation of such plans. Consequently, the development of this area of the law under section 2033 has been limited; most typical employee survivor benefit plans are taxed under section 2039 so that the government need not resort to section 2033.

### (10) Statutory Benefits

As distinguished from private, contractual benefit plans, survivor benefits under various types of social welfare legislation are ***not includible*** under section 2033. Examples include Social Security payments, benefits under the Railroad Retirement Act of 1937, and Workers' Compensation awards. [Rev. Rul. 67–277, 1967–2 C.B. 322]

#### (a) Rationale—Not "Owned at Death"

The decedent owns no interest in statutory benefits payable to certain survivors from funds produced by taxes.

| TYPES OF PROPERTY INCLUDIBLE UNDER SECTION 2033 | GILBERT |
|---|---|
| INCLUDIBLE UNDER SECTION 2033 | NOT INCLUDIBLE UNDER SECTION 2033 |
| ***Debts to the decedent,*** even if cancelled | ***Self-cancelling installment notes*** |
| | ***Tax-exempt bonds,*** etc. |
| Claims that ***survive the decedent's death*** | ***Wrongful death claims*** |
| ***Contract*** for insurance on the life of someone ***other than the policy owner*** | |
| Income-producing property owned at death | |
| ***Income produced*** from property ***before*** the decedent's death | ***Income produced*** from property ***after*** survivor's benefits under employment related plans the decedent's death |
| ***Right to unearned income*** when the ***right is the property,*** discounted to present value | ***Right to unearned income*** when such right is ***included with*** the property (but may affect property's value) |
| ***Liquidation payment*** from the decedent's business | ***Profits*** accruing ***after*** the decedent's death |
| ***Survivor's benefits*** | |
| ***Partnership earnings*** paid to ***extinguish the decedent's partnership interest*** | |
| Benefits paid ***per employment contract*** | ***Voluntary payments*** made by employer |
| | ***Statutory benefits*** (e.g., Social Security benefits) |

### d. Nature of Ownership Required for Tax

The "ownership" required by the statute is ***beneficial ownership.*** Technical legal title is not subject to the estate tax. [Treas. Reg. § 20.2033–1] Thus, for example, if the decedent holds legal title to property as trustee for another but has no beneficial interest in the property, it is not included in the decedent's gross estate.

#### (1) Transfers Void Under Local Law

One who makes a transfer of property that is absolutely void under local law has not parted with beneficial ownership; hence, the property remains taxable in the transferor's estate under section 2033. [**City National Bank v. United States,** 383 F.2d 341 (5th Cir. 1967)] On the other hand, property ***received*** in a transfer that is void under local law is ***not included*** in the transferee's estate (because the transferee has never acquired beneficial ownership).

#### (2) Expectancies

An "expectancy" is not an interest in property. Consequently, the possibility, or even the likelihood, that a decedent or the decedent's estate may receive property under a will, under the laws of intestate succession, or as a (revocable) beneficiary under a life insurance policy on the life of another is ***not*** included in the decedent's gross estate.

### e. Impact of State Law

The nature of an individual's interest in property is defined by the law of the state in which the property is located, and since imposition of the estate tax depends upon the nature of the decedent's interest, the resolution of federal estate tax issues often calls for reference to local law. At the same time, however, local law does not define the ***scope*** of federal tax law—whether an interest in property or a transfer is taxable (or a claim is deductible) is a matter of federal tax law, to be resolved by a federal administrative agency or the federal courts. Stated more simply, ***local law*** defines a person's rights, obligations, privileges, and powers with respect to property; whereas ***federal tax*** law defines whether those rights, etc., give rise to imposition of the estate tax (or allowance of an estate tax deduction).

#### (1) Determination of State Law

Given the relationship between local law and the federal tax law, the issue arises as to how the federal institutions resolve the relevant local law question.

##### (a) Where General Rule of Law Applies

The resolution of this issue is relatively simple where a general rule of local property law, promulgated by a state statute or by the state's highest court as a matter of common law, is clearly applicable. Absent conflicting federal law, the federal authority will follow the state law.

e.g. **Example:** A donor granted property to a donee for life, remainder to the donee's heirs. If the Rule in Shelley's Case is followed in the state in which the property is located, the donee has a fee simple interest, and the property will be included in the donee's gross estate. However, if the state has repudiated the Rule, the property will not be included in the donee's gross estate because the donee's interest is a life estate which is extinguished at death.

##### (b) Where Interpretation of State Law Required

Where the question involves the interpretation of state law and its application to a specific situation, and where the specific issue has ***not*** been adjudicated by a state court, the IRS or a federal court must undertake to interpret and apply the local law itself.

e.g. **Example:** Prior to death, Howard endorsed certain securities to Anna and placed them in his safe deposit box. At the same time, Howard wrote to Anna advising her that, "I have endorsed certain securities over to you this day as a gift and have placed them in my safe deposit box for safekeeping. Stop by at your convenience, and we will go to the bank to get them." Howard died before Anna came for the securities. Under local law, "delivery" of property to the donee is required for a completed lifetime gift. Assuming that no local authority addresses the issue of whether endorsement of securities and notification to the donee of the purported gift, under the circumstances recited, satisfies the delivery requirement, the IRS or a federal court must make its own determination in order to ascertain whether Howard owned the securities at death or had made a completed gift, thereby divesting himself of all interest in the securities prior to death.

### (2) Effect of Prior State Court Determination

A difficult question arises where a lower state court has adjudicated the specific property rights: To what extent is the IRS or a federal court ***bound*** by that determination? For example, suppose in the above example that the probate court had determined that delivery to Anna had been completed, so that she was the owner of the securities at Howard's death and that the securities were not part of Howard's probate estate. Neither party appeals, and the decision becomes final. Does this final determination of the probate court conclusively settle the question of whether the securities are subject to tax under section 2033?

#### (a) Former Conflicting Views

Prior to 1967, there were at least three differing views on this issue: (i) the state court's determination, which bound the parties in interest, ***also bound the federal court*** addressing the federal tax issue, (ii) the state court's determination was binding ***unless procured by fraud or collusion,*** or (iii) the state court's determination was binding only if the federal court found that the issue was ***fairly presented*** by opposing parties **and *fairly litigated* in** the state court proceedings.

#### (b) The *Bosch* Case—Lower Court Decisions Not Binding

The Supreme Court finally resolved the conflict in 1967, adopting a rule reminiscent of that applied in diversity litigation under **Erie Railroad v. Tompkins,** 304 U.S. 64 (1938). The Court *in Bosch* held that, in addressing a federal tax question turning upon a question of local property law, the IRS and federal courts are only bound by the decisions of the ***highest court of the state*** because "the state's highest court is the best authority on its own law." [**Commissioner v. Estate of Bosch,** 387 U.S. 456, 465 (1967)] According to the Court, state lower court decisions, on the other hand, need only be given ***"proper regard."*** Hence, the federal authority is in effect "sitting as a state court," and it is not bound by the lower court decision but rather can decide the matter as it believes the state's highest court would decide it.

**EXAM TIP** GILBERT

For exam purposes, remember that the determination of whether a decedent owned a particular piece of property is similar to the choice of law principles in civil procedure—a federal court ***must apply the property law of the state in which the decedent lived,*** and it is ***bound by the highest state court decisions.***

##### 1) Impact of *Bosch*

In federal tax cases, the federal court decision is only final as to the tax issue, but it does not determine property rights of the parties under the state law. Thus, under the *Bosch* decision, one party (Anna in the example above) may be finally determined to be the legal owner of property by a state court, while another party (Howard in the example above) may be treated as the owner for estate tax purposes!

## 3. Section 2034—Dower or Curtesy Interests

Section 2034 of the Code includes in the decedent's gross estate "the value of all property to the extent of any interest therein of the surviving spouse, existing at the time of the decedent's death as dower or curtesy, or by virtue of the statute creating an estate in lieu of dower or curtesy."

### a. Effect—No Deduction for Marital Interests

Property owned by the decedent at death is included at its ***full value*** without any reduction for the surviving spouse's marital interests therein. [Treas. Reg. § 20.2034–1]

### b. Background and Analysis

This section is more a clarification of legislative intent than a substantive taxing provision. It was enacted in 1918 (two years after the predecessor of section 2033) simply to make clear that if property is subject to tax under section 2033, its full value is to be included in the gross estate; this is so even though an argument might be made that the property is not freely transferable by the decedent to the extent that it is subject to the surviving spouse's dower, curtesy, or statutory "forced share" rights.

#### (1) Note

The above principle (precluding reduction of the gross estate to the extent of such marital "claims" against the estate) is consistent with other provisions of the statute that deny that marital rights constitute adequate consideration either to prevent classification of a transfer as "gratuitous." [*See* I.R.C. § 2043(b)]

### c. Release of Interest

Moreover, section 2034 cannot be avoided by substitution of a contractual obligation to pay an amount in lieu of dower or curtesy [**Empire Trust Co. v. Commissioner,** 94 F.2d 307 (4th Cir. 1938)] or by the surviving spouse's release of dower or curtesy rights in lieu of a legacy in the decedent's will. [**Mayer v. Reinecke,** 130 F.2d 350 (7th Cir. 1942)]

### d. Distinguish—Community Property Rights

Dower and curtesy are not vested interests, but mere expectancies in the property of the other spouse. On the other hand, in community property states each spouse is treated as owning a present, undivided one-half interest in the community assets. The result is that on the death of either spouse, ***only his or her one-half is includible*** in the gross estate. The other half belongs to the surviving spouse and is not includible in the gross estate.

### e. Effect of Marital Deduction

The importance of section 2034, requiring the inclusion of dower and curtesy interests, is greatly offset by the marital deduction. [*See* I.R.C. § 2056] As will be discussed later, the marital deduction operates to take out of the taxable estate most of the property included therein under section 2034.

**EXAM TIP** GILBERT

On your exam, be careful to distinguish between ***dower, curtesy, and forced shares*** on one hand, and rights under ***community property laws*** on the other. Dower, curtesy, and forced shares ***must be included in the decedent's gross estate,*** given that they are not currently vested interests. However, a community property interest is treated as currently vested, and thus ***need not be included in the decedent's estate*** under section 2034.

## 4. Section 2035—Gifts Made Within Three Years of Death

The estate tax cannot reach property that was the subject of a completed gift during the decedent's life. Thus, to prevent easy avoidance of the estate tax by "deathbed transfers," the estate tax has subjected gifts made shortly before death to taxation.

### a. Background

#### (1) Former Tax on Transfers "in Contemplation of Death"

Prior to 1977, a completed gift made by the decedent during life was exposed to the estate tax if made ***"in contemplation of death."*** The operative element for taxation was the ***subjective intent*** or motive of the decedent at the time of the transfer.

##### (a) Proof of Transferor's Intent—Presumptions

Intent or motive is essentially a factual question, always difficult to resolve. It is made even more difficult when one is called upon to ascertain the subjective intent of a person who is now dead. In order to reduce these administrative problems, the statute has always included a presumption that transfers within a certain period prior to death would be deemed to have been made in contemplation of death.

###### 1) Conclusive Presumptions and *Heiner v. Donnan*

From 1916 until 1926, the statutory presumptions could be rebutted upon showing absence of the requisite motive. The conflicts and controversies this produced prompted Congress, in 1926, to enact a ***conclusive*** presumption that transfers in excess of $5,000 made within two years of the decedent's death were made in contemplation of death. However, in **Heiner v. Donnan,** 285 U.S. 312 (1932), the Supreme Court held this presumption constitutionally invalid as a violation of the Due Process Clause of the Fifth Amendment insofar as it established an arbitrary classification for taxation of certain transfers (within two years of death) while others (made before that time) escaped tax.

###### 2) Viability of a Conclusive Presumption Today

Although ***Heiner*** has never been overruled, it is felt that a conclusive presumption can survive constitutional attack today. Over the years, the Supreme Court has been more willing to uphold objective guidelines for imposition of the tax, on the theory that they are reasonable and necessary for the effective administration of the tax and thus not arbitrary classifications. This was the theory urged, unsuccessfully, by the dissent in ***Heiner***.

#### 3) Presumptions Under the 1954 Code

Prior to its amendment in 1976, the 1954 Code contained two presumptions:

a) A ***rebuttable*** presumption that transfers made within three years of death were made in contemplation of death; and

b) A ***conclusive*** presumption that transfers made more than three years before death were ***not*** in contemplation of death.

### (2) 1976 Tax Reform Act Amendment

Under the Tax Reform Act of 1976, any inter vivos transfer, in trust or otherwise, made by the decedent after December 31, 1976, was included in the decedent's gross estate if the decedent died within three years of the transfer. Therefore, the amendment dictated ***automatic*** inclusion in the decedent's gross estate of gifts made ***within three years of death.***

#### (a) Constitutionality

Despite any lingering vitality of **Heiner v. Donnan,** the Committee Reports support the constitutionality of this approach. The amendment did not establish a conclusive presumption of subjective intent but, rather, provided a rule of law as to the scope of the estate tax which would be applied uniformly to all taxpayers without regard to intent.

### (3) Limited Taxation of "Deathbed Gifts" Under the 1981 Act

As noted in Chapter One, the 1976 Act "unified" the gift and estate tax rates and credits, and it provided that all lifetime transfers be taken into account in determining the marginal rates of tax that would be applied to the decedent's estate. The effect of these provisions was substantially to reduce the need to ***include*** deathbed gifts in the gross estate of a decedent, since such gifts would be taxed under the gift tax when made (using the same rate schedule as the estate tax) and would be added to the estate tax base for the purpose of determining the estate tax. In effect there would be no difference in the total taxes paid, whether or not such gifts were included in the decedent's gross estate, except: (i) if the property appreciated substantially between the date of the gift and the decedent's death (within three years), and (ii) to the extent that the annual exclusion was applicable to the gift.

#### (a) Outright Gifts Excluded

Congress was persuaded that the unification of the transfer taxes thus made the tax avoidance potential of most deathbed gifts quite negligible, and this negligible fiscal effect did not justify the time and cost required to assure that all of such gifts were reported and to undertake a second appraisal and valuation of the property transferred. Consequently, the 1981 Act amended section 2035 so as to eliminate most outright gifts from inclusion in the decedent's gross estate. [I.R.C. § 2035(a)]

#### (b) Continuing Major Impact of Section 2035

Section 2035 continues to operate and have a major impact in two very important areas:

#### 1) "Gross-Up Rule"

Although a gift made within three years of death is not included in the decedent's estate, any gift taxes paid or payable with respect to such gifts ***are*** included. [I.R.C. § 2035(b)]

#### 2) Transfer or Release of Taxable "Strings"

If the decedent possessed or retained a taxable interest or power with respect to certain property which would result in the inclusion of the subject property in the decedent's estate under section 2036, 2037, 2038, or 2042, the transfer or release of the taxable power or interest within three years of death will be ineffective to preclude estate taxation of the property. Consequently, section 2035 continues to interact with these other sections so as to include in the gross estate property that would have been included if the transfer or release had not occurred within the three-year period. [I.R.C. § 2035(a)(2)] This rule is inapplicable to bona fide sales for "adequate and full consideration in money or money's worth." [I.R.C. § 2035(d)]

**EXAM TIP** GILBERT

For your exam, remember that, although most outright gifts need not be included in the decedent's gross estate, two important exceptions exist: First, ***taxes paid or payable as a result of the gift*** are included in the donor's gross estate. Second, ***if another provision would have called for the gifted property to be included*** in the decedent's gross estate had the gift not taken place within the three-year period, the property must be included in the decedent's gross estate.

### b. Gift Taxes Paid by Decedent on Inter Vivos Gifts Also Included ("Gross-Up" Rule)

A decedent's gross estate includes the amount of any gift tax paid by the decedent or the decedent's estate with respect to any gifts made within three years of death. [I.R.C. § 2035(b)]

#### (1) Purpose

Without this rule, it would be advantageous for a decedent to make death-bed gifts: the payment of related gift taxes would reduce the decedent's gross estate since, if the decedent paid the taxes, the amount would not be in the decedent's estate, and the estate would be entitled to a credit for gift taxes. [*See* I.R.C. § 2001 and Treas. Reg. § 20.2053–6(d)] The "gross-up" rule eliminates this opportunity for tax avoidance. The impact of section 2035 on the payment of gift taxes cannot be avoided by a gift to the spouse who in turn immediately makes a gift and then pays gift taxes with the gifted funds. The "step transaction" doctrine will permit the IRS to ignore the intermediate transfer to the spouse and treat the transaction as one in which the decedent made a gift and payment of gift taxes within three years of death. [**Brown v. United States,** 329 F.3d 664 (9th Cir. 2003)]

#### (2) Example

Dakota died in 2022 and had made five taxable gifts totaling $4 million between 2020 and 2022. Dakota had already used the applicable exclusion amount before making the gifts in 2020. Dakota paid a total of $1.6 million in gift taxes on the five gifts. Since these five gifts were made within three years of Dakota's death, the $1.6 million paid in gift taxes will be included in Dakota's gross estate under the "gross-up" rule.

#### (3) Application of Gross-Up Rule to a Spouse's Gifts

The "gross-up" rule also applies to gift taxes paid by the decedent (or decedent's executor) with respect to gifts made by the decedent's spouse that are "split" with the decedent under section 2513 within three years of the decedent's death. Gift splitting is discussed in Chapter Four.

#### (4) Application of Gross-Up Rule Where a Donee Pays Gift Tax

In **Estate of Sachs v. Commissioner,** 88 T.C. 769 (1987) (reversed on separate issue), a gift made within three years of the donor's death was conditioned on the donee paying the donor's gift tax liability—a "net gift" situation. The Tax Court held that the gift tax, even though paid by the donee, was includible in the donor's estate under the gross-up provision. The rationale for including the gift tax in the donor's gross estate is to disincentivize the donor from making deathbed transfers to reduce the estate tax base by an amount equal to the gift taxes. Significantly, in **Steinberg v. Commissioner,** 145 T.C. 184 (2015), the court determined that donees' assumption of the section 2035(b) liability reduced the fair market value of the gift because it constituted consideration in money or money's worth under section 2512(b).

### c. Relation of Section 2035 to Other Taxing Sections—Release of Taxable Interests Within Three Years of Death

With the exception of section 2040, which taxes joint tenancy property, section 2035 interacts with the other specific taxing sections of the Code to produce a tax under those sections if a taxable interest or incident of ownership ***is transferred, released, or relinquished within three years of death.*** [I.R.C. § 2035(a)(2)]

#### (1) Basis for Interaction

Prior to 1981, this interaction was specifically provided for in certain of the other taxing provisions, such as sections 2038 and 2041, or was developed by judicial authorities as a matter of statutory interpretation based upon principle and apparent congressional intent [*see, e.g.,* **United States v. Allen,** 293 F.2d 916 (10th Cir.), *cert. denied,* 368 U.S. 944 (1961)]. The 1981 amendment of section 2035 specifically provides that this section will continue to interact with sections 2036, 2037, 2038, and 2042. Also, section 2041 continues to interact with section 2035 by virtue of section 2041(a)(1)(B) and (a)(2).

e.g. **Example:** Ten years ago, D transferred property to X but retained a life estate. Two years before death, D transferred the retained life estate to X. Section 2036(a)(1) taxes transfers during life where the transferor retained a life interest in the property, and section 2035, as amended, continues to operate where a retained life estate is transferred within three years of death. It is not the life interest alone which will be taxed under section 2035 but, by the interaction of sections 2035 and 2036(a)(1), the ***full value*** of the property. In effect, section 2035 operates to permit a tax under section 2036(a)(1) just as if D's life interest persisted until D's death.

e.g. **Example:** Moreover, the court in ***Allen*** held that where the decedent ***sold*** a retained life estate to the holder of the remainder within three years of death, the full value of the property (less the consideration received for the transfer) was included in the decedent's estate by virtue of sections 2035 and 2036(a)(1). [***Rationale:*** Even though there was "full and adequate consideration" for the transfer of the life estate, the consideration paid was negligible when compared to the value of the property which the decedent, by this device, hoped to remove from taxation under section 2036(a)(1). Congress clearly intended to tax the full value of property transferred subject to a retained interest that persists until death or that is relinquished within three years of death, and the court refused to allow this intent to be frustrated by a transfer within three years of death for a consideration inadequate when compared to the value of the property potentially subject to tax.

#### (2) Limitation—Coextensive Interaction

Where section 2035 interacts with another specific taxing section, the substantive provisions of ***both*** sections must apply for a tax to result; the interaction neither adds to nor reduces the scope of the substantive provisions.

e.g. **Example:** If, in the above example, D transferred the retained life interest to X ***four years*** before death, no estate tax would result since, under section 2035, transfers more than three years prior to death are not taxed and, under section 2036(a)(1), a retained life interest will not produce a tax if the life estate is transferred or relinquished before death. Likewise, if the life estate had not been retained by D but rather, had been ***granted to D*** by another, a transfer within three years of death would not produce a tax, since a life estate granted to the decedent by a third party is not taxable under section 2036(a)(1). ***Section 2035 does not add to the scope of other taxing sections.***

#### (3) Exception—Grantor Trusts Under I.R.C. § 676

Any transfer from a portion of a trust that is revocable and taxed to the grantor of the trust under section 676 is treated as being transferred by the grantor and not from the trust, thereby making section 2035 inapplicable. [I.R.C. § 2035(e)]

## 5. Section 2036—Transfers with Retained Life Interests

Under section 2036 of the Code, a tax is imposed upon any inter vivos transfer made by a decedent "under which he has retained for his life or any period not ascertainable without reference to his death or for any period which does not in fact end before his death—(i) the possession or enjoyment of, or the right to income from, the property, or (ii) the right either alone or in conjunction with any person, to designate the persons who shall possess or enjoy the property or the income therefrom." Section 2036 is inapplicable where there is a bona fide sale for an adequate and full consideration in money or money's worth. [*See* I.R.C. § 2036(a)]

### a. Historical Background

This section (as well as sections 2037 and 2038), derives from the Revenue Act of 1916 which imposed an estate tax upon lifetime transfers "intended to take effect in possession or enjoyment at or after" the transferor's death. Sections 2036 through 2038 codified the intended scope and thrust of this rather obscure phrase and, for the most part, addressed what were at first very restrictive and later quite expansive interpretations of that phrase by the Supreme Court.

### (1) Transfers with Retained Life Estates Held Not Taxable

It had always been assumed that a transfer with a reserved life estate was clearly within the intendment of the statutory language taxing transfers "intended to take effect in possession and enjoyment at or after" the transferor's death. State courts, interpreting identical language in state inheritance tax laws, had consistently so held, and the Supreme Court, in **Reinecke v. Northern Trust Co.,** 278 U.S. 339 (1929), had so implied. It therefore came as quite a surprise when the Supreme Court held, in **May v. Heiner,** 281 U.S. 238 (1930), that such transfers were ***not*** subject to the estate tax. The Court's theory was that the transfer to the owner of the remainder occurred at the time of the original grant, not upon the transferor's death; the remainder was already vested, and death merely extinguished the intervening interest. Thus, the words "intended" and "possession and enjoyment" were effectively read out of the statute, the Court insisting that a transfer from the decedent at death was required.

### (2) Congressional Reaction—the 1931 Joint Resolution and the 1932 Act

On March 2, 1931, the Supreme Court reaffirmed its position in ***Heiner.*** However, Congress responded the next day with a Joint Resolution specifically taxing transfers with a reserved life estate. This provision was subsequently clarified and refined in the Revenue Act of 1932.

#### (a) Limitation—Prospective Operation Only

It is important to note that Congress limited the provisions of both the Joint Resolution and the 1932 Act to prospective application only. Thus, transfers prior to the effective date of the Joint Resolution (March 4, 1931) are not taxed; and transfers between that date and the effective date of the 1932 Act (June 7, 1932) are taxed under the more limited provisions of the Joint Resolution.

#### (b) Substantive Changes

The 1932 Act contained four modifications, two of which were considered substantive ***without retroactive effect:*** (i) the addition of "for any period not ascertainable without reference to [the transferor's] death" to the time periods for which an interest must be retained in order to incur the tax; and (ii) the imposition of the tax when the decedent retained the power to designate income "either alone or in conjunction with any person."

#### (c) Clarifying Changes

On the other hand, two changes were deemed to be merely clarifying and declaratory of prior law: (i) the substitution of the phrase "for any period which does not in fact end before his death" for the language of the Joint Resolution "for any period not ending before his death," and (ii) substituting "the right to income" for "the income."

### (3) Later Developments—May v. Heiner Overruled

In **Commissioner v. Church's Estate,** 335 U.S. 632 (1949), the Supreme Court overruled ***Heiner.*** And, while the decision had little impact on transfers with reserved life estates after 1931, it did expose pre-1931 transfers to tax under the "intended to take effect" language which was still part of the Code in 1949.

(a) **Effect of Section 2036(c) of the 1954 Code—1931 Cut-Off Date**

The tax on the pre-1931 transfers was not long lived. With the passage of the 1954 Code, Congress provided (under section 2036(c)) that the tax will ***not*** reach transfers made prior to the effective date of the Joint Resolution, and transfers between that date and the effective date of the 1932 Act will be taxed only if they would have been taxed under the Joint Resolution.

**b. Introductory Analysis**

On its face, section 2036(a) specifies four requirements for taxation:

**(1) Transfer**

A decedent must have made an inter vivos transfer of property or an interest in property (to a trust or otherwise).

**(2) Retained Interest**

At the time of the transfer, the decedent must have retained certain interests in or powers over the property.

**(3) Time Periods**

The taxable interests or powers must be retained for one of three time periods:

(a) For ***life;***

(b) For a period of time other than life if the period ***cannot be determined without reference to the decedent's death;*** or

(c) For a period of time other than life if ***in fact the decedent dies before the end of that period.***

**(4) Taxable Interests or Powers**

The interests or powers retained must be either:

(a) ***The possession or enjoyment*** of, or a ***right to income from,*** the property; or

(b) ***The right to designate who shall possess or enjoy*** the property or its income.

**(5) Comments**

**(a) Bona Fide Sale Exception**

Section 2036(a) includes a bona fide sale exception. Under this exception, even if a transferor retains a life estate in transferred property but there is a "bona fide sale for an adequate and full consideration in money or money's worth," [I.R.C. § 2036(a)] the property will not be included in the transferor's gross estate under section 2036.

**1) Attempts to Structure Transfer as a Bona Fide Sale—Application of Substance over Form**

Transferors attempt to avoid section 2036 by making it appear that a transfer is a bona fide sale. In **Estate of Maxwell v. Commissioner,** 3 F.3d 591 (1993), a mother sold her home to her son and daughter-in-law and took back a promissory note. She continued to reside in the home as a "tenant" and immediately forgave a portion of the loan equal to the annual exclusion. The rent essentially equaled the interest payments on the loan.

There were no payments made on the principal. Under the mother's will, executed a few days after the transfer, she forgave the loan. The court determined that the taxpayer must demonstrate that at the time of the transaction there was a real expectation of repayment when the bona fides of a promissory note are at issue. After analyzing this issue, the court concluded that the home was included in the mother's gross estate under section 2036 because there was not a bona fide sale for adequate and full consideration.

### (b) Overlap of Requirements

For purposes of this Summary, analysis of the scope and thrust of section 2036 follows the above four taxation requirements. It should be noted, however, that the interpretative authorities frequently cross categories. For example, the issue of whether a taxable interest or power has been ***retained*** may merge with the issues of whether it is the decedent who made the ***transfer*** of property and whether the decedent has a "right" to possession or to income.

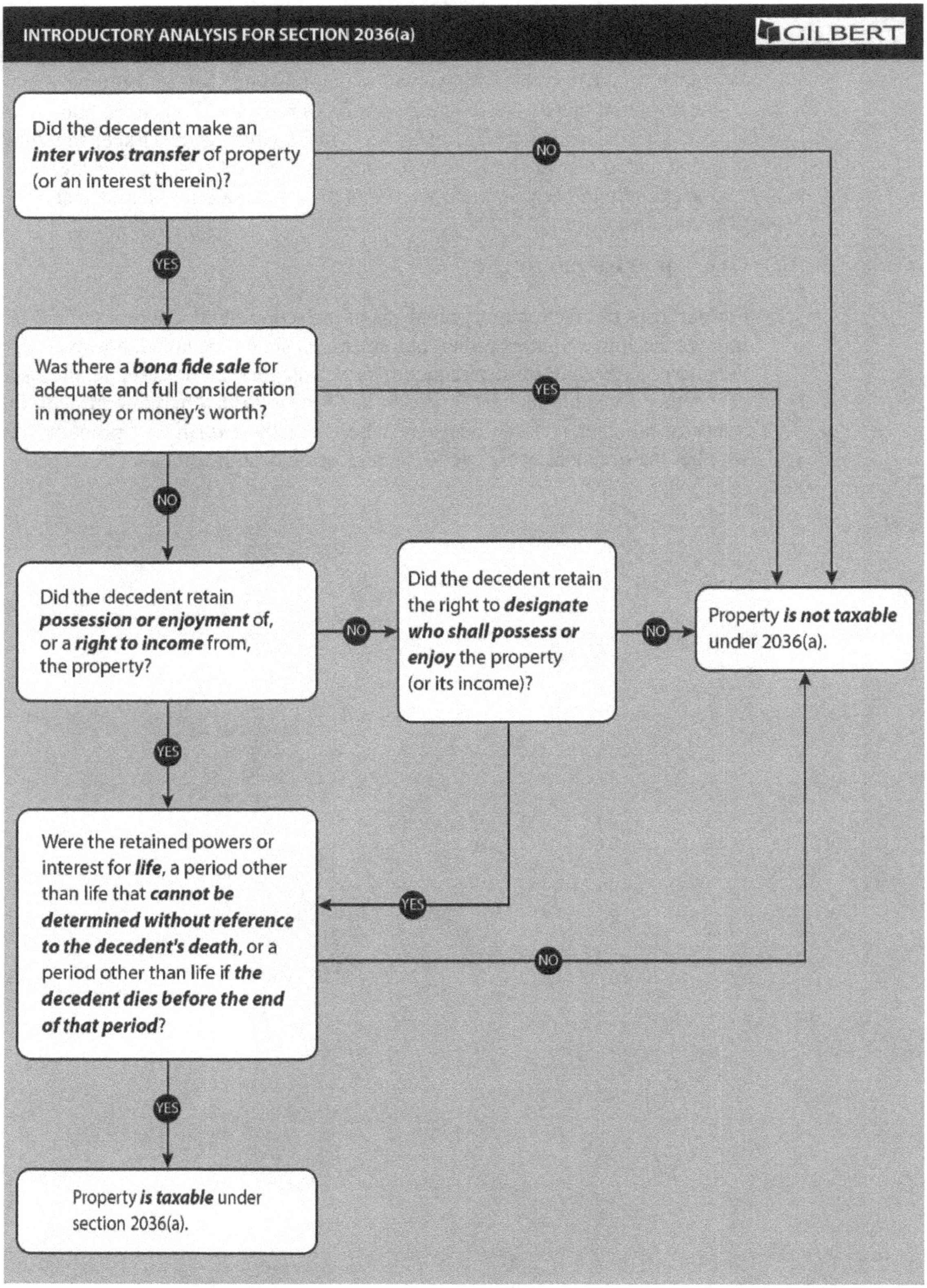


### c. Requirement of a Transfer

For purposes of taxation under section 2036, it is insufficient that the decedent possesses a life estate in property or a special power with respect to property. Rather, the property to which the life estate or power relates must have been "transferred" by the decedent during life.

#### (1) Transfers in General

The term "transfer" applies to the conveyance of any property, on trust or otherwise. It also applies to any expenditure made by a decedent during life for the purpose of having a third person convey property to a donee. In addition, it includes the relinquishment of an interest or incident of ownership or the exercise or release of a taxable power of appointment. These notions of "transfer" are applicable, directly or by analogy, to the transfer requirement under section 2036. Additionally, some other transfer issues have been addressed by the courts with specific reference to section 2036.

#### (2) Life Insurance Settlement Options

If a beneficiary under a life insurance policy on the life of another is entitled to receive the proceeds upon the death of the insured but elects a settlement option under which the company retains the proceeds, paying the electing beneficiary interest on the fund for life and distributing the retained proceeds to the beneficiary's designee upon the beneficiary's death, it has been held that the beneficiary has made a ***transfer of the proceeds*** reserving a right to income, which is taxable under section 2036. It is immaterial that the settlement option was elected prior to or upon the death of the insured. [**Pyle v. Commissioner,** 313 F.2d 328 (3d Cir. 1963)]

##### (a) Distinguish—Insured's Election

Where the ***insured*** elects this type of settlement option for the beneficiary, and the beneficiary has no right or power to modify the same, the result is contra. Here, the beneficiary has not made a "transfer," and hence the proceeds are not taxable to the beneficiary's estate. [**Minotto v. Commissioner,** 9 T.C.M. 556 (1950)]

#### (3) Community Property Election

In community property states, a surviving spouse may elect, pursuant to a provision in the deceased spouse's will, to take a life estate in all the community property in lieu of the survivor's own vested fee interest in one-half of the community property. If such an election is made, the survivor is treated as having transferred the survivor's vested one-half interest while reserving a life estate therein. [**Gregory v. Commissioner,** 39 T.C. 1012 (1963)]

##### (a) Note

The survivor is not deemed to have made a transfer of the ***deceased*** spouse's interest, and since the survivor possessed only a life estate therein, at death it is not taxed in the survivor's estate.

##### (b) And Note

The "widow's election" cases under section 2036 are complicated by the issue of consideration. Since the "transfer" by the survivor is in consideration of the life estate in the property of the deceased spouse, the value of the property transferred for purposes of tax under section 2036 must be reduced by the value of the life interest.

#### (4) Who Is the Transferor

Ordinarily, in assessing tax consequences, the ***substance*** of transactions, rather than mere ***form,*** controls. For example, suppose Paul were to purchase property from

Sam and direct Sam to transfer a life estate in the property to Paul with a remainder to Darla; or suppose Paul were to transfer property to Sam with the understanding that Sam would immediately thereafter transfer that same property to a trust naming Paul the life income beneficiary with remainder to Sam (or another). In both cases, Sam is the formal or nominal transferor of the property in which Paul enjoys a life estate but, clearly, Paul is the actual transferor. And in both cases, the tax law would treat Paul as the transferor of the property in which the life estate was reserved.

### (a) Application—Reciprocal Trusts

The above principle that the substance rather than form determines who is the transferor is well illustrated by the "reciprocal trust doctrine."

e.g. **Example:** Two brothers (John and Bobby) transferred equal amounts of property on separate irrevocable trusts. The trust established by John provided that Bobby should enjoy the income for his life with remainder to his issue. The trust established by Bobby was identical, but reciprocal in its terms, providing for income to John for life, remainder to his issue. The court found that the trusts were in consideration of each other so that John was to be treated as the actual transferor of the trust nominally established by Bobby, and conversely. Thus, upon John's death, the value of the Bobby trust—which John was deemed to have established—was included in John's gross estate because of the "retained" life estate which John had in that trust. [**Lehman v. Commissioner,** 109 F.2d 99 (2d Cir.), *cert. denied,* 310 U.S. 637 (1940)]

#### 1) When Are Trusts Deemed "Reciprocal"?

##### a) Background—Spousal Reciprocal Trusts

At one time, problems were experienced in taxing reciprocal trusts between spouses. Outside of interspousal arrangements, the authorities had emphasized consideration as the touchstone for determining the actual, substantial transferor; but when the reciprocal settlors were spouses, it was difficult to find a technical, common law consideration. Thus, prior to 1969, many courts refused to apply the reciprocal trust doctrine between spouses, reasoning that the trusts were merely a mutual division of family property and were not created in consideration of each other. [**Newberry's Estate v. Commissioner,** 201 F.2d 874 (3d Cir. 1953)]

##### b) Consideration Not Required

However, the Supreme Court has since eliminated the notion of consideration as a critical element on the theory that " 'consideration,' in the traditional legal sense, simply does not normally enter into such intrafamily transfers." Rather, "application of the reciprocal trust doctrine requires only that the trusts be ***interrelated*** and that to the extent of mutual value, leave the settlors in approximately the ***same economic position*** as they would have been in had they created the trusts naming themselves as life beneficiaries." [**United States v. Grace,** 395 U.S. 316 (1969)]

**EXAM TIP** GILBERT

On your exam, be careful to watch out for the ***reciprocal trust doctrine.*** If two trusts are interrelated, and if the settlors are in approximately ***the same economic position*** as they would have been in had they created the trusts naming themselves as life beneficiaries, the reciprocal trust doctrine most likely applies, and the settlors ***will be deemed to have retained a life estate in the trust established by the other,*** making it taxable to their respective estates.

c) **Comment**

Presumably, *Grace* does not stand for the proposition that consideration is irrelevant, but rather that the reciprocal trust doctrine may be applied even though technical legal consideration is absent. However, in resolving one issue, *Grace* opens up others. For example, is the Court's rule subjective insofar as it speaks of the "interrelationship" of the trusts (which suggests an intent to interrelate), or is it objective insofar as it speaks of no effective change in the parties' economic position (which can be detected by objective observation of the result)? [*See* **Bischoff v. Commissioner,** 69 T.C. 32 (1977) (concurring opinion suggests that *Grace* requires an ***intended*** interrelationship)]

d) **Dissimilar Trust Terms**

The reciprocal trust doctrine will not apply if the trusts in question are substantially different. [*See* **Estate of Levy v. Commissioner,** 46 T.C. Memo 1983–453 (1983) (determining that the reciprocal trust doctrine did not apply where the decedent and his spouse created similar trusts because the decedent's wife had a special power of appointment, but the wife's trust did not grant one for the decedent)]

(5) **Time of the Transfer**

Since section 2036 does not reach transfers prior to the effective date of the 1931 Joint Resolution, it may be important to determine precisely when a transfer is deemed made. The general rules may be summarized as follows:

(a) **Outright Gifts**

Where a gift is made outright, the transfer occurs when title passes from the transferor.

(b) **Gifts on Irrevocable Trust**

The passing of title is the critical time as to gifts on trust. The fact that signatures are later added to the trust agreement does not alter the effective transfer date, but merely signifies the signer's acquiescence to a transfer previously made. [**Commissioner v. Henry,** 161 F.2d 574 (3d Cir. 1947)]

1) **Note**

It has also been held that a transfer is complete upon delivery of the deed of trust, even though the trust property was not given to the trustee until a later date. [**Farnum v. Commissioner,** 14 T.C. 884 (1950)]

#### (c) Gifts on Revocable Trusts

Where the trust is ***revocable*** the authorities are in conflict. The Tax Court adopts the position that the transfer is made at the time the property is transferred to the trustee [**Canfield v. Commissioner,** 34 T.C. 978 (1960), *aff'd,* 306 F.2d 1 (2d Cir. 1962)], while the Court of Claims and the Fourth Circuit have held that the transfer does not occur until the power to revoke lapses or is released [**Smith v. United States,** 139 F. Supp. 305 (Ct. Cl. 1956); **Commissioner v. Talbott,** 403 F.2d 851 (4th Cir. 1968), *rev'g* 48 T.C. 271 (1967), *cert. denied,* 393 U.S. 1022 (1969)]

#### (d) Additions to Trust

Even though a trust was created prior to March 3, 1931, ***additions*** to the trust made after that date may result in proportionate taxation of the trust corpus under section 2036. For example, if D transferred $80,000 on trust in 1930, reserving a right to trust income for life, and then transferred $100,000 to the trustee of this trust in 1940 (at which time the previously transferred corpus had appreciated in value to $100,000), one-half of the trust corpus would be exposed to the estate tax under section 2036 on the theory that the added property was "transferred" after the cut-off date.

### d. Requirement That the Interest or Power Be Retained

For the tax to attach under section 2036, it is ***not*** sufficient that the taxable interest or power be possessed by the decedent at death. Rather, the decedent must have ***retained*** the interest or power in connection with the inter vivos transfer.

#### (1) Limitation—Interest Must Be Retained in Property Transferred; Annuities

The retained interest or power must be in the ***very property*** transferred; hence, transfers solely in return for the transferee's promise to pay an ***annuity*** to the transferor are usually treated as the purchase of an annuity, not the reservation of a life estate in the conveyed property.

**Example—Transfer for Annuity:** The decedent, along with her husband and son, had transferred property to a trustee, directing the trustee to liquidate the trust property and purchase annuities for the beneficiaries. Specifically, the decedent was to receive an annuity paying her $10,000 per year for life. Until the property could be liquidated in an orderly manner and the annuities purchased, the trustee was authorized to hold the property and pay the decedent up to $10,000 per year. The decedent died before any annuities were purchased but for over 10 years received approximately $10,000 per year from the trust. The Tax Court held that the decedent's portion of the trust property (to the extent necessary to produce $10,000 of income per year) was taxable under section 2036(a)(1). However, the Seventh Circuit reversed, finding that the transfer was in consideration of an agreement to pay an annuity of $10,000 per year and there was no retained interest in the property transferred. [**Becklenberg v. Commissioner,** 273 F.2d 297 (7th Cir. 1959)]

**Example—Transfer Held Reserved Life Estate:** Taxpayers transferred closely held stock to trust for an "annuity" calling for payment of $75,000 annually for their lives. The trustee then sold the stock for $1 million (payable in 10 years) with annual interest of $75,000. The court held that in substance the taxpayers had reserved a life estate in the property transferred on trust. [**Lazarus v. Commissioner,** 513 F.2d 824 (9th Cir. 1975); *see also* **Ray v. United States,** 762 F.2d 1361 (9th Cir. 1985) (transfer on trust was held ***not*** to be a transfer for an annuity because, on the facts, no exhaustion of the principal would ever be required to pay the fixed monthly amount reserved by the transferor)]

#### (a) Annuity-Life Insurance Package

Decedent, who was uninsurable, purchased an "annuity-life insurance package" for a single premium of $350,000 and then assigned the insurance policies to a trust for her children. For all practical purposes, the face amount of the life insurance was approximately equal to the single premium paid, and the annuity payments were approximately equal to the income that that premium could be expected to earn, less an amount that the insurance company would take as its profit. The government asserted that this agreement was really a transfer with the reservation of a life interest, but the Supreme Court disagreed, holding that the annuity and life insurance contracts were technically two separate contracts and thus two separate properties. The straight life annuity which ended at Decedent's death was not taxable under section 2033; the life insurance was not taxable under section 2042 since Decedent retained no incidents of ownership in the policy; and there could be no tax under section 2036 since Decedent's annuity contract (which was retained) represented an interest neither in the property transferred (the premium paid) nor in the separate life insurance contract. [**Fidelity-Philadelphia Trust Co. v. Smith,** 356 U.S. 274 (1958)]

##### 1) Note

This rather transparent tax avoidance scheme is now forestalled by section 2039.

### e. Period of Retention

The interest or power must be retained for one of three time periods: (i) for the ***transferor's life;*** (ii) for a period ***not ascertainable without reference to the transferor's death;*** or (iii) for a period of time that does ***not in fact end before the transferor's death.***

#### (1) For Life

The first period, "for life," is self-explanatory and usually quite obvious. Recall that the decedent need not be actually enjoying the property during life or in fact be able to exercise a power to designate during life.

#### (2) Period Not Ascertainable Without Reference to Death

This time period is apparently designed to assure that a tax will be imposed under section 2036 even though a person does not technically reserve an interest or power "for life"—as long as the life or death of the transferor is the critical limitation upon the continuation of the retained interest or power.

e.g. **Example:** A son transfers property to his mother, reserving the right to receive the income therefrom in quarterly payments, with a provision that no part of the income between the last quarterly payment and the date of the son's death is to be received by the son or his estate. Since the period for which the income is retained is "not ascertainable without reference to his death," the transfer is includible in the son's estate. [*See* Treas. Reg. § 20.2036–1(b)(1)(i)]

#### (3) Period That Does Not in Fact End Before Death

For this period of retention, the transferor sets a specific term for the transferor's use or possession of the property, such as 10 years. This does not refer to the transferor's death and is not a life estate, but if the transferor dies within the 10-year term, the term does not end before death and the result will be the property being included in the transferor's gross estate.

**Example:** At age 40 and while in excellent health, Darla irrevocably transferred property on trust for the benefit of Alan but reserved the right to direct the trustee to pay some or all of the income to herself (Darla) for five years. In the fourth year following the creation of the trust, Darla is killed in an automobile accident. Even though it does not appear that Darla ***intended*** to retain a right in the income ***for her life,*** the right to income which she did retain did not, in fact, end before her death; hence, the value of the trust property is included in her estate under section 2036(a)(1).

**Example:** A parent makes a gift of income-producing property to a minor child under the Uniform Transfers to Minors Act. The parent serves as the custodian. The child dies before reaching the majority age. The property is includible in the parent's gross estate under section 2036(a)(2) because the parent retained for a period which does not end before the parent's death.

### f. Nature of Interest Retained Under Section 2036(a)(1)

Section 2036(a)(1) requires retention of a beneficial interest in the property: A decedent must retain ***"possession or enjoyment"*** of, or ***"the right to income"*** from, the property. Apparently, the retention of both possession or enjoyment and the right to income is not required, although from an economic perspective these elements frequently merge (i.e., a right to income from the property connotes enjoyment of it and possession or enjoyment implies a lifetime access to its economic potential).

#### (1) Subsequent Reconveyance of Interest

Section 2036 will ***not*** apply where the decedent ***reacquires*** an interest in the property subsequent to the transfer. For example, if D made an outright gift of property during D's lifetime and the donee later—without prearrangement—reconveyed to D's a life estate therein, D does not have a "retained" life estate, and the transfer will not be included under section 2036. [*See* **Estate of Uhl v. Commissioner,** 241 F.2d 867 (7th Cir. 1957)]

#### (2) Distinguish—Prearranged Reconveyance

##### (a) Significance—Tax Avoidance Forestalled

To be distinguished from the above situation are cases where the donee's subsequent reconveyance was prearranged. The Regulations provide that "an interest or right is treated as having been retained or reserved if at the time of the transfer there was an understanding, express or implied, that the interest or right would later be conferred." [Treas. Reg. § 20.2036–1(a)] This position is crucial to prevent the tax avoidance that would otherwise result through transfers with no apparent retained interest but which are made with the clear understanding that such an interest will be conferred upon the transferor. Indeed, the same rule obtains where the understanding was not legally enforceable but was, in fact, carried out.

**e.g.** **Example:** A father transferred income-producing property to his children upon an oral understanding that he would continue to receive all the rents until he died. Pointing out that the "retention" need not be expressed in the instrument of transfer, the court found that even though the oral understanding was unenforceable under local law, it was sufficient for inclusion under section 2036 when coupled with the fact that the father did collect the income for life. [**McNichol v. Commissioner,** 265 F.2d 667 (3d Cir. 1959), *cert. denied,* 361 U.S. 829 (1959)]

### (3) Non-Income-Producing Property

Since the retention of possession or enjoyment is sufficient to attract the tax, it is not necessary that the property be income-producing. Thus, if a donor gives certain works of art to a donee, but retains possession for life, the value of the works of art is taxable to the donor under section 2036(a)(1) simply because of retained possession; one need not resort to economic niceties to find some "right to income" from this non-income-producing property.

### (4) Contingent Interests—Secondary Life Estates

As a general proposition, actual possession or enjoyment during life is required; a retained reversionary interest would be taxed under section 2033 but probably not under section 2036. However, a retained right to income will produce a tax under section 2036 even though the decedent was not receiving income at the time of death. According to the Committee Reports that accompanied the 1932 Act, this was the thrust of the clarifying amendment inserting "right to income" for "the income." Moreover, the retention of a secondary life estate after the death of a primary life tenant will produce a tax even though the decedent dies before the primary life tenant. [Treas. Reg. § 20.2036–1(b)(ii); *see also* **Commissioner v. Estate of Arents,** 297 F.2d 894 (2d Cir.), *cert. denied,* 369 U.S. 848 (1962)]

### (5) Possession or Enjoyment

As previously noted, section 2036 will apply even though the decedent retained no legal ***right*** to lifetime possession and enjoyment. However, the mere fact of possession is apparently ***not*** sufficient to attract the tax; there must also exist some ***understanding or agreement*** between the decedent and the transferee that the decedent should be entitled to enjoy possession for one of the requisite time periods. [Treas. Reg. § 20.2036–1(a)]

#### (a) Inferring an Understanding from Possession

In a number of cases where the decedent transferred a personal residence to a spouse or children, but continued to live in the residence until death, the Service contended that an understanding or agreement should be inferred from the fact of continued possession.

##### 1) Intraspousal Transfers

However, in cases involving transfers between spouses, this position did not meet with success [*see, e.g.,* **Gutchess v. Commissioner,** 46 T.C. 554 (1966), *acq.* 1967–1 C.B. 2], and in 1970, the Service announced that "continued occupancy by the donor spouse along with the donee spouse will not normally give rise to an inference that an understanding or agreement exists." [Rev. Rul. 70–155, 19701 C.B. 189]

2) **Other Transfers—Exclusive Possession Test?**

On the other hand, continued occupancy of a residence given to other persons (usually children) frequently has been held to create an inference that an "understanding" existed, thus supporting a tax on the value of the residence under section 2036. A comparison of two cases suggests that a critical factor giving rise to this inference is the exclusive occupancy of the donor. [*See* **Linderme, Sr. v. Commissioner,** 52 T.C. 305 (1969) (property taxed as donor's exclusive occupancy emphasized); **Diehl v. United States,** 21 A.F.T.R.2d 1607 (1967) (jury verdict for taxpayer where the decedent continued to reside in residence with donees, his children)]

(b) **Inferring an Understanding from Transfer to a Trust**

Similarly, the requisite "understanding" has been inferred where the decedent makes a transfer to a trust and, regardless of the trust terms, continues to beneficially enjoy the transferred property.

e.g. **Example:** The decedent transferred property to a trust, the income to be paid to his wife for life with remainder to his children. The trust was ostensibly irrevocable, and for purposes of this issue, no interest or power was retained. However, the evidence indicated that the decedent's wife never directly received any income from the trust, that the beneficiaries were only vaguely aware of the existence of the trust but not of its terms or the identity of the trustee, and that the trustee, in fact, distributed income and corpus at the decedent's direction and request and principally to the decedent for his benefit. Finding that the dealings raised an inference of a prearrangement that the decedent should retain control for his benefit until death, the court held that the decedent had retained possession and enjoyment during his life and imposed a tax on the property under section 2036(a)(1). [**McCabe v. United States,** 475 F.2d 1142 (Ct. Cl. 1973)]

(c) **Gift and Leaseback**

A gift of property followed by a "leaseback" to the donor, allowing the donor to use the property for the balance of the donor's lifetime by paying a nominal "rent," is nothing more than a disguised life estate and is fully taxed in the "tenant's" estate. [**Estate of DuPont v. Commissioner,** 63 T.C. 746 (1975)]

(6) **Right to Income**

Just as "possession and enjoyment" does not require a legally enforceable right, neither does the "right to income." The term "right" was added by the Revenue Act of 1932, not to limit the scope of this taxing provision but to clarify that property can be taxed even though the decedent is not receiving the income if the decedent has a right to the income. As discussed above, the Regulations suggest that "right" is to be interpreted as including an "understanding, express or implied"; and judicial authorities have held that the tax attaches under section 2036(a)(1) if the decedent is in fact receiving the income pursuant to some understanding with the donee even though the understanding is not legally enforceable.

(a) **Inference of Retained Right from Fact of Continued Receipt**

In **Strangi v. Commissioner,** 85 T.C.M. (CCH) 1331 (2003), the Tax Court held that a transfer of 98% of the decedent's wealth to a limited partnership by means of his son-in-law's exercise of a power of attorney was a change of form and not a sale for full and adequate consideration. It was a mere recycling of value. The court did say that some intangible factors (e.g., the presence of independent partners or investors) could take it out of this treatment, but that was not present in the case before it. The court also read into the arrangement an implied agreement that the decedent would retain the same relationship to the transferred assets relative to income that he had prior to the transaction. The decedent's estate appealed the decision, but the Fifth Circuit Court of Appeals agreed with the Tax Court that the wealth transferred to the limited partnership should be included in the decedent's gross estate under Section 2036(a)(1). [*See* **Strangi v. Commissioner,** 417 F.3d 468 (5th Cir. 2005)]

### (b) Indirect Beneficial Interests

The "right to income" is not limited to situations where the decedent personally collects or receives the income. So long as the income is to be used for the ***benefit of the transferor*** during life, a retained right to income may be found.

#### 1) Discharge of Legal Obligations

Thus, if income from property transferred on trust is to be used, or may be used, to discharge the transferor's legal obligations, this retained beneficial interest is clearly treated as a "right to income." [Treas. Reg. § 20.2036–1(b)(2)]

##### a) Contingent Obligations

It is not entirely clear whether payments made on an obligation for which the decedent was only ***contingently*** liable will support taxation of the trust property in the decedent's estate.

**i.** At least one case suggests that the income must be used to discharge a primary liability of the decedent. Thus, where decedent transferred mortgaged property to a trust with directions that the income from the property be used to pay off the mortgage, even though the decedent was personally liable to pay the mortgage note, the court held that there was no "right to income" retained. ***Rationale:*** There had been a complete and irrevocable transfer of the property for the benefit of others, and the primary obligation for the discharge of the mortgage was that of the donee, not the donor who was only secondarily liable; therefore, application of the income to this purpose was for the benefit of the trust and beneficiaries, not the donor/decedent. [**Hays v. Commissioner,** 181 F.2d 169 (5th Cir. 1950)]

#### 2) Support Trusts

Where a decedent creates a trust, the income from which is to be used during the decedent's life to fulfill his legal obligation of support, the decedent has retained a "right to income." For example, a trust is taxable under section 2036(a)(1) where the income is payable to the decedent's spouse for family and joint living expenses and for the spouse's support. [**Helvering v. Mercantile-Commerce Bank & Trust Co.,** 111 F.2d 224 (8th Cir.), *cert. denied,* 310 U.S. 654 (1940); *see also* **Commissioner v. Dwight's Estate,** 205 F.2d 298 (2d Cir.), *cert. denied,* 346 U.S. 871

(1953); **Estate of Gorkey v. Commissioner,** 72 T.C. 721 (1979), *aff'd as to this issue,* 735 F.2d 1367 (7th Cir. 1984)]

#### 3) Transfers Under Uniform Transfers to Minors Act

A transfer to children under the Uniform Gifts to Minors Act (the donor/parent acting as custodian) was included in the transferor's estate, since the Act authorized application of the income for the support of the minor. [**Prudowsky v. Commissioner,** 55 T.C. 890 (1971), *aff'd,* 465 F.2d 62 (7th Cir. 1972)] The same result will obtain under the newer Uniform Transfers to Minors Act.

#### 4) Distinguish—Transfers Extinguishing Support Obligation

Where property is transferred to ***extinguish*** any further support obligation (e.g., alimony trust created by the decedent to discharge alimony owing to ex-spouse), the payments are no longer deemed attributable to the decedent's continuing legal obligation and hence the transfer is not includible in the decedent's estate. [**National Bank of Commerce v. Henslee,** 179 F. Supp. 346 (M.D. Tenn. 1959)] Rather, it is treated as a transfer for consideration and is not taxable under section 2036(a)(1).

**EXAM TIP** GILBERT

Note this distinction: A trust that is used to ***fulfill*** a support obligation of the decedent ***is included*** in the decedent's gross estate, but a trust that is used to ***extinguish*** a support obligation is not.

### (c) Discretionary Trusts

As long as the settlor is not a trustee and cannot otherwise compel the use of the trust property or income for the settlor's benefit, the fact that the trustee has discretionary power to so use the income will not cause the trust property to be taxed under section 2036(a)(1). [*See* **Chrysler v. Commissioner,** 44 T.C. 55 (1965), *rev'd on another issue,* 361 F.2d 508 (2d Cir. 1966); *see also* **Mitchell v. Commissioner,** 55 T.C. 576 (1970), *acq.,* 1971–2 C.B. 3] This is true even if the trustee is given discretion to make payments directly to the settlor. [*See* **Commissioner v. Irving Trust Co.,** 147 F.2d 946 (2d Cir. 1945)]

#### 1) Caution—Prearrangement?

Courts may imply a retention of a right to income from continued discretionary distribution to the decedent. For example, where the property transferred was the decedent's sole source of income, and after the transfer the trustee paid all of the income to the decedent, a prearrangement may be inferred even though the instrument recited that the trustee had "absolute discretion" regarding payments. [**Skinner v. United States,** 316 F.2d 517 (3d Cir. 1963)]

#### 2) Distinguish—Where Settlor Can Compel Exercise of Discretion

Even though a trustee is given discretion to make payments to the settlor, if the settlor can compel exercise of this discretion in the settlor's favor, a "right to income" will be deemed to exist. For instance, where the standards governing the exercise of discretion are vague (e.g., a direction to distribute "such income as may be necessary for the comfort and happiness" of the settlor) the settlor could presumably enlist the aid of a court to compel the trustee to make distribution to him. Moreover, even where the standards governing the exercise of discretion are definite and ascertainable (e.g., to distribute "such income as may be necessary for the support, maintenance and welfare" of the settlor), the settlor could compel the exercise of the trustee's discretion in the settlor's own favor and, hence, has retained a "right to income." Similarly, where the decedent was settlor of a trust in which creditors of the decedent could have reached trust income and principal under state law to satisfy debts of the decedent, the decedent has retained an interest taxable under section 2036. [**Estate of Paxton v. Commissioner,** 86 T.C. 785 (1986); *see also* Tech. Adv. Mem. 199917001]

#### (d) Transfer of Stock Coupled with Employment Contract

Where stock is transferred by gift and, in connection therewith, the transferor enters into an "employment contract" with the corporation which provides for a "salary" in an amount likely to and which does absorb all the corporate profits, and which is to be paid to the transferor for the transferor's life without regard to services rendered, the transaction may be treated as a transfer of stock reserving a right to income. [**Holland v. Commissioner,** 47 B.T.A. 807 (1942)]

##### 1) Distinguish—Bona Fide Employment Contract

Where the employment contract represents reasonable compensation for services actually rendered by the transferor, it has been held that the tax will not attach under section 2036(a)(1). [**Hofford v. Commissioner,** 4 T.C. 542 (1945)]

## g. Nature of Power Retained Under Section 2036(a)(2)

Section 2036(a)(2) exposes to the estate tax any property transferred by the decedent wherein there was retained "the right, either alone or in conjunction with any person, to designate the persons who shall possess or enjoy the property or the income therefrom."

### (1) In General—Power vs. Interest

This provision pertains to retention of a ***power*** with respect to the property rather than an interest in the property or its income. However, most of the substantive rules applicable to retained interests are applicable, by analogy, to retained powers.

#### (a) Transfer and Retention

The issues and principles considered in connection with the requirements that there be a "transfer" and that the interest or power be "retained" apply equally to retained interests under section 2036(a)(1) and retained powers under section 2036(a)(2).

#### (b) Contingent Powers Included

Even though the exercise of the power is contingent upon the happening of an ***event beyond the control of the transferor*** and ***which has not occurred*** at the time of the decedent's death, the property is subject to tax under section 2036(a)(2). [Treas. Reg. § 20.2036–1(b)(3)(iii)]

**e.g.** **Example:** A decedent created a discretionary trust and appointed trustees. The decedent had the power to appoint successor trustees in the event of a vacancy but did not have the power to remove a trustee (that is, the decedent could not create a vacancy). Under state law, this power included the power to appoint the decedent unless disclaimed in the governing instrument (which it was not). Even though there was no vacancy at the decedent's death, the power required that the trust assets be included in the decedent's estate under section 2036(a)(2) because the trustees had the right to control beneficial enjoyment. [**Estate of Farrell v. United States,** 553 F.2d 637 (Ct. Cl. 1977)]

**1)** While a decedent's power to appoint himself or herself as a successor trustee, even if subject to a contingency that has not yet occurred will cause inclusion in the gross estate under section 2036, a power to remove a corporate trustee and appoint another corporate trustee is not a power that will cause inclusion in the estate under section 2036. [**Estate of Wall v. Commissioner,** 101 T.C. 300 (1993)] The Service has agreed that a power to remove a trustee and appoint another that is not "related or subordinate" to the transferor will not cause inclusion in the gross estate under section 2036. [Rev. Rul. 95–58, 1995–2 C.B. 191]

**2)** An analogy may be made here to retained secondary life estates. Recall that such retained interests will expose the transferred property to taxation under section 2036(a)(1) even where the decedent dies before the primary life tenant (i.e., before the retained interest is enjoyed by the decedent). A retained power is similarly taxable under section 2036(a)(2) even though the power was not exercisable by the decedent at death because a stated contingency had not occurred.

### (c) Beneficial Power in Favor of the Transferor Not Required

It is not necessary that the power be exercisable in favor of the transferor. If the transferor has power to designate the possession or enjoyment by others, section 2036(a)(2) applies despite the fact that the decedent could not have exercised the power so as to secure a personal economic benefit. [*See, e.g.,* **Yawkey v. Commissioner,** 12 T.C. 1164 (1949)]

**e.g.** **Example:** Brandon transferred property to a trust for the benefit of his children, Bentley and Kade, appointing himself as trustee. The income from the trust was to be distributed to the children, but Brandon retained the discretionary power to invade the principal for the benefit of his grandchildren. Even though Brandon's power could not be used to obtain economic benefit for himself, the trust property would be included in his gross estate because as trustee he retained the power to designate the possession or enjoyment of the property.

### (d) Joint Powers Included

It does not matter that a power is exercisable by the decedent only jointly or with the consent of another person. Moreover, the fact that the person whose consent is required enjoys a beneficial interest in the property that will be adversely affected by its exercise ***does not*** prevent taxation under section 2036(a)(2). [*See* Treas. Reg. § 20.2036–1(b)(3)]

**EXAM TIP** GILBERT

Property is included under section 2036(a)(2) even if the transferor's control of beneficial enjoyment is exercisable only in conjunction with someone with an adverse interest. This rule is inconsistent with gift taxation. For gift tax purposes, a transfer is complete if the transferor's control is exercisable in conjunction with someone with an adverse interest (e.g., a transferor can revoke a transfer in conjunction with the beneficiary). [*See* Treas. Reg. § 25.2511–2(e)]

#### (e) Capacity in Which Power Exercisable

If the requisite power is retained, the capacity in which it is exercisable is immaterial. For instance, the fact that the power is exercisable by the decedent in a fiduciary capacity as trustee will not prevent taxation.

#### (f) Form of the Power

The retained power need not specifically authorize a designation or shifting of enjoyment. Any power having this effect is within the scope of section 2036(a)(2).

##### 1) Power to Accumulate

Section 2036(a)(2) applies to any transfer to a trust in which the settlor has retained the power to direct the accumulation of trust income during the settlor's lifetime because such accumulation would ***divert the income*** from the income beneficiary to the owner of the remainder. In other words, the accumulation of income operates as a "silent" transfer to corpus, thus enlarging the remainder interest. [**United States v. O'Malley,** 383 U.S. 627 (1966)]

###### a) Nonexercise of Right Immaterial

Note that the mere ***retention*** of such a power makes the transfer taxable, regardless of whether any accumulation was ever directed by the settlor.

**EXAM TIP** GILBERT

Don't be fooled by a fact pattern that has a settlor who has retained, but not exercised, a power to control the distribution of trust assets. The ***mere retention*** of such a power is sufficient to ***bring the trust under section 2036(a)(2),*** resulting in the trust being included in the settlor's gross estate.

##### 2) Power to Encroach

A similar result follows where the settlor retains the power to invade or encroach upon the corpus for the benefit of the income beneficiary (at the expense of the owner of the remainder). The retention of such power to shift beneficial enjoyment makes the trust corpus taxable in the settlor's estate, whether or not the power was ever exercised. [**Commissioner v. McDermott's Estate,** 222 F.2d 665 (7th Cir. 1955)]

3) **Power to Allocate ("Sprinkle")**

If the settlor retains the power to direct the allocation of trust income among various beneficiaries, the property transferred ss taxable to the settlor's estate under section 2036(a)(2). [**Industrial Trust Co. v. Commissioner,** 165 F.2d 142 (1st Cir. 1947)]

## (2) Power to Affect Possession or Enjoyment

### (a) Power Must Affect Beneficial Enjoyment or Possession

Section 2036(a)(2) is inapplicable if the power does not affect the enjoyment of the income received or earned or possession of the trust property during the decedent's life.

e.g. **Example:** A settlor creates an inter vivos irrevocable trust and transfers an apartment building to the trust with income payable to the settlor's daughter for life and the corpus payable to the settlor's son upon the daughter's death. The settlor reserves the power to distribute the corpus to the daughter at any time. The settlor dies while both the daughter and son are alive. Section 2036(a)(2) is inapplicable because the reserved power does not affect beneficial enjoyment. Conversely, if the settlor reserves the power to pay the trust income to the son at any time, section 2036(a)(2) applies because the settlor's power affects beneficial enjoyment. As will be discussed later in this chapter, section 2038 applies in both situations.

### (b) Shifting of Economic Enjoyment Not Required

Clearly, the power to shift possession or enjoyment of the property or its income from one party to another is taxable (above); however, this is not essential. Section 2036(a)(2) will also apply where decedent has retained the power to affect the ***time and manner*** of a single beneficiary's possession and enjoyment.

e.g. **Example:** The decedent created certain inter vivos trusts for her children. As a co-trustee, she had the power, in conjunction with the other trustees, to accumulate the income or distribute it currently to the designated income beneficiary. Upon her death, the trusts would terminate, and the corpus and any accumulated income was to be distributed to the beneficiary or to his or her estate. Each trust had a single income beneficiary who also owned the remainder so that, in any event, the beneficiary of each trust was assured of receipt of all the income and the property. Although the decedent had no power to shift economic enjoyment, the trusts were held taxable under section 2036(a)(2). ***Rationale:*** The decedent was able to affect the time and manner of beneficial enjoyment by exercising her power (retained as co-trustee) to accumulate income during her life rather than distributing it currently. [**Struthers v. Kelm,** 218 F.2d 810 (8th Cir. 1955); *see also* **Lober v. United States,** 346 U.S. 335 (1953) (dealing with a similar question under the predecessor of section 2038)]

**EXAM TIP** GILBERT

It is important to distinguish between the gift and estate tax rules related to ***time and manner*** of a beneficiary's possession and enjoyment. Under the regulations, a gift is not considered incomplete, merely because the donor retains the right to change the manner or time of enjoyment. [*See* Treas. Reg. § 25.2511–2(d)]

### (c) Limitation—Power Must Be Exercisable During Decedent's Life

However, the power must be one that will affect possession or enjoyment of the income or property ***during the decedent's lifetime.*** Thus, for example, if the power to designate is exercisable only by will, it will not be included in the decedent's gross estate under section 2036(a)(2). [Treas. Reg. § 20.2036–1(b)(3)]

#### 1) But Note

A power to affect post-death enjoyment ***is taxable*** under section 2038.

### (d) Limitation—Nonbeneficial Power Must Be Discretionary

Where the power in question is to designate possession or enjoyment ***of another,*** it must be ***a discretionary*** power. Consequently, if the transferor is the trustee of a trust that ***requires*** the distribution of income to A for life with remainder to B, the transferor has no "power" to designate income or possession.

#### 1) Power Limited by Ascertainable Standard

If the exercise of a power to accumulate or distribute income or to invade corpus is governed by an ***ascertainable standard,*** the power is not discretionary; rather, it is in substance a mandatory direction. [*See* **Jennings v. Smith,** 161 F.2d 74 (2d Cir. 1947)]

##### a) "Ascertainable Standards"

"Ascertainable standards" are those that identify a reasonably objective circumstance that will govern the exercise of the power. Typically accepted as ascertainable standards are support, education, health or medical needs, maintenance according to one's accustomed standard of living, etc.

#### 2) Discretionary Standards

In contrast, where an apparent standard governing exercise of the power cannot be reasonably related to some objective circumstance, it does not effectively limit or mandate exercise of the power and thus leaves the power discretionary.

e.g. **Example:** A power remains fully discretionary where its exercise is subject to such vague guidelines as "happiness," or "comfort and happiness."

#### 3) Mixed Standards

If a "discretionary" standard is included among "ascertainable" standards, the power remains discretionary. For example, a power governed by "support, maintenance, welfare, ***and happiness***" is discretionary. On the other hand, a "discretionary" standard may be so limited as to become an ascertainable standard (e.g., "reasonable comfort according to one's accustomed manner of living").

### (e) Right to Veto Exercise of Power

If a power is (i) ***purely discretionary,*** (ii) ***exercisable solely by another person,*** and (iii) the ***decedent had no right or power to compel its exercise in his favor,*** there will be no inclusion in the decedent's gross estate under section 2036. [**Commissioner v. Irving Trust Co.,** 147 F.2d 946 (2d Cir. 1945)] However, if the decedent retains a right to consent to the trustee's proposed exercise of a discretionary power, the decedent will be treated as having retained the power purportedly granted to the trustee. The law refuses to give any effect to the technical distinction that the trustee must initiate action, while the decedent is limited to exercising a veto. [*Cf.* **Thorp v. Commissioner,** 164 F.2d 966 (3d Cir. 1947), *cert. denied,* 333 U.S. 843 (1948)]

### (f) Administrative Powers

The statute, in designating for taxation those retained powers that would affect possession and enjoyment, is qualitatively limited to ***dispositive or distributive powers,*** not those relating solely to the management and administration of the property or investment of trust funds. However, it is arguable that administrative powers can affect possession or enjoyment. For example, broad powers of investment conceivably might permit the trustee (decedent) to invest entirely in unproductive property, thereby shifting enjoyment from the current income beneficiary to the remainderman.

#### 1) The *"State Street Trust* Doctrine"

In **State Street Trust Co. v. United States,** 263 F.2d 635 (1st Cir. 1959), the court held that the broad investment powers retained by the decedent as trustee of the trust he created were the equivalent of the power to designate possession or enjoyment of income insofar as the decedent might, through selection of investments, benefit one beneficiary to the detriment of others. The court rejected the trustee's argument that fiduciary restraints imposed by state law would prevent such shifting of economic benefits under the guise of exercising administrative powers as to trust investments.

##### a) *State Street Trust* Overruled

But the *"State Street Trust* doctrine" was, in fact, never followed because subsequent cases were always distinguished on the facts. In 1970, the First Circuit overruled its eleven-year-old opinion. [*See* **Old Colony Trust Co. v. United States,** 438 F.2d 684 (1st Cir. 1970)] ***Rationale:*** The principle that the fiduciary must be impartial and serve all beneficiaries, coupled with the power of all beneficiaries to enlist the aid of the courts to enforce compliance with this principle, gainsays any discretionary "power" in a trustee to improperly use administrative powers to affect beneficial enjoyment.

## 2) Retention of Voting Rights in Transferred Stock

### a) Former Rule—Section 2036 Inapplicable

Prior to the 1976 Tax Reform Act, mere retention of voting control over shares of a closely held corporation transferred on trust was not considered a "power to designate," and hence did not result in taxation of the shares in the transferor's estate. [**United States v. Byrum,** 408 U.S. 125 (1972)]

#### i. *Byrum* Case

The decedent owned 71% of the stock of three corporations. He transferred a portion of this stock on trust for his children, retaining the power to vote the stock, to veto its sale or exchange, and to replace the trustee. The government argued that the decedent's power to vote the transferred stock, when viewed in light of the voting power of the retained stock, amounted to a retention of enjoyment of the property transferred (control of the corporation) which was taxable under section 2036(a)(1), and also effectively gave the decedent power to control the dividend policy and income flow, thus amounting to a power to designate who shall possess or enjoy the income from the property which was taxable under section 2036(a)(2).

#### ii. Holding

Over the dissent of Justice White, the Supreme Court held that administrative powers, however broad, were not taxable under section 2036. Citing **Reinecke v. Northern Trust Co.,** 278 U.S. 339 (1929), the court reasoned that fiduciary restraints (here imposed upon corporate directors) prevented the administrative powers from being viewed as discretionary distributive or dispositive powers.

### b) "Anti-*Byrum*" Amendment

An amendment intended legislatively to overrule the *Byrum* decision was passed as part of the Tax Reform Act of 1976, but it was so flawed in purpose and effect that within two years a completely new "anti-*Byrum*" amendment was substituted by the Revenue Act of 1978. Under section 2036(b), a donor will be considered to have retained the "enjoyment" of stock transferred during life under section 2036(a)(1) if the donor ***retains the right to vote the transferred shares*** and, if at any time within three years of the donor's death, the donor ***"controls" the corporation*** whose shares were given away.

#### i. Retention of Voting Rights

Although the statutory language is somewhat obscure, the Committee Reports make it clear that inclusion in the gross estate will occur only if the right to vote the stock transferred is retained. Thus, a 100% shareholder could give away 49% of the corporate stock, retain control through ownership of the retained

51%, but avoid estate tax upon the stock transferred if the power to vote that stock was not retained. Alternatively, a controlling shareholder may retain control but avoid any estate tax upon the transfer of the nonvoting shares.

#### ii. Control Requirement

Under subsection (b)(1), "control" is defined as ownership of 20% or more of the voting stock of the issuing corporation.

a. Note that the decedent-transferor need not ***retain*** control. It is sufficient if the decedent possesses the requisite control at any time within three years of death.

b. For purposes of the control requirement, the "constructive ownership rules" of section 318 are applicable. Hence, any stock owned directly or indirectly by the decedent's parents, spouse, children, or grandchildren, and any stock owned by certain entities, such as trusts, estates, partnerships, or controlled corporations, is attributed to the decedent.

#### iii. Comment

As noted above, the government's theory in *Byrum* (and in Revenue Ruling 67–54, 1967–1 C.B. 269, which involved a gift of ***nonvoting*** stock by a controlling shareholder) rested upon the element of substantial retained control whereby the shareholder could personally enjoy the perquisites of corporate proprietorship during life and affect (through this control) the beneficial enjoyment by donees of the proprietary and financial perquisites of stock ownership.

a. Under the government's theory, retention of voting power in the transferred stock was not critical as long as the shareholder otherwise retained ***control*** through, for example, continued ownership of a controlling block of stock. The government urged in *Byrum* that it was concerned with ***control***, not an "insignificant minority interest."

b. By requiring retained voting rights in the stock transferred, the amendment permits the retention of control by a major shareholder as long as the subject of the gift is of a minority interest (in which voting rights are not retained) or is of nonvoting stock. On the other hand, by defining "control" at such a low level as 20% of voting power, the statute embraces minority interests with which the government may not have been concerned.

### h. Amount Includible

As a general rule, the ***entire value*** of the property subject to the retained interest or power is taxable under section 2036. The tax is not limited to the value of the specific interests affected.

**Example:** Ronald transferred property to a trust for George for life, remainder to Debra, reserving the power to add or substitute other income beneficiaries. Even though Ronald's power affects only the income interest, not that of the owner of the remainder, the full value of the property is taxable in Ronald's estate.

#### (1) Retention of Right in a Portion of the Property

However, where the retained right relates only to a ***portion*** of the property, ***only that portion is taxed.***

**Example:** Where the decedent transfers property reserving a life interest in the income from ***one-half*** of the property, the value of one-half the property, as of the decedent's death (or the alternate valuation date), is subject to tax.

**Example:** Assume that a decedent's right to income is limited to $500 a month for life or "whatever income is necessary for my support and maintenance." Only that portion of corpus that would be required to produce that amount of income would be taxable to the decedent's estate under section 2036(a)(1). [**Estate of Uhl v. Commissioner,** 241 F.2d 867 (7th Cir. 1957)]

#### (2) Retained Right Subject to Intervening Estate

If the retained interest or power relates to possession or income after an intervening estate which cannot be affected by the retained interest or power, the amount taxable is reduced by ***the value of the intervening estate.***

**Example:** John transferred property to Bill for life, then to himself for life, remainder to Albert. Should John predecease Bill and Albert, the value of the property less the value of Bill's remaining life estate is taxable in John's estate.

#### (3) Retention of Power to Accumulate Income

Where the decedent retains the power to direct accumulation of income, and the applicable taxing provision is section 2036 both the property ***and the accumulated income*** earned therefrom are subject to tax. [**United States v. O'Malley,** 383 U.S. 627 (1966)]

### i. Relinquishment or Transfer of Retained Interest or Power

If the decedent divests whatever retained rights or powers with respect to transferred property during life, the estate tax will ordinarily not attach to the property under section 2036. However, as already discussed, the property will be brought back into the decedent's gross estate under section 2035 if the decedent relinquishes the retained section 2036 rights or powers within three years of death. Please note that with respect to retained voting rights, section 2036(b)(3) specifically provides that the relinquishment of voting rights within three years of death will be treated as a transfer of property by the decedent. Therefore, the stock remains taxable under section 2036(b).

## 6. Section 2037—Transfers Taking Effect at Death

Section 2037 includes in the decedent's gross estate the value of any property transferred by the decedent during the decedent's lifetime (on trust or otherwise), where (i) the transferee's possession and enjoyment of the property is contingent upon ***surviving*** the decedent-transferor; ***and*** (ii) the decedent-transferor has retained ***a reversionary interest*** in the property ***valued at more than 5%*** of the value of the property at the time of the decedent's death. Section 2037 is inapplicable to "a bona fide sale for an adequate and full consideration in money or money's worth."

### a. Historical Background

Transfers taking effect at death were also within the contemplation of the tax on lifetime transfers "intended to take effect in possession or enjoyment at or after" the transferor's death under the 1916 Act. Section 2037 now specifies the taxability of such transfers (focusing on arrangements often referred to as "*Hallock*-type" transfers) and, with the enactment of its predecessor in 1949, the broad and troublesome language of the 1916 Act was eliminated from the Code.

#### (1) Review of Supreme Court Decisions

A survey of the relevant Supreme Court decisions is particularly helpful for a thorough understanding of section 2037.

##### (a) Klein v. United States

In *Klein,* D transferred property to A for life retaining a reversion after A's life estate, but if D predeceased A, then A would take the property in fee. A survived D and the Court held the property taxable in D's estate under the "intended to take effect" language of the 1916 Act. [**Klein v. United States,** 283 U.S. 231 (1931)]

###### 1) Rationale

D retained a reversion after A's life estate, and A was required to survive D in order to secure the property. A's fee interest was held in abeyance until D's death. Thus, the Court found a transfer from D to A which would only be effective upon D's death.

##### (b) Helvering v. St. Louis Union Trust Co.

D transferred property to a trust to A for life, with the provision that if D outlived A, the property would return to D, but if A outlived D, the remainder would go to X (or, in a companion case, vest in A absolutely). D predeceased the remaindermen, and the transfers were held ***not*** taxable. [**Helvering v. St. Louis Union Trust Co.,** 296 U.S. 39 (1935)]

###### 1) Rationale

Although these situations were, as a practical matter, identical to that in *Klein,* the Court found a subtle property law distinction: X (or A) had a vested remainder subject to divestment, and D had a possibility of reverter if A predeceased D (whereas in *Klein,* only a life estate was vested, D having retained a reversion). Consequently, D's death "passed no interest to any of the beneficiaries of the trust and enlarged none beyond what was conveyed by the indenture. His death simply put an end to what, at best, was a mere possibility of reverter. . . ."

##### (c) Helvering v. Hallock

This decision grew out of a consolidation of three cases, two of which posed facts similar to *St. Louis Union Trust Co.,* and one in which the facts were similar to *Klein.* This time, however, the Supreme Court found no essential difference between the cases and held all the transfers taxable, thereby overruling *St. Louis Union Trust Co.* [**Helvering v. Hallock,** 309 U.S. 106 (1940)] At the same time, the precise basis for its decision and the rationale for taxing such transfers was left unclear. Specifically:

1) Did the tax attach because the transferor had a reversionary interest, or because the beneficiary's possession or enjoyment was conditioned upon surviving the transferor, or both?

2) Was it necessary that the reversionary interest be expressly reserved, or would it be sufficient if it arose by operation of law?

3) Was it sufficient if the reversionary interest was remote and contingent, or must there be some significant possibility of reverter?

#### (d) Spiegel's Estate v. Commissioner

After almost a decade of litigation in the lower courts, the Supreme Court finally answered the questions left open in *Hallock*. [**Spiegel's Estate v. Commissioner,** 335 U.S. 701 (1949)] Briefly:

1) The reversionary interest is critical, and a condition of survivorship for the beneficiary to take is required (although the Court's decision is not entirely clear on this latter point).

2) It is sufficient if the reversionary interest exists—contrary to conventional wisdom (which assumed an express reservation was required) it is immaterial whether it is expressly reserved or arises by operation of law.

3) Even a remote reversionary interest is enough for taxation (in fact, the value of D's reversionary interest in *Spiegel's Estate* was less than .004 of the value of the corpus).

### (2) Congressional Reaction

The broad interpretation given by *Spiegel's Estate* to the taxation of "*Hallock*-type" transfers prompted statutory clarification and modification in the Technical Changes Act of 1949. These provisions were further refined in section 2037 of the 1954 Code, the general provisions of which are set forth below in the "introductory analysis."

## b. Introductory Analysis

For analytical purposes, section 2037 may be viewed as establishing ***four requirements for taxation***:

### (1) Condition of Survivorship

The decedent's inter vivos transfer of an interest in the property must be such that the beneficiary can obtain possession or enjoyment of the property ***only by surviving the decedent.*** [I.R.C. § 2037(a)(1)]

### (2) Reversionary Interest

It must be shown that the decedent retained a reversionary interest in the property. [I.R.C. § 2037(a)(2)]

#### (a) Note

With respect to transfers made ***prior to October 8, 1949***, the reversionary interest must be expressly reserved. [I.R.C. § 2037(a)(2)] However, for ***post-October 7, 1949*** transfers, it is sufficient if the reversionary interest arises by operation of law. Thus, the rule in *Spiegel* operates prospectively only.

### (3) De Minimis Rule

Moreover, section 2037 will only apply if the value of decedent's reversionary interest ***exceeds*** 5% of the value of the transferred property immediately before decedent's death. [I.R.C. § 2037(a)(2)]

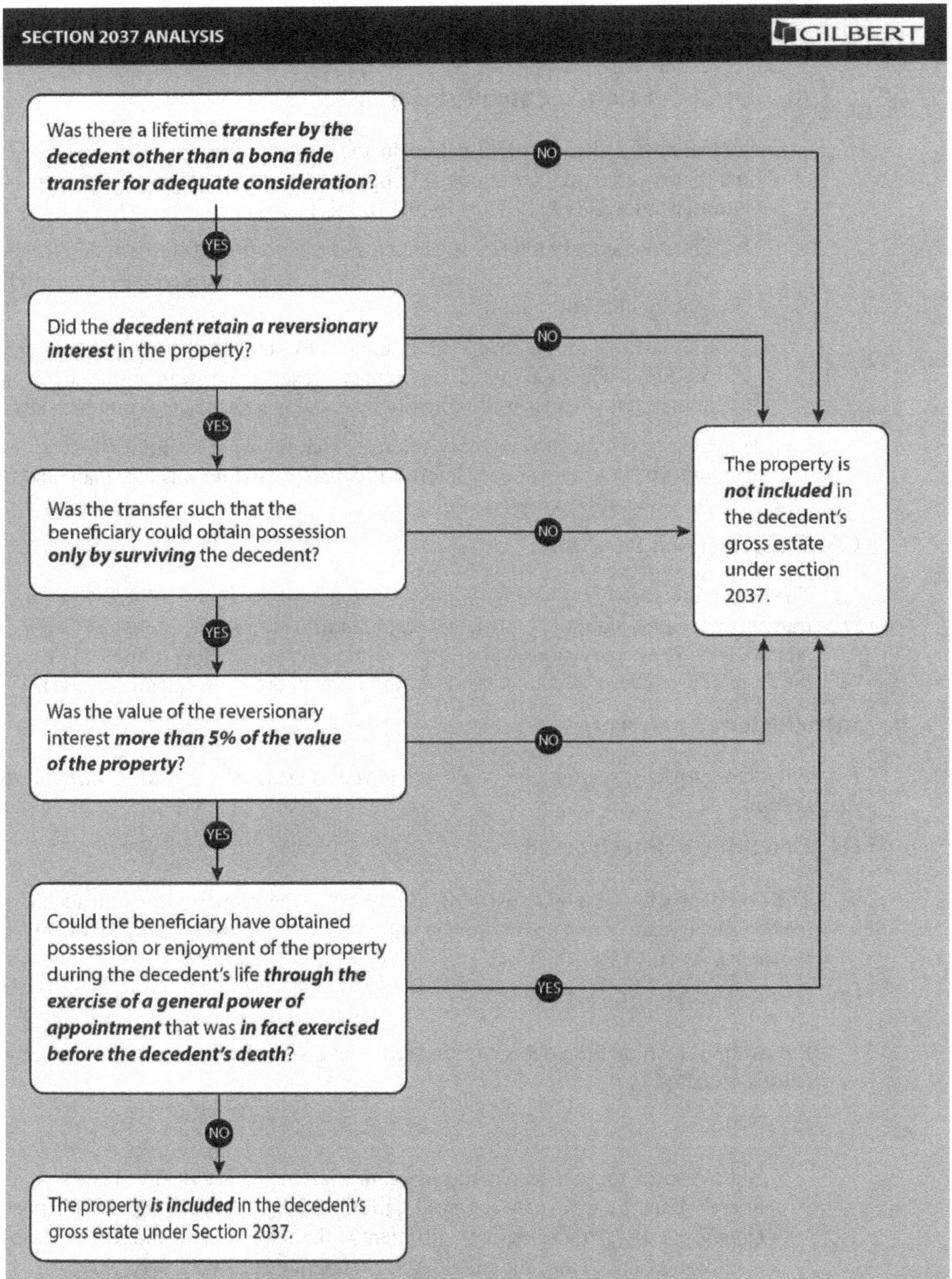

#### (4) Power in a Third Party (the "Negative Requirement")

Finally, the last sentence of section 2037(b) imposes a so-called negative requirement: "Notwithstanding the foregoing, an interest so transferred shall not be included in the decedent's gross estate under this section if possession or enjoyment of the property could have been obtained by any beneficiary during the decedent's life through the exercise of a general power of appointment (as defined in section 2041) which in fact was exercisable immediately before the decedent's death." [I.R.C. § 2037(b)]

#### (5) Collateral Aspects

In addition to the above four basic requirements, three collateral matters should be considered:

(a) ***The requirement of a transfer*** by the decedent;

(b) ***The amount taxable*** under this section; and

(c) ***The relationship of section 2037 to other taxing sections.***

### c. The Transfer Requirement

The nature and scope of the transfer requirement under this section is similar to that under section 2036. Keep in mind that the property must have been transferred ***by the decedent*** during life. The tax under section 2037 will not reach property transferred by another—even though possession or enjoyment may be dependent upon surviving the decedent and the decedent possesses a "reversionary interest" (e.g., a remainder or a reversion inherited from the actual transferor).

#### (1) Limitation—Transfer of Entire Interest Outside Statute

A reversionary interest must be ***"retained"*** by the decedent. It would be insufficient if the decedent transferred the entire interest in the property and subsequently reacquired a reversionary interest in the form of a remainder from the owner of the remainder.

#### (2) Time of the Transfer

Because this statute operates differently with respect to transfers before October 8, 1949, and those after October 7, 1949, it may be important to determine the time at which the transfer was made. This issue is resolved under the same principles that govern the similar issue under section 2036.

### d. The Survivorship Requirement

It is essential to the operation of section 2037 that a beneficiary's ***possession and enjoyment*** be ***contingent solely*** on ***surviving the transferor.***

#### (1) Analytical Approach

In determining whether this requirement is met, it may be helpful to ask the following questions:

(i) Is the interest of any beneficiary ***contingent?***

(ii) If so, is it ***contingent on surviving*** the transferor?

(iii) If so, is it contingent ***solely*** on surviving the transferor—rather than some other person or alternate event?

**EXAM TIP** GILBERT

On your exam, if you are having difficulty resolving whether the section 2037 survivorship requirement has been met, you might be able to simply ask the question: ***"Does it make any difference to the beneficiary whether the transferor lives or dies?"***

#### (2) Distinguish Property Law

Note that it is a beneficiary's ***possession or enjoyment*** which must be conditioned on surviving the decedent. The statute does not focus upon whether a future interest is technically contingent or vested under property law. Thus, for purposes of section 2037, a survivorship condition may exist in the case of a vested remainder subject to divestment as well as in the case of a contingent remainder, since, in both instances, whether the beneficiary will ever ***possess or enjoy*** the property is held in abeyance.

e.g. **Example:** The terms of a trust created by Kevin provides "to Mary Ann for life, reversion to Kevin, or, if Kevin is not living at Mary Ann's death, to Rose or Rose's estate." Rose's interest will vest if Kevin fails to survive Mary Ann, irrespective of whether Rose predeceases Mary Ann and Kevin. However, Rose cannot ***possess or enjoy*** the property unless she survives Kevin. Hence, the transfer is included in Kevin's estate under section 2037 if the reversionary interest is more than 5% of the value of the property.

#### (3) Transferor Must Be Measuring Life

The fact that the transferee must survive some third person in order to possess or enjoy the property is not enough to result in taxation under section 2037. Section 2037 applies only to transfers conditioned upon the transferee surviving the ***transferor.***

e.g. **Example:** Lauren transfers property to a trust with the income payable to Archie for life and, upon Archie's death, remainder to Archie's surviving children and if Archie leaves no surviving children, then to Lauren or to Lauren's estate. Since Archie's children can possess or enjoy the property without surviving Lauren (they need only survive Archie), the transfer is not taxable under section 2037. Lauren has an implied reversion. However, that the value of Laurens's reversion is taxed under section 2033.

e.g. **Example:** Montgomery transfers property to a trust with the income payable to Homer for life and at Homer's death, remainder to Homer's surviving children and if none of Homer's children survive, then to Montgomery, but if Montgomery is then dead, to Max. As in the prior example, Homer's interest and that of Homer's children are not dependent upon surviving Montgomery. However, Max can only come into possession or enjoyment by outliving Montgomery. Hence, the requirements of section 2037 are satisfied provided that Montgomery's reversionary interest is more than 5% of the value of the property.

#### (4) Effect of Alternative Event

Since the beneficiary's possession or enjoyment must be dependent ***solely*** on surviving the transferor, a condition of survival will not support inclusion under section 2037 if the beneficiary can take upon the happening of some ***alternative event.*** [Treas. Reg. § 20.2037–1(b)] e.g. **Example:** Stan transferred property to a trust with income to be accumulated until Oliver is 50 years of age and then to distribute the property and any accumulated income to Oliver. However, if Stan died before Oliver reached age 50, the trust was to terminate and the trustee was to distribute the property to Oliver; provided, however, that if Oliver died before attaining age 50, the trust property was to revert to Stan or his estate. Here, Oliver will be able to obtain possession and enjoyment of the property if he lives to age 50 even though Stan is also alive at that time. Thus, since Oliver's possession or enjoyment is not dependent ***solely*** on surviving Stan, section 2037 does not apply.

cf. **Compare:** Bill transferred property to a trust with income to be accumulated until Al was 50 years old and then to distribute the property and accumulated income to Al, if Bill were then dead. But if Bill were still living when Al attained 50 years of age, the trustee was to continue to accumulate the income until Bill died and then distribute the trust property to Al provided that if Al died before reaching 50 years of age, or if Al predeceased Bill, the trust property reverts to Bill or his estate. Here, section 2037 ***does*** apply. Al's possession or enjoyment is contingent on attaining age 50 ***and*** surviving Bill, whichever occurs ***last.*** Thus, in any event, Al must survive Bill in order to possess and enjoy the property.

#### (a) Caution—"Unreal" Alternative Event

If the alternative event under which the beneficiary may take is so extreme as to be "unreal," it may be disregarded. [Treas. Reg. § 20.2037–1(b)] Thus, if the decedent transfers property to a trust with directions to accumulate the income from the trust and to distribute the entire trust property to another "if he survives me or, even if I am then living, at such time as he is elected President of the United States," it is likely that the alternative event upon which the possession or enjoyment is conditioned will be disregarded and, assuming the reversionary interest requirement is met, the property will be included in the decedent's gross estate under section 2037.

### (5) Expectation That Beneficiary Must Survive Not Enough

Suppose that the decedent, having a life expectancy of five years, transfers property to a trust with directions to accumulate the income for 30 years and then to distribute everything to A or her estate. Although it is clear that the decedent intended to defer A's possession or enjoyment until after the decedent's death, the Supreme Court has held that such a transfer is not one "intended to take effect in possession or enjoyment at or after" the decedent's death. [**Shukert v. Allen,** 273 U.S. 545 (1926)] This case has never been overruled nor modified by statute; hence, neither section 2037 (nor sections 2036 or 2038) will reach this type of transfer.

## e. The Reversionary Interest Requirement

In addition to the survivorship requirement, the decedent/transferor must have retained a "reversionary interest" in the property.

### (1) What Constitutes a "Reversionary Interest"?

For purposes of section 2037, a "reversionary interest" ordinarily includes all reversionary interests identified by property law—reversions, possibilities of reverter, or rights of reentry or powers of termination. However, the term is not limited to reversionary interests in the technical, property law sense. Rather, it encompasses any sort of right or power, vested or contingent, under which there *is*

***any possibility that the property transferred may return to the transferor, or the transferor's estate, or be subject to a power of disposition by the transferor (to the transferor or any third person).*** [I.R.C. § 2037(b)] Thus, powers to revoke or to withdraw, or powers to compel exercise of the trustee's discretion in the transferor's favor (e.g., for the transferor's support) are within the scope of section 2037. [*See* **Valentine v. Commissioner,** 54 T.C. 200 (1970)]

#### (a) Exception—Reversionary Interest in Income Alone

It is specifically provided that a mere right to receive or dispose of ***only the income*** from the transferred property does ***not*** constitute a "reversionary interest." [I.R.C. § 2037(b); Treas. Reg. § 20.2037–1(c)(2)]

##### 1) Distinguish—Taxation Under Section 2036

However, such a retained right or power will result in taxation of the property under section 2036.

##### 2) Rationale

As already noted, Congress expressly provided that section 2036 would only apply to transfers made after March 3, 1931. Section 2037, however, operates with respect to transfers made before that date. Thus, to assure that transfers wherein a life interest in income or a power to dispose of income was retained would be taxed only if made after March 3, 1931, it was necessary to exclude such transfers from the scope of section 2037.

#### (b) Possibility That the Property May Return—Limitations

Although "reversionary interest" is defined very broadly, the term is also subject to some well-established limitations:

##### 1) Technical Reversions

A grant of alternative contingent remainders is said to create a technical reversion because under the law of future interests some future interest must be vested. However, regardless of such a technical reversion, it is impossible that possession or enjoyment will return to the transferor; therefore, the reversionary interest requirement is not met.

e.g. **Example:** Monica transfers property to Phoebe for life, remainder to Ross if Ross is then living, otherwise to Rachel. Under property law, Ross and Rachel have alternative contingent remainders and there is a technical reversion in Monica. But, since either Ross or Rachel (or Rachel's estate) necessarily will possess or enjoy the property upon the death of Phoebe, Monica has not retained a reversionary interest within the meaning of section 2037. Nor in this case is the survivorship requirement met.

##### 2) Expectancies

The interest must be more than a mere expectancy. For example, the possibility that the transferor might reacquire the property by inheritance (or by bequest or gift) from the transferee or another is ***not*** a sufficient reversionary interest to render it taxable under section 2037. [Treas. Reg. § 20.2037–1(c)(2)]

### 3) Discretionary Power in Third Party

The possibility that the property might return to the transferor by reason of a third party's (e.g., the trustee's) authority to distribute all or any portion of the transferred property to the transferor is not taxable under section 2037 as long as the third party's power is ***purely discretionary.*** [**Estate of Uhl v. Commissioner,** 241 F.2d 867 (7th Cir. 1957)]

#### a) Distinguish—Nondiscretionary Power

Where the transferor may compel the exercise of a third party's discretion in his favor (e.g., where the exercise of the third party's discretion is governed by an enforceable, ascertainable standard) the requisite reversionary interest is present. [**Valentine v. Commissioner,** 54 T.C. 200 (1970)]

## (c) Subject to Power of Disposition

If a power of disposition is retained, the property will be taxed under section 2037. It is not necessary that the retained power be a beneficial one (i.e., one that would allow the transferor to possess or enjoy the property). Thus, if a transferor of a trust retained a power to designate beneficiaries, to add to or substitute beneficiaries, to shift enjoyment of the property among beneficiaries, or to require that corpus be paid to beneficiaries designated in the transferor's will, the property is taxable in the transferor's estate.

### 1) Fiduciary Capacity Does Not Affect Taxability

This result under section 2037 is not affected by the fact that the transferor reserved the taxable power in a fiduciary capacity (e.g., as trustee). But, if the power is one to designate possession or enjoyment of third parties, it must be ***discretionary.*** [**Estate of Klauber v. Commissioner,** 34 T.C. 968 (1960)]

### 2) Joint Powers

Unlike sections 2036 and 2038, section 2037 does not specifically provide that a power of disposition is taxable if it is exercisable "either alone or in conjunction with any person." Thus, it appears that joint powers are outside the scope of section 2037, particularly if the person whose consent is required to exercise is an adverse party. [*See* **Reinecke v. Northern Trust Co.,** 278 U.S. 339 (1929)]

#### a) Note

Quite apart from the language of the statute, a joint power probably would not result in taxation under section 2037 because, in such a case, the value of the reversionary interest could not be determined actuarially. It is unlikely that actuarial science can determine the probability of the exercise of a discretionary power by a third party. Since the value of the "reversionary interest" would not be ascertainable, it would not meet the requirement that its value be more than 5% of the value of the property. [*See* **Estate of Klauber v. Commissioner,** 34 T.C. 968 (1960)]

### (2) Express Terms vs. Operation of Law

For post-October 7, 1949 transfers, it is immaterial whether the "reversionary interest" arises by the express terms of the instrument or by operation of law. However, for transfers made before October 8, 1949, the reversionary interest must be expressly created by the instrument of transfer.

#### (a) Purpose

The limitation regarding pre-October 8, 1949, transfers is intended to overrule, to this extent, *Spiegel's Estate* discussed earlier in this chapter.

#### (b) Express Terms of the Instrument

A reversionary interest arises by the express terms of the instrument not only where it is specifically identified but also, according to the Regulations, where the instrument "contains an express disposition which affirmatively creates a reversionary interest." [Treas. Reg. § 20.2037–1(f)(2)]

e.g. **Example:** Montgomery transferred property to a trust for Homer for life, remainder to such of Homer's children who survive Montgomery, remainder in default of such surviving children to Montgomery's next of kin. If, under local property law, the limitation to Montgomery's next of kin creates a reversion in Montgomery, a reversionary interest is deemed reserved under the express terms of the instrument.

e.g. **Example:** Suppose Montgomery conveyed property to Homer for life, remainder to Homer's heirs at law "as determined by the present laws of this state," and under the applicable inheritance statute then in force, Montgomery was Homer's only heir at law. If the limitation is construed to be to the heirs at law at the ***time the life tenant dies,*** any reversionary interest arises by ***operation of law,*** not by the express terms of the instrument; but if the limitation is interpreted as applying to the life tenant's heirs at law at the ***time of the transfer,*** and the ***transferor*** is the heir at that time, the reversionary interest would be by the ***express terms*** of the instrument. [**Estate of Marshall v. Commissioner,** 16 T.C. 918 (1951), *aff'd,* 203 F.2d 534 (3d Cir. 1953) (finding that by designating present law, the decedent effectively incorporated that law in the instrument of transfer and, thus, "affirmatively created a reversionary interest")]

##### 1) Collateral Documents

Although the reversionary interest must be expressly reserved for pre-October 8, 1949, transfers, the reservation need not be in the specific instrument of conveyance. A reservation in a collateral document will support taxation under section 2037 if that collateral document is necessarily ***related to the transfer.***

e.g. **Example:** Assume that Don transferred property to Alice for life, remainder to whomever Alice should appoint by will, remainder in default of appointment to Alice's children. Assume further that in connection with the transfer Don entered into a contract with Alice where Alice agreed, in consideration of the transfer of the property to herself, that she would make the testamentary appointment to Don if Don were then living, remainder passing to contingent appointees (or to the takers in default) if Don were dead at the time of Alice's death. This collateral, enforceable agreement creates a reversionary interest in Don arising by the express terms of the instrument. [**Gilbert v. Commissioner,** 14 T.C. 349 (1950)]

##### (c) Operation of Law

A reversion arises by operation of law where, for instance, the decedent transfers property under circumstances in which a reversion, possibility of reverter, or right of reentry or power of termination would arise under property law. For example, if Don transfers property "to Alice for life, remainder to Ben, provided that Ben survives Don," Don has retained a reversionary interest by operation of law that vests if Ben predeceases Don.

### f. De Minimis Rule—Reversionary Interest Must Exceed Five Percent of Property's Value

The statute expressly provides that a transfer will be taxable only if the reversionary interest retained by the decedent/transferor is valued ***at more than*** 5% of the total value of the property transferred. [I.R.C. § 2037(a)(2)]

#### (1) Time and Method of Valuation

The value of the reversionary interest is determined on the basis of the decedent's life expectancy immediately prior to death. [Treas. Reg. § 20.2037–1(c)(3)] For this purpose, actuarial calculations which take into account standard mortality tables are used. [I.R.C. § 2037(b)]

#### (2) Mortality Tables Conclusive?

It is not clear under the statute whether mortality and actuarial principles are the exclusive means for ascertaining value or whether circumstances peculiar to an individual case may be considered. One case has held that where the particular facts and circumstances demonstrate that the decedent's life expectancy, immediately prior to death, was less than that projected in standard mortality tables (e.g., where decedent was suffering from a terminal illness), value can be computed on the basis of the actual facts and standard mortality tables ignored. [**Hall v. United States,** 353 F.2d 500 (7th Cir. 1965)]

##### (a) Service's Position

The IRS maintains that the valuation question should turn exclusively upon the use of standard mortality tables. [Treas. Reg. § 20.7520–3(b)(3)(ii); *see also* **Estate of Roy v. Commissioner,** 54 T.C. 1317 (1970)] This appears to be the better view since adherence to the decision in *Hall* would render taxation under section 2037 virtually impossible. It would be the unusual case in which the facts and circumstances immediately prior to a decedent's death would not indicate a morbid condition, thereby reducing the decedent's life expectancy to a negligible factor, in effect, the statute would only reach cases of sudden or unexpected death. It certainly does not appear that Congress intended to enact such an illusory taxing provision. [*See* **Robinson v. United States,** 632 F.2d 822 (9th Cir. 1980) (adopting the IRS position and rejecting the interpretation in *Hall*)]

#### (3) Five Percent of What?

In determining whether the 5% limitation is met, the value of the reversionary interest is compared to the value of the entire property that would revert to the decedent. [Treas. Reg. § 20.2037–1(c)(4)]

##### (a) Alternate Valuation Ignored

The property's value as of the decedent's death governs, even though the executor might elect to value the property, for estate tax purposes, at the alternate valuation date, six months after the decedent's death. [Treas. Reg. § 20.2037–1(c)(3)]

##### (b) Immaterial That Portion of Property Not Subject to Tax

Although only a portion of the property is includible in the decedent's gross estate under section 2037, it is the value of the ***entire property*** to which the reversion relates which is the term for comparison. For example, suppose D transferred property on trust to pay the income to A for life, remainder to X, but if D was alive at A's death, then the property was to revert to D. If D dies before A and X, the value of D's reversion (immediately before death) is compared to the value of the entire trust corpus, even though there is included in D's gross estate only the value of the remainder (total value less the value of A's life estate), since A's interest is not dependent upon survivorship. [*See* Rev. Rul. 76–178, 1976–1 C.B. 273; Treas. Reg. § 20.2037–1(c)(4)]

### g. The Negative Requirement—Power of Appointment in Another

Notwithstanding the fact that the survivorship and reversionary interest requirements are met, section 2037 will not apply to a transfer "if possession or enjoyment of the property could have been obtained by any beneficiary during the decedent's life through the exercise of ***a general power of appointment*** (as defined in section 2041) which in fact was exercisable immediately before the decedent's death." [I.R.C. § 2037(b)] A general power of appointment is one that would allow the holder of the power to appoint the property subject to the power to the holder, the holder's estate, the holder's creditors, or the creditors of the holder's estate. [I.R.C. § 2041(b)(1)]

#### (1) Must Be a Taxable Power

The reference to section 2041 means that the power must be one that will result in taxation of the property in the holder's estate under section 2041.

#### (2) Power to Appoint to a Beneficiary

The statute requires that the power be of a type that will allow the holder to appoint the property to some beneficiary of the present transfer.

#### (3) Effect of Special Powers of Appointment

Although the grant of a special power to a third person will not automatically preclude taxation (because not a "taxable power"), arguably the existence of such a power will reduce the value of the reversionary interest below the 5% requirement insofar as it cannot be determined actuarially whether a person will or will not exercise a discretionary power. Thus, the existence of a special power of appointment in another may indirectly remove the transfer from the reach of section 2037.

### h. Amount Taxable

It is not necessarily the entire value of the property transferred that is subject to tax under section 2037. Rather, only the ***value of the interest that is dependent upon survivorship*** is included in the transferor's gross estate; in other words, those interests that are not contingent on surviving the transferor are not taxed under this section. [Treas. Reg. § 20.2037–1(e), examples (3) & (4)]

e.g. **Example:** David transfers property on trust with directions to pay the income to Andy for life, remainder to Xavier if David dies before Andy, but otherwise the property is to revert to David. Only the value of Xavier's remainder interest is taxable in David's estate, because it is the only interest contingent on surviving David. [*See* Rev. Rul. 76–178, 1976–1 C.B. 273]

e.g. **Example:** David transfers property on trust with directions to accumulate the income during David's life and upon David's death to distribute the entire property and accumulated income to Xavier; but if Xavier predeceases David, then the property and accumulated income is to be paid to David's estate. If David predeceases Xavier, the entire property must be included in David's estate because of the wording of this gift: Xavier gets the entire property by surviving David, all income having been accumulated.

### i. Relation of Section 2037 to Other Taxing Sections

It was previously noted that section 2035 (transfers within three years of death) continues to interact with section 2037 to produce a tax under that latter section. Thus, if a transfer is otherwise taxable under section 2037, the decedent cannot avoid the tax by a transfer of the reversionary interest within three years of his death.

#### (1) Section 2033

Although a reserved reversionary interest may not be taxable under section 2037 because, for example, the requisite condition of survivorship is not present or the value of the reversionary interest is less than 5% of the property, section 2033 can still include in the decedent's gross estate the value of the reversionary interest itself.

#### (2) Section 2036

While retention of a reversionary interest in (or power to dispose of) income alone from transferred property will not produce a tax under section 2037, if the transfer occurs after March 3, 1931, the property in which such an interest or power is retained will be taxable under section 2036.

#### (3) Section 2038

A power to revoke, or power to alter or amend, constitutes a reversionary interest or a power to dispose of the property, respectively, and where such powers are retained, a condition of survivorship necessarily exists. Consequently, with respect to these powers, sections 2037 and 2038 overlap.

## 7. Section 2038—Revocable Transfers

Also taxable in the decedent's gross estate is the value of any property that the decedent has transferred during the decedent's lifetime, on trust or otherwise, where ***at the date of death*** the transfer was subject to a ***power to alter, amend, revoke or terminate, exercisable by the decedent*** alone or in conjunction with any other person. Section 2038 is inapplicable to "a bona fide sale for an adequate and full consideration in money or money's worth."

## a. Historical Development of Section 2038

Many substantive aspects of section 2038 are best explained and analyzed in terms of its historical development.

### (1) Taxation of Revocable Transfers Under Early Revenue Acts

Although Congress intended revocable transfers to be taxed under the "intended to take effect in possession and enjoyment" language of the 1916 Act, concern with possible restrictive interpretations by the Supreme Court prompted enactment of a provision specifically taxing revocable transfers as part of the Revenue Act of 1924. The relevant provisions of the 1924 Act are similar to those presently found in paragraph (2) of section 2038(a).

#### (a) What About Pre-1924 Transfers?

The tax treatment of transfers made prior to the 1924 Act is well illustrated by the decision in **Reinecke v. Northern Trust Co.,** 278 U.S. 339 (1929), wherein the Supreme Court addressed four principal issues. That case involved seven trusts, two of which were created prior to the Revenue Act of 1916 and five of which were created in 1919. The decedent died in 1922.

##### 1) Shifting of Enjoyment at Death

The decedent reserved no beneficial interest in the 1919 trusts, but it was provided that they should terminate and the remainder take effect five years after the decedent's death. Even though the trusts were limited to take effect in possession or enjoyment after the decedent's death, the transfers were held not taxable because the decedent retained no interest, and nothing "passed" from the decedent at death. Essentially, the Court held that a mere shifting of enjoyment at or after death was insufficient to attract the tax. This basic rule persists today.

##### 2) Administrative Powers

The decedent also reserved broad administrative powers over the 1919 trusts, including the power to invest and reinvest trust funds, vote shares of stock owned by the trust, control leases of trust property, and appoint successor trustees. But the Court said that administrative powers alone will not attract the tax. According to the Court, what is necessary is a power to shift economic enjoyment, and "the shifting of the economic interest . . . was [here] complete as soon as the trust was made."

##### 3) Power to Revoke

With respect to the pre-1916 trusts, the decedent reserved a life income interest in and a power to revoke the trusts. The unqualified power to revoke was held to render the trusts taxable, even though they were created prior to the first estate tax.

###### a) Constitutionality

The Court found the tax constitutional on the theory that a transfer had in fact taken place ***after*** passage of the applicable taxing statute. The taxable transfer did not occur until the power to revoke lapsed at the decedent's death, so that the statute was not retroactive in effect.

b) **Contemporary Application**

The decision to tax revocable transfers remains in effect today under the present Code. Where an unlimited power to revoke is reserved with respect to a transfer and the power is in existence at the transferor's death, the property is taxable under section 2038.

4) **Power to Alter with Consent of Adverse Party**

The decedent also reserved a power to alter or amend the trusts created in 1919, but the power could only be exercised with the consent of certain beneficiaries whose interests could be adversely affected by the exercise of the power. The Court held that since the consent of an adverse party was required, for all practical purposes the transfers were complete and thus not taxable under the 1916 Act. Note that this holding is affected by the 1924 Act discussed below.

(b) **Joint Powers**

Under the rule of **Reinecke v. Northern Trust Co.,** 278 U.S. 339 (1929), a joint power, which is otherwise taxable, will result in a tax ***if*** the co-holder of the power is not an adverse party; but, for ***pre-1924*** transfers, the tax will not attach to the interest of a ***beneficiary*** whose consent is required for the exercise of an otherwise taxable power. [Treas. Reg. § 20.2038–1(d)]

1) **Post-1924 Transfers—Consent of Adverse Party Immaterial**

The 1924 Act extended the estate tax to transfers wherein the transferor reserved a power to revoke or amend "alone or in conjunction with any person"; and the Supreme Court thereafter held the statute applicable even where the co-holder of the power was an adverse party. [**Helvering v. City Bank Farmers Trust Co.,** 296 U.S. 85 (1935) (stating that "any person" includes a person whose interest might be adversely affected by exercise of the power]

2) **Rescission by Consent of All Parties**

But, where the power to revoke, amend, or terminate is exercisable by the decedent and ***all*** the beneficiaries of the trust, and under local law the settlor and the beneficiaries are allowed to rescind the trust by mutual consent, the transfer is not taxable. ***Rationale:*** The reservation of such a power adds nothing to the rights already conferred upon the parties by law and thus does not make an otherwise irrevocable trust "revocable" in the tax sense. [**Helvering v. Helmholz,** 296 U.S. 93 (1935); Treas. Reg. § 20.2038–1(a)(2)]

(2) **Extension of Taxing Scope by the 1936 Act**

The provisions of the 1936 Revenue Act relating to revocable transfers (presently embodied in paragraph (1) of section 2038(a)) amended the tax under the 1924 Act (embodied in paragraph (2) of section 2038(a)) as follows: (i) addition of the parenthetical phrase "in whatever capacity exercisable" relating to the decedent's power; (ii) addition of the parenthetical phrase "without regard to whom or from what source the decedent acquired such power" relating, again, to the decedent's power; and (iii) inclusion of the power to "terminate" in the list of taxable powers.

### (a) Source of the Power

The amendment referring to the source of the decedent's power makes clear that for purposes of section 2038 a retained power is not essential. Thus, as long as the power is exercisable by the decedent at the date of death, it is immaterial how the decedent acquired the power.

#### 1) Background

This addition was prompted by the Supreme Court decision in **White v. Poor,** 296 U.S. 98 (1935). In that case, the decedent created an irrevocable trust, retaining no power or interest, but granting the trustees the power to alter and terminate the trust. Although the decedent originally served as one of the trustees, she later resigned. However, upon the resignation of another trustee, the decedent was reappointed and served as trustee until her death. The Court held the trust property not taxable under the 1924 Act because the power the decedent possessed at death was not reserved but had been acquired by virtue of the action of others in reappointing her as trustee.

#### 2) Prospective Application Only

Although the amendment overrules ***White***, it operates prospectively only and thus is limited to transfers made after June 22, 1936. [I.R.C. § 2038(a)] The Second Circuit, in **Estate of Skifter v. United States,** 468 F.2d 699 (2d Cir. 1972), indicated in dicta that it might hold that a power which was not originally retained but transferred back might not be includible under section 2038, a conclusion to which the Fifth Circuit, in **Rose v. United States,** 511 F.2d 259 (5th Cir. 1975), also in dicta, disagreed. Both cases involved section 2042.

### (b) Capacity in Which Exercisable

The 1936 Act also makes certain that the statute applies without regard to the "capacity" in which the power is exercisable by the decedent. Thus, even though the decedent possessed the power as trustee and was therefore subject to certain fiduciary restraints, the property is includible in her gross estate.

#### 1) Purpose

This issue had not been specifically addressed by the Supreme Court cases dealing with transfers under the 1924 Act. However, the provision was apparently added as a precautionary measure lest the Court find that the capacity in which the power is exercisable bears upon taxation.

#### 2) Retroactive Effect

Subsequent cases established that the tax would attach even though the decedent's power was exercisable only in a fiduciary capacity. Thus, this amendment is ***not*** limited to prospective application; it is merely declaratory of prior law and therefore reaches transfers made prior to the 1936 Act.

### (c) Power to Terminate

In **White v. Poor,** 75 F.2d 35 (1st Cir. 1935) (discussed above), the court had expressed some concern as to whether a power to terminate was the equivalent of a power to alter or amend. To resolve any doubt, the power to terminate was expressly added in the 1936 Act to the list of taxable powers.

## b. Analytical Approach Under Section 2038

As noted above, section 2038 is inapplicable to "a bona fide sale for an adequate and full consideration in money or money's worth." Provided that there was not a bona fide sale, analysis of the scope of section 2038 focuses on the following issues:

(1) ***Whether the decedent "possesses" the taxable power*** at death or, stated another way, whether the power is ***exercisable by the decedent*** at the date of death.

(2) ***The nature of the taxable powers.***

(3) ***Certain collateral*** questions including:

   (a) ***The requirement of a transfer*** by the decedent;

   (b) ***The amount taxable;***

   (c) ***The effect of a release*** of a taxable power within three years of death; and

   (d) ***The relationship of section 2038 to other taxing sections,*** in particular section 2036(a)(2).

## c. Requirement of a Transfer

As in the case of sections 2035 through 2037, a threshold requirement for taxation under section 2038 is that the decedent must have made an inter vivos transfer of property. The principles governing this issue are identical to those under sections 2036 and 2037.

## d. The Power Must Be Exercisable at Death

The tax is imposed upon transfers where the enjoyment of the transferred property is subject, at the date of the transferor's death, to any change through the exercise of a power by the decedent. [I.R.C. § 2038(a)] Thus, the power must either be "possessed" or "exercisable" by the decedent ***at the time of death.***

### (1) Contingent Powers

A power that is subject to some contingency before it can be exercised is not a taxable power under section 2038 if: (i) the contingency is **not within control** of the decedent and (ii) the ***contingency has not occurred at the time of the decedent's death.*** [Treas. Reg. § 20.2038–1(b); *see also* **Jennings v. Smith,** 161 F.2d 74 (2d Cir. 1947)]

e.g. **Example:** Alexis transferred property to a trust with directions to pay the income to Jose for life, then to Kramer for life, remainder to George. Alexis reserved the right to designate additional income beneficiaries or remaindermen if she survived Jose. If Alexis predeceases Jose, no part of the property is taxable under section 2038 since Jose's death is not within the control of Alexis and the condition did not occur by the time of Alexis's death.

#### (a) Note

The transfer will be included in Alexis's gross estate under section 2036(a)(2) because the right to designate additional income beneficiaries affects beneficial enjoyment, and the contingency does not need to occur prior to Alexis's death.

#### (b) Exception—Ministerial Conditions

Where the exercise of the power is subject only to a ministerial condition—such as the giving of notice or the expiration of a certain period of time before the amendment to the transfer will become effective—taxation is not precluded. However, for purposes of computing the amount includible in the gross estate, the value of the property subject to the power is discounted for the period required to elapse between the date of the decedent's death and the date when the alteration, amendment, revocation, or termination could take effect. [Treas. Reg. § 20.2038–1(b)]

#### (c) Distinguish—Inability or Disability Preventing Exercise

A disability which prevents the decedent from exercising the power will not affect the applicability of section 2038 as long as the power is "possessed" by the decedent and is technically "exercisable" by the decedent. Hence, the property will be included in the gross estate even though the decedent is incompetent to exercise the power at the decedent's death. [*See* **Round v. Commissioner,** 332 F.2d 590 (1st Cir. 1964); **Hurd v. Commissioner,** 160 F.2d 610 (1st Cir. 1947); **Inman v. Commissioner,** 18 T.C. 522 (1952), *rev'd on another issue*]

**EXAM TIP** GILBERT

Don't be led astray by facts in an exam question that indicate that the decedent was unable to exercise the power to change the disposition of previously transferred property. The ***mere possession*** of such a power ***by itself*** would be sufficient to mandate inclusion of the property in the decedent's gross estate.

### (2) By Whom Power Exercisable?

Section 2038 applies where a taxable power is exercisable by the ***decedent*** or by the ***decedent and another.***

#### (a) Joint Powers

The statute expressly provides that a transfer is taxable under section 2038 whether the taxable power is exercisable by the decedent ***alone or in conjunction with any other person.*** [I.R.C. § 2038(a)] It is immaterial that the co-holder may have an adverse interest (e.g., a beneficiary). However, recall that the tax will not attach where all parties with an interest consent to revocation and local law permits recission. [*See* Treas. Reg. § 20.2038–1(a)(2)]

#### (b) Power Exercisable Solely by Another

Unless the ***decedent*** has the right to exercise the power, a transfer subject to such power is not includible in the decedent's gross estate. This is true even where the power is vested in one who lacks a substantial adverse interest to the decedent, such as a trustee or even a subordinate party (e.g., transferor's spouse). [**Commissioner v. Irving Trust Co.,** 147 F.2d 946 (2d Cir. 1945)]

### (3) Indirect Access to the Power Sufficient

The decedent need not technically possess the power. As long as the decedent has ***access*** to the power or can ***compel its exercise***, the statute will apply.

##### (a) Power to Replace Trustee

If a trustee is granted a power that in the hands of the decedent will be a taxable power and the decedent has the right to remove the trustee and appoint a successor trustee, including the decedent, the decedent is deemed to have "access" to the power and therefore to "possess" the power. [Treas. Reg. § 20.2038–1(a)(3)] On the other hand, a power to remove a corporate trustee and appoint another corporate trustee is not a power that will cause inclusion in the estate under section 2038. [**Estate of Wall v. Commissioner,** 101 T.C. 300 (1993)] The Service has agreed that a power to remove a trustee and appoint another that is not "related or subordinate" to the transferor will not cause inclusion in the gross estate under section 2038. [Rev. Rul. 95–58, 1995–2 C.B. 191]

##### (b) Power to Compel Exercise

The decedent is treated as possessing the power where, although it is technically reposed in a trustee, the decedent can compel exercise of the trustee's discretion.

#### (4) Source of the Power

As noted above, transfers made after June 22, 1936, are subject to the tax whether or not the decedent retained the power. It is sufficient that the power is exercisable by the decedent at the decedent's death.

### e. Nature of the Taxable Power

Section 2038 enumerates the principal types of powers that render a transfer taxable under this section: ***powers "to alter, amend, revoke, or terminate."*** Any of these powers render the transfer taxable. It is immaterial whether the powers are exercisable by will or inter vivos or both. It is also immaterial whether the power is ever exercised. Although such powers occur most frequently with respect to transfers to a trust, a non-trust transfer subject to such a power is equally taxable. [Treas. Reg. § 20.2038–1 (a)]

#### (1) General Considerations

##### (a) Administrative vs. Dispositive or Distributive Powers

To be taxable, the power must be one that can ***affect enjoyment.*** It must be a power to affect the disposition or distribution of the property. A purely administrative power (e.g., power to add to the trust estate or to direct trust investments) which does not affect enjoyment of any beneficial interest will not expose the transfer to the tax. [**Central Trust Co. v. United States,** 167 F.2d 133 (6th Cir. 1948)]

##### (b) Beneficial Power Not Necessary

A power that allows the decedent to beneficially enjoy the property or its income is taxable, such as a power to reacquire the property through exercise of a power to revoke, or a power to add or substitute the decedent as income beneficiary through exercise of a power to amend. However, a beneficial power is not essential for taxation. The decedent's ability to affect the enjoyment of others through exercise of the power is sufficient. [**Walter v. United States,** 295 F.2d 720 (6th Cir. 1961)]

##### (c) Discretionary vs. Nondiscretionary Powers

Only ***discretionary*** powers will render the transfer taxable. Where distributions to others are mandated by the terms of the instrument or are controlled by ***fixed, ascertainable standards***, the "power" is not discretionary and is not taxable. [**Jennings v. Smith,** 161 F.2d 74 (2d Cir. 1947)]

e.g. **Example—Power Subject to Ascertainable Standard:** Darby created a trust and declared herself as the trustee. Under the terms of the trust, the trustee must pay income to Arthur during Arthur's life and distribute the corpus to Xavier after Arthur's death provided, however, that the trustee may invade the corpus and make distributions to Arthur "to the extent necessary to maintain Arthur in his accustomed manner of living." Since there is a fixed ascertainable standard (Arthur's accustomed manner of living), the exercise of the power is nondiscretionary, and the transfer is not includible in Darby's estate.

###### 1) Distinguish—Vague Standards

A power to invade, "when the circumstances so require," leaves the trustee with too much discretion, and if the decedent had such discretion, the transfer would be taxable. [**Hurd v. Commissioner,** 160 F.2d 610 (1st Cir. 1947)]

###### 2) Distinguish—Beneficial Power

A fixed ascertainable standard will not prevent taxation where the power is beneficial. Thus, if a trustee is granted power to invade corpus "to the extent necessary to maintain the ***transferor*** in her accustomed manner of living," the transfer is taxable since the transferor can compel exercise of the power in the transferor's favor.

#### (2) Powers to Revoke

Any power under which the decedent had the right to repossess the property transferred, directly or indirectly, is a taxable "power to revoke." The form of the power and the manner in which it arises is irrelevant as long as the decedent had beneficial access to the property.

##### (a) Right of Rescission

Certain transfers by minors, which are absolute in form, can be rescinded by the minor. This right of rescission is a "power to revoke" for purposes of section 2038. Similarly, gifts made pursuant to a power of attorney that did not specifically include the power to make gifts are revocable under state law and therefore includible in the gross estate of the transferor under section 2038. [**Estate of Swanson v. United States,** 46 Fed. Cl. 388 (2000)]

##### (b) Right to Set Aside Transfer of Community Property

A spouse's power under community property laws to set aside a gift or other improper transfer of his or her share of community property by the other spouse is treated as a power to revoke.

#### (c) Power to Deal with Trust Property

The power to borrow the entire trust corpus without adequate security, or to "repurchase" the corpus for a purely nominal consideration is a taxable power to revoke. [**Commonwealth Trust Co. v. Driscoll,** 50 F. Supp. 949 (W.D. Pa.), *aff'd,* 137 F.2d 653 (3d Cir. 1943), *cert. denied,* 321 U.S. 764 (1944)]

### (3) Power to Terminate

A power to end a trust and cause a distribution of trust property before expiration of the term specified in the trust agreement is a taxable power to "terminate."

#### (a) Pre-1936 Transfers

Recall that the addition of the power to terminate under the 1936 Act was not a substantive change, but simply a clarification of preexisting law so that such transfers are taxable even if made before June 22,1936.

e.g. **Example—Power Affecting Beneficial Interests:** The decedent established separate trusts for the decedent's minor children, each of which was to terminate after 15 years with distribution of the trust property to the beneficiaries at that time. The trust also provided for gifts over should a child die before the end of the trust term without leaving living descendants. In addition, the decedent reserved a power to terminate the trust and cause immediate distribution to the beneficiary prior to the end of the term. The Supreme Court rejected the argument that the trusts were not taxable because created prior to the 1936 Act. The decedent's power was held to be the equivalent of a power to alter or amend the trusts under the 1924 Act, insofar as exercise of the power would assure the beneficiary of enjoyment of the property, which otherwise might be shifted to another under the provision for a gift over in the event the child did not survive the 15-year term. [**Commissioner v. Estate of Holmes,** 326 U.S. 480 (1946)]

#### (b) Power to Affect Time and Manner of Enjoyment

Although the power to terminate a trust will often cause a shifting of beneficial enjoyment, this is not required. A power simply to accelerate the time of enjoyment of the trust property is also a taxable power of termination.

e.g. **Example—Termination in Favor of Existing Beneficiaries:** The decedent established separate trusts for his children under which the corpus and any accumulated income were to be distributed to the beneficiary at age 25 or the beneficiary's estate if the beneficiary died prior to reaching the age of 25. The decedent reserved a power to direct the termination of the trusts prior to expiration of the stated term. However, no gifts over were provided, so that each beneficiary (or the beneficiary's estate) was assured of receiving all of the property and income from the beneficiary's separate trust because the exercise of the decedent's power could not shift beneficial enjoyment. The Supreme Court held the trusts taxable in the decedent's estate since the power enabled the decedent to affect the ***time and manner*** of enjoyment of the trust property. [**Lober v. United States,** 346 U.S. 335 (1953)] Note that for ***gift tax*** purposes there is a ***completed gift*** where the reserved power merely affects the time and manner of enjoyment. [Treas. Reg. § 25.2511–2(d)]

#### (4) Power to Alter or Amend

There is no apparent difference between a power to "alter" and a power to "amend" for purposes of section 2038. Both contemplate any discretionary power, the exercise of which will affect the beneficial enjoyment of the property transferred. This includes the power to change the share of income or corpus that a beneficiary will receive, to substitute or add new beneficiaries, to invade corpus for the benefit of an income beneficiary or another, or to invade corpus for the benefit of the remainderperson. [**Cook v. Commissioner,** 66 F.2d 995 (3d Cir. 1933), *cert. denied,* 291 U.S. 660 (1934); **Commissioner v. Chase National Bank,** 82 F.2d 157 (2d Cir.), *cert. denied,* 299 U.S. 552 (1936)]

##### (a) Power to Accumulate Income

The power to direct the accumulation or distribution of income is a taxable power to alter or amend. This is true even though accumulated income will not be added to corpus (where it will increase the beneficial interest of the owner of the remainder) but must ultimately be distributed to the income beneficiary since this power will affect the ***time and manner*** of the income beneficiary's enjoyment. [**United States v. O'Malley,** 383 U.S. 627 (1966)]

##### (b) Transfers Under Uniform Transfers to Minors Act

Property transferred to a minor child under the Uniform Transfers to Minors Act will be included in the donor-parent's estate where the parent serves as custodian since, as custodian, the parent has discretionary power to apply custodial property or income derived therefrom for the benefit of the minor. [**Prudowsky v. Commissioner,** 55 T.C. 890 (1971)] Such gifts are also taxable under section 2036.

### f. Amount Taxable

The amount includible in the decedent's gross estate under section 2038 is the value of the ***interest*** that is subject to the taxable power. Thus, if the decedent retained a taxable power affecting the entire property transferred, its entire value is includible. But, if the exercise of a power would affect only a particular beneficiary's interest, only the value of that interest is taxable in the transferor's estate. [**Commissioner v. Bridgeport City Trust Co.,** 124 F.2d 48 (2d Cir. 1941)]

e.g. **Example—Distribution of Income:** The decedent transferred property on trust with directions to pay the income to the decedent's three children until the youngest child attained the age of 30, at which time the trust was to terminate and the corpus was to be distributed to the children (or their estates) equally. The decedent reserved the right to direct how much of the income was to be paid to each child. Since the income interest alone is affected by the decedent's power, section 2038 only taxes the value of the income interest as of the date of the decedent's death.

cf. **Compare—Taxation Under Section 2036:** However, under section 2036(a)(2), the entire trust property will be included in the decedent's gross estate because the decedent retained the power to designate who shall possess or enjoy the income from the property.

#### (1) Distribution of Corpus

If a decedent has the power to direct invasion of corpus and distribution to the ***owner of the remainder*** (or another), the entire value of the trust property is includible since the power affects not only the interest of the owner of the remainder but also that of the income beneficiary, insofar as it decreases the amount of income that the reduced corpus will produce. If, however, the power is limited to invasion and distribution for the benefit of the ***income beneficiary***, apparently only the value of the remainder interest is taxable since, in any event, the income beneficiary will receive all of the income from the property. [*See* **Walter v. United States,** 341 F.2d 182 (6th Cir. 1965)]

### g. Relationship Between Section 2038 and Other Taxing Sections

#### (1) Section 2036(a)(2)

There is considerable substantive overlap between sections 2038 and 2036(a)(2) in that the comprehension of powers to "designate who shall possess or enjoy the property or the income therefrom" is essentially the same as that of powers to "alter, amend, revoke, or terminate." Indeed, most transfers taxable under section 2036 will be taxable under section 2038. However, at the same time, there are certain differences in the taxing scope of these sections:

##### (a) Time of the Transfer

Section 2036 will not reach transfers made prior to March 3, 1931. However, section 2038 reaches "revocable" transfers whenever made.

##### (b) Source of the Power

Taxation under section 2036 is limited to ***retained*** powers. However, as to transfers made after June 22, 1936, section 2038 will operate without regard to the source of the decedent's power.

##### (c) Enjoyment After Decedent's Death

Section 2036 is limited to powers that will affect enjoyment of the income or property during the decedent's lifetime. However, section 2038 applies even though the power will affect enjoyment of interests after the decedent's death.

##### (d) Contingent Powers

Section 2038 will not operate where the decedent's power was subject to a contingency beyond the decedent's control which had not occurred at the time of the decedent's death. However, section 2036 will apply in such a case.

##### (e) Amount Includible

Section 2038 only includes the specific interest that is subject to the taxable power. Section 2036, on the other hand, reaches the entire property to which the retained interest or power relates.

##### (f) Power to Change the Owner of the Remainder Only

Section 2036 is inapplicable where the decedent retained only the power to change only the owner of the remainder. Section 2038 applies to such a power.

#### (2) Section 2035—Relinquishment of Power Within Three Years of Death

Section 2038 specifically provides for taxation where a power to alter, amend, revoke, or terminate "is relinquished during the three-year period ending on the decedent's death." This interaction is also specified in section 2035(a)(2). Further, any transfer from a portion of a trust which is revocable and taxed to the grantor of the trust under section 676 is treated as being transferred by the grantor and not from the trust, thereby making section 2035 inapplicable.

(3) **Section 2037**

Section 2038 also overlaps with the tax on transfers "taking effect at death" under section 2037. For example, a taxable power to revoke, or to alter or amend, would effectively create a condition of survivorship with respect to those beneficiaries whose interests may be affected by the power. Likewise, a power to terminate could create a condition of survivorship where the power would shift enjoyment if exercised. If the decedent also retained a reversionary interest in the property worth more than 5% of its value, section 2037, as well as sections 2036 and 2038, will apply. However, where the sections do overlap, inclusion is usually urged under the more straightforward section 2038 or section 2036.

## 8. Section 2039—Annuities

A decedent's gross estate includes the value of amounts receivable by a beneficiary under a contract or agreement where the decedent, during life, was receiving or had a right to receive payments under the contract or agreement.

### a. Background

The taxation of certain survivor benefits and annuity-type survivor benefits under section 2033 and other specific taxing sections was often troublesome. As a result of the difficulty, section 2039 was added to the 1954 Code, providing definitive rules for the taxing of survivor benefits under annuity or annuity-like contracts.

#### (1) Taxation of Annuities Apart from Section 2039

A review of the application of other taxing provisions to certain types of annuity contracts may be helpful toward an understanding of the basic rationale of section 2039 and its relation to other taxing sections.

##### (a) Straight Life Annuity

If the decedent receives an annuity during life that terminates on the decedent's death, nothing is includible in the decedent's estate on account of the annuity under section 2039 or any other provision of the estate tax because decedent's interest is extinguished by the decedent's death.

##### (b) Straight Life Annuity—Benefits Payable to Another

Similarly, if the decedent purchases an annuity for ***another,*** ordinarily nothing is included in the decedent's estate since the decedent has no interest in the contract. However, if the decedent retains some power with respect to the contract (e.g., the power to change the beneficiary or to cash in the contract) the value of the contract will be taxable under section 2038.

##### (c) Refund Annuity—Payable to Decedent's Estate

If the decedent purchases a refund annuity (an annuity for life that provides a certain number of payments that are guaranteed), the amount of any refund payable to the decedent's estate is taxable under section 2033 (as property owned at death). However, it is not taxable under section 2039 because the refund is not payable to a surviving beneficiary. For example, the decedent purchases a contract calling for a $500 monthly payment to the decedent for life, but if the decedent dies before receiving back as much as the decedent paid for the annuity, the balance is to be refunded to the decedent's estate and taxable under section 2033. If the decedent outlives the refund period so that no refund is owing, nothing is included in the decedent's estate.

### (d) Refund Annuity—Payable to Another

If the refund is payable to another and the decedent has a right to change the beneficiary designation, the amount of the refund is taxable under section 2038 as a revocable transfer. [**Old Colony Trust Co. v. Commissioner,** 102 F.2d 380 (1st Cir. 1939)] And, even if the beneficiary cannot be changed, the annuity payment might be taxable under section 2036, on the theory that the decedent essentially reserved a life estate (the annuity) in the property transferred (the premiums which will be refunded). Even so, however, such an annuity is now clearly taxable under section 2039.

### (e) Joint and Survivor or Self and Survivor Annuity

Joint and survivor annuities are those in which payments are made to the purchaser and another jointly during their lives, with benefits continuing in favor of the survivor during life. Under a self and survivor annuity plan, the primary annuitant receives payments during life, and after death the payments continue to a designated beneficiary. For estate purposes, both types of plans present the same problems.

#### 1) Possible Treatment

Unless the decedent has a right to change the survivor beneficiary designation [I.R.C. § 2038], there are technical difficulties in taxing these survivor's benefits apart from section 2039. Upon the decedent's death, the decedent's interest in the contract is extinguished so that the decedent technically has no interest in the survivor's benefits which can be taxed under section 2033. Moreover, since the insurance company's obligation to pay annuity benefits to the survivor may be viewed as a contractual obligation separate from its obligation to make payments to the primary annuitant(s), it is arguable that the decedent has retained no interest in the ***property transferred*** for purposes of section 2036, although some cases suggested that taxation under section 2036 is possible in this case. [*See, e.g.,* **Forster v. Sauber,** 249 F.2d 379 (7th Cir. 1957)]

#### 2) Note

However, survivor's benefits under these types of annuities are now clearly taxable under section 2039.

## (2) Scope of Section 2039

Although section 2039 is entitled "Annuities," the label is somewhat misleading. As will be seen below, the statute also extends to contractual arrangements that are beyond the typical commercial annuity contract, and, as noted above, certain types of annuity contracts are not taxed under section 2039 but may be taxable under other provisions of the estate tax.

### b. Nature of the Survivor's Interest

Section 2039(a) taxes "the value of an ***annuity or other payment*** receivable by any beneficiary ***by reason of surviving the decedent*** under any form of ***contract or agreement*** entered into after March 3, 1931 (other than as insurance under policies on the life of the decedent). . ."

#### (1) Annuity or Other Payment

The survivor's benefit does not need to be in the form of an annuity. Any payment or payments, other than as proceeds of life insurance, that become payable to a survivor are includible in the decedent's estate (if the other requirements are met).

##### (a) Exception for Life Insurance Proceeds

Where life insurance is part of an annuity-type plan, payments to the survivor that are in the nature of life insurance proceeds are not taxable under section 2039. However, if the decedent retained "incidents of ownership" in the policy, life insurance payable under an annuity may be included in the decedent's estate under section 2042.

##### (b) Determination of Whether Benefit Is Life Insurance

For federal tax purposes, whether payments are "life insurance proceeds" turns on whether a ***"life insurance risk"*** exists at the date of the decedent's death. A life insurance risk is present if the reserve value under the contract (premiums paid plus earnings allocated to the cash value of the contract) is less than the proceeds that become payable to the beneficiary upon the death of the primary annuitant (insured). [Treas. Reg. § 20.2039–1(d)]

e.g. **Example:** Dora purchased an annuity contract that provided that when Dora reached age 65, the insurance company would pay her $300 per month for life and, upon Dora's death a similar payment would be made to Dora's designated beneficiary for the beneficiary's life. The contract also provided that should Dora die before reaching age 65, a lump sum in the amount of $100,000 would be paid to Dora's designated beneficiary. If Dora dies before age 65 and if the reserve value of the annuity contract does not equal the $100,000 lump sum benefit (which it normally would not until Dora is 65), the lump sum benefit is treated as life insurance and is not taxable under section 2039.

###### 1) All or Nothing Rule

Whether a benefit is life insurance is determined on an all-or-nothing basis. Thus, in the example above, if Dora died one month before attaining age 65, when the reserve value of the annuity contract was $99,975, the proceeds would be treated as life insurance. It is immaterial that the difference between the reserve value and the amount of the proceeds payable is very small.

#### (2) Receivable by Reason of Surviving the Decedent

The annuity payable to the beneficiary after the decedent's death must be "by reason of surviving the decedent." If benefits are payable to a beneficiary at a scheduled time or upon the happening of an event, irrespective of whether the decedent is then living or dead, they are not taxable under section 2039, even though the decedent may be dead at the time scheduled for payment. [Treas. Reg. § 20.2039–1(b)]

#### (a) Need Not Be Solely Dependent upon Survivorship

Although this survivorship requirement is reminiscent of that under section 2037, unlike section 2037, section 2039 does not require that the beneficiary's interest be conditioned ***solely*** on surviving the decedent. If, for example, benefits became payable to the beneficiary upon the death of the decedent or upon the beneficiary attaining age 70, and the decedent dies before the beneficiary reaches age 70, the survivor's benefits are taxable under section 2039. However, if the primary annuitant is alive when the beneficiary attains age 70, payments thereafter made to the beneficiary are, presumably, not subject to tax under section 2039 because not receivable "by reason of surviving the decedent."

#### (b) Payment Need Not Correspond to Decedent's Interest

Also, there is no requirement that the annuity or other payment to the beneficiary correspond in form or amount to that payable to the decedent under the contract.

### (3) Receivable Under a Contract or Agreement

The benefits must be receivable "under any form of contract or agreement entered into after March 3, 1931. . . ."

#### (a) Nature of Contract

The reference to "***any form*** of contract or agreement" makes it clear that taxation under section 2039 is not limited to a formal, commercial annuity. According to the Regulations, section 2039 reaches "any arrangement, understanding or plan, or any combination of arrangements, understandings or plans arising by reason of the decedent's employment." [Treas. Reg. § 20.2039–1(b)(1)]

##### 1) Private Annuities Included

Although the Regulations specifically refer to employment-related plans, informal arrangements arising independently of the decedent's employment (e.g., "private annuities") apparently are subject to tax under section 2039.

#### (b) The 1931 Cut-Off Date

The March 3, 1931, cut-off date is reminiscent of the same cut-off date under section 2036. Presumably, Congress had a reserved life estate analogy in mind in enacting section 2039 and thus felt it appropriate to limit this latter section to the same extent that it limited the taxation of transfers with reserved life estates.

##### 1) What About Premium Payments After 1931?

Even though a trust with retained life estate is created before March 3, 1931, section 2036 reaches any ***additions*** to the trust made by the decedent after the 1931 cut-off date. However, it is unclear whether an analogy can be drawn to section 2039. Because section 2039 refers to contracts or agreements ***entered into*** after March 3, 1931, it may be that the statute does not tax premium payments made with respect to annuities entered into prior to the 1931 cut-off date. Neither the Code nor the Regulations indicate when a contract or agreement is "entered into" for purposes of this section.

#### (c) Separate Contracts Do Not Preclude Taxation

The rights of the decedent and the survivor need not arise under the same contract or agreement. However, if the benefits are payable under separate contracts, it must appear that they are part of a single, integrated arrangement. [Treas. Reg. § 20.2039–1]

## c. Nature of Decedent's Interest

The survivor's benefit is taxable under section 2039(a) "if, under such contract or agreement, an annuity or other payment was payable to the decedent, or the decedent possessed the right to receive such annuity or payment, either alone or in conjunction with another for his life or for any period not ascertainable without reference to his death or for any period which does not in fact end before his death."

### (1) Decedent's Interest in the Contract

The decedent's interest must be in the contract or agreement under which the survivor's benefits are payable. But, as noted above, section 2039 will tax survivor's benefits even though payable under a contract that was technically separate from the contract under which the decedent was receiving or was entitled to receive payments, ***if*** the separate contracts form an ***integrated plan.***

#### (a) Employment Related Plans

Separate arrangements under employment related plans need not be entered into simultaneously or with the intention that they be treated as a single contract. It is sufficient that the plans constitute a single "package" of employment benefits.

e.g. **Example:** Suppose an employer establishes a pension plan for its employees that will pay a certain amount to retired employees for their lives. Subsequently, the employer establishes a plan that will pay a lump sum to an employee's designated survivor if the employee should die before retirement. Still later, the employer sets up another plan providing for certain payments to a designated survivor if the employee dies after retirement. Under the Regulations, these three plans would be considered part of a single package of employment related benefits and thus would be "integrated." [Treas. Reg. § 20.2039–1(b)(2), example (6); *see also* **Estate of Bahen v. United States,** 305 F.2d 827 (Ct. Cl. 1962)]

##### 1) Theory of Integration Questioned

Although it distinguished *Bahen* on the facts, the Second Circuit, in **Schelberg v. Commissioner,** 612 F.2d 25 (2d Cir. 1979), questioned whether the *Bahen* rule and its extension in later cases was supported by the statutory language and the Committee Reports that accompanied the 1954 Code. *Schelberg* was rejected by a district court considering benefits received by another taxpayer under the same (IBM) employment-related plans. [**Looney v. United States,** 569 F. Supp. 1569 (M.D. Ga. 1983)]

### (b) Insurance—Annuity "Packages"

Annuity-life insurance arrangements have also been treated as one integrated plan, thus producing a tax under section 2039. For example, where the decedent purchased an annuity/insurance package and assigned the life insurance to another, the Fifth Circuit found the life insurance and annuity contracts to be a single integrated plan, so that the "life insurance" proceeds were includible in the decedent's estate under section 2039. [**Montgomery v. Commissioner,** 458 F.2d 616 (5th Cir.), *cert. denied,* 409 U.S. 849 (1972)]

#### 1) Distinguish—Taxation Under Section 2036

However, prior to the *Montgomery* case, the government sought to tax a similar arrangement under section 2036. Its argument rested on the premise that the two contracts were integrated, so that the decedent had in substance transferred a "life insurance" contract to the assignee with a reserved life interest (the annuity). The Supreme Court disagreed. It held that the life insurance and annuity contracts were separate investments; therefore, the insurance proceeds were not taxable under section 2036 because the decedent retained no interest in that contract. [**Fidelity-Philadelphia Trust Co. v. Smith,** 356 U.S. 274 (1958)]

### (2) Annuity or Other Payment

Just as in the case of the survivor's benefit, the interest of the decedent need not be in the form of an annuity; any form of payment will satisfy the requirements of section 2039.

#### (a) Exception—Salary

However, the Tax Court has held that the term "other payment" does not include compensation that the decedent was receiving or was entitled to receive at the time of the decedent's death. Rather, the term is "qualitatively limited to post-employment benefits." [**Estate of Fusz v. Commissioner,** 46 T.C. 214 (1966), *acq.* 1967–2 C.B. 2]

#### (b) Distinguish—Retirement Benefits Disguised as Salary

However, section 2039 cannot be avoided simply by designating post-employment benefits as continuing compensation. Thus, for example, payments for "consultation services" to be made to a person following withdrawal from full time employment will be scrutinized to determine whether they are in fact compensation for services or merely a disguised form of post-retirement benefit. [*See, e.g.,* **Silberman v. United States,** 333 F. Supp. 1120 (W.D. Pa. 1971); Rev. Rul. 71–507, 1971–2 C.B. 331; *but compare* **Kramer v. United States,** 406 F.2d 1363 (Ct. Cl. 1969)]

### (3) Payable to Decedent—Right to Receive

The statutory requirement is met if the decedent was actually receiving payments under the contract or agreement or if the decedent had a right to receive payments in the future. For instance, if the decedent was entitled to receive a pension upon retirement, with a death benefit payable to a designated survivor, and the decedent died before retirement, the survivor's benefit is includible in the decedent's estate under section 2039.

#### (a) Contingent Right

The "right to receive payment" has been broadly interpreted, so that the statute may be satisfied even when decedent's right to future payment is subject to a remote contingency.

e.g. **Example:** The decedent's employer established a plan under which the decedent's survivor would receive certain annuity payments. The decedent was not entitled to receive any payments ***unless*** the decedent became totally and permanently disabled prior to retirement. The decedent died before retirement and had never become disabled. The court held that this contingent right to receive payments in the future was sufficient to meet the "right to receive" requirement of section 2039. [**Estate of Bahen v. United States,** 305 F.2d 827 (Ct. Cl. 1962); *but compare* **Schelberg v. Commissioner,** 612 F.2d 25 (2d Cir. 1979)]

#### (b) Payments Terminating Prior to Death—the Gap in Section 2039

On the other hand, if a decedent has received ***everything*** the decedent is entitled to receive under the contract, benefits payable to the decedent's survivor under the contract are not taxable under section 2039. Thus, suppose the decedent is entitled to receive a lump sum upon retirement and a designated survivor is entitled to receive payments upon decedent's death. If the decedent dies after retirement and after having received the lump sum payment, the survivor's benefit is not taxable under section 2039 since, at death, the decedent was neither ***receiving*** payments nor did he have any ***right to receive*** payments in the future. [Treas. Reg. § 20.2039–1(b)(2), example (5)]

### (4) Joint Interests Produce Tax

The decedent's right to receive payments need not be exclusive (as evidenced by the statutory language "either alone or in conjunction with another"). Accordingly, the survivor's benefits are fully taxable to the decedent even though lifetime payments are made jointly to the decedent and another.

### (5) Time Periods

The payments (or right to payments) must persist for the decedent's "life or for any period not ascertainable without reference to his death or for any period which does not in fact end before his death." The intention of these alternative time periods is the same as that for the identical time periods under section 2036.

## d. Amount Includible

The estate tax is imposed upon that value of the survivor's benefit that is proportionate to contributions made by the decedent. [I.R.C. § 2039(b)]

### (1) Valuation of Survivor's Benefits

Valuation of the taxable benefit is made as of the date of the decedent's death. If the benefit is in the form of a lump sum payment, the amount of the payment would be the amount of survivor's benefit. But if the benefit is in the form of an annuity or other deferred payments, the amount of the benefit is the present value of the right to receive these payments, determined actuarially.

#### (2) Proportionate Inclusion

It is not necessarily the entire value of the survivor's benefit that is includible; rather, only the amount that is proportionate to the decedent's contributions toward the purchase price of the contract is taxable.

##### (a) Determining Decedent's Contributions—Attribution Rule

However, under the general rule of section 2039(b), any contributions to the purchase price made ***by the decedent's employer are treated as contributions made by the decedent.***

e.g. **Example:** Assume that the value of the survivor's benefit is $100,000, that the decedent contributed $10,000 of the purchase price, the decedent's employer contributed $60,000, and the survivor contributed $10,000. The decedent and the employer contributed 87.5% of the purchase price ($70,000 divided by $80,000). Thus, $87,500 is included in the decedent's estate.

## 9. Section 2040—Joint Interests

Co-tenancies with a ***"right of survivorship"*** are included in the gross estate of the first joint tenant to die. However, the estate tax consequences may differ radically according to the nature of the ownership interests involved.

### a. Background

Because of the peculiar incidents of ownership and property rights that attach to tenancies with a right of survivorship, a special provision is necessary for their taxation. Under technical property law, when the first joint tenant dies, nothing "passes" to the survivor; rather, the decedent's undivided interest is extinguished by death and the survivor "survives" to sole ownership of the property. At the same time, however, it is clear that joint tenancies can be, and frequently are, used as substitutes for testamentary giving.

#### (1) The Revenue Act of 1916

The first estate tax act specifically provided for the taxation of tenancies by the entirety and joint tenancies with right of survivorship. These provisions were virtually identical to those presently found in section 2040(a) of the 1954 Code.

#### (2) Husband-and-Wife Joint Tenancies

The 1976 Tax Reform Act first provided special rules for husband-and-wife joint tenancies. Modified in the Revenue Act of 1978 and substantially revised in the Revenue Act of 1981, these special rules are now embodied in section 2040(b).

### b. Introductory Analysis

Analysis of the scope of section 2040 may be broken down into ***five principal elements***:

(1) ***Determination of the type of co-tenancies*** to which section 2040 is applicable;

(2) ***The general rule of inclusion*** provided for by section 2040(a);

(3) ***The required nature of the survivor's contribution*** which may allow a portion of the value of joint tenancy property to be excluded from the estate of the first joint tenant to die;

(4) ***The relation of section 2040 to other taxing sections;*** and

(5) ***Special spousal rules for "qualified joint interests" under section 2040(b).***

## c. Section 2040 Applies Only to Co-Tenancies with a Right of Survivorship

Section 2040 reaches those forms of joint ownership having, as one of their incidents, a "right of survivorship" (joint tenancies, tenancies by the entirety, joint bank accounts, etc.).

### (1) Taxation of Tenancies in Common, Etc. and Community Property

Forms of co-ownership ***without*** survivorship rights (e.g., tenancies in common and community property) are ***not*** taxable under section 2040. However, the decedent's interest in such property is taxable under section 2033 as property owned at death.

**EXAM TIP** GILBERT

On your exam, be careful to consider ***all*** relevant sections when determining whether property must be included in the decedent's gross estate. For example, although property with an ownership form without a right of survivorship ***is not*** includible under ***section 2040,*** the property ***may be included*** under ***section 2033.***

### (2) Form of Joint Tenancy

The specific form of the joint tenancy (what it might be called under property law or under a specific mode of title registration) is irrelevant. The critical factor is the ***right of survivorship,*** and all forms of co-ownership that have a right of survivorship are subject to section 2040. Thus, in addition to common law joint tenancies or tenancies by the entirety, such forms of co-ownership as joint bank accounts, joint registration of securities or personal property, United States Savings Bonds registered in the name of "D, P.O.D. [payable on death] to X," and joint brokerage accounts are within the scope of section 2040. [*See* Rev. Rul. 69–148, 1969–1 C.B. 226]

## d. General Rule of Inclusion

The estate tax is not limited to the value of the decedent's undivided interest. Rather, it extends to the ***full value*** of the joint tenancy property ***except*** "such part thereof as may be shown to have originally belonged to . . . [the survivor] and never to have been received or acquired by the [survivor] from the decedent for less than an adequate and full consideration in money or money's worth" [I.R.C. § 2040(a)]

### (1) Original Consideration or Contribution—in General

Thus, to the extent the property or a portion thereof originally belonged to the survivor, or to the extent the survivor furnished all or a part of the consideration for its acquisition, the property is not includible in the decedent's estate. However, in order to obtain the exclusion, the taxpayer (estate) has the burden of proving what part of the property (or the consideration therefor) was contributed by the survivor (usually referred to as proof of an "original contribution" by the survivor).

#### (a) Proportionate Exclusion

The amount excluded from the decedent's estate is ***not*** the amount that the survivor contributed, but rather an amount ***proportionate*** to the survivor's contribution. In **Estate of Goldsborough v. Commissioner,** 70 T.C. 1077, *aff'd*, 673 F.2d 1310 (4th Cir. 1982), the court applied the following formula to determine the value that should be excluded from the decedent's gross estate where the donee realizes taxable gain upon the sale of the gifted property:

$$\text{Amount Excluded} = \text{Entire value of property (on the date of death or alternate valuation date)} \times \frac{\text{Survivor's consideration}}{\text{Entire consideration paid}}$$

**Example:** Al and Bill acquired property as joint tenants for $10,000 and Al paid the entire price. At Al's death, the property is worth $20,000. The full value of the joint tenancy property is included in Al's estate.

**Example:** Same situation as above, but Bill made an original contribution of $2,000 to the purchase price of $10,000. Under ***Goldsborough's*** consideration furnished test, since 20% of the consideration was furnished by Bill ($2,000 divided by $10,000), upon Al's death, 20% of the value of the property ($20,000), or $4,000, is excluded from Al's estate; 80% ($8,000 divided by $10,000) of the property's value ($16,000) is included.

### (2) Joint Interests Created by Another

Where the joint tenancy interest was acquired by gift, bequest, devise, or inheritance from a ***third party,*** only the value of the fractional interest of the deceased joint tenant is included in the decedent's gross estate. [I.R.C. § 2040(a)] In effect, each joint tenant is treated as the original owner of the joint tenant's fractional interest in the whole. [Treas. Reg. § 20.2040–1(a)(1)]

### (3) Distinguish—Improvements Made to Joint Tenancy Property

If the survivor has paid for improvements on the property after its acquisition, only the ***actual cost*** of the improvements may be excluded from the decedent's gross estate. The apportionment rule is limited to contributions made to the ***creation or acquisition*** of the joint tenancy; it does not apply to improvements. [**Estate of Peters v. Commissioner,** 386 F.2d 404 (4th Cir. 1967)]

**EXAM TIP**

Sometimes, the intuitively "right" answer is not the correct exam answer. For example, remember that only the ***actual cost*** of improvements (rather than their proportionate value) that the survivor pays for may be excluded from the decedent's gross estate, ***even if the improvement greatly enhances the value of the property.***

## e. Required Nature of the Survivor's Contribution

The critical problem in applying the proportionate exclusion rule is determining whether a portion of the property ***originally belonged to the survivor*** or, where the survivor paid part of the purchase price, whether the consideration furnished by the survivor ***originated with the survivor*** and was not acquired by or received by the survivor, at any time, from the decedent **"*for less than an adequate and full consideration in money or money's worth.*"** [I.R.C. § 2040(a)]

### (1) Prior Gifts or Bequests from Third Party

Any money or property that the survivor acquired from a third party which is used as consideration for the acquisition of a joint tenancy between the survivor and the decedent is consideration that originates with the survivor. It is not necessary that the survivor "earn" the money or property that the survivor furnishes (although the survivor's earnings or the product thereof will, of course, qualify).

### (2) Prior Gifts from Decedent

Property that the survivor originally received as a gift from the decedent cannot be claimed as an "original" contribution by the survivor. For example, if D gives separately owned property to X, who then conveys the property back to "D and X as joint tenants with right of survivorship," at D's death, the full value of the property is includible in D's estate since the entire property "originated" with D. [**United States v. Jacobs,** 306 U.S. 363 (1939)]

#### (a) Distinguish—Consideration Furnished

Although property is received from the decedent, to the extent the survivor paid full and adequate consideration in money or money's worth, it will be deemed to originate with the survivor.

e.g. **Example:** Dale conveyed property worth $15,000 to Xavier for $5,000. Subsequently, Xavier conveyed the property to "Dale and Xavier as joint tenants with right of survivorship." Upon Dale's death, one-third of the value of the property is excludible from Dale's estate. Although Xavier furnished consideration for the original transfer, he did not pay ***full*** consideration in money or money's worth; thus, to the extent that the original transfer from Dale to Xavier was a gift (two-thirds), the property originated with Dale and is includible in Dale's estate.

### (3) Income from Gifted Property

Although property given by the decedent to the survivor remains attributable to the donor, any ***income*** derived from the gifted property after the date of the gift belongs to and is attributable to the survivor. Moreover, this rule normally applies even if the income derives from joint tenancy property created by the decedent; one-half of the income belongs to each joint tenant and if the income is used to acquire other joint tenancy property, one-half of the consideration for the acquisition of that joint tenancy is attributable to the survivor.

e.g. **Example:** Theresa gives securities to Laura. Thereafter, Laura collects and accumulates the dividends and interest and contributes the accumulated income as part of the consideration for the acquisition of joint tenancy realty by Theresa and Laura. Theresa dies. The income contributed by Laura is an "original contribution" for purposes of section 2040(a).

e.g. **Example:** Theresa pays the entire consideration for the acquisition of an apartment building, taking title in the name of Theresa and Laura as joint tenants. Accumulated rents from the building are subsequently used to purchase Whiteacre in joint tenancy. Theresa dies. The full value of the apartment building is included in Theresa's estate; however, only one-half of the value of Whiteacre is included in Theresa's estate since one-half of the rents from the apartment building (which were the source of the purchase price) are attributable to Laura as an original contribution.

### (4) Profits Realized from Appreciation in Value of Gifted Property

It is reasonably well accepted now that when one person gives property to another, any profits realized by the donee that are attributable to appreciation in value of the gifted property subsequent to the date of the gift may constitute an original contribution by the donee to the acquisition of joint tenancy property. Note, however, that this rule extends only to profits attributable to ***post-gift appreciation*** in value, not to the taxable gain that the donee may realize upon sale of the gifted property. [**Harvey v. United States,** 185 F.2d 463 (7th Cir. 1950)].

e.g. **Example:** Sean buys securities for $2,000. Three years later, he gives the securities to Charlotte. At the time of the gift, the securities are worth $6,000. Several years later, Charlotte sells the securities for $10,000 and uses the entire proceeds to purchase joint tenancy real estate with Sean. Charlotte's taxable gain upon the sale of the securities is $8,000 ($10,000 minus $2,000). [*See* I.R.C. §§ 1001 and 1015] Charlotte dies when the real estate is worth $15,000. Under the ***Goldsborough*** consideration furnished test, $3,000 is excluded from Charlotte's gross estate under section 2040 ($15,000 times $2,000/$10,000).

#### (a) Exception—No Exclusion Where Same Property Reconveyed in Joint Tenancy

According to the Regulations, if the donee reconveys the same property into joint tenancy with the donor, post-gift appreciation may not be attributed to the donee as an original contribution. [Treas. Reg. § 20.2040–1(c), example (4)]

e.g. **Example:** In the example above, if Charlotte reconveyed the securities to Sean and Charlotte as joint tenants, and Sean died before Charlotte, the entire value of the securities would be includible in Sean's estate.

#### (b) Exception—Reinvestment of Joint Tenancy Property

Don purchased stock with his own funds and had the stock issued to Don and Alice as joint tenants. Subsequently this stock was sold at a profit and the proceeds were invested in other stock, which was also issued to Don and Alice as joint tenants. Upon Don's death, the full value of the "new" stock was included in Don's estate; Alice's one-half of the profit on the sale of the original stock was not accepted as an "original contribution" by Alice. According to **Endicott Trust Co. v. United States,** 305 F. Supp. 943 (N.D.N.Y. 1969), "changing the character of the property but not the character of the ownership will not . . . permit an escape from taxation as joint property." According to *Endicott*, the property was never owned outright by the surviving joint tenant but was always owned as joint tenancy property with the decedent.

### (5) Assumption of Mortgage as Original Contribution

If both joint tenants assume a mortgage with respect to joint tenancy property, one-half of the mortgage is attributable to each as an original contribution. [**Bremer v. Luff,** 7 F. Supp. 148 (N.D.N.Y. 1933)]

e.g. **Example:** Mike and Cathy acquire real property as joint tenants. Mike pays the entire down payment of $4,000, and both Mike and Cathy jointly assume a mortgage of $16,000. Mike dies before any payments are made in amortization of the mortgage principal. In this case, Mike's contribution is $12,000 ($4,000 down payment plus one-half of the $16,000 mortgage), and Cathy's contribution is $8,000 (one-half of the outstanding mortgage). Thus, 40% ($8,000 divided by $20,000) is excludible from Mike's estate.

#### (a) Amortization of Jointly Assumed Mortgage

As a jointly assumed mortgage is paid off, the proportionate "original contribution" will vary unless both joint tenants contribute equally to the payments.

e.g. **Example:** In the example above, suppose that before his death, Mike made payments on the mortgage, reducing the balance to $10,000. Mike's contribution would be $15,000 (the $4,000 down payment, the $6,000 payments amortizing the mortgage, and one-half of the $10,000 mortgage that remains outstanding); and Cathy's contribution would be $5,000 (one-half of the outstanding mortgage). Hence, only 25% of the value of the joint tenancy property ($20,000 divided by $5,000) is excludible from Mike's estate.

#### (b) Income from Property Used to Pay off Mortgage

If a jointly assumed mortgage is paid off with ***income derived from the property,*** each joint tenant will be treated as having made equal contributions to the amortization of the mortgage.

e.g. **Example:** In the example above, if the income from the jointly held property was used to reduce the mortgage from $16,000 to $10,000 before Mike dies, 40% of the value of the joint tenancy property is excludible from Mike's estate; Cathy's contribution would be in the amount of $3,000 (one-half of the mortgage payments) plus $5,000 (one-half of the balance due), which is 40% of the acquisition cost.

### (6) Burden of Proof

As noted earlier, the burden of establishing that consideration originated with the survivor is upon the decedent's estate. The Internal Revenue Service and the courts insist on a very strict tracing requirement. For example, if both parties made deposits to and withdrawals from a jointly held bank account, the entire account balance was held taxable in the estate of the first to die because it could not be proven that it was not the survivor's deposits that were withdrawn! [**Estate of Drazen v. Commissioner,** 48 T.C. 1 (1967)]

## f. Special Rule for Spousal Joint Tenancies

Section 2040(b) provides a special rule for joint tenancies between the decedent and the decedent's spouse. It is applicable to all decedents dying after 1981, without regard to the time the joint tenancy was created. A review of some of the authorities suggests that the rationale for the enactment of section 2040(b) is that while joint tenancy investments by spouses frequently represent the joint contributions of both spouses, it is usually extremely difficult for the survivor to prove an "original contribution" to the property's acquisition.

### (1) "Qualified Joint Interests"

As amended by the 1981 Act, section 2040(b) provides that in the case of a "qualified joint interest" only one-half of the value of the property is includible in the gross estate.

#### (a) Definition

A "qualified joint interest" is any interest held by a decedent ***and the decedent's spouse*** that is either: (i) a tenancy by the entirety, or (ii) a joint tenancy with right of survivorship, ***but only if the decedent and decedent's spouse are the only joint tenants.*** Note that a tenancy by the entirety can only exist where the only co-tenants are spouses.

**EXAM TIP** GILBERT

For your exam, you should remember that a qualified joint interest under section 2040 may be held ***only*** by the decedent and the decedent's spouse. If ***any other person*** is included, there is not a "qualified joint interest," and the general rule under section 2040(a) applies.

### (b) Effect

Where a qualified joint interest exists, one-half of the value of the property will be included in the estate of the first to die, without regard to which co-tenant furnished the consideration at the time of the joint tenancy's creation. Thus, if the donor dies first, only one-half of the property's value is included in the donor's estate, whereas under the general rule the entire value would be taxed. But, if the donee dies first, one-half will be included in the donee's estate, even though under the general rule nothing would have been included. Of course, the full value of the property is included in the estate of the surviving joint tenant who has survived to sole, fee simple ownership. [I.R.C. § 2033]

e.g. **Example:** A spouse purchases land for $100,000 as a joint tenant with her husband. The spouse provides all of the consideration for the land. Three years later, the husband dies. Under section 2040(b), one-half of the land's value is included in the husband's gross estate. It is irrelevant that the spouse provided all of the consideration.

### (c) Interaction with 100% Marital Deduction

Although the one-half inclusion rule under section 2040(b) responds to some anomalies that attended joint ownership of property by spouses under prior law, it offers dubious relief. The 1981 Act also allows a 100% marital deduction, and the joint tenancy property will qualify for this allowance without regard to who dies first, or how much is included in the decedent's estate under I.R.C. § 2056. Thus, no additional estate tax liability is incurred in any event. In **Gallenstein v. United States,** 975 F.2d 286 (6th Cir. 1992), involving a joint tenancy that was created prior to 1977, and where the decedent contributed 100% of the purchase price, the court held that the decedent could use the prior law of contribution and include 100% in the decedent's estate, thereby getting a full stepped up basis under I.R.C. § 1014 and paying no tax on the property because of the 100% marital deduction.

## g. Community Property

Section 2040 does not apply to community property. However, since community property does represent a form of concurrent ownership, the estate tax aspects are appropriately considered at this point.

### (1) Nature of Community Property; General Application of Estate Tax

In most community property states, each spouse is recognized as having a present, vested one-half interest in all community assets. In turn, on the death of either spouse, only the deceased spouse's one-half of the community property is taxable under section 2033. Thus, in determining the tax status of community property, the extent to which it is "attributable" to the decedent is immaterial. [**United States v. Goodyear,** 99 F.2d 523 (9th Cir. 1938)] Note that the form in which property is held is not controlling. An asset may well be "community property" (and taxed as such) even though title is held in some other form of co-tenancy. For example, property acquired with one spouse's earnings during marriage (community property) can be a "community" asset even though title is taken in joint tenancy.

### h. Services as Consideration

Many of the cases involve spouses. Although it is clear that an economic value can be placed upon one spouse's services to another spouse or to the family, such services—at least if they are of an ordinary domestic nature—were not deemed to constitute consideration "in money or money's worth" or an "original contribution" to the acquisition of joint tenancy property. [*See, e.g.,* **Bushman v. United States,** 8 F. Supp. 694 (Ct. Cl. 1934), *cert. denied,* 295 U.S. 756 (1935)]

#### (1) Nondomestic Services

The same result obtained where one spouse rendered gratuitous services in the business of the other spouse. [*See, e.g.,* **Rogan v. Kammerdiner,** 140 F.2d 569 (9th Cir. 1944)] Of course, if the spouse was paid ***a reasonable salary*** for the services, the earnings would constitute an original contribution on that spouse's part. Or, if the spouse worked in the other spouse's business under a definite ***agreement*** for reimbursement for services by way of an interest in jointly held property, the agreed upon reimbursement might have been considered an original contribution by that spouse. [*See* **Richardson v. Helvering,** 80 F.2d 548 (D.C. Cir. 1935)] However, it did not occur to most to formalize the employment arrangement.

#### (2) Informal Partnerships

Taxpayers scored a few victories where the surviving spouse (joint tenant) was able to convince a court that a business in which the surviving spouse materially and continuously participated with the deceased spouse constituted a business partnership and that the partnership profits (to which the survivor was entitled to one-half) were used to acquire the joint tenancy property. [*See* **United States v. Neel,** 235 F.2d 395 (10th Cir. 1956); **Otte v. Commissioner,** T.C. Memo. 1972–76] However, the burden of proof was quite difficult to overcome.

### i. Relationship of Section 2040 and Other Statutory Provisions

As will be seen by the cases illustrated below, section 2040 does not ordinarily interact with other specific sections of the estate tax; indeed, where it is applicable, it generally ***supersedes*** these other sections.

#### (1) Severance of Joint Tenancy—in General

When a joint tenancy is severed prior to death, section 2040 is inapplicable, and the full value of the property is no longer subject to tax in the decedent's estate. However, if the decedent retains an interest as a tenant in common, that interest will be taxed under section 2033.

#### (2) No Interaction with Section 2035

As previously discussed, estate taxation under section 2035 is now limited to: (i) gift taxes paid or payable with respect to gifts made within three years of death, and (ii) the transfer or release of certain interests or powers that would produce taxation under other specific estate tax provisions. Because section 2040 is not among the provisions specified for continued interaction with section 2035, no estate tax will attach if joint tenancy property is transferred within three years of a joint tenant's death.

**Example:** Ten years ago, Diane purchased property and took title in the names of Diane and Alex as joint tenants. On her death bed, Diane conveys her one-half undivided interest to Alex. Assuming no gift tax liability resulted from this death-bed gift, no portion of the value of the joint tenancy property will be included in Diane's estate. Except for the gift, the full value of the property would be subject to the estate tax.

# 10. Section 2041—Powers of Appointment

Under general property law, a "power of appointment" is a power granted by a "donor of the power" to a "donee of the power" by virtue of which the donee of the power may dispose of the property subject to the power even though it is "owned" by another. Under technical property law, the grant of a power of appointment does not give the donee an "interest" in the property subject to the power. At the same time, however, a person who has, for example, a life estate in property and a power to appoint the property to whomever the person chooses, virtually owns that property outright. Consequently, section 2041 includes the value of the property subject to the power in the gross estate of the holder of such a power.

## a. Background

The first estate tax (under the 1916 Act) did not specifically include property subject to a power of appointment in the holder's gross estate. However, the Revenue Act of 1918 made certain powers of appointment subject to the estate tax. As it turned out, this action was a wise precaution, because the Supreme Court later held that absent a specific provision taxing a power of appointment, the property subject to the power could not be subject to the estate tax. **[United States v. Field,** 255 U.S. 257 (1921)]

### (1) Taxation of Powers of Appointment Under the 1918 Act

The first provision taxing powers of appointment was limited to ***general powers*** (defined under section 2041(b)(1)) that were ***exercised*** by the decedent.

#### (a) Unexercised Powers Not Taxed

The government sought to tax unexercised powers under the predecessor of section 2033, arguing that a person who held a life estate coupled with a general power of appointment in the property was, in effect, the "substantial owner." However, the Supreme Court rejected this argument. **[Helvering v. Safe Deposit & Trust Co.,** 316 U.S. 56 (1942)]

### (2) The Revenue Act of 1942

The Supreme Court's decision in the *Safe Deposit & Trust* case was offset by the passage of the Revenue Act of 1942. Under this Act, powers of appointment created on or before October 21, 1942, the effective date of the Act, were taxed as before (i.e., the Act operated prospectively only). Powers created after October 21, 1942, however, were included in the gross estate whether or not exercised and, indeed, the Act imposed a tax on many special powers of appointment. The Act also gave a time frame in which the donee of a pre-1942 general power of appointment could be partially released to be a nongeneral power so that the exercise of the power would not be taxable, which time frame was from time to time extended by later legislation.

#### (3) The Powers of Appointment Act of 1951

Persuaded that the extensive taxation of post-1942 powers under the 1942 Act was inappropriate, in 1951 Congress limited the tax upon post-1942 powers to ***general*** powers of appointment. Such powers, however, remain taxable whether or not exercised. The Act also extended to November 1, 1951, the time in which pre-1942 general powers of appointment could be partially released to be a nongeneral power so that the exercise of the power would not be taxable.

#### (4) The 1954 Code

Section 2041 of the 1954 (and 1986) Code is simply a refinement of the system of taxing powers of appointment adopted in the 1951 Act.

### b. Introductory Analysis

The treatment of section 2041 may be broken down into four basic issues:

(1) ***Determination of the date of the power's creation;***

(2) ***The nature*** of the taxable power;

(3) ***Special rules relating to preexisting powers***; and

(4) ***Special rules relating to post-1942 powers.***

### c. Date of Creation of the Power

Given the fact that pre- and post-October 21, 1942, powers are taxed differently, it is important to determine when the power is created.

#### (1) Direct Transfers

Where a power of appointment is granted with respect to property not transferred to a trust (an unusual situation today), the power is deemed created on the date it is granted to the donee. And, since powers of appointment are usually granted together with some other interest in the property (such as a life estate), the date of the creation of the power will usually be the same as the date upon which the interest in the property is transferred.

#### (2) Transfers to a Trust

Powers of appointment granted with respect to property transferred to a trust are deemed created on the same date that the trust came into existence by a transfer of property to the trustee.

#### (3) Revocable Trusts

With respect to revocable trusts, it is uniformly held that the date of creation of the power is the date upon which the property is transferred to the trustee (rather than when the power to revoke lapses or is released). [*See* **United States v. Merchant's National Bank,** 261 F.2d 570 (5th Cir. 1958); Treas. Reg. § 20.2041–1(e)]

#### (4) Powers Granted Under Will

If the power is created by will, the date of decedent's death (when the will "speaks") is the date of the creation of the power. However, section 2041(b)(3) provides a special rule for wills executed on or before October 21, 1942. If the will was not republished after that date and if the decedent died before July 1, 1949, the power will be treated as a pre-1942 power.

### d. Nature of the Taxable Power of Appointment

Inclusion in a powerholder's gross estate under section 2041 is limited to ***general*** powers of appointment. [I.R.C. § 2041(a)]

#### (1) Definition of "General Power"

The statute defines a general power of appointment as "a power which is exercisable in favor of the ***decedent, the decedent's estate, the decedent's creditors,*** or the ***creditors of the decedent's estate.***" [I.R.C. § 2041(b)(1)] Note that it is not necessary that the decedent be able to appoint the property to all of the permissible appointees; a power is general if it ***can*** be exercised ***in favor of any one of them.*** And, as long as the decedent can appoint the property to any one of the permissible appointees, it is immaterial that the decedent may also be able to appoint the property to others.

##### (a) Special/Nongeneral Powers Distinguished

A "special power" is any power of appointment that is not a general power. For example, a power to appoint property to or among a designated class of persons, ***not including*** the decedent or the decedent's estate, etc., is a special or nongeneral power of appointment. Hence, property subject solely to a special power is not taxable in the decedent's estate under section 2041.

e.g. **Example:** The power to appoint "to whomever D chooses" is a general power of appointment, as is a power to appoint "to D's children or D's estate."

cf. **Compare:** A power to appoint to a limited class of persons ***not including*** the decedent, the decedent's creditors, the decedent's estate, or the creditors of the decedent's estate (e.g., "to D's children") is not a general power of appointment.

POWERS OF APPOINTMENT — GILBERT

| TYPE | DEFINITION | TAXABLE UNDER SECTION 2041? |
|---|---|---|
| **GENERAL** | Power ***can be*** exercised in favor of:<br>• Decedent;<br>• Decedent's estate;<br>• Decedent's creditors; ***or***<br>• Creditors of decedent's estate | Yes |
| **SPECIAL (NONGENERAL)** | Power can be exercise in favor of any person or class ***other than*** listed above. | No |

##### (b) Testamentary or Lifetime Power

It is generally sufficient that the power be exercisable either during life or by will. It need not be exercisable both during life and by will.

### (c) Exception for Certain Powers to Consume Which Are Limited by an Ascertainable Standard

The statute provides that "a power to consume, invade, or appropriate property for the benefit of the decedent which is limited by an ascertainable standard relating to ***health, education, support, or maintenance of the decedent***" is not a general power of appointment. Such a limited power is not a general power of appointment even though it enables the decedent to appoint the property to the decedent or the decedent's creditors. [I.R.C. § 2041(b)(1)(A)]

## (2) Form of the Power

For federal tax purposes, it is not necessary that the power be in any particular form. Many rights, powers, and authorities over property are classified as powers of appointment even though they may not be so defined under state property law. For example, powers to withdraw property from a trust, or to consume property (whether held on trust, or otherwise) are powers of appointment since they allow the person who possesses the "power" to obtain beneficial enjoyment of the property.

### (a) Capacity in Which Exercisable

The capacity in which the power is exercisable is immaterial. For example, the fact that a general power is exercisable by the decedent as trustee will not prevent taxation under section 2041.

### (b) Indirect Access to the Power

Moreover, the power need not technically lie with the decedent. Thus, the decedent will be deemed to possess a general power of appointment if the decedent has authority to compel exercise of a power held by another for the decedent's benefit.

### (c) Contingent Powers

Since the power must be "exercisable" by the decedent [I.R.C. § 2041(b)(1)], it would appear that a contingent power is not taxable if the contingency is beyond the decedent's control and has not occurred at the time of the decedent's death.

### (d) Administrative Powers

For purposes of section 2041, the power must be such that the decedent can benefit the decedent, either directly or indirectly (e.g., by appointing to the decedent's creditors). Thus, mere powers of management, investment, etc., with respect to the property are not "powers of appointment."

## (3) Limited to Donated Powers

Section 2041 applies only to powers ***donated*** to the decedent by some third party, not to powers that the decedent ***retained*** or ***reacquired*** in connection with property the decedent formerly owned. Retained or reacquired powers with respect to property may be taxable under some other section, but they are not "powers of appointment" within the scope of section 2041. [*See* I.R.C. §§ 2036(a)(2) and 2038]

e.g. **Example:** Diane transferred property to a trust for Alex for life, with the corpus to be distributed to such of Alex's children as Diane shall appoint.

This power reserved by Diane is not a taxable power of appointment under section 2041. However, it would be taxable under section 2038.

**cf.** **Compare:** If Diane had given Alex the power to determine which children the property would go to after Alex's death, Alex's power over the remainder would be a power of appointment. However, the property would not be taxable in Alex's estate because it was not a ***general*** power of appointment.

**(4) Direct or Indirect Benefit**

A "general power" exists where property may be appointed, ***directly*** or ***indirectly,*** for the decedent's benefit.

**(a) Power to Discharge Own Obligations**

If the holder can utilize the power to discharge the holder's legal obligations, it is deemed exercisable for the holder's benefit and is a general power. In effect, the holder has the power to appoint to the property to the holder's creditors.

**(b) Power Exercisable to Support Another**

A decedent has a general power where the decedent may exercise a power (or compel its exercise) to use property for the support of a person whom the decedent is legally obligated to support. [*See* Treas. Reg. § 20.2041–1(c)(1)]

**e. Preexisting Powers—Special Rules**

A power created on or before October 21, 1942 (preexisting powers), is included in the gross estate under section 2041 only if it is ***exercised.*** [I.R.C. § 2041(a)(1)]

**(1) Exercise by Will**

Under the Code, if a power is created on or before October 21, 1941, the exercise of a general power of appointment by will is included in a decedent's gross estate. [I.R.C. § 2041(a)(1)(A)] Moreover, under the law of many states, a decedent's residuary clause will exercise a general power of appointment even though no reference to the power nor intent to exercise it is expressed. In such case, the general power is deemed "exercised" by the decedent's will for federal estate tax purposes.

**(2) Exercise During Life**

If a general power created on or before October 21, 1941 is exercised during the life of the decedent, the property will be included in the decedent's gross estate only if it would have been included under sections 2035 through 2038 had the property subject to the power been transferred by the decedent.

**e.g.** **Example:** If a decedent is granted a life estate in property created on or before October 21, 1941 with a general power to appoint the remainder, and four years before the decedent's death, the decedent appoints the property to a trust and reserves the right to revoke the trust, the property is includible in the decedent's gross estate. [I.R.C. §§ 2041(a)(1)(B), 2038]

**(3) Lapse or Release of Preexisting Powers**

Since a preexisting power must be exercised to be taxed, a failure to exercise the power, or a lapse or release of the power, will ***not*** cause inclusion of the property in the decedent's gross estate.

#### (4) Reduction of Power and Exercise of Special Power

If a preexisting general power was reduced to a special power (e.g., by a partial release) before November 1, 1951, a subsequent exercise of the special power is not deemed to be an exercise of a general power of appointment. [I.R.C. § 2041(a)(1)]

#### (5) Joint Powers

A preexisting power granted to the decedent and another, jointly, is ***not*** included in the decedent's gross estate under section 2041. [I.R.C. § 2041(b)(1)(B)] It is immaterial whether the co-holder of the power is an adverse party.

### f. Post-1942 Powers—Special Rules

Unlike preexisting powers, a power created after October 21, 1942, will be included in a decedent's gross estate whether exercised ***or unexercised.*** In other words, property subject to a post-1942 general power of appointment will be included in the decedent's gross estate if the decedent merely ***possessed*** the general power at the time of the decedent's death. The very existence of the power renders the property taxable. [I.R.C. § 2041(a)(2)]

#### (1) Inability to Exercise

Since exercise of the power is not crucial, it is immaterial that the decedent was under a legal disability to effectively exercise the power or was otherwise unable to exercise it. Indeed, it has been held that section 2041 will apply even where the decedent was unaware of the power. [**Freeman v. Commissioner,** 67 T.C. 202 (1976); **Alperstein v. Commissioner,** 613 F.2d 1213 (2d Cir. 1979). *But see* **Finley v. United States,** 404 F. Supp. 200 (S.D. Fla. 1975)]

**EXAM TIP** GILBERT

On your exam, be sure to remember that ***the mere holding of a general power of appointment*** over a subject property ***will be sufficient to cause the property to be included in the decedent's gross estate*** for powers created after October 21, 1942.

#### (2) Lapse or Release

The lapse (failure to exercise within a specified time) or affirmative release of a power is treated as an "exercise" of the power. [I.R.C. § 2041(a)(2), (b)(2)] Accordingly, property subject to a power that lapsed or was released is includible in the decedent's estate if a lifetime exercise of the power would have produced taxation—if the lapse or release occurred under circumstances where property transferred by the decedent would be includible under sections 2035 through 2038.

##### (a) Limitation on Includability for a Lapse of General Power

However, where the decedent had a noncumulative power to withdraw funds from a trust annually, a failure to exercise the power (i.e., a lapse of the annual power) is treated as the exercise of a general power only to the extent of the greater of \$5,000 or 5% of the value of the property to which the power relates. [I.R.C. § 2041(b)(2)] ***Rationale:*** This is a relief provision designed to allow a certain flexibility in estate planning.

e.g. **Example:** A grantor transfers \$900,000 in stocks to a trust to Mary for life, remainder to Katie, and grants Mary a power to compel distribution of the corpus to herself up to $50,000 per year. If Mary does not exercise the power in any given year, the power lapses for that year. Under the general rules of section 2041, the lapse will be treated as an exercise of the power in favor of the owner of the remainder (Katie), and the property will be taxed in Mary's estate because she is deemed to have reserved a life estate in the property "transferred." However, the special exception for lapsed powers limits inclusion in Mary's estate to the amount by which $50,000 exceeds the greater of $5,000 or 5% of the value of the corpus at the time each annual power lapses. In this example, that amount is $5,000 ($900,000 times .05 = $45,000; $50,000 less $45,000). Even so, in ***the year of Mary's death,*** the full amount of the property subject to the power ($50,000) is included. The special rule does not apply to this amount. It is taxed to Mary's estate not because the power lapsed, but because there was a taxable power to appoint this amount which was in existence at Mary's death.

#### (3) Distinguish—Renunciation or Disclaimer

A qualified disclaimer (defined under section 2518) is neither an exercise, lapse, or release of the power—even if the renunciation or disclaimer is made within three years of the death of the disclaimant. [Treas. Reg. § 20.2041–3(d)(6)]

#### (4) Joint Powers

In contrast to preexisting powers, a power created after October 21, 1942, will be taxed even though exercisable only with the concurrence of another person, ***unless*** the co-holder of the power is the ***donor*** (creator) of the power or a person who has ***a substantial interest in the property*** (adverse party). [I.R.C. § 2041(b)(1)(C)(i), (ii)]

##### (a) Permissible Appointee Not Adverse Party

For this purpose, a person who, ***after the decedent's death,*** will be able to exercise a power of appointment in that person's own favor (by succeeding to the decedent's power) is an adverse party. [I.R.C. § 2041(b)(1)(C)(ii)]

## 11. Section 2042—Life Insurance

Proceeds of life insurance policies on the decedent's life are includible in the gross estate if the proceeds are: (i) payable to (or for the benefit of) ***decedent's estate;*** or (ii) payable to any other beneficiary, but only if the ***decedent possessed "incidents of ownership"*** in the policy at the time of death.

### a. Background

Life insurance is patently "testamentary" in nature. At the same time, however, since the insured will never receive the proceeds, it is difficult to find that the insured has an "interest" in the proceeds; and since the premiums paid by the insured bear no necessary relation to the proceeds payable to the beneficiary, it is difficult to find a "transfer" by the insured during life or upon death. For these reasons, taxation under the Revenue Act of 1916, which contained no specific provision taxing life insurance proceeds, was troublesome.

#### (1) The Revenue Act of 1918

The deficiency in the first estate tax was remedied with passage of the 1918 Act, expressly providing for the taxation of life insurance to the estate of the insured. The

1918 scheme is similar to the present statute insofar as it divides the taxation of life insurance proceeds into two categories: proceeds payable to the decedent's estate and proceeds payable to some other beneficiary.

#### (a) Proceeds Payable to Estate

When payable to the insured's estate, the proceeds of life insurance were fully taxable.

#### (b) Proceeds Payable to Another

When payable to some beneficiary other than the estate, the 1918 Act imposed a tax on the proceeds if the insurance contract was "taken out by the decedent" on her own life. It also provided a special $40,000 exemption.

##### 1) "Taken out by the Decedent"

The meaning of this phrase was a source of much confusion. Although it was conceded that the decedent need not have originally applied for the policy, beyond this the interpretations varied.

**a)** The initial Regulations under the 1918 Act maintained that the test was whether the decedent had paid the premiums for the insurance, but subsequently, the Treasury limited taxation to situations where the decedent ***both*** paid the premiums ***and*** possessed incidents of ownership in the policy. Still later, the Regulations were amended to provide that the premium payments and incidents of ownership tests would be applied in the alternative.

**b)** Finally, in 1941, the Regulations returned full cycle and adopted the premium payments standard as the exclusive test for taxability.

### (2) The 1942 Act

Responding to the confusion generated by the Regulations, Congress adopted, as part of the 1942 Act, the premium payments and incidents of ownership criteria as ***alternative*** tests for taxability. In addition, the Act repealed the $40,000 exemption.

### (3) The 1954 Code

With passage of the 1954 Code, the standard for taxation changed once again. Proceeds payable to beneficiaries other than the estate of the insured are now taxed only if the insured possessed ***incidents of ownership*** in the policy at her death. [I.R.C. § 2042(2)]

#### (a) Scope of Section 2042

Section 2042 applies only to proceeds from life insurance on the ***decedent's*** life. It has no application to insurance policies on the lives of other persons or to the proceeds therefrom. However, insurance policies owned by a decedent on the lives of others constitute "property owned by the decedent" and so are includible under section 2033.

## b. Introductory Analysis

Analysis of section 2042 raises five principal topics:

**(1)** ***What constitutes "life insurance"?***

**(2)** ***The taxation of life insurance payable to the estate.***

(3) ***The taxation of proceeds payable to someone other than the estate.*** **This is, in fact, the major area of concern and is subdivided into two elements:**

(a) The scope of the term ***"incidents of ownership."***

(b) The determination of ***whether the decedent possessed incidents of ownership*** at the time of death (which requires analysis of the effect of assignment of incidents of ownership during life).

(4) ***The amount includible.***

(5) ***The taxation of life insurance that is subject to community property laws.***

## c. What Constitutes Life Insurance?

For insurance contracts written after December 31, 1984, I.R.C. § 7702 provides that life insurance must be a ***life insurance contract under applicable state law*** and must meet ***three additional tests:*** (i) a ***cash value accumulation*** test, which states the cash value cannot exceed the net single premium cost for the coverage provided; (ii) the premiums paid ***cannot exceed a "guideline premium limitation";*** and (iii) the death benefit ***must fall within the "cash value corridor."*** The death benefit cannot be less than a percentage of the cash value that ranges from 250% for an insured under age 40 to 100% for an individual between the ages of 90 and 95. As to any contract that is a life insurance contract under applicable state law but does not meet all of the three additional requirements listed above, the excess of the death benefit over the cash surrender value will be deemed to be life insurance for purposes of the estate and gift tax.

## d. Prior Law

Under prior law, neither the Code nor Regulations specifically defined life insurance for purposes of section 2042, and the courts had been hesitant to frame a precise and exclusive definition.

### (1) "Life Insurance Risk" Test

According to the Supreme Court, the critical issue in determining whether a particular arrangement amounts to "life insurance" is whether that arrangement comprehends a "life insurance risk." In other words, the economic risk of death must be shifted or distributed. [**Helvering v. LeGierse,** 312 U.S. 531 (1941)]

### (2) Commercial Contract Not Necessary

It is not required that the death benefit be payable under a typical life insurance contract purchased from a commercial insurance company. Any arrangement that ***shifts or distributes the economic risk of death*** may be taxable under section 2042. [*See* Treas. Reg. § 20.2042–1] I.R.C. § 2042 applies to death benefits "of every description," including funeral and death benefits paid by fraternal societies. [Treas. Reg. § 20.2042–1(a)] Note that Treas. Reg. § 20.2042–1 has not been amended to reflect the enactment of I.R.C. § 7702.

e.g. **Example:** The death benefit payable to the survivor of a member of the New York Stock Exchange has been held to be "life insurance," on the theory that the economic risk of death was distributed among the members of the Exchange who were previously assessed to provide a fund for payment of the benefits. [**Commissioner v. Treganowan,** 183 F.2d 288 (2d Cir.), *cert. denied,* 340 U.S. 853 (1950)]

**DETERMINING WHETHER A POLICY IS "LIFE INSURANCE" UNDER SECTION 7702**

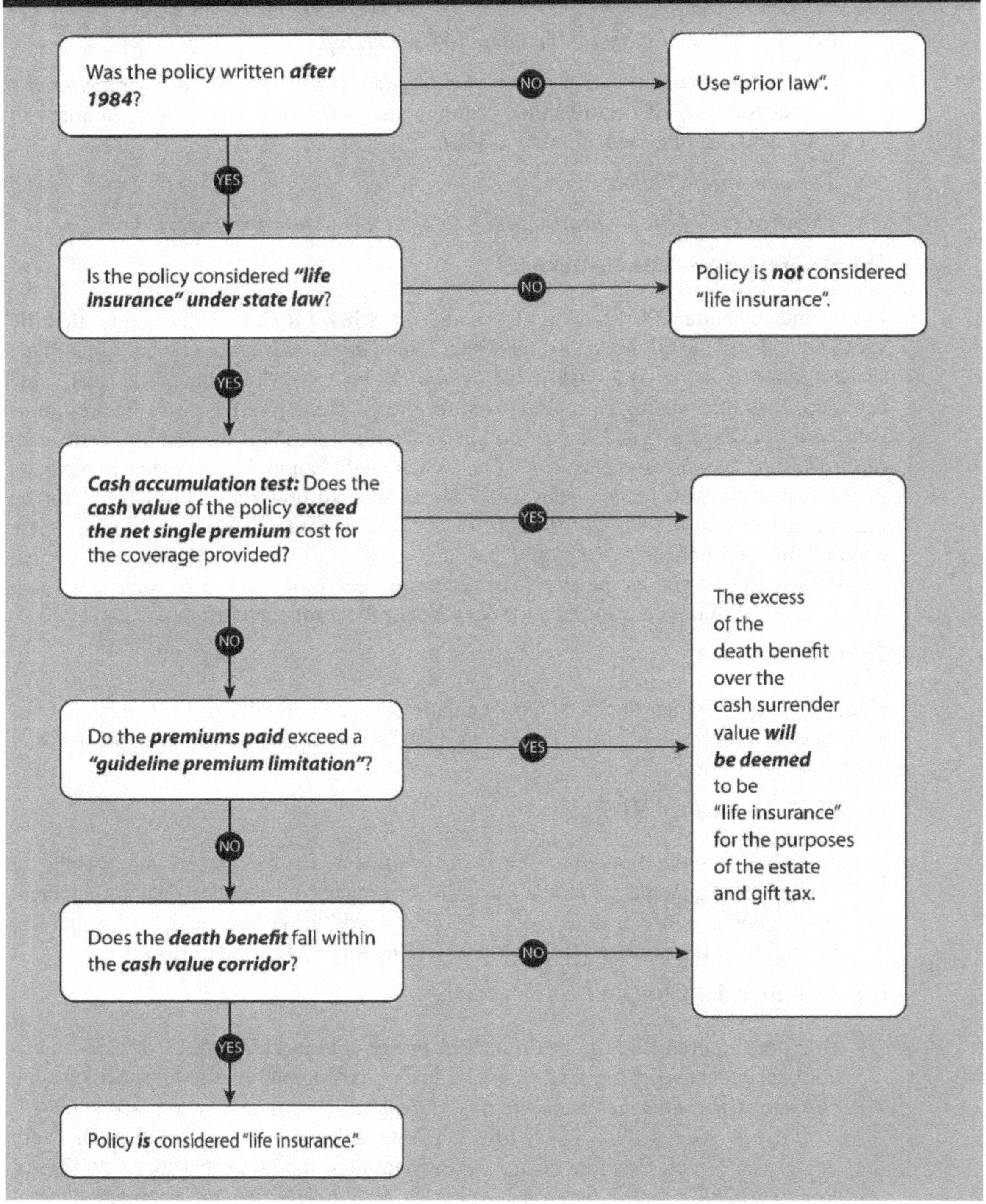


### (3) Accidental Death Policies

The Supreme Court has refused to limit the term "life insurance" to insurance that covers the ***inevitable*** risk of death. Thus, benefits payable for death by certain accidental causes—whether pursuant to specific accident insurance or double indemnity clauses under regular life insurance (which double the amount of the proceeds payable in the event death should result from accidental causes)—are within the scope of section 2042. **[Commissioner v. Estate of Noel,** 380 U.S. 678 (1965) (finding that accidental death benefits under "flight insurance" policy purchased by the decedent shortly before fatal air crash includible under section 2042(2)]; *see also* Rev. Rul. 83–44, 1983–1 C.B. 228 (determining that death benefits payable under no-fault automobile insurance policy are "life insurance proceeds" for purposes of section 2042)]

### e. Life Insurance Payable to Insured's Estate

Proceeds of life insurance policies made payable to the insured's estate (or to the insured's executor, administrator, etc.) are included in the decedent's gross estate. [I.R.C. § 2042(1)] This is true regardless of whether the insured paid the premiums or retained any incidents of ownership in the policy.

#### (1) Payable "for the Benefit of the Estate"

Proceeds payable to some other beneficiary will be included under section 2042(1) if that beneficiary is legally bound to apply the proceeds to ***discharge obligations of the insured's estate.*** Thus, if the proceeds are payable to a trustee but the trustee is obliged to remit to the decedent-insured's executor "such amounts as may be necessary to pay death taxes, administration expenses, funeral expenses, etc.," the proceeds will be included in the insured's estate even though the decedent did not possess any incidents of ownership in the policy. [Treas. Reg. § 20.2042–1(b)(1)]

#### (2) Effect of State Law

In some states, life insurance payable to the insured's estate or executor is not administered and distributed as part of the decedent's estate but is immediately distributable to certain designated beneficiaries and is not subject to claims of creditors. In this case, it has been held that the proceeds are payable to beneficiaries ***other than the estate*** and so are ***not*** taxable unless the insured retained incidents of ownership in the policy. [*See* **Webster v. Commissioner,** 120 F.2d 514 (5th Cir. 1941)]

### f. Life Insurance Payable to Other Beneficiaries

Insurance benefits payable to named beneficiaries other than the estate are taxable in the decedent-insured's estate only if the insured possessed ***incidents of ownership*** in the policy at the time of death. [I.R.C. § 2042(2)]

#### (1) What Are "Incidents of Ownership"?

Other than certain reversionary interests discussed below, the Code does not define "incidents of ownership." However, the Regulations and other authorities make it clear that the phrase is not limited to ownership of the contract but extends to any right or interest in the policy whereby the insured has the practical power, directly or indirectly, to ***control the existence of the policy,*** to ***rearrange the economic interests therein,*** or to ***affect the benefits payable thereunder.*** [*See* Treas. Reg. § 20.2042–1(c)(2)] The Regulations provide examples of incidents of ownership, including "the power to change the beneficiary, to surrender or cancel the policy, to assign the policy, to revoke an assignment, to pledge the policy for a loan, or to obtain from the insurer a loan against the surrender value of the policy."

e.g. **Example:** Rose had a life insurance policy. She was unable to change beneficiaries on the insurance policy, but she still held the power to surrender or cancel the policy at her death. Because she held the power to surrender or cancel the policy at her death, she had incidents of ownership and the proceeds of the policy would be included in her gross estate.

e.g. **Example:** Luis had a life insurance policy that would be paid out to his three daughters upon his death. Luis could not change beneficiaries, cancel or surrender the policy, assign the policy, or pledge it for a loan. Without the power to do any of these Luis did not have any incidents of ownership in the policy and thus the proceeds from the policy will not be included in his gross estate.

### (b) Right to Affect Time and Manner of Enjoyment

The right to select a settlement option and thus affect the time and manner of a beneficiary's enjoyment of the proceeds is considered an incident of ownership [**Estate of Lumpkin v. Commissioner,** 474 F.2d 1092 (5th Cir. 1973)]

### (c) Employer Group Insurance

Employer-furnished group term insurance is includible in the employee's estate if the employee possesses any incidents of ownership at death. [Rev. Rul. 69–54, 1969–1 C.B. 2211]

#### 1) Power to Terminate Employment

It has been held that an employee's power to affect the cancellation of the employer-owned policy by quitting the job is ***not*** an incident of ownership. [**Estate of Lumpkin v. Commissioner,** 56 T.C. 815 (1971), *rev'd on another issue,* 474 F.2d 1092 (5th Cir. 1973)] The Service now follows this rule. [Rev. Rul. 72–307, 1972–1 C.B. 307]

#### 2) Assignment of Term Insurance

Where allowed under state law and the terms of the insurance contract, an assignment by the employee of all incidents of ownership in the contract, including the right to retain the insurance after termination of employment and the right to convert the term insurance into permanent coverage, is effective to remove the proceeds from exposure to the estate tax. [Rev. Rul. 69–54; Rev. Rul. 72–307]

### (d) Reversionary Interests

The Code specifically provides that a reversionary interest is an incident of ownership if the value of such interest exceeds 5% of the value of the policy immediately prior to the insured's death. For this purpose, a reversionary interest is any possibility that the policy or its proceeds may return to the decedent or to the estate or be subject to a power of testamentary disposition by the decedent. [I.R.C. § 2042(2)]

e.g. **Example:** Insured transfers the policy on her life to a trust for the benefit of B provided he survives the insured. This contingency creates a reversionary interest in the insured and if the value of this interest (computed by actuarial tables just before the insured's death) is in excess of 5% of the value of the policy, the proceeds are taxable in her estate.

e.g. **Example:** As part of a divorce settlement, D agrees to maintain a life insurance policy on D's life in which D's ex-spouse is to be named beneficiary until such time as the ex-spouse dies or remarries. Since the ex-spouse could marry or die before D, D has a reversionary interest in the policy; hence, it is includible in D's gross estate even though D has no power to change the beneficiary or cancel the policy and the proceeds are paid to the ex-spouse upon D's death. [Rev. Rul. 76–113, 1976–1 C.B. 276]

**EXAM TIP** GILBERT

If an exam question requires you to determine whether life insurance proceeds are includible in the decedent's gross estate, recall that you need to check the facts to see if:

(i) ***The policy is made payable to the decedent's estate*** (or the decedent's executor or administrator). If so, the proceeds are taxable as part of the estate. Note, however, that a policy that names the decedent's ***spouse or children as beneficiaries*** is ***not*** the same thing and does ***not*** make the proceeds taxable to the decedent's estate; or

(ii) ***The decedent possessed incidents of ownership*** in the policy at the time of death. Here look for things such as the right to change beneficiaries or borrow, surrender, or cancel the policy. If you see such rights, the proceeds are included in the decedent's estate.

### (2) What Constitutes "Possession" of Incidents of Ownership?

The insured need not have ***retained*** incidents of ownership, as where the insured owned the policy originally and transferred it to another with a reservation of certain rights. All that is required is that the incidents of ownership be ***possessed*** by the insured at death. For example, where X applies for and at all times is the owner of a policy on D's life, the proceeds are taxable in D's estate if X gave D any incidents of ownership.

#### (a) Joint Powers Taxable

The statute specifically provides that the insurance proceeds will be taxed whether the incidents of ownership are exercisable by the insured-decedent "alone or in conjunction with any other person." [I.R.C. § 2042(2)] Thus, it is of no consequence that the concurrence of an adverse party may be required.

#### (b) Insurance Trusts

If a policy is placed on trust, the terms of both the policy and the trust instrument will determine whether the insured possesses incidents of ownership. For example, where a life insurance policy was irrevocably assigned to the trustee of a trust, but the insured possessed the power to alter or amend the trust, the insured was held to possess incidents of ownership in the policy at death. [**Commissioner v. Estate of Karagheusian,** 233 F.2d 197 (2d Cir. 1956)]

#### (c) Inability to Exercise Incidents of Ownership

The fact that the insured was unable to exercise any right or power with respect to the policy at the time of death is immaterial. Thus, for example, the proceeds of a flight insurance policy were taxed in the decedent-insured's estate because he reserved the power to change beneficiaries; it was of no effect that he did not have the policy in his possession after boarding the aircraft and so could not have exercised his power to change the beneficiary designation by written endorsement on the policy. [**Commissioner v. Estate of Noel,** 380 U.S. 678 (1965)]

##### 1) Legal Disability

Similarly, it is ordinarily deemed immaterial that the insured is incompetent or cannot exercise incidents of ownership because of an agreement with some third party. Whether the insured ***possessed any*** incidents of ownership is determined under the insurance contract itself ("policy facts"). [*See* **United States v. Rhode Island Hospital Trust Co.,** 355 F.2d 7 (1st Cir. 1966); **Nance v. United States,** 430 F.2d 662 (9th Cir. 1970]

#### 2) Economic Interest Limitation

However, in one case, life insurance proceeds were not included in the insured's estate where, although he was technically the owner of the policy, the beneficiary had been irrevocably designated, the policy was within the control of the beneficiary, and the insured had never paid any premiums. ***Rationale:*** In effect, there had been a full assignment of the policy since not only was the insured unable to exercise any incidents of ownership but, in the court's view, he was precluded from doing so insofar as he had no economic interest in the policy ("intent facts"). [**Morton v. United States,** 457 F.2d 750 (4th Cir. 1972)]

### (d) Buy-Sell Agreements

Frequently, the owners of closely held businesses enter into agreements under which the remaining owners or the business entity itself will purchase the interest of a principal who dies. This is done through two methods, the entity purchase agreement and cross purchase agreement. Both of these buy-sell agreements are funded by insurance. The life of each principal is insured and upon a principal's death the proceeds of the insurance are collected and paid over to the insured's estate in consideration for the transfer or liquidation of the decedent's interest in the business.

#### 1) Entity Purchase Agreement

With an entity purchase agreement, the business entity will take out a life insurance policy, and the proceeds will be paid to the business entity upon the death of the first co-owner. Since the business entity holds all of the incidents of ownership for the policy, the proceeds will not be included in the deceased co-owner's gross estate under section 2042. However, the proceeds may increase the value of the entity.

##### a) Include Insurance but Not Business Interests?

In **Tompkins v. Commissioner,** 13 T.C. 1054 (1949), a partnership carried life insurance on the life of the principals, payable to itself, in order to fund a partnership liquidation agreement. Upon the death of the insured decedent, the partnership collected the proceeds of the insurance and paid them over to the decedent's estate in complete liquidation of the decedent's partnership interest. The insurance proceeds were held taxable in the partner-insured's estate since the insured possessed incidents of ownership in the policy jointly with the other partners. However, the court refused also to include the value of the partnership interest (under section 2033) since this would in effect result in double taxation.

##### b) Include Value of Interest but Not Insurance?

However, in a later case, the Tax Court held that policies transferred by the decedent to his partnership were not includible in the decedent's estate since the decedent had not retained any incidents of ownership in an individual capacity, but only in the capacity as a partner. **[Estate of Knipp v. Commissioner,** 25 T.C. 153 (1955), *aff'd on other grounds,* 244 F.2d 436 (4th Cir.), *cert. denied,* 355 U.S. 827 (1957)] The capacity in which incidents of ownership must be exercised is ordinarily immaterial. The ***IRS acquiesced*** in this result to avoid double taxation—i.e., taxation of the life insurance proceeds owned by the partnership under section 2042, and taxation of the value of the partner's interest (augmented by the insurance proceeds) under section 2033. [Rev. Rul. 83–147, 1983–2 C.B. 158] It follows that, if the partnership owns insurance on the life of a partner that is not payable to the partnership, it is taxable in the estate of the insured under general principles of the deceased partner holding incidents of ownership exercisable jointly.

#### 1) Cross Purchase Agreement

In a cross purchase agreement, each co-owner will take out a life insurance policy on the life of the other co-owners, which will be payable to the co-owner who takes out the policy. When one of the co-owners dies the proceeds from the policy will be used to purchase the deceased co-owner's interest in the business. Since the co-owner who takes out the policy has all the incidents of ownership the proceeds from the policy will not be included in the deceased co-owner's gross estate.

### (e) Incidents of Ownership Held as Trustee

According to the Regulations, it is of no consequence that incidents of ownership are held as a trustee, and this is true whether the insured transferred the policy to the trust or the policy was assigned to the trust by another. [Treas. Reg. § 20.2042–1(c)] However, some modification of this general rule has developed as a result of a series of court decisions:

#### 1) Leading Case

In **Estate of Fruehauf v. Commissioner,** 427 F.2d 80 (6th Cir. 1970), the insured's wife transferred policies she owned on the life of her husband to a testamentary trust in which the insured was named co-trustee. The court reasoned that the husband possessed incidents of ownership as the trustee and by exercising his power of administration and investment, he could have cashed in the policy, borrowed against the policy, etc. Hence, the proceeds were includible in his gross estate.

#### 2) Tax Court Distinguishes

**In Estate of Skifter v. Commissioner,** 56 T.C. 1190 (1971), *aff'd,* 468 F.2d 699 (2d Cir. 1972), the insured's role as trustee of his wife's testamentary trust—which included policies of insurance on his life—did not support inclusion of the proceeds in his estate. The court distinguished *Fruehauf* on the ground that Mr. Skifter did not have an economic interest in the trust, whereas Mr. Fruehauf was one of the trust beneficiaries. The court also reasoned that the decedent's "power" was not reserved and was purely administrative.

#### 3) Fifth Circuit Rejects Tax Court Rationale

The Fifth Circuit added to the confusion in **Rose v. United States,** 511 F.2d 259 (5th Cir. 1975), where the insured was named as trustee of a trust created by his brother for the benefit of the insured's children and used trust funds to purchase life insurance on his life. Here the insurance proceeds were found includible in the insured's estate. The court squarely rejected the holding and reasoning in *Skifter*. It stated that section 2042 does not require that the insured have some personal economic interest in the policy; it is sufficient if the insured can merely affect the time and manner of enjoyment.

#### 4) Service Ruling

Based upon its analysis of the legislative history of section 2042, the Service has adopted a position that strikes a balance between *Fruehauf Rose,* and *Skifter*: A decedent will not be deemed to have incidents of ownership over an insurance policy that is held by a trust if: (i) the decedent's powers are held in a fiduciary capacity as trustee; (ii) the powers cannot be exercised for the decedent's personal benefit; (iii) the decedent did not transfer the policy to the trust; (iv) the decedent did not furnish the consideration for purchasing or maintaining the policy; and (v) the devolution of powers to the decedent was not part of a prearranged plan involving the decedent. [Rev. Rul. 84–179, 1984–2 C.B. 195]

### (f) Policy Owned by Controlled Corporation

For many years, the Service has taken the position that proceeds from insurance owned by a corporation that is solely owned by the insured are includible in the insured's estate since the insured indirectly possessed incidents of ownership through an ability to control the corporation. By reason of an amendment to the Regulations, the same result now obtains where the insured, although not sole owner, owns more than 50% of the stock of the corporation. [Treas. Reg. § 20.2042–1(c)(6)]

## g. Assignment of Incidents of Ownership

If the insured has made a complete and effective inter vivos gift of all ownership and beneficial interest in the insurance policy, retaining ***no incidents of ownership***, the proceeds are normally not taxable in the estate. If the insured transfers incidents of ownership within three years of death, the proceeds will be taxed in the insured's estate under section 2035(a)(2).

e.g. **Example:** In 2015, a decedent took out an insurance policy on the decedent's life. The decedent designated the daughter as the beneficiary and assigned all incidents of ownership to the daughter. However, the decedent retained the power to designate a new beneficiary. During 2020, the decedent relinquished the right to designate a new beneficiary. The decedent died in 2022. The insurance proceeds will be included in the decedent's gross estate under section 2035 because the decedent relinquished the ability to designate a new beneficiary (an incident of ownership) within three years of the decedent's death.

## h. Amount Includible

In general, section 2042 taxes the entire value of the insurance proceeds. Thus, where the proceeds are payable in a lump sum, the lump sum amount is included in the insured's estate. If the proceeds are payable in installments, the taxable amount is the present fair market value of the installment obligation.

### i. Life Insurance and Community Property States

When the insurance policy on a decedent's life is purchased with community property funds, it is treated as a community asset—i.e., one in which each spouse is deemed to have an existing, one-half interest. This is true even though the policy itself names the insured as the "sole owner" because the spouse's ownership rights arise by operation of law.

#### (1) Treatment if Insured Dies First

One-half of the proceeds are included in the insured's estate under section 2042, since the insured is the owner of a one-half interest in the policy. The other half belongs to the surviving spouse as a matter of community property law—even though the insured has named someone else (e.g., a child) as beneficiary under the policy. But, if the surviving spouse ***consents*** to payment of the insurance proceeds to the third-party beneficiary, the surviving spouse is deemed to have made a ***taxable gift*** of one-half interest in the proceeds. [**Commissioner v. Chase Manhattan Bank,** 259 F.2d 231 (5th Cir. 1958)]

#### (2) Treatment if Spouse Dies First

The spouse's one-half interest in insurance on the other spouse's life is "property owned by the decedent," taxable under section 2033. However, it is not one-half of the proceeds that would be taxed but, rather, one-half of the present value of the insurance (measured by its replacement cost). [**United States v. Stewart,** 270 F.2d 894 (9th Cir. 1959)]

##### (a) What Happens When Insured Subsequently Dies?

All of the proceeds ***attributable to premiums paid by the insured*** are included the insured's gross estate. Thus, if 80% of the insurance premiums were paid with community funds while the uninsured spouse was still alive (40% attributable to each spouse), and 20% of the premiums are paid by the insured after the spouse's death, 60% of the proceeds are taxed in the insured's estate when that spouse later dies. [**Scott v. Commissioner,** 374 F.2d 154 (9th Cir. 1967)]

#### (3) Effect of Inter Vivos Transfer of Ownership

Different results may follow where the insured has made a valid inter vivos transfer to the insured's spouse of the insured's one-half interest in the insurance policy.

##### (a) On Death of Insured Spouse

Nothing is included in the insured's estate since the insured did not have any incidents of ownership, ***provided*** that community funds are not thereafter used for premium payments.

##### (b) If Spouse Predeceases Insured

Since the spouse owned the policy, the full replacement value of the policy would be included in the spouse's estate under section 2033.

## 12. Section 2043—Consideration

The estate tax and the gift tax reach ***gratuitous*** transfers only. Accordingly, transfers for "a full and adequate consideration in money or money's worth" are not taxed.

### a. Partial Consideration

Provision is made, however, for a transaction that is in part a sale and in part gratuitous where property is transferred "for a consideration in money or money's worth, but is not a bona fide sale for an adequate and full consideration in money or money's worth, there shall be included in the gross estate only the excess of the fair market value at the time of death of the property otherwise to be included on account of such transaction, over the value of the consideration received therefor by the decedent." [I.R.C. § 2043(a)] Section 2043 applies to any transfers under sections 2035 to 2038 and section 2041.

e.g. **Example:** A parent owned a condominium unit. When the unit was worth $200,000, the parent conveyed it to the parent's adult child. The child felt uncomfortable to accept it without giving the parent some money for it. As a result, the child gave the parent $50,000 for the unit. The parent continued to live in the condominium until death. As a result, the condominium is included in the parent's gross estate under section 2036(a)(1). Under section 2043, the amount included is $150,000, the difference between the fair market value of the unit and the amount of consideration that the child paid to the parent.

### b. Measure of Consideration—"Money or Money's Worth"

For tax purposes, it is not enough that the consideration be adequate to support a binding contract. Rather, it must be measurable in terms of money or money's worth. It must constitute the ***economic equivalent*** of the property transferred.

e.g. **Example:** An ***antenuptial agreement*** based upon a promise of marriage or upon the actual entering into of a marriage contract, or ***an agreement not to contest a decedent's will,*** may constitute adequate consideration for a binding contract. However, since such promises and the performances of such promises cannot be specifically reduced to economic terms, they do not constitute "money's worth" and thus will not insulate transfers pursuant to such contracts from the estate or gift taxes. **[Latty v. Commissioner,** 62 F.2d 952 (6th Cir. 1933)]

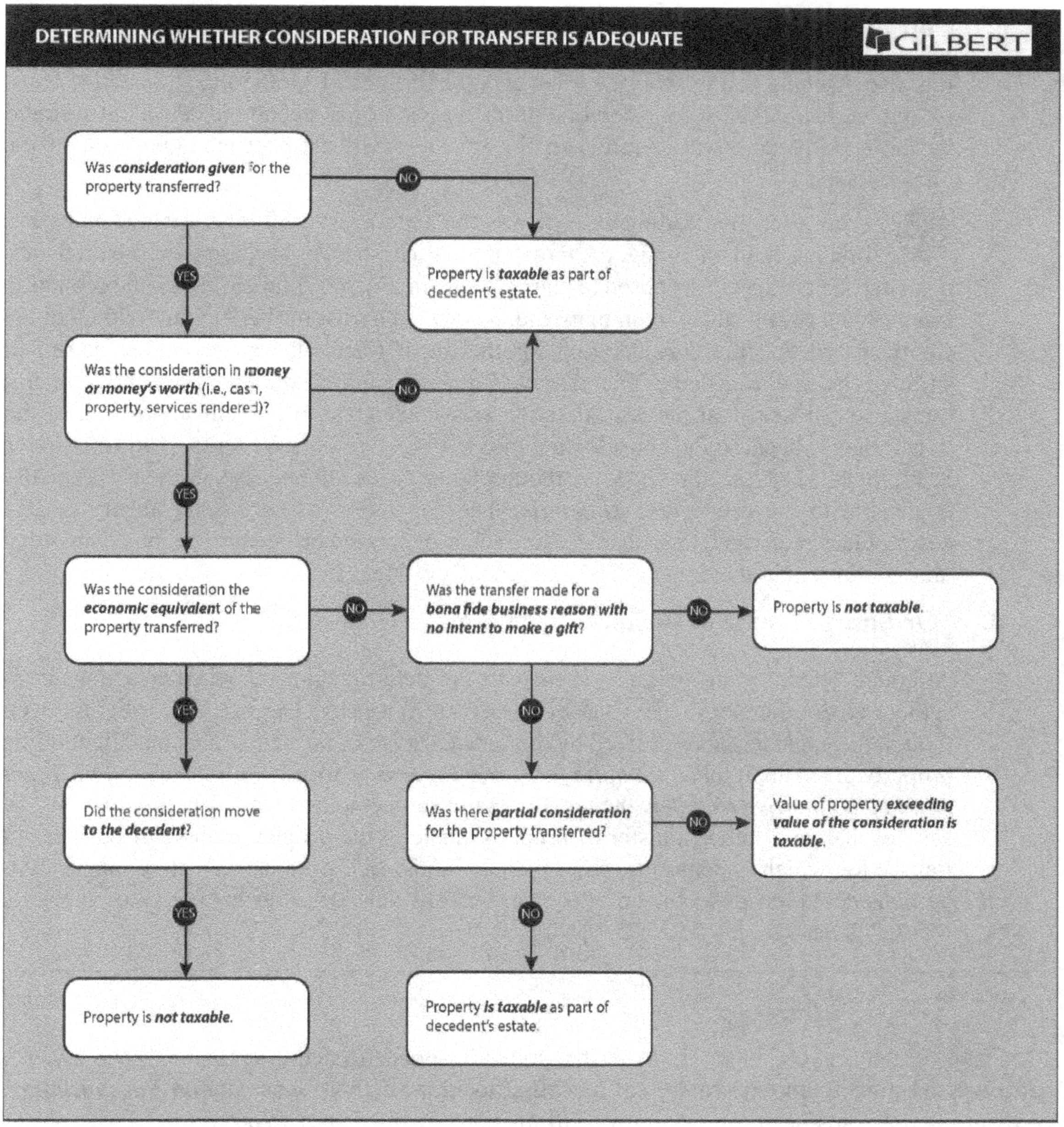


## (1) Rationale—Depletion of the Estate

If the consideration received is the economic equivalent of the property transferred, there is no reduction in the transferor's net worth and thus no reduction of the estate that is subject to the transfer taxes; but if the economic equivalent is not received in exchange, the transferor's estate is depleted, and the transfer is treated as gratuitous in order to prevent avoidance of taxes.

## (2) Form of Consideration

It is not essential that the consideration be cash as long as it is measurable in economic terms. Thus, in addition to cash and property, services rendered to the transferor that can be translated into economic terms also constitute consideration "in money's worth."

### c. Consideration Must Move to the Transferor

It is also essential that the consideration take the form of a benefit to the transferor. Thus, a payment to another in consideration of the transfer, or an economic detriment suffered by the transferee in consideration of the transfer, will not prevent imposition of the transfer taxes.

e.g. **Example:** In a leading case, X was the beneficiary of a trust established by her first husband but, under the terms of the trust, she would cease to be a beneficiary upon her remarriage. D proposed to marry X and, in order to compensate for the economic loss that she would suffer upon marriage, he created a trust for her benefit. Although the Court agreed that the consideration for the transfer included an economic detriment suffered by the transferee (X) that was the economic equivalent of the property transferred, it held that the consideration was inadequate to prevent imposition of the transfer taxes because the consideration did not move to the transferor. [**Commissioner v. Wemyss,** 324 U.S. 303 (1945)] Although *Wemyss* is a gift tax case, its theory is equally applicable to the estate tax. ***Rationale:*** The "depletion of the estate" theory is also applicable here. Even if the consideration can be expressed in "money or money's worth," unless it moves to the transferor, the decedent's estate is depleted by the transfer.

### d. "Ordinary Course of Business Exception"

Although donative intent is not critical to the determination of whether a transfer is subject to the transfer taxes, "bad bargains" are not subject to tax. Accordingly, even though the consideration received by the transferor is not the economic equivalent of the property given up, if there is ***a bona fide business reason*** for such a transfer and ***no intent to make a donative transfer***, the transfer is not subject to tax. Under the Regulations, "a sale, exchange or other transfer of property made in the ordinary course of business (a transaction which is bona fide, at arm's length, and free from any donative intent), will be considered as made for an adequate and full consideration in money or money's worth." [Treas. Reg. § 25.2512–8]

**EXAM TIP** GILBERT

Don't be fooled on your exam by facts that make it appear that the decedent "gave away" property by making an extremely bad business decision. If there was a ***bona fide business reason*** for the transfer and ***no donative intent,*** the transfer ***is not taxed*** on the decedent's death. The same principle applies for gift tax purposes.

### e. Release of Marital Rights

Section 2043(b)(1) provides that the relinquishment marital rights or of dower or curtesy is ***not*** considered to be consideration in "money or money's worth." This is a logical corollary to section 2034, which includes in the decedent's estate the value of all interests possessed by the surviving spouse under laws relating to dower, curtesy, or a statutory forced share. Thus, section 2043(b) precludes decedents from circumventing section 2034 by contracting to transfer property in consideration of the spouse's release of marital rights.

#### (1) Application to the Gift Tax

**(a)** The gift tax statute does not expressly contain a rule similar to section 2043(b). However, in **Merrill v. Fahs,** 324 U.S. 308 (1945), the Supreme Court determined that the same rule applied to the gift tax because the estate and gift taxes should be construed consistently ("in pari materia"). Hence, the release of marital rights is not considered to be money or money's worth for purposes of the gift tax.

#### (2) Contrast—Support Rights

It has been held that the "other marital rights" under section 2043(b) refer only to post-death rights in the decedent's estate that are analogous to dower, curtesy, or statutory forced shares. Accordingly, the release of a spouse's right to be ***supported*** by the other spouse may be deemed adequate consideration for transfer tax purposes. [Rev. Rul. 68–379, 1968–2 C.B. 414]

##### (a) Comment

Whether or not a spouse's support rights can effectively be released during life may be questionable. Even if such a release is possible, the valuation of such support rights may be troublesome. The taxpayer has the burden of proving the value of the consideration. [*See* **United States v. Past,** 347 F.2d 7 (9th Cir. 1965)]

#### (3) Property Settlements

A transfer in discharge of marital rights that is part of a ***divorce settlement*** and is incorporated into the decree of divorce is not a taxable transfer for estate and gift tax purposes. [**Estate of Watson v. Commissioner,** 20 T.C. 386 (1953); **Harris v. Commissioner,** 340 U.S. 106 (1950)] This rule has been extended by statute to divorce settlements provided that they are not subject to the gift tax under section 2516. [I.R.C. § 2043(b)(2)]

#### (4) Distinguish—Community Property

The relinquishment or other disposition of community property is always sufficient consideration for a transfer of property of equivalent value, since each spouse has an existing, vested one-half interest in the community assets.

#### (5) Transfers Between Other Co-Tenants

Transfers of property between co-tenants (holding title as joint tenants or tenants in common) is a transfer for adequate consideration. [**Sullivan's Estate v. Commissioner,** 175 F.2d 657 (9th Cir. 1949)]

## 13. Section 2044—Certain Marital Deduction Property

### a. Marital Deduction Allowed for QTIP Elections

The 1981 Revenue Act amended the estate and gift tax marital deduction provisions to allow for a spouse or the spouse's executor to elect to claim the marital deduction where the donee or surviving spouse receives qualified terminable interest property (QTIP). [*See* I.R.C. §§ 2056(b)(7) and 2523(f)]

### b. Inclusion Required Under Section 2044

Without section 2044, the QTIP property will not be subject to transfer tax. The donor spouse will not be subject to estate or gift tax because of the unlimited marital deduction. Moreover, the donee/surviving spouse is not required to include the property in the gross estate under any other estate tax provision. Section 2044 requires property that qualifies for the marital deduction after a QTIP election to be included in the donee/surviving spouse's estate upon death. [I.R.C. § 2044(a), (b)(1)]

e.g. **Example:** A donor owned an office building. The donor transferred the building to a trust with all rental income payable to the donor's spouse for life, and the spouse was given the right to appoint the corpus/building at death to any of their children or grandchildren. On the donor's gift tax return, the donor elected the marital deduction under section 2523(f) as the gift was QTIP property. The spouse died several years later and appointed the couple's son and daughter as recipients of the corpus. The office building will be included in the spouse's gross estate under section 2044.

### c. Exception if Section 2519 Applies

The donee/surviving spouse is subject to gift tax under section 2519 if the donee/surviving spouse disposes of ***any portion*** of the QTIP property before death. For example, if the donee/surviving spouse gives the income interest from the QTIP property (e.g., dividends) to another person, the donee/surviving spouse has made a completed gift of the income under section 2501 and a gift of the property (e.g., stock) under section 2519. To prevent double taxation, the donee/surviving spouse is not required to include the QTIP property in the gross estate under section 2044. [I.R.C. § 2044(b)(2)]

e.g. **Example:** Based on the same facts above, assume that the spouse notified the trustee to give 50 percent of the rental income to the son and daughter. The spouse has made a completed gift of the income interest to the son and daughter under section 2501 and a gift of the office building under section 2519. When the spouse dies, the property is not included in the spouse's gross estate per section 2044(b)(2). If included, the spouse would be subject to double taxation.

## 14. Section 2045—Prior Interests

This section provides, essentially, that an interest in property or powers with respect to property that result in inclusion of the property in the gross estate under the estate tax provisions will, except as otherwise specifically provided, produce that result without regard to when the particular transfer, interest, right, or power was made, created, exercised, etc.

e.g. **Example—Joint Interests:** A joint tenancy created prior to the first estate tax will be taxed in the estate of the first to die under section 2040(a) since that section contains no limitation regarding the date of the joint tenancy's creation. [*See* **United States v. Jacobs,** 306 U.S. 363 (1939)]

cf. **Compare—Transfers with Retained Life Estate:** However, where the decedent transferred property reserving a life estate prior to March 3, 1931, no estate tax will attach under section 2036 because that section is specifically limited to transfers made on or after March 3, 1931. [I.R.C. § 2036(c)]

## 15. Section 2046—Disclaimers

A disclaimer or renunciation (an unqualified refusal to accept a transfer of property) is not a "transfer" for estate or gift tax purposes, even though other persons may acquire an interest in the property as a result of the disclaimer.

### a. Uniform Rule Under Tax Reform Act

As part of the Tax Reform Act of 1976, Congress enacted section 2518, under the gift tax, which establishes a uniform rule as to when a disclaimer or renunciation will be effective for federal tax purposes (i.e., when a disclaimer will not be treated as a "transfer"). Section 2046 incorporates the rule of section 2518 for estate tax purposes. The disclaimer rules are fully discussed in Chapter Four.

# B. Deductions

## 1. Introductory Analysis

Five deductions are allowed under the estate tax:

(i) ***Certain expenses of and claims against the estate*** [I.R.C. § 2053];

(ii) ***Certain losses*** incurred during the period of administration [I.R.C. § 2054];

(iii) ***Certain transfers to charity*** [I.R.C. § 2055];

(iv) The ***marital deduction*** [I.R.C. § 2056]; and

(v) ***State death taxes*** [I.R.C. § 2058].

**EXAM TIP** GILBERT

Of the five deductions above, ***the marital deduction is of principal importance*** in estate planning (and thus on your exam) and is also the most complex.

## 2. Section 2053—Expenses, Indebtedness, and Taxes

A deduction is allowed for various types of expenses incurred or paid by the estate and for various types of claims against the estate, including debts and taxes owed by the decedent. Specifically, subsection (a) lists four categories of deductible items: (i) ***funeral*** expenses; (ii) ***administration*** expenses; (iii) ***claims against the estate***; and (iv) "***unpaid mortgages*** on, or any indebtedness in respect of, property where the value of the decedent's interest therein, undiminished by such mortgage or indebtedness, is included in the value of the gross estate."

### a. Expenses of Administering Nonprobate Assets

A further deduction is authorized under subsection (b) of section 2053 for expenses related to the administration of property that is not part of the decedent's probate estate but which is included in the gross estate for federal estate tax purposes (i.e., property taxable under sections 2035 through 2042).

#### (1) Scope of Deduction

These expenses are deductible "to the same extent that such expenses would be allowable as a deduction . . . if such property were [administered as part of the probate estate]." Thus, the nature of the deductible expenses must be similar to those allowable under subsection (a), those occasioned by the decedent's death and incurred in settling the decedent's interest in the property or vesting good title to the property in the beneficiaries. [Treas. Reg. § 20.2053–8(b)]

##### (a) Note

The rules relating to deductions of executor's and attorney's fees and miscellaneous administration expenses "are applied in determining the extent to which trustee's commissions, attorney's and accountant's fees and miscellaneous administration expenses are allowed in connection with the administration of property not subject to claims." [Treas. Reg. § 20.2053–8(c)]

### (2) Time Limitation

Such expenses are only deductible if paid before expiration of the statute of limitations relating to the estate tax return, normally three years after the date upon which the return is filed. [I.R.C. § 2053(b); *see also* I.R.C. § 6501]

## b. Funeral Expenses

Such expenses include the amounts actually spent to inter (or cremate) the decedent, as well as reasonable amounts paid for a tombstone, monument or mausoleum, or for a burial lot (for the decedent or the family), and reasonable expenditures for future care of the lot. Also included is the cost of transporting the decedent to the place of burial. [Treas. Reg. § 20.2053–2]

### (1) Limited to Amounts Actually Expended

Unlike the deduction for administration expenses, where reasonable estimates of such expenses are deductible, the deduction for funeral expenses is limited to amounts ***actually paid*** before the estate tax return is filed. [Treas. Reg. § 20.2053–2]

### (2) Limitation Under Community Property Law

If the community property law of the state imposes a charge for funeral expenses upon the entire community, not merely the property interests of the decedent, only one-half of the funeral expenses are deductible. [Rev. Rul. 70–156, 1970–1 C.B. 190; Rev. Rul. 71–168, 1971–1 C.B. 271]

## c. Administration Expenses

This deduction is limited to expenses that are ***actually and necessarily incurred*** in the administration of the decedent's estate (i.e., in the collection of assets, payment of debts, and distribution of property to the persons entitled thereto). [Treas. Reg. § 20.2053–3(a)] The Regulations divide administration expenses into: (i) executor's commissions; (ii) attorney's fees; and (iii) miscellaneous expenses.

### (1) Executor's Commissions

Executor's fees may be deducted if they have been paid or it is expected that they will be paid but no deduction may be taken if commissions are not anticipated. [Treas. Reg. § 20.2053–3(b)(1)]

#### (a) Limited to Estate Administration

The deduction only extends to fees relating to administration of the decedent's ***estate.*** It cannot be taken for fees associated with services that are in the nature of trust administration.

##### 1) Note

Fees of a trustee under a revocable inter vivos trust that relate to services normally performed by an executor (collection of assets, payments of debts and distribution to beneficiaries) are deductible. **[Commissioner v. Bronson,** 32 F.2d 112 (8th Cir. 1929)] But a testamentary trustee's fees relating to trust investment and administration are not deductible; and this limitation also extends to situations where the decedent's executor unduly deferred distribution of the estate and undertook to perform services in the nature of a trustee's duties.

2) **Expenses Benefiting Heirs or Legatees**

Likewise, expenses incurred for the benefit of heirs or legatees that are not essential to the proper settlement of the estate are ***not deductible*** as administration expenses. [Treas. Reg. § 20.2053–3(b)(1)]

**(b) Reasonable Estimates Allowed**

Administration of the estate will normally extend beyond the time at which the estate tax return must be filed (nine months after the decedent's death). To accommodate for this, the Regulations allow a deduction for a reasonable estimate of the fees to be paid the executor. [Treas. Reg. § 20.2053–3(b)(1)]

**(2) Attorney's Fees**

Attorney's fees relating to legal counsel to the executor, the collection or settlement of claims against the estate, and litigation expenses, including litigating estate tax deficiencies, are deductible. However, legal services incurred in protecting the interests of a particular beneficiary, rather than for the benefit of the estate as a whole, are not deductible. And, again, reasonable estimates of attorney's fees that will be paid are deductible. [Treas. Reg. § 20.2053–3(c)]

**(3) Miscellaneous Expenses of Administration**

In addition to executor's commissions and attorney's fees, various other administration costs are deductible. Court costs, accountant's fees, appraiser's fees, costs of storing or maintaining the property of the estate, and the cost of selling estate assets where such sales are necessary for payment of debts or for the orderly distribution of the estate are deductible. [Treas. Reg. § 20.2053–3(d)]

**d. Claims Against the Estate**

Debts and other claims asserted against the estate are deductible if they represent personal obligations of the decedent that existed at the time of death. [Treas. Reg. § 20.2053–4(a)(1)]

**(1) Must Be Legally Enforceable**

However, no deduction is allowed unless the claim was legally enforceable against the decedent ***and*** is legally enforceable against the decedent's estate. Thus, for example, claims on which the statute of limitations has run cannot be deducted, nor can claims that are filed with the executor after the time allowed by state law. [Treas. Reg. § 20.2053–4; *but compare* **Russell v. United States,** 260 F. Supp. 493 (N.D. Ill. 1966) (allowing a deduction for a claim filed and paid after the nonclaim period); *see also* Rev. Rul. 75–24, 1975–1 C.B. 306 (allowing deduction of an unfiled claim settled with the consent of all beneficiaries)]

**(2) Liabilities Created by Law**

Claims arising as a result of the decedent's torts, including court ordered support claims, and certain tax claims are deductible. [*See* **Harris v. Commissioner,** 340 U.S. 106 (1950)]

### (3) Contingent Claims

No deduction is allowed if it appears that the claim may never be paid by the decedent's estate. Thus, claims on which the decedent was only secondarily or contingently liable (e.g., as a guarantor) are not deductible unless it is shown that the person primarily liable has defaulted so that the decedent's liability has become fixed and immediate. [**DuVal's Estate v. Commissioner,** 152 F.2d 103 (9th Cir. 1945)]

### (4) Tax Claims

The decedent's liability for tax claims, including income taxes, gift taxes, and property taxes that accrued prior to death are deductible as claims against the estate. [Treas. Reg. § 20.2053–6]

#### (a) Distinguish—Taxes Accruing After Death

Taxes that accrue after the decedent's death cannot be deducted. [I.R.C. § 2053(c)(1)(B)] Accordingly, estate or inheritance taxes are generally not deductible since they accrue at the decedent's death, and not ***before.***

#### (b) Foreign Death Taxes

Section 2053(d) allows the executor to elect to deduct foreign death taxes imposed upon property that is also included in the decedent's gross estate for federal estate tax purposes.

### (5) Contractual Claims

If the claim is ***"founded on a promise or agreement"*** (i.e., a contractual claim), it ***must be supported by "adequate and full consideration in money or money's worth."*** [I.R.C. § 2053(c)(1)(A)] This requirement is to prevent the decedent from diminishing the taxable estate by creating "obligations" which are really gifts.

#### (a) Marital Rights as Consideration

For this purpose, the relinquishment of marital rights is ***not*** deemed a consideration "in money or money's worth." [I.R.C. § 2053(e)] The rationale for this limitation is similar to that of section 2043(b), which generally denies that the release of marital rights is sufficient consideration to immunize a transfer from the transfer taxes.

#### (b) Special Exception for Charitable Pledges

The decedent's promise or agreement to make a charitable contribution is deductible as a claim despite the fact that the pledge was gratuitous, but only to the extent that a bequest to the charity would be allowed as a charitable deduction under section 2055. [I.R.C. § 2053(c)(1)(A)]

### (6) Community Debts

Since only the decedent's half of community property assets are taxable in the decedent's gross estate, only half of the community debts are deductible.

### e. Unpaid Mortgages

The amount of any mortgage, trust deed, or other lien against property included in the decedent's gross estate is deductible if the ***full value of the property,*** unreduced by the amount of the lien, ***is included in the decedent's estate.*** [I.R.C. § 2053(a)(4)]

#### (1) Application—Decedent Personally Liable

If the decedent is personally liable on the mortgage note, the full value of the property is includible in his estate, and then a deduction is allowed under section 2053. [Treas. Reg. § 20.2053–7] Consequently, the estate can deduct the full amount of the liability even though it might exceed the value of the encumbered property.

#### (2) Application—Decedent Not Personally Liable

In contrast, if the decedent is not personally liable on the mortgage, only the ***net value*** of the property (value less amount of encumbrance) is included in the decedent's estate and, hence, no deduction is allowed. [Treas. Reg. § 20.2053–7] Thus, if the encumbrance exceeded the value of the property, nothing would be includible or deductible.

### f. Special Limitations on Deductions

In addition to the limitations relating to specific types of expenses, the statute imposes three special limitations:

#### (1) Allowable Under Local Law

Claims and expenses related to the probate assets are deductible only if they are "allowable by the laws of the jurisdiction . . . under which the estate is being administered." [I.R.C. § 2053(a)]

##### (a) Determination of When Allowable

State law governs whether a particular claim or expense is "allowable." [Treas. Reg. § 20.2053–1(a)(1)] However, the fact that the state probate court allows (or disallows) a particular claim or item of expense is not necessarily dispositive. Rather, under the rule of **Commissioner v. Estate of Bosch,** 387 U.S. 456 (1967), the federal courts, in resolving the estate tax issue, are not bound by lower state court decisions but may ***independently*** determine whether or not a claim is allowable under the governing state law. [*See* **First National Bank v. United States,** 422 F.2d 1385 (10th Cir. 1970)]

##### (b) Nonprobate Assets

This limitation is not reiterated as to expenses relating to nonprobate assets. [*See* I.R.C. § 2053(b)] However, since such deductible expenses must be of a nature similar to those expenses that are allowed as deductions to the probate estate, it can be inferred that they must also be allowable under state law. [*See* Rev. Rul. 68–611, 1968–2 C.B. 410]

#### (2) Insolvent Estate

Generally, expenses and claims against the decedent's probate estate are deductible only to the extent of the value of the assets in the probate estate. If such expenses and claims exceed the value of the probate assets, the excess may be deducted (and the deduction applied against the value of the non-probate assets included in the decedent's gross estate) ***only if*** these excess claims are actually paid before the date for filing of the estate tax return. [I.R.C. § 2053(c)(2); Treas. Reg. § 20.2053–1(c)] Expenses and claims relating to non-probate assets (but which are included in the decedent's gross estate) are not subject to this limitation; such expenses and claims are deductible as long as they are paid before the statute of limitations for reassessment of tax expires.

**(3) No Double Deductions**

Most administration expenses and claims deductible under section 2053 could also be taken as deductions on the estate's ***income tax return.*** However, both deductions are not ordinarily allowed—the executor must ***elect*** whether to claim the deductions against the estate's income ***or*** against the gross estate. [I.R.C. § 642(g)]

**(a) Exception—"Income in Respect of Decedent"**

However, if the gross estate includes "income in respect of a decedent" (income earned prior to death but not payable until after the date of death), the expenses paid by the estate attributable to such income, including business expenses, interest, and taxes are allowable ***both*** as deductions for income tax purposes and as claims against the estate for estate tax purposes. [Treas. Reg. § 1.642(g)–2]

**(b) Selling Expenses**

Prior to 1976, expenses incurred in selling estate property were deductible under section 2053 even though they were also applied to offset the taxable gain realized upon the sale. The theory was that section 642(g) was limited, by its terms, to expenses that were ***"deductible"*** for both income and estate tax purposes and did not extend to nondeductible capital expenditures even though such expenditures operated to reduce the amount of taxable gain realized. [**Estate of Bray v. Commissioner,** (1966), *aff'd,* 396 F.2d 452 (6th Cir. 1968)] However, the 1976 Tax Reform Act eliminated the opportunity for such a double "deduction." As amended, section 642(g) now requires that the executor elect to apply such expenses against the gross estate or against the taxable gain realized on the sale of the property.

## 3. Section 2054—Deductions for Losses

Although generally captioned "losses," the deduction under section 2054 is limited to ***casualty or theft losses*** that are ***not*** compensated for by insurance or otherwise.

**a. No Double Deduction**

Such losses may be deductible against the estate's income tax return under as well as against the gross estate under section 2054. However, as with deductions for expenses and claims, the executor must elect whether to deduct casualty or theft losses against the estate's income or from the gross estate—again, double deductions are disallowed. [I.R.C. § 642(g)]

**EXAM TIP** GILBERT

Be sure to distinguish estate tax deductions from income tax deductions. For example, "losses" in the estate tax context are ***only casualty or theft*** losses. Losses incurred upon the sale of property during the course of administration may be deducted (or may offset gains) for ***income tax*** purposes, but they are ***not*** deductible for estate tax purposes.

# 4. Section 2055—the Charitable Deduction

Section 2055 allows a deduction for the value of all property transferred by the decedent for specified public, religious, educational, or other charitable purposes.

## a. Charitable Object

Note that not all inter vivos gifts or charitable bequests qualify: The gift must be to an organization operated ***exclusively*** for a ***recognized religious, scientific, literary, educational,*** or ***other charitable*** purpose. [I.R.C. § 2055(a) and Treas. Reg. § 20.2055–1(a)(2)] Unlike the charitable deduction for income tax purposes under section 170, the charitable organization need not be organized or created in the United States (foreign charities qualify).

## b. Property Transferred Inter Vivos

Deductions are available not only with respect to transfers under the decedent's will, but also for any inter vivos transfers made by the decedent to the extent that they are taxable in her gross estate. [*See* Treas. Reg. § 20.2055–1(a)]

e.g. **Example:** If the decedent made an inter vivos transfer of a remainder interest in the decedent's personal residence to a charity, reserving a life estate, the value of the residence would be included in the decedent's gross estate under section 2036(a)(1), but that same amount would be allowed as a deduction under section 2055. The effect is to wash out any tax on inter vivos transfers to charity.

### (1) Special Rules for Powers of Appointment

Similarly, if the property is included in a decedent's gross estate under section 2041 (relating to powers of appointment), the appointment of the property to a charity is treated as a transfer and therefore qualifies for the charitable deduction. [I.R.C. § 2055(b)]

## c. Limitations on Deductible Amount

The amount of the deduction is limited to the value of the property that is transferred to the charity. [I.R.C. § 2055(a)] Furthermore, two special limitations apply:

(1) ***The amount of the deduction cannot exceed the value of the transferred property*** that is included in the decedent's gross estate; [I.R.C. § 2055(d)] and

(2) ***If the property transferred to the charity is burdened with an obligation to pay any death taxes*** imposed upon the decedent's estate, the charitable deduction will be reduced by the amount of such taxes, since the outstanding obligation also reduces the amount that actually passes to the charity. [I.R.C. § 2055(c)]

(a) ***This reduction of the deductible amount may operate to increase the amount of death taxes,*** certainly federal estate taxes, and possibly state inheritance taxes. And, to the extent that the increased death taxes burden the charitable bequest, the deduction is further reduced, with a further increase in death taxes, and so on, and so on!

### d. Split-Interest Gifts

Interests in the same property may be given to both an individual with a life estate interest and the remainder interest to a charity ("charitable remainder gifts") or a term of years to a charity followed by a remainder to an individual ("charitable lead gifts"). In either case, the charitable deduction is generally limited to the value of the interest actually transferred to the charity. [I.R.C. § 2055(a)]

(1) Under the Tax Reform Act of 1969, charitable remainder or charitable lead gifts are deductible only if the split-interest gift is made in certain designated forms:

#### (a) Form Required

The statute requires that the gift be in the form of an ***"annuity trust,"*** a ***"unitrust,"*** or a ***"pooled income fund."*** [I.R.C. § 2055(e)(2)(A)]

##### 1) Annuity Trust

This is a trust in which the trustee is required to distribute annually to the noncharitable beneficiary a specified sum that is at least 5% and not more than 50% of the original value of the trust assets. [I.R.C. § 664(d)]

##### 2) Unitrusts

Under a "unitrust," the trustee must distribute annually a sum that is either a fixed percentage (at least 5% and not more than 50%) of the trust estate (determined annually) or the entire trust income, whichever is less. [I.R.C. § 664(d)]

##### 3) Pooled Income Fund

This is a trust where a public charity is trustee, and several donors contribute property to the trust, each reserving for himself or herself a life estate in a proportionate share of the combined property. The public charity must have an irrevocable remainder. [I.R.C. § 642(c)(5)]

#### (b) Limitations

Even if an annuity trust or unitrust otherwise qualifies, no deduction is allowed if another, noncharitable remainder precedes the charitable remainder; or the income interest is for a term of years (rather than a life estate), and the term exceeds 20 years. [I.R.C. § 664(d)]

#### (c) Exceptions

The special forms required by the 1969 Act do not apply to certain split-interest gifts. [I.R.C. §§ 2055(e)(2), 170(f)(3)(B)] The principal types of split interests excepted are:

1) ***An undivided interest in the property***—(e.g., a tenancy in common); and

2) ***A remainder interest in a personal residence*** or a farm following ***a legal life estate.***

# 5. Section 2056—the Marital Deduction

A deduction is also allowed for property that passes to the surviving spouse upon the decedent's death. Formerly, the maximum allowable deduction was 50% of the adjusted gross estate; however, with passage of the 1981 Revenue Act a deduction is allowed for ***all property*** passing to the spouse (i.e., a 100% deduction).

## a. Background

Prior to the allowance of the marital deduction, decedents' estates in community property jurisdictions enjoyed a singular advantage. Because one-half of the property was already "vested" in the surviving spouse, only the decedent's half was taxable on death. The marital deduction was enacted in 1948 for the purpose of securing approximately equal estate tax treatment of decedents' estates in community property and non-community property jurisdictions.

### (1) Impact on Substantive Requirements

This focus upon equalizing the treatment of residents of common law and community property states shaped the substantive requirements of the deduction.

#### (a) Quantitative Limitation

Since one-half of the community property was effectively excluded from the gross estate of a community property state resident decedent, a ***quantitative*** limitation (50% of the adjusted gross estate) was imposed upon the amount of separate property that could be "excluded" from tax by means of the marital deduction. Also, since community property enjoyed this "exclusion" ipso facto, the one-half of community property that *was* included in the decedent's estate could not be taken into account in determining the 50% ceiling.

#### (b) Qualitative Limitation

Since the one-half interest in community property owned by the surviving spouse was owned outright, and this would be includible in the surviving spouse's estate upon death, the Code provided a ***qualitative*** limitation on the type of interests that would qualify for the deduction. Essentially it was required that in order to be deductible to the decedent, the interest passing to the survivor must be of a type that was potentially includible in the surviving spouse's estate upon death.

### (2) Should Marital Transfers Be Taxed at All?

In a very real sense, transfers of property between spouses represent little more than a shifting of marital wealth within a single community of economic interest. Thus, whether such transfers should be taxed at all is an important policy question.

#### (a) Comment

As noted above, this question was not a paramount consideration in the 1948 allowance of the marital deduction; rather, parity between common law and community property jurisdictions was the primary concern.

#### (b) Distinguish—1981 Act

Over the years, however, the policy question was addressed by commentators and "law reform" groups, and occasionally by committees of Congress. It received a generally sympathetic hearing in connection with the formulation of the Tax Reform Act of 1976, but a full 100% deduction did not emerge in that Act because of concern with anticipated revenue losses it would occasion. However, the substantial tax reductions proposed (and enacted) in the 1981 Act persuaded Congress to answer the policy question in the affirmative, despite the (relatively insignificant) revenue loss that the 100% marital deduction would produce.

### b. General Scope of the Deduction

Section 2056(a) allows a deduction in an "amount equal to the value of any interest in ***property which passes or has passed from the decedent***" to a surviving spouse.

#### (1) Value of Property Passing to Surviving Spouse

The marital deduction is limited to the ***net*** value of the property interests passing to the surviving spouse.

##### (a) Encumbrances

Thus, if the property bequeathed to the surviving spouse is subject to a mortgage or other encumbrance that is not released by a payment from the estate, the value of the property for purposes of the marital deduction is reduced by the amount of the encumbrance. [I.R.C. § 2056(b)(4)(B)]

##### (b) Death Taxes

Similarly, the value of the interest passing to the surviving spouse must be reduced by any federal estate or other death taxes payable by the spouse or payable out of the interest passing to the spouse. [I.R.C. § 2056(b)(4)(A)]

###### 1) Note

If the marital portion is reduced by death taxes, a circular computation may result: The maximum marital deduction that was used to compute the federal estate taxes in the first instance is reduced by those taxes; the reduction of the marital deduction then increases the estate taxes payable which, in turn, reduces the amount of the marital deduction—and so forth.

##### (c) Conditional Bequests

Moreover, the marital deduction is limited to property that the surviving spouse receives ***unconditionally.*** Consequently, if the decedent's will requires the surviving spouse to relinquish some right or property in order to take under the will, only the excess of the value of the property received under the will over what the spouse was required to relinquish is deductible. [**United States v. Stapf,** 375 U.S. 118 (1963)]

#### (2) Maximum Allowed

As noted above, there is no longer any quantitative limitation upon the marital deductions. The value of ***all*** property passing to the surviving spouse is deductible—as long as it meets the requirements discussed below.

#### (3) Effect of Community Property

There is no longer any further differential treatment of community property for purposes of the marital deduction. A bequest of a decedent's one-half interest in community property to the surviving spouse qualifies for the marital deduction to the same extent as a bequest of separate property.

## c. Overview of Requirements for Marital Deductions

There are five basic requirements for allowance of the marital deduction.

### (1) Citizens Only

No marital deduction is allowed if the surviving spouse is not a citizen of the United States, even though the decedent was a citizen. [I.R.C. § 2056(d)(1)]

#### (a) Rationale

The underlying rationale of the marital deduction is that the interest passing to the surviving spouse must be potentially includible in the surviving spouse's estate at death. However, if the surviving spouse is not a citizen, there is a possibility that the property ***could escape taxation*** because the property of a nonresident alien is subject to the federal estate tax only if it is located in the United States. To avoid this risk, the Code does not allow the marital deduction for property passing to a noncitizen surviving spouse.

#### (b) The Qualified Domestic Trust Exception

The marital deduction will be allowed to the estate of the decedent spouse (citizen or resident alien) if the otherwise qualifying interest passes to a "qualified domestic trust." [I.R.C. § 2056(d)(2)]

##### 1) Definition

A qualified domestic trust is defined as a trust: (i) that requires at least ***one trustee to be a citizen*** or domestic corporation; (ii) that provides that no distribution may be made from the trust ***unless the citizen-trustee withholds the tax*** imposed by section 2056A; (iii) with respect to which the ***citizen-decedents executor elects to have the trust qualify*** as a qualified domestic trust; and (iv) that otherwise ***meets requirements*** established by the Treasury Department. [I.R.C. § 2056A(a)]

##### 2) Tax Imposed

Under section 2056A(b), a tax is imposed on any and all distributions from a qualified domestic trust ***except*** distributions of income and hardship distributions to the surviving spouse. [I.R.C. § 2056A(b)(1)(A), (b)(3)] Also, a tax is imposed on the value of any property remaining in the trust on the date of the surviving spouse's death. [I.R.C. § 2056A(b)(1)(B)]

##### 3) Amount of Tax

The tax is that amount by which the citizen-decedent's estate tax would have been increased if the amount taxable (the amount of the distribution or amount remaining on trust at the surviving spouse's death) had been included as part of the citizen-decedent's taxable estate. And, for this purpose, any previous taxable distributions from the qualified domestic trust must be taken into account. [I.R.C. § 2056A(b)(2)(A)]

### (2) Inclusion in Gross Estate

The property passing to the surviving spouse must have been included in the decedent's gross estate. [I.R.C. § 2056(a)] This is a logical limitation. The estate should not receive a deduction with respect to a transfer of property that was never subject to the estate tax in the first place.

### (3) Surviving Spouse

The decedent must have been married at the time of death, and the spouse must survive the decedent.

#### (a) "Spouse"

Historically, ***same-sex marriages*** were not recognized under the Internal Revenue Code. However, in 2013, the Supreme Court determined that the Defense of Marriage Act (1 U.S.C.S. Chap. 1, § 7), which had barred recognition of same sex marriage for federal tax purposes, was unconstitutional. [**United States v. Windsor,** 570 U.S. 744 (2013)] Hence, a decedent spouse in a same-sex marriage is entitled to claim the marital deduction for transfers made to a surviving spouse.

#### (b) "Survived"

In determining whether the spouse survived the decedent, the presumptions (or reversal of the presumptions) under the Uniform Simultaneous Death Act are taken into account. [Treas. Reg. § 20.2056(c)–2(e)]

### (4) Passing Requirement

An interest in property must have "passed" from the decedent to the surviving spouse—by will, by operation of law, or otherwise. The marital deduction is ***not*** limited to property passing from the decedent to the surviving spouse by way of will or intestacy. Rather, the "passing" requirement includes just about all situations where the surviving spouse acquired property from the decedent to the extent such property is included in the decedent's gross estate. [I.R.C. § 2056(c)]

#### (a) Marital Shares

Interests acquired as dower, curtesy, or a statutory forced share are deemed to "pass" from the decedent to the surviving spouse. [I.R.C. § 2056(c)(3)]

#### (b) Inter Vivos Transfers

Inter vivos transfers made to a spouse and which are includible under sections 2035 through 2038 (reserved life estates, etc.) "pass" to the surviving spouse for purposes of the marital deduction. [I.R.C. § 2056(c)(4)]

#### (c) Other Includible Interests

Joint interests, property appointed under a power of appointment, and life insurance received by the surviving spouse are considered to have passed from the decedent to the surviving spouse and deductible if and to the extent they are included in the decedent's gross estate. [I.R.C. § 2056(c)(5)–(7); *see also* I.R.C. §§ 2040–2042 (providing the estate tax inclusion rules for these interests)]

### (d) Will Contests

Any interest that a surviving spouse receives pursuant to a settlement or compromise of a will contest "passes" to that spouse, provided that such settlement resulted from a "bona fide recognition of enforceable rights of the surviving spouse in the decedent's estate." [Treas. Reg. § 20.2056(c)–2(d)(2)]

### (e) Effect of Disclaimers

Under prior law, if within nine months of the decedent's death any other beneficiary disclaimed an interest in the decedent's estate and the surviving spouse became entitled to that interest (under the decedent's will or by intestacy), such an interest was deemed to "pass" to the surviving spouse. On the other hand, property disclaimed ***by the surviving spouse*** did ***not*** "pass" to that spouse. The subsection of section 2056 that specified this rule was repealed by the 1976 Act. However, it appears that the disclaimer rules of section 2518 (incorporated in the estate tax by section 2046) secure the same results.

## (5) The Interest Must Be a "Deductible Interest"

Only ***deductible*** interests that pass to the surviving spouse qualify for the marital deduction. In general, there are four types of ***nondeductible*** interests:

### (a) Interest Not Included in Gross Estate

As noted above, the deduction is limited to interests that are subject to tax in the decedent's gross estate. Thus, for example, property received by the surviving spouse upon exercise of a nontaxable, special/nongeneral power of appointment does not qualify for the marital deduction.

e.g. **Example:** A parent created an inter vivos trust and transferred income-producing stock to the trust. Under the terms of the trust, income was payable to the parent's daughter for life. The daughter had the power to appoint the remainder to her spouse or children under the terms of her will. At death, the daughter appointed the remainder to her spouse. The daughter is not entitled to the marital deduction because the daughter exercised a nongeneral power of appointment.

### (b) Interests Deductible Under Section 2053

Interests passing to the surviving spouse, but which are properly deductible under section 2053, may not also be taken as a marital deduction. For example, payments from the estate in satisfaction of a bona fide loan that the spouse had made to the decedent, or fees the spouse receives for services as executor of the decedent's estate, are only deductible under section 2053. [Treas. Reg. § 20.2056(a)–2(d)(2)]

### (c) Losses

If property passing to a surviving spouse is subject to a casualty or theft loss during the course of administration, the value of that property does not qualify for the marital deduction to the extent that a deduction for the loss was claimed under section 2054. [Treas. Reg. § 20.2056(a)–2(b)(3)]

#### (d) Nondeductible Terminable Interests

The disallowance of any deduction for certain "terminable interests" is one of the most significant and complex limitations on the marital deduction and is discussed in detail below.

| GILBERT |
|---|
| **SUMMARY OF REQUIREMENTS FOR THE MARITAL DEDUCTION** |
| **THE FIVE BASIC REQUIREMENTS FOR THE MARITAL DEDUCTION ARE:** |
| ☑ The surviving spouse must have been a ***United States citizen;*** |
| ☑ The property passing to the surviving spouse ***must have been included in the decedent's gross estate;*** |
| ☑ The decedent ***must have been married*** (including a same sex marriage) at the time of death, and the spouse ***must survive the decedent;*** |
| ☑ An interest in the ***property must have "passed" from the decedent to surviving spouse*** by will, intestacy, ***or otherwise*** (e.g., dower/curtesy, statutory forced share, reserved life estate, etc.); and |
| ☑ The interest ***must be deductible interest.*** Generally, an interest will be eligible for the marital deduction ***unless*** the interest (i) was ***not included*** in the decedent's gross estate; (ii) is ***deductible under sections 2053 or 2054;*** or (iii) is a ***nondeductible terminable interest.*** |

### d. The "Nondeductible Terminable Interest" Rule

The marital deduction is not allowed for certain "terminable interests" that pass to the surviving spouse.

#### (1) Rationale

In community property states, the surviving spouse's share of the community assets passes to the spouse in fee (i.e., absolutely) and will ordinarily be included in the spouse's estate and taxable upon the spouse's death. Since the marital deduction was designed to approximate the estate tax treatment between spouses in community property and common law jurisdictions, it was deemed inappropriate to allow the deduction for interests that would be extinguished prior to or upon the death of the surviving spouse. To allow a deduction for a terminable interest would permit complete estate tax avoidance (i.e., the interest would neither be taxed in the decedent's estate nor in the surviving spouse's estate), and this was not the purpose of the marital deduction. Nor is it presently the purpose of the marital deduction, despite the 100% deduction of the 1981 Act.

#### (2) What Is a "Terminable Interest"?

Terminable interests are those that will terminate upon lapse of time or the failure or happening of some event or contingency. [I.R.C. § 2056(b)] Examples of terminable interests include a life estate, a term for years, or a defeasible fee.

### (a) Property with Limited Life

A patent, which will expire after a certain period of time, is not a terminable interest. Therefore, the marital deduction is allowed for a devise of a patent to a surviving spouse.

### (b) Bonds, Notes, Etc.

The Internal Revenue Code specifically provides that an interest shall not be considered terminable "merely because it is the ownership of a bond, note, or similar contractual obligation, the discharge of which would not have the effect of an annuity for life or for a term." [I.R.C. § 2056(b)(1)]

### (c) Estate Trusts

An estate trust is one in which the surviving spouse is made sole beneficiary during life with the corpus to be distributed to that spouse's estate upon death. Since no one other than the surviving spouse or the surviving spouse's estate acquires an interest in the trust, the interest passing to the surviving spouse is deductible.

### (d) Special Rules for Support Allowances

Almost every state has provision in its probate law for payment of a support allowance to a widow or widower out of the deceased spouse's probate estate. Whether the money so paid qualifies for the marital deduction depends upon the following factors:

(i) ***The time for determining whether such payments are "terminable"*** is the date of the decedent's death—not the date when the allowance is ordered by the probate court. [**Jackson v. United States,** 376 U.S. 503 (1964)]

(ii) ***If local law provides the surviving spouse a fixed and indefeasible right*** to a specific sum of money or a fixed percentage of the decedent's estate for support during the period of probate administration, the payments will qualify for the marital deduction.

(iii) ***If (as is far more typical) the spouse has no vested rights*** to such payments at the time of the decedent's death but merely acquires a right to payments if and when ordered by the probate court, the payments are deemed terminable on the theory that the survivor would get no allowance if the surviving spouse died or remarried before it is granted. [**Jackson v. United States** (discussed above)] The Tax Court agreed with the Sixth Circuit that even if the surviving spouse must petition the court for the allowance, it will not preclude the marital deduction. [*See* **Estate of Green v. United States,** 441 F.2d 303 (6th Cir. 1971) and **Estate of Watson v. Commissioner,** 94 T.C. 262 (1990)] The court in *Watson* cited *Green* for the following proposition:

> To hold that an interest is terminable only because legal procedures are invoked to enforce an interest which is otherwise vested at the date of the husband's death, is to hold that all elective rights, such as the widow's allowance and the statutory interest in lieu of dower, are disqualified as marital deductions.

***Watson,*** 94 T.C. at 280.

(iv) ***If the allowance is for an indefinite period*** (no fixed amount) ***or is dependent upon the spouse surviving*** throughout the period of allowance, it is a terminable interest and does not qualify for the deduction. [**Estate of Cunha v. Commissioner,** 279 F.2d 292 (9th Cir. 1960)]

## e. Exceptions to the "Terminable Interest" Rule

There are five exceptions in which an interest although technically classifiable as a "nondeductible terminable interest" will nonetheless qualify for the marital deduction. The exceptions are discussed in this part.

### (1) Survivorship Exception

In general, bequests to a spouse conditioned upon surviving a period of time after the death of the decedent or surviving some event that would occur after the death of the decedent are nondeductible terminable interests. However, the Code recognizes a limited exception where the condition is restricted to surviving the decedent for a period of not more than ***six months*** ("to my spouse A, provided A survives for five months after my death"), *or* not dying from ***a common disaster*** ("provided that A does not die in the same disaster in which I lose my life"). Where these limited contingencies are used, the interest granted to the survivor is deductible—provided, of course, that the surviving spouse in fact outlives the prescribed period or does not die as a result of such common disaster. [I.R.C. § 2056(b)(3)]

#### (a) Contingency Must Necessarily Occur Within Six Months

It is not enough that the event upon which survivorship is conditioned (other than death by common disaster) may ***possibly*** occur within the six-month period. For example, a bequest conditioned upon surviving distribution of the decedent's estate ("to my spouse if living at the time of distribution of my estate") is ordinarily not considered to be within the statutory survivorship exception, even though distribution may conceivably occur within the six-month period. The fact that the distribution can occur after the six-month period removes this type of bequest from the statutory exception—even if the distribution is in fact made within the six-month period. [**Hanson v. Vinal,** 413 F.2d 882 (8th Cir. 1969)]

#### (b) Distinguish—Immediate Vesting

However, it has been held that such a bequest is deductible if, under local property law, the interest is deemed to vest in the surviving spouse immediately upon the decedent's death. [*See* **Kellar v. Kasper,** 138 F. Supp. 738 (D.S.D. 1956)]

### (2) Life Estate with Power of Appointment Exception

A transfer in which the surviving spouse is to receive all the income from the property during the surviving spouse's life (or all the income from a specific portion of the property) *and* is granted an unqualified power to appoint the property (or a specific portion thereof) to the surviving spouse or the surviving spouse's estate will qualify for the marital deduction. [I.R.C. § 2056(b)(5)] This provision forms the basis for the marital deduction trust, which was predominately used prior to 1982, and is still widely used today.

### (a) Income Requirement

To invoke this exception, it is essential that the surviving spouse be entitled to ***all*** of the income from the property or a portion thereof payable at least annually. If the trustee has any power to accumulate or withhold income beyond the period of administration (below), the trust will not qualify ***unless*** the survivor is granted an unlimited power to demand that the income be distributed. [Treas. Reg. § 20.2056(b)–5(f)(8)]

#### 1) The Surviving Spouse's Right to Receive Income Must Be Unconditional

The surviving spouse must be entitled to receive all income payable at least annually. If the trustee has the discretion to distribute income, the marital deduction is not allowed. For example, if the trustee has sole discretion to distribute income for "care and support in the style and manner of living" to which the spouse has become accustomed, the marital deduction is not allowed because the trust does not meet the income requirement. [**Wisely v. United States,** 893 F.2d 660 (4th Cir. 1990)]

#### 2) The Specific Portion Rule

If the surviving spouse is entitled to income from a specific portion of the property or has the power to appoint a specific portion of the property (e.g., income from one-half or the power to appoint one-half of the property), the marital deduction will be allowed under the "specific portion rule." However, the amount of the marital deduction is limited to percentage of the value of the property transferred on trust. [Treas. Reg. § 20.2056(b)–5(b)]

##### a) Application

It is the ***lowest*** portion or fraction to which the spouse is entitled that determines the deductible amount. Thus, if the surviving spouse was bequeathed one-half of the income and a power to appoint one-fourth of the corpus, the deduction would be limited to one-fourth of the value of the property transferred.

##### b) Fractional vs. Dollar Amount

The specific portion must be expressed as a fraction or percentage of the total trust income or corpus and not as a fixed dollar amount. [I.R.C. § 2056(b)(10)]

#### 3) Income During Administration of Estate

The Regulations provide that the income requirement is met even though the executor is authorized to accumulate income from the marital portion during the period of administration, as long as the executor cannot delay settlement of the estate beyond a reasonable period of time. [Treas. Reg. § 20.2056(b)–5(f)(9)]

#### 4) Effect of Administrative Powers

Normal administrative powers conferred on a trustee—e.g., to apportion receipts and expenses between income and corpus, etc.—do not disqualify the trust for marital deduction purposes. [Rev. Rul. 69–56, 1969–1 C.B. 224]

#### 5) Stub Income

Upon the death of the surviving spouse, income accruing from the last payment date to the date of death may either be subject to a general power of appointment or paid to the estate of the surviving spouse to meet the all-income requirement. [Treas. Reg. § 20.2056(b)–(5)(f)(8)] Note that the stub income requirement is different from that of the QTIP trust. QTIPs are discussed below in this section.

### (b) Power of Appointment Requirement

It is also crucial that the surviving spouse have the power to appoint the property to the surviving spouse or the surviving spouse's estate, and this power must be exercisable by the surviving spouse alone and in all events. Moreover, no other person may have the power to appoint the property away from the surviving spouse. [I.R.C. § 2056(b)(5)]

#### 1) Nature of the Power

Although the required power is frequently referred to as a "general power," it is more specific than the "general power of appointment" definition under section 2041. Under section 2041, it is sufficient if a powerholder has a power to appoint to the powerholder, powerholder's creditors, powerholder's estate, or the creditors of the powerholder's estate. However, for purposes of section 2056, the power must be exercisable in favor of ***the surviving spouse or surviving spouse's estate.***

#### 2) Ability to Exercise

It is generally immaterial whether the surviving spouse is capable of exercising the power. The surviving spouse's incompetence will not preclude allowance of the marital deduction. [Rev. Rul. 55–518, 1955–2 C.B. 384; *but compare* **Stockdick v. Phinney,** 16 A.F.T.R.2d 6202 (1965)]

#### 3) Formalities

Moreover, limitations of a formal nature (e.g., requiring that the holder make specific reference to the power) will not disqualify an interest. [Treas. Reg. § 2056(b)–5(g)(4)]

#### 4) Powers to Consume

Although an unlimited power to withdraw the trust corpus is a sufficient power to appoint to oneself, it has often been held that powers to consume are not enough to qualify the interest since such a power is limited to withdrawals for one's own needs, whereas the power required under the statute must be one that is freely exercisable for any purpose. [*See* **Estate of Pipe v. Commissioner,** 241 F.2d 210 (2d Cir.), *cert. denied,* 355 U.S. 814 (1957); **Commissioner v. Ellis,** 252 F.2d 109 (3d Cir. 1958)]

#### 5) Joint Powers

The statute specifies that the requisite power be exercisable by the surviving spouse ***alone.*** Thus, the marital deduction is not allowed if the power is a joint power.

#### 6) Contingent Powers

The power must be exercisable by the surviving spouse "in all events." Accordingly, any condition or limitation upon its exercise will disqualify the interest. Indeed, it has been held that even though the competence of the surviving spouse is immaterial, where the power of appointment has been granted in such a way that it is to cease if the surviving spouse becomes incompetent or a guardian or conservator is appointed for the surviving spouse, the power is not exercisable "in all events," and the marital deduction is not allowed. [**Starrett v. Commissioner,** 223 F.2d 163 (1st Cir. 1955)]

#### 7) No Power in a Third Party

It is equally essential that no person have the power to appoint property away from the surviving spouse. However, a third party's power to appoint property ***to*** the surviving spouse is not fatal to the marital deduction. [Treas. Reg. § 2056(b)–5(j)] And, the Regulations permit a third party power to appoint trust property as long as the power is not "in opposition" to that of the surviving spouse. [Treas. Reg. § 20.2056(b)–(5)(j)]

e.g. **Example:** A spouse gives the surviving spouse a life interest in income and a general testamentary power to appoint the corpus to any person, including the surviving spouse's estate. The trust provides that to the extent that the surviving spouse fails to appoint the corpus, a named third party can appoint the corpus to anyone. The marital deduction is allowed even though a third party can appoint the corpus after the surviving spouse's death in the event that the spouse has not exercised the power.

### (3) Exception for "Qualified Terminable Interest Property"

Section 2056(b)(7) allows the marital deduction in the case of "qualified terminable interest property." [I.R.C. § 2056(b)(7)(A)] The "qualified terminable interest property" exception to the nondeductible terminable interest rule was enacted under the Revenue Act of 1981. This type of interest became known by the acronym "QTIP."

#### (a) Definitions

##### 1) "Qualified Terminable Interest Property"

A QTIP is defined as property or an interest therein that ***passes*** from the decedent, in which the ***surviving spouse*** has a ***qualifying income interest for life,*** and with respect to which the decedent's executor makes an ***election*** to have the property qualify as a QTIP interest. [I.R.C. § 2056(b)(7)(B)(i) & (iii)]

#### 2) "Qualifying Income Interest"

The surviving spouse has a "qualifying income interest for life" if the surviving spouse is entitled to ***all of the income*** from the property or a specific portion thereof payable at least annually, and ***no*** person (including the surviving spouse) ***has a power to appoint*** any part of the property ***to anyone other than the surviving spouse, except*** that the surviving spouse (or some other person) may be granted a power of appointment if this power is exercisable only at or after the surviving spouse's death [I.RC. § 2056(b)(7)(B)(ii) & (iv)].

### (b) Election

An affirmative election by the decedent's executor is a substantive requirement for allowance of the deduction. It must be made on the decedent's estate tax return filed by the executor and, once made, the ***election is irrevocable***. [I.R.C. § 2056(b)(7)(B)(v)]

### (c) The "Passing" Requirement

This is the same as the general passing requirement of section 2056(a) discussed in part d above.

### (d) The "Income" Requirement

This is the same as the income requirement under the life estate with power of appointment exception. In **Estate of Nicholson v. Commissioner,** 94 T.C. 666 (1990), the trustee was directed to pay income to the spouse "as she may from time to time require to maintain. . .her usual and customary standard of living. . ." Significantly, the local court granted an order to modify the trust language to require all income to be paid to the surviving spouse at least quarterly effective as of the decedent's death. However, the Tax Court in *Nicholson* determined that ***federal courts are not required give effect to local court modifications after the IRS has acquired revenue rights even though the modifications are binding between on the parties.***

#### 1) Stub Income

"Stub income" may be paid to the estate of the surviving spouse or to the next beneficiaries in interest. [Treas. Reg. § 20.2056(b)–(7)(d)(4)]

#### 2) Income Interest Contingent on Election

Making the spouse's income interest contingent upon the executor's election of QTIP treatment will not disqualify the property for QTIP treatment. [**Spencer's Estate v. Commissioner,** 43 F.3d 226 (6th Cir. 1995); **Clack's Estate v. Commissioner,** 106 T.C. 131 (1996)—acquiescing in result]

### (e) No Right to Appoint Property to Another Person

No person (***including*** the surviving spouse) may have a power to appoint the property away from the surviving spouse under the QTIP exception. [*See* **Estate of Bowling v. Commissioner,** 93 T.C. 286 (1989) (disallowing the QTIP exception where the trustee could invade the corpus of the trust for the "emergency needs" of ***any*** beneficiary)]

#### 1) Distinguish—Power to Appoint to Surviving Spouse

Another person ***may*** be granted a power to appoint the property ***to*** the surviving spouse and the surviving spouse may be granted a limited (nongeneral) power to consume. However, if the surviving spouse was granted a general power of withdrawal, the marital deduction would be allowed under the life estate with power of appointment exception.

#### 2) Note

Some other party may be granted a power to appoint the property (limited/nongeneral or general) as long as the power may not be exercised until the surviving spouse's death. [I.R.C. § 2056(b)(7)(B)(ii) (flush language)]

### (f) Effect of Election

The initial effect of the election is to allow the QTIP interest to qualify for the marital deduction in the decedent's estate. The ultimate effect is to expose the surviving spouse to transfer taxes, even though the surviving spouse possesses only a limited interest in the property.

#### 1) Property Taxed in Surviving Spouse's Estate

Upon the death of the surviving spouse, the QTIP property will be included in the surviving spouse's gross estate. [I.R.C. § 2044] It is the value of the entire property, not just the spouse's income interest, that is included in the gross estate.

e.g. **Example:** A decedent created a testamentary trust in which the surviving spouse received income for life payable quarterly, and the surviving spouse had the right to appoint the property at death to any or all of their two children. The executor made a QTIP election on the decedent's tax return. The actuarial value of the surviving spouse's life estate interest was $500,000, and the value of the corpus was $2,000,000 at the time of the decedent's death. The surviving spouse designated the death to go the two children equally under the terms of her validly probated will. At the time of the surviving spouse's death, the property was worth $2,200,000. Pursuant to section 2044, the fair market value of the property at the surviving spouse's death ($2,200,000) is included in the surviving spouse's gross estate.

#### 2) Property Subject to Gift Taxes

If the surviving spouse makes a lifetime transfer of the income interest in the QTIP property, the full value of the property (not just the value of the income interest) will be treated as a taxable gift by the surviving spouse. [I.R.C. § 2519]

### (g) Partial Elections Permitted

The election is not an "all or nothing" option. The executor may elect to qualify all ***or any portion*** of the QTIP property. Moreover, the executor may make a partial election in the form of a formula, such as qualifying "so much of the property as may be necessary to reduce the federal estate tax liability to $0, after taking into account all other allowable deductions and credits" [Priv. Ltr. Rul. 8301050 (September 30, 1982)]

#### (h) Comparison with Power of Appointment Exception

The QTIP exception is more flexible than the life estate with power of appointment exception. If an interest to a surviving spouse meets the life estate with power of appointment exception, the marital deduction is mandatory, whether or not it results in tax savings for the decedent. Conversely, where the surviving spouse receives a qualifying income interest for life, the decedent's executor can assess the situation at the time of the decedent's death to determine whether it is beneficial to claim the marital deduction. Further, a QTIP provides the decedent with the right to designate the beneficiaries who will take the property upon the surviving spouse's death. For example, if the decedent creates a life estate with a general power of appointment in favor of the surviving spouse, the surviving spouse may remarry, have children with the new spouse, and exercise the power of appointment in their favor instead of any children the decedent and surviving spouse may have had together.

### (4) Insurance Settlement Exception

Certain interests passing to a surviving spouse in the proceeds of life insurance, endowment, and annuity contracts held by the insurer are not considered terminable where conditions similar to the life estate with power of appointment exception are satisfied. Under this exception, if the surviving spouse has a right to all interest or installment payments with respect to the insurance proceeds (or to a specific portion of such payments) during the surviving spouse's life ***and*** has an unqualified power to appoint the entire residue (or a specific portion of the proceeds) to the surviving spouse or the surviving spouse's estate, the marital deduction is allowed. [I.R.C. § 2056(b)(6)]

#### (a) Distinguish—Balance Payable to Third Party

If upon the death of the surviving spouse, remaining unpaid benefits are payable to another, the entire amount is a nondeductible terminable interest. Thus, where a settlement option provided for an annuity to be paid to the surviving spouse with 120 payments guaranteed, and further provided that any balance should be paid to another, no part of the proceeds qualified for the marital deduction—not even the part related to the surviving spouse's life expectancy. [**Meyer v. United States,** 364 U.S. 410 (1960)]

### (5) Exception for Certain Charitable Remainder Trusts

The 1981 Act also introduced a special exception for qualified charitable remainder trusts. A marital deduction will be allowed for the value of the ***income interest*** passing to a surviving spouse if the surviving spouse is the only noncharitable beneficiary of a trust that qualifies as a charitable remainder annuity trust or unitrust. [I.R.C. § 2056(b)(8)]

## f. Estate Planning Technique—"Equalization Clauses"

When both spouses have independent wealth, it may be preferable not to take the maximum marital deduction but, rather, leave only that amount of property to the surviving spouse that will increase the estate to the point where it is equal to the estate of the first to die. To secure this equalization, the will may contain a formula clause (e.g., I give to my spouse only so much of my property which, when added to the value of the property owned by my spouse, will make the spouse's estate equal in value to that of my estate). ***Note that the portability of a deceased spouse's unused exclusion amount has lessened the need for equalization clauses.***

#### (1) Service Challenges Equalization Clauses

In **Estate of Smith v. Commissioner,** 66 T.C. 415 (1976), *aff'd,* 565 F.2d 455 (7th Cir. 1977), the Service disallowed the marital deduction in the case of such an equalization clause. Its position was, essentially, that since the executor could value both estates (for purposes of equalization) either at the date of the decedent's death or at the alternate valuation date allowed by section 2032(b) (six months after death), the executor in effect possessed a power to appoint property away from the surviving spouse, and thus, the interest passing to the surviving spouse was a nondeductible terminable interest.

#### (2) Court Approval of Clauses

The Tax Court and appellate court rejected the Service's theory. Both courts reasoned that the value of the surviving spouse's interest was ***determinable*** under the equalization formula as of the date of the decedent's death, even though it could not be ***determined*** until the executor elected date-of-death or alternate valuation date values, and this election was one granted by the estate tax law. [*See* I.R.C. § 2032(b)] Thus, the statutory election did not create a terminable interest or a "power" to appoint property away from the spouse, any more than it would do so in the case of any formula bequest. [**Estate of Smith v. Commissioner** (discussed above) *see also* **Estate of Meeske v. Commissioner,** 72 T.C. 73 (1979); **Estate of Laurin v. Commissioner,** T.C. Mem. 1979–145, *aff'd,* 645 F.2d 8 (6th Cir. 1981)]

#### (3) Service Acceptance

The Service has agreed to follow the case law and allow the marital deduction for property passing under an equalization clause even though the executor has the option of valuing the surviving spouse's estate, for equalization purposes, at the alternate valuation date. [Rev. Rul. 82–23, 1982–1 C.B. 139]

## 6. Section 2058—Deduction for State Death Taxes

Under section 2058, a deduction is allowed for inheritance, legacy, estate, and succession taxes actually paid to any state of the United States (or territory or the District of Columbia). This replaces the credit for state death taxes under section 2011.

### a. Limitations

The state death tax deduction is subject to the following two principal limitations.

#### (1) Property Taxable in Estate

A deduction is not allowed for state death taxes paid on property that is not included in the decedent's gross estate for federal estate tax purposes; therefore, the deduction is limited to property subject to both federal and state death taxes. [I.R.C. § 2058(a)]

#### (2) Time of Payment

Generally, the deduction is allowed if the state death taxes are actually paid within a period of four years following the filing of the estate tax return, and deduction from the gross estate must be claimed within the same four-year period. [I.R.C. § 2058(b)]

## SUMMARY OF ESTATE TAX DEDUCTIONS GILBERT

### THE FIVE DEDUCTIONS ALLOWED UNDER THE ESTATE TAX ARE:

☑ ***Expenses and Claims against the estate:***

- ***Funeral expenses***
- Expenses ***actually and necessarily incurred in administration*** of the estate (e.g., executor's and attorney's fees, court costs, appraiser's fees, etc.)
- ***Legally enforceable claims against the estate*** including taxes that accrued prior to death
- ***Unpaid mortgages*** on property included in gross estate

☑ ***Losses: Casualty and theft losses*** not compensated by insurance

☑ ***Charitable deductions:*** Value of property donated to recognized ***religious, scientific, literary, educational, or other charitable organization***

☑ ***Marital deduction: Net value*** of property passing to ***surviving spouse*** (i.e., less encumbrances, federal death taxes payable by spouse)

☑ ***State death taxes:*** The deduction is limited to property ***subject to both federal and state death taxes;*** and the state death ***taxes must be paid,*** and the ***claim*** for a deduction from the gross estate ***must be made, within a four-year period.***

# Chapter Three

# Substantive Aspects of the Gift Tax

CONTENTS PAGE

# Chapter Approach

The gift tax is imposed upon "taxable gifts." [I.R.C. §§ 2501, 2502] This is defined as the total amount of gifts made during the calendar year less allowable deductions. [I.R.C. § 2503(a)] Thus, to determine gift tax liability, you need to determine:

## 1. "Gifts"

Is there a transfer under section 2501?

Is the transfer in the ordinary course of business?

Did the donor receive adequate and full consideration in money or money's worth?

Is the gift completed?

## 2. Allowable Exclusions

What qualifies for the annual exclusion?

What qualifies for the education exclusion?

What qualifies for the medical exclusion?

## 3. Allowable Deductions

Are there any allowable gift tax deductions?

Is there a gift that is subject to the charitable deduction?

Is there a gift that is subject to the marital deduction?

Note that as a matter of terminology, the first issue is commonly referred to as what transfers are "taxable gifts," even though, as mentioned, this phrase technically refers to the ***total amount of gifts less allowable deductions.***

# A. Taxable Gifts

## 1. Introductory Analysis

Unlike the estate tax—where a number of specific Code sections define the types of property and types of transfers that are subject to the tax—the subject matter of the gift tax is, for the most part, simply but broadly defined as "the transfer of property by gift." [I.R.C. §§ 2501, 2511] Accordingly, the primary focus must be on the authorities that have interpreted this broad statement of the tax base. At the same time, however, chapter 12 of the Code (the gift tax) does contain certain specific provisions relating to taxable gifts, which must also be examined.

## 2. Elements of a Taxable Gift

The gift tax attaches to "the transfer of property by gift . . . by any individual. . . ." [I.R.C. § 2501(a)(1)] Section 2511(a) elaborates upon this principle by adding that the tax "shall apply whether the transfer is in trust or otherwise, whether the gift is direct or indirect, and whether the property is real or personal, tangible or intangible. . ." For purposes of analysis, these concepts may be best understood by considering the four basic elements of a taxable gift:

(1) The ***identity and capacity*** of the donor or donee;

(2) The ***subject matter of the gift*** under I.R.C. § 2501;

(3) The ***sufficiency of a transfer*** for gift taxation; and

(4) The lack of ***adequate and full consideration***

## 3. Background on Donor and Donee

The tax is imposed only on gifts made "by any individual." [I.R.C. § 2501(a)(1)]

### a. Donor

A donor can be an individual or an entity. The Regulations take the position that a gift by an entity is taxable to the persons who have a beneficial interest in the entity. Thus, a gift made by a partnership is taxable to the partners in proportion to their partnership interest; and a corporate gift is taxable to the shareholders in proportion to their financial equity. [Treas. Reg. § 25.2511–1(g)] Nonresident aliens ae subject to the tax only on gifts of property located in the United States. [I.R.C. § 2511(a)] Moreover, transfers of ***intangible*** property by nonresident aliens are not subject to the gift tax at all. [I.R.C. § 2501(a)(2)]

#### (1) Beneficial Owner

The transfer must be made by a person who ***owns a beneficial interest*** in the property transferred. Thus, a trustee whose only interest in the property is the legal title that is held in a fiduciary capacity does not make a "gift" when the trustee distributes property from the trust. [Treas. Reg. § 25.2511–1(g)(1)] This is true whether the distribution is required or is pursuant to a discretionary power granted to the trustee. Note, however, that a different result may obtain if the trustee is also a beneficiary of the trust. Moreover, there are different tax consequences if the discretionary power is deemed to be a power of appointment as discussed in Chapter 4.

#### (2) Identity of Donor

The gift tax is imposed upon the ***actual owner*** and transferor of the property, not upon one who is merely a nominal transferor.

e.g. **Example—Indirect Gifts:** The statute expressly provides for the taxation of indirect as well as direct gifts. [I.R.C. § 2511(a)] Thus, if Alex transfers property to Baker on the condition that Baker transfers the property to Charlie, Alex is the actual transferor of the property to Charlie. Or, if Alex transfers $20,000 to Baker on the condition that Baker transfers $10,000 to Charlie, Alex has made a gift of $10,000 each to Baker and Charlie. [Treas. Reg. § 25.2511–1(h)]

e.g. **Example—Reciprocal Trusts:** As in the case of the estate tax, the substance rather than the form of reciprocal or crossed-trusts determines the identity of the transferor. Thus, if Alex transfers $100,000 in trust for Baker's children, and, in consideration of the transfer, Baker creates a similar trust for Alex's children, Alex and Baker will each be treated as having made an indirect gift to their own children. [**Commissioner v. Warner,** 127 F.2d 913 (9th Cir. 1942); **Sather v. Commissioner,** 251 F.3d 1168 (8th Cir. 2001)]

### b. Donee

Although a gift is taxable only if made "***by***" an individual, the statute does not require that the ***donee*** be an individual. Note, however, that a gift to an entity is treated as a gift to the individuals who own beneficial interests in the entity.

(1) **Transfers to a Trust**

A gratuitous transfer to a trust is not treated as a single gift to the trustee but, rather, as a gift to the several trust beneficiaries. The value of each beneficiary's interest, determined actuarially, is the amount of the gift to each of them. [**Helvering v. Hutchings,** 312 U.S. 393 (1941)]

(2) **Gifts to a Corporation or Partnership**

A gift to a corporation has been held to be a gift to the individual shareholders of the corporation, the value of the separate gifts being proportionate to the interests of the shareholders. [**Heringer v. Commissioner,** 235 F.2d 149 (9th Cir.), *cert. denied,* 352 U.S. 927 (1956)] The same rule applies in the case of gifts to a partnership.

**EXAM TIP** GILBERT

If on your exam you see a gift ***by a corporation or partnership,*** keep in mind two things:

(1) Although the gift tax statute appears to cover only gifts made ***"by an individual,"*** the Regulations make sure that gifts by an artificial entity do not escape taxation. The gift is taxable, ***not to the entity*** but to the ***individuals who have a beneficial interest*** in the entity (i.e., the shareholders, partners, etc.), in proportion to their interest in the entity.

(2) Where a gift is made ***to a corporation or partnership,*** the same approach is taken: The ***individual shareholders or partners*** are considered to be the recipients, not the entity.

(3) **Identity of the Donee**

There is no requirement that the donee be identified or ascertained. Thus, a gratuitous transfer to an unascertained person or to persons not yet in being ("to my grandchildren") is a taxable gift. [**Robinette v. Helvering,** 318 U.S. 184 (1943)]

## 4. The Subject Matter of the Gift Under I.R.C. § 2501

The gift tax is imposed upon transfers of ***property.*** [I.R.C. § 2501(a)(1)]

### a. Property—in General

For purposes of the gift tax, property is defined broadly, and in the most comprehensive sense, to include ***any type*** of interest "real or personal, tangible or intangible." [I.R.C. § 2511(a)]

(1) **Equitable Interests**

The transfer of equitable interests, as well as legal interests, is subject to the gift tax. Thus, the transfer by a trust beneficiary of the beneficiary's interest in the trust (if alienable) is a taxable gift of the interest. [Treas. Reg. § 25.2511–1(f)]

(2) **Future Interests**

Gifts of future interests (remainders, reversions, etc.) as well as present interests may be the subject matter of taxable gifts. [Treas. Reg. § 25.2511–1(f)]

#### (3) Contingent Interests

Moreover, as long as the gift is otherwise complete, the fact that the transferred interest is subject to a condition precedent or may be divested upon the happening of a condition subsequent, does not prevent imposition of the tax.

##### (a) Valuation

Contingent interests are valued actuarially. For example, if the gift is contingent on survivorship, actuarial valuation is made on the basis of standard mortality tables. If the condition is one that does not permit actuarial valuation, or if the value of the interest is not otherwise ascertainable, the retained interest will be assigned a value of zero unless the taxpayer meets the burden of establishing the value of the interest. [*See* **Robinette v. Helvering,** 318 U.S. 184 (1943)]

### b. Types or Property

Special attention should be given to the taxation of certain types of property.

#### (1) Foreign Real Estate

A gift of real property located outside of the United States is a taxable gift if it is made by a ***United States citizen or resident.*** [I.R.C. § 2501(a)(1)] Recall that nonresident aliens are subject to the gift tax only on transfers of property located in the United States. [I.R.C. § 2511(a)]

#### (2) Tax-Exempt Securities

The fact that various government bonds and other securities are declared "exempt from taxes" does not affect the taxability of a gift of such securities because the gift tax is a tax on the ***transfer*** of property, not on the property itself. [*See* **Blodgett v. Holden,** 275 U.S. 142 (1927); Treas. Reg. § 25.2511–1(a); *see also* **United States v. Wells Fargo Bank,** 485 U.S. 351 (1988)]

**EXAM TIP** GILBERT

On your exam, don't let the fact that a government bond or security may be "tax-exempt" throw you for a loop. Recall that such securities ***are*** taxable for ***gift tax purposes,*** because the tax is on the ***transfer, not*** the security itself.

#### (3) Debts

##### (a) Checks and Notes

A gratuitous transfer of the donor's own note or check is not taxable until the donee cashes the check or collects the note, because until then it is merely an unenforceable indebtedness of the donor, unsupported by consideration. [Rev. Rul. 67–396, 1967–2 C.B. 351] But a gift of a ***third party's*** note or check would be a taxable transfer of property—a chose in action. [Rev. Rul. 84–25, 1984–1 C.B. 191]

##### (b) Payment of Another's Debt

The payment of the debts of another is as much a gift as actually giving the money to the debtor and, hence, is taxable accordingly.

#### (c) Forgiveness of Indebtedness

The forgiveness of a debt, with the intent to make a gift to the debtor, is a taxable gift to the debtor. [Treas. Reg. § 25.2511–1(a)] However, one who forgives a debt in a bona fide business transaction does not make a taxable gift.

### (4) Promise to Make a Transfer in the Future

The assumption of a legal obligation to transfer property at some time in the future is treated as a ***present*** gift of property. The value of the gift is the present discounted value of the right to receive the amount of property that the donor is obliged to transfer at the future date. [Rev. Rul. 69–347, 1969–1 C.B. 227] Note that this principle applies to a promise supported by adequate ***contractual*** consideration, but not to a promise for consideration that prevents the transfer from being a taxable gift.

### (5) Gifts of Income

The gratuitous transfer of a right to receive income from property is a taxable gift. For example, if a settlor creates a trust to pay the income from the trust principal to a beneficiary for 10 years, there is a gift by the settlor to the beneficiary of the right to receive income for 10 years. The value of the gift is the present discounted value of the right to receive the income payments, determined under actuarial tables prescribed by the Regulations. [*See* Treas. Reg. § 25–2512–5, Table B].

### (6) Life Insurance

One who transfers a life insurance policy to another, or purchases a life insurance policy for another, makes a taxable gift of the value of the insurance contract (its cost or replacement value). [Treas. Reg. § 25.2512–6] Moreover, if the donor thereafter pays the annual premiums on the policy, each premium payment is also a taxable gift. [**Commissioner v. Boeing,** 123 F.2d 86 (9th Cir. 1941)]

### (7) Annuities

Similarly, the gratuitous transfer or purchase of an annuity is a taxable gift. The irrevocable designation of a beneficiary (primary or survivor) is a taxable gift of the value of the benefits, determined actuarially. [Treas. Reg. § 25.2511–2(f)]

### (8) Disposition of Life Estate in Marital Deduction ("QTIP") Property

For purposes of the estate ***and*** gift taxes, the 1981 Act permits certain "qualified terminable interest property" to qualify for the marital deduction to the donor or to the decedent's estate. Recall that, despite the fact that the donee/surviving spouse only has a life estate in such property, the full value of the property will be included in the estate if the spouse dies while still enjoying the life interest. Similarly, if the spouse disposes of the life interest during the spouse's lifetime, the spouse will be treated as having made a gift of the ***full value of the property*** to which the interest relates, not just the life interest itself. [*See* I.R.C. § 2519]

## c. Performance of Personal Services

Although the gratuitous performance of services for another may constitute a "transfer" of a valuable economic benefit, a "gift" of services is ***not subject to the gift tax.*** [*See* Rev. Rul. 56–472, 1956–2 C.B. 21; **Commissioner v. Hogle,** 165 F.2d 352 (10th Cir. 1947)]

#### (1) Rationale—No Estate Tax Avoidance

The theory is that a gift of services, unlike a gift of property, does not deplete the donor's estate and thus is not within the essential purpose of the gift tax. In other words, to prevent avoidance of the estate tax, the gift tax attaches to transfers that reduce or ***deplete*** the donor's estate; however, the transfer taxes do not require a person to ***augment*** her estate by charging for services rendered.

#### (2) Distinguish—Third Party Payment for Services Rendered

On the other hand, if one pays for services rendered by a third party to another, the payment may constitute an indirect gift to the recipient of the services and, thus, be a taxable gift. [Treas. Reg. § 25.2511–1(h)(3)]

### d. Right to Use Property

Although an economic benefit can be conferred by allowing another to use premises rent-free or by lending money to another without charging interest, the authorities had generally held that such arrangements did not result in a taxable gift. The rationale was similar to that of gratuitous personal services. In neither case had the estate been depleted; rather, the donor had simply not undertaken to augment her estate by charging rent or interest. [*See* **Johnson v. United States,** 254 F. Supp. 73 (N.D. Tex. 1966); **Crown v. Commissioner,** 67 T.C. 1060 (1977), *non. acq*. 1978–1 C.B. 2, *aff'd,* 42 A.F.T.R.2d 6503 (1978)]

#### (1) Supreme Court View—Taxable Gift

The United States Supreme Court has held that an ***interest-free loan*** by parents to their son and to a closely held family corporation constituted taxable gifts to the extent of the reasonable value of the use of the money lent. **[Dickman v. Commissioner,** 465 U.S. 330 (1984)] The Court reasoned that the "no obligation to augment one's estate" argument "misses the mark" in this instance. While it is true that one is not obliged to put one's property to productive use, when one "chooses not to waste the use value of money. . .but instead transfers the use to someone else," a taxable event has occurred.

##### (a) Demand Loans

According to the Supreme Court, the fact that the loan is a demand loan may affect the value of the gift but does not gainsay that there has been a taxable gift.

##### (b) Application

The *Dickman* case appears to be applicable to the gratuitous, ***rent-free use*** of tangible property as well as the interest-free use of money.

## 5. Sufficiency of Transfer

For there to be a taxable transfer, there must have been "a ***transfer*** of property." [I.R.C. § 2501(a)(1)]

### a. Form of Transfer

The transfer need not be in any particular form. Any type of transaction by which property rights are passed to or conferred upon another is regarded as a "transfer" for gift tax purposes. [Treas. Reg. § 25.2511–1(a)]

#### (1) Indirect Gifts

Indirect as well as direct transfers are subject to the gift tax. Gifts that are indirectly made whereby property rights or interests are "gratuitously passed or conferred upon another, regardless of the means or device employed." [**Goodman v. Commissioner,** 156 F.2d 218]

A common scenario whereby an indirect gift might occur is where the transferor receives less than adequate and full consideration in money or money's worth from the person receiving the benefit. [I.R.C. § 2512(b)]. [*See* **United States v. Marshall,** 771 F.3d 854]

#### (2) Delivery and Donative Intent

Neither delivery nor donative intent are necessary elements for federal gift tax purposes. [*See* Treas. Reg. § 25.2511–1(g)(1)]. At the same time, however, since a gratuitous transfer will not be effective under property law where these elements are absent, they do bear upon the sufficiency of the transfer for gift tax purposes. This is another illustration of how local law, although not determinative of the federal tax question, affects the tax issue insofar as it establishes the property rights upon which the federal taxes focus.

### b. Complete vs. Incomplete Transfer

One of the essential elements of a taxable gift is that the transfer be ***complete.*** Thus, to the extent that some interest in the property is retained, there is no gift of that interest—even though there may be a taxable gift of other interests in the property. To the extent that the donor has retained powers with respect to the disposition of the property, the gift may be incomplete and not taxable. [*See* Treas. Reg. § 25.2511–2]

#### (1) Categories of Incomplete Transfers

For purposes of analysis, there are three general categories of incomplete transfers:

##### (a) Retained Interests

An interest retained in transferred property is not taxable because it has not been "transferred." Accordingly, the amount of the taxable gift is the value of the property less the value of the retained interest. [**Smith v. Shaughnessy,** 318 U.S. 176 (1943)]

##### (b) Revocable Transfers

In **Burnet v. Guggenheim,** 288 U.S. 280 (1933), the Supreme Court held that the creation of a trust, which was revocable by the settlor without the concurrence of anyone having a substantial adverse interest in the trust was incomplete and nontaxable. This is true whether the power to revoke is expressly reserved or arises by operation of the law (e.g., a transfer by a minor where local law grants the minor a power to rescind within a reasonable time after attaining majority; or a state law that makes all trusts revocable where the settlor has not expressly made them irrevocable).

##### (c) Power to Alter or Amend

Subsequently, the Supreme Court went beyond the *Guggenheim* case and held that the settlor's reservation of the mere power to change the beneficiaries under the trust made the transfer "incomplete" and nontaxable, even though the settlor retained no power to revoke the trust or to become a beneficiary. **[Sanford's Estate v. Commissioner,** 308 U.S. 39 (1939)]

## (2) Nature of Retained Powers That May Render a Gift Incomplete

### (a) Similarities to Estate Tax

In a number of ways, the types of retained powers that will render a transfer incomplete (and nontaxable) for gift tax purposes are similar to those powers to revoke or alter or amend that will render a lifetime transfer incomplete (***and taxable***) for estate tax purposes.

#### 1) Power Must Affect Beneficial Enjoyment

As with the estate tax, the power must be one that ***affects beneficial enjoyment.*** Thus, a purely administrative power will not render the gift incomplete. **[Du Pont v. Commissioner,** 2 T.C. 246 (1943)] However, administrative powers which ***do not*** affect beneficial enjoyment of a trust by its beneficiaries, if held in a fiduciary capacity, will not cause transferred property to be includible in the gross estate. [**Old Colony Trust Co. v. United States,** 423 F.2d 601 (1st Cir. 1970)].

#### 2) Capacity in Which Exercisable

The capacity in which the power is held is immaterial. The gift is incomplete where a power to alter or amend beneficial enjoyment is held by the settlor as trustee. [*See* Treas. Reg. § 25.2511–2]

#### 3) Discretionary vs. Nondiscretionary Powers

In order for the gift to be incomplete, the power must be ***discretionary.*** A mandatory direction to make certain distributions to third parties is not a discretionary power, nor is a power that is governed by ***fixed or ascertainable standards.*** [*See* Treas. Reg. § 25.2511–2(g)]

#### 4) Access to the Power

A discretionary power held by a ***third party*** does ***not*** render the gift incomplete. However, the gift would be incomplete if the settlor retained the right to compel exercise of the power by the trustee or to remove the trustee and appoint a successor trustee. [*See* Treas. Reg. § 25.2511–2(b)]

### (b) Differences from Estate Tax

There are also some substantial differences between the estate tax law and the gift tax law.

#### 1) Power to Affect Time or Manner of Enjoyment

A gift is ***complete for gift tax purposes*** even though the settlor has retained power to affect the time and manner of enjoyment of the property by the designated beneficiaries. [Treas. Reg. § 25.2511–2(d)] The property is ***included in the gross estate*** for estate tax purposes under sections 2036(a)(2) and 2038 even though it is complete for gift tax purposes. [**Lober v. United States,** 346 U.S. 335 (1953); **Struthers v. Kelm,** 218 F.2d 810 (8th Cir. 1955)]

#### 2) Contingent Powers

For purposes of the gift tax, the fact that exercise of the reserved power is contingent upon the happening of an event beyond the grantor's control will not render the gift incomplete. To this extent, gift tax law is similar to the treatment under section 2038 but differs from the estate tax treatment under section 2036. [*Cf.* **Griswold v. Commissioner,** 3 T.C. 909 (1944); Rev. Rul. 54–537,1954–2 C. B. 316]

#### 3) Joint Powers

Unlike the result under sections 2036 and 2038 of the estate tax, a transfer that can be altered or revoked by the settlor only with the consent of a person possessing a ***"substantial adverse interest"*** is a complete transfer and a taxable gift. However, if the co-holder of the power does not possess a substantial adverse interest, the gift is incomplete. [*See* Treas. Reg. § 25.2511–2(e); **Higgins v. Commissioner,** 129 F.2d 237 (1st Cir. 1942)]

##### a) Persons with a "Substantial Adverse Interest"

Ordinarily, the beneficiaries of the trust, as well as their successors in interest, are deemed to have the requisite adverse interest. The trustee, on the other hand, does not have a substantial adverse interest.

###### i. Distinguish—Duty to Support Beneficiary

The cases are split as to whether those under a legal duty to support the beneficiary (but who are not themselves beneficiaries—e.g., parent, guardian) have a substantial adverse interest. [*See* **Fleischmann v. Commissioner,** 40 B.T.A. 672 (1939); **Commissioner v. Prouty,** 115 F.2d 331 (1st Cir. 1940)]

##### b) Amount Taxable

As indicated above, to the extent that the settlor can alter or amend the trust without the concurrence of an adverse party, the gift is incomplete. Accordingly, only the ***value of the adverse party's interest*** is subject to the gift tax.

e.g. **Example:** A transfers property to a trust with income payable to B for life and the remainder to C. If A reserves a right to alter or amend the trust with the consent of B (the life income beneficiary), the value of the life income interest is a taxable gift; but the value of the remainder interest to C is treated as an incomplete and nontaxable transfer since B has no interest adverse to the exercise of a power to revoke the remainder. [*See* **Camp v. Commissioner,** 195 F.2d 999 (1st Cir. 1952)]

| RETAINING POWERS—DIFFERENCES BETWEEN ESTATE TAX AND GIFT TAX | | GILBERT |
|---|---|---|
| **POWER RETAINED BY SETTLOR** | **ESTATE TAX RAMIFICATION** | **GIFT TAX RAMIFICATION** |
| **To Affect Time or Manner of Enjoyment** | The property must be ***included in the decedent's gross estate*** under section 2036(a)(2) or section 2038 | ***Gift is complete,*** and a gift may be imposed |
| **Contingent on an Event Beyond Settlor's Control** | The property must be ***included in the decedent's gross estate*** under section 2036(a)(2) but not under section 2038. | ***Gift is complete,*** and a gift tax may be imposed |
| **Joint Power with Another Whose Interests are Adverse to Those of Settlor** | ***Gift is incomplete,*** and the property must be ***included in the decedent's gross estate*** under either section 2036 or section 2038 | ***Gift is complete,*** and a gift tax may be imposed |

#### (3) Payments Made Under an Incomplete Trust

Although the reservation of a power to alter or revoke may render a transfer on trust "incomplete" and nontaxable at the time of its creation, any distributions of income (or corpus) ***actually made*** to the beneficiaries under such a trust are taxable gifts to the beneficiaries at the time of the distribution. [Treas. Reg. § 25.2511–2(f); **Commissioner v. Warner,** 127 F.2d 913 (9th Cir. 1942)]

#### (4) Relinquishment of Powers

A gift that is incomplete because of powers retained by the donor becomes complete—and taxable—if the donor subsequently relinquishes the power, or the donor's right to exercise it terminates. For example, if A reserves power to revoke a trust "until 10 years from the date this trust is created," the gift is complete and becomes taxable upon expiration of the 10-year period (unless previously revoked). [Treas. Reg. § 25.2511–2(f)]

## 6. Treatment of Concurrent Interests in Property

### a. Creation of Concurrent Interests

In general, the basic rules of the gift tax govern in determining whether there has been a taxable gift. If property is acquired in co-tenancy, there is a taxable gift to the extent that the value of the undivided interest acquired by one co-tenant exceeds what he or she contributed to the purchase price.

#### (1) Exception for Certain Revocable Joint Interests

However, if the concurrent interest is "revocable" by the donor, there is not a complete gift, and thus, no gift tax exposure. Examples of "revocable" concurrent interests include joint bank accounts, joint brokerage accounts, and United States Savings Bonds registered in a form of joint ownership.

#### (2) Prior Law—Exception for Real Property Acquired by Spouses

Prior to 1982 (and after 1954), the creation of a tenancy by the entirety or a joint tenancy between spouses in real property was not treated as a taxable gift to any extent unless the donor-spouse elected to treat it as such at the time the joint tenancy was created. The creation of such joint tenancies after 1981 may constitute taxable gifts, but any gift is completely offset by the marital deduction.

### b. Termination of Concurrent Interests

If the creation of a concurrent interest was a taxable gift, a later severance will not produce a second taxable gift, provided each co-tenant receives his or her share of the property. But a transfer of a concurrent interest by the co-tenants to a third party is treated as a gift by each co-tenant of his or her undivided interest.

#### (1) Special Rule Where Creation of a Joint Tenancy Was Not a Taxable Gift

Where creation of the concurrent interest was not a taxable gift, a severance will be a taxable gift unless the donor receives the entire property or proceeds of its sale.

#### (2) Application of Special Rule

Where co-tenants are husband and wife, the taxable gift that may result from the severance will be fully deductible under the gift tax marital deduction to the extent that there is a technical transfer from one spouse to the other.

## 7. Adequate and Full Consideration

A "gift" is defined under section 2512(b) in terms of the type of consideration that will prevent a transfer from being treated as gratuitous. The requisite consideration is the same as that under the estate tax—"adequate and full consideration in money or money's worth." Thus, a transfer is a taxable gift to the extent that this consideration is absent. [Treas. Reg. § 25.2512–8]

### a. "Money or Money's Worth"

The nature of the consideration required for gift tax purposes is virtually identical to that required under the estate tax.

#### (1) Monetary Terms

Consideration that supports a simple contract may not be sufficient; rather, it must be measurable in ***monetary terms.*** [Treas. Reg. § 25.2512–8] Consideration in the form of love and affection or a promise, which may be upheld under local law for contract purposes, is insufficient for gift tax purposes. [Treas. Reg. § 25.2512–8]

#### (2) More than Mere Detriment

Even though expressible in monetary terms, the consideration must ***move to the transferor.*** A mere detriment to the transferee will not prevent a transfer from falling within the gift tax. [**Commissioner v. Wemyss,** 324 U.S. 303 (1945)] The consideration must be of ***economic benefit*** to the transferor and more than ***mere detriment*** to the transferee.

### b. Effect of Partial Consideration

Section 2512(b) makes it clear that where some consideration is paid (but not "full" consideration) only the excess of the value of the property transferred over the consideration received by the transferor is subject to the gift tax.

### c. Marital Rights as Consideration

Although the gift tax provisions do not specifically preclude the release of dower, curtesy, or other marital rights as "consideration," the Supreme Court has held that the gift and estate tax should be construed together in this regard. Consequently, the Court has read into the gift tax the rule of section 2043(b), which states that the release of such rights is not to be treated as consideration "in money's worth." [**Merrill v. Fahs,** 324 U.S. 308 (1945)]

#### (1) Exception Where Section 2516 Applies

Under section 2516, the transfer of property in ***settlement of marital rights*** is considered to be made for an ***adequate and full consideration*** in money or money's worth provided that it is pursuant to a written agreement, and the divorce takes place within a three-year period beginning on the date of the divorce. Hence, the divorce must take place within one year prior to the divorce or two years after it.

**Example:** On May 19, 2022, a formerly married couple entered into a written settlement agreement that required one spouse to transfer stock worth $500,000 to the other spouse in settlement of marital and property rights. Under section 2516, the divorce must take place between May 19, 2021 and May 19, 2024 for the transfer to be considered as made for an adequate and full consideration in money or money's worth.

### d. Ordinary Course of Business Exception

Transfers that occur in the ordinary course of business are not taxable as gifts.

#### (1) Transfers That Occur in the Ordinary Course of Business

As with the estate tax, Congress did not intend to tax business-motivated transfers as gifts, even where the transfer was made for less than an "adequate and full consideration in money or money's worth." Consequently, transfers that are a product of ***bona fide,*** arm's length negotiations and that are ***free from donative intent*** are not taxable gifts, regardless of the adequacy of consideration. [Treas. Reg. § 25.2512–8]

##### (a) Economic Considerations

If it appears that the transferor was motivated by economic considerations, the transfer will not be taxed as a gift (e.g., employee bonuses, "gifts" to customers or suppliers, sales below market value of property due to necessity, or merely a bad business bargain). [*See, e.g.,* **Anderson v. Commissioner,** 8 T.C. 706 (1947); Rev. Rul. 68–558, 1968–2 C.B. 415]

##### (b) Settlement of Bona Fide Disputes

Amounts paid in settlement of a bona fide dispute are not taxable gifts. This rule has been extended in some cases to the settlement of a will contest. [**Estate of Friedman v. Commissioner,** 40 T.C. 714 (1963)]

##### (c) Family Transactions

The fact that the parties to a transfer are related does not preclude arm's length business negotiations. However, the Service and the courts ***closely scrutinize transfers between family members*** so as to assure that the transaction is not a disguised gift. [*See* Rev. Rul. 73–61,1973–1 C.B. 408; **Giannini v.**

**Commissioner,** 2 T.C. 1160 (1943), *aff'd,* 148 F.2d 285 (9th Cir.), *cert, denied,* 326 U.S. 730 (1945)]

## ELEMENTS OF A TAXABLE GIFT—SUMMARY OF KEY POINTS

GILBERT

### IDENTITY AND CAPACITY OF DONOR AND DONEE

**DONOR**

- Transfer by an ***"individual";*** but in gifts by ***corporations or partnerships, shareholders or partners*** are deemed to be the donors, not the entity
- ***Nonresident Aliens***—tax only on gifts of ***tangible property located in United States***
- ***Competency*** of owner determined by ***local law***
- **Actual owner,** not nominal transferor (e.g., agent, trustee) is donor

**DONEE**

- Does ***not*** have to be an individual
- ***Beneficial owner*** (trust's beneficiaries, corporation's shareholders) is donee

### SUBJECT MATTER OF GIFT

- "Transfer of ***property***"
- ***Any type*** of property, including equitable, future, or contingent interests, and income interests, annuities, life insurance
- ***Foreign property*** subject to tax if donor is a ***citizen or resident of United States***
- ***Tax-exempt securities*** are taxable (tax is on ***transfer***)
- ***Payment of another's debt or forgiveness of debt*** is taxable
- But **gift of personal services is not taxable**

### SUFFICIENCY OF TRANSFER

- "***Transfer*** of property"
- ***Direct or indirect transfers*** subject to tax
- ***Delivery and donative intent not technically necessary*** *but* "gift" is defined under local law and those elements are usually required
- ***Retained interests, revocable transfers, and power to alter*** make transfer **incomplete** and not taxable

### LACK OF CONSIDERATION

- Lack of ***"adequate and full consideration"***
- Consideration must be ***in money or money's worth;*** contract consideration may not be sufficient
- Consideration must ***move to transferor***
- ***Partial consideration*** will exempt part of gift from tax
- ***Ordinary course of business exception*** (no donative intent) applies

# B. Exclusions

## 1. Introductory Analysis

For some donors, they utilize an annual exclusion and the gifts made are entirely excluded from the application of the gift tax. The gifts do not become taxable gifts and do not absorb any portion of the donor's applicable exclusion amount.

## 2. The Annual Exclusion

Once the total value of all gifts made during the year has been determined, the allowable annual exclusion reduces "gross gifts." However, although the annual exclusion of section 2503(b) operates like a deduction, it is an exclusion: If a gift does not exceed the specified amount, no gift tax return need be filed at all, and the gift tax deductions are applied after the annual exclusion against "gross gifts." [I.R.C. §§ 6019(a), 2524]

### a. Amount of Exclusion

The first $10,000 of gifts (indexed for inflation)—***other than gifts of future interests***—given by a donor to any single donee in any calendar year is excluded in the computation of the donor's taxable gifts. [I.R.C. § 2503(b)]

(1) ***If the donor's gift to any particular donee is less than the annual exclusion,*** the balance of the exclusion is lost; there is no carryover to other donees or to any other years.

(2) ***Conversely, if a gift is more than $10,000,*** only the excess is taxable.

(3) ***Commencing in 1998,*** the $10,000 figure is ***indexed for inflation*** in increments of $1,000. The figure was first adjusted in 2002 (to $11,000) and is ***$16,000 as of 2022.***

(4) If the gift is to a spouse who is not a citizen of the United States, an annual exclusion of $100,000 (adjusted for inflation) is allowed instead of a marital deduction. [I.R.C. § 2523(i)(2)] The amount allowed for 2022 is $164,000.

### b. Effect—Optimum Availability for Tax-Free Gifts

Since the exclusion is an ***annual*** amount ***per donee,*** a donor can give away, tax-free, a substantial amount of the donor's estate each year by simply dividing gifts into amounts of under $16,000 each and giving them to a large number of donees. There is no limit on the number of exclusions which a donor can utilize in any year.

**EXAM TIP** GILBERT

For your exam, remember that the annual exclusion for gifts is $16,000 ($32,000 for a married couple) ***per donee.*** Thus, donors can avoid gift taxes by making ***many small*** (under $16,000/$32,000) gifts to ***different*** donees. (*Note:* The $16,000 and $32,000 amounts are the inflation-adjusted figures).

### c. Identity of Donees

Because the annual exclusion is allowed on a ***per donee*** basis, the identity (and number) of donees must be ascertained. But note that the donees need not be identified for a gift to be complete and taxable.

(1) **Gifts Made to a Trust**

Recall that where a gift is made to a trust having several beneficiaries, the beneficiaries, not the trustee, are the real donees of the gift. Thus, the donor is entitled to an annual exclusion for each beneficiary's interest, so long as the interest is a "present" interest. [**Helvering v. Hutchings,** 312 U.S. 393 (1941)]

(2) **Discretionary Distributions**

If distributions (of income or corpus) are to be made in the trustee's discretion, the ***annual exclusion will not be allowed***. This is true even though the trustee's discretion is governed by an ascertainable standard. [**Van Den Wymelenberg v. United States,** 272 F. Supp. 571 (E.D. Wis. 1967)]

---

**EXAM TIP** GILBERT

Be careful to watch for a reciprocal gift issue where, for example, two siblings give the maximum annual exclusion gifts to their own children and ***to each other's children.*** This may be particularly evident when the total gifts across family lines are equal but the amounts per child are not. (A gives B's one child $16,000 and B give A's two children $8,000 each).

---

d. **Present Interest Requirement**

The annual exclusion is not allowed in the case of a gift of a "future interest in property." [I.R.C. § 2503(b)] A present interest is defined as an ***unrestricted right to the immediate use, possession, or enjoyment of property or the income from property.*** [Treas. Reg. § 25.503–3(b)] If the beneficiary's right to income is restricted or deferred in any way, the income right is a future interest and does not qualify for the exclusion.

(1) **What Is a "Future Interest"?**

The Regulations define the term "future interest." [Treas. Reg. § 25.2503–3]

For purposes of the annual exclusion, a future interest is either:

(a) ***Any interest or estate***, whether vested or contingent, that is ***limited*** to commence in use, possession, or enjoyment at a ***future date;*** or

(b) ***Any interest or estate,*** whether vested or contingent, that is ***subject to the will of some other person.***

(2) **Examples of "Present" and "Future" Interests**

(a) **Reversions, Remainders, Possibilities of Reverter, Etc.**

Whether vested or contingent, these are clearly "future" interests. [**United States v. Pelzer,** 312 U.S. 399 (1941)]

(b) **Life Estates**

A life estate is ordinarily a "present" interest. But where it is limited to commence at some time in the future (even one year from the date of the gift), or at the will of another, it is a "future" interest. [*See* **Fondren v. Commissioner,** 324 U.S. 18 (1945)]

### (c) Right to Income from a Trust

A life income interest under an existing trust is a "present" interest, even though the actual distribution of income will occur annually. The value of this interest is the present value of the right to receive income over the term of the interest (for life or a term of years), determined actuarially. [*See* Treas. Reg. § 25.2512–6]

#### 1) Distinguish—Discretionary Distributions

However, if the trustee has discretion concerning the distribution of income to the beneficiary, the interest is a "future" interest for which no annual exclusion is allowed.

#### 2) Right to Corpus

Where the life income beneficiary is also to receive distributions of corpus (whether upon termination of the trust or at the discretion of the trustee), her income interest is a "present" interest, but any right to corpus is a "future" interest. **[Fondren v. Commissioner,** 324 U.S. 18 (1945)]

##### a) Distinguish—Third-Party Distributions

If the trustee has ***discretion to distribute corpus for the benefit of another,*** the income beneficiary's interest is a ***"future"*** interest since her right to income is dependent upon the will of the trustee. By distributing corpus to the third party the trustee can reduce or eliminate the amount of income payable to the income beneficiary.

### (d) Contract Rights

Gifts of bonds or rights under executory contracts are gifts of "present" interests, even though redemption under the contracts will take place in the future; it is the contract right itself which constitutes the subject matter of the gift. Likewise, a gift of insurance or annuity contracts is a present interest. [Treas. Reg. § 20.2503–3(a)]

## (3) Exception to Present Interest Requirement—Gifts to Minors

As explained with the present interest requirement, an ***outright gift to a minor,*** like an outright gift to an adult, is a gift of a present interest even though state law may require the appointment of a guardian to take charge of the property. Similarly, an outright gift to a custodian under the ***Uniform Transfers to Minors Act*** is a gift of a present interest. However, it is usually preferred to make gifts to minors on trust with discretionary distributions of income. This will allow the trustee to distribute such income (or corpus) as may be necessary for the minor's support, but to accumulate any income not needed for support for ultimate distribution at a more mature age. Prior to 1954, the annual exclusion would not be allowed for such discretionary trusts, the gift being of a "future" interest under the general rules of section 2503(b).

### (a) Section 2503(c) Trusts

#### 1) Requirements

An annual exclusion for property transferred to a trust for a minor is authorized if at all times the property and the income therefrom:

a) *May* be expended for the benefit of the minor before the minor attains age 21, ***as long as*** the property and any accumulated income will be distributed to the minor at age 21 or,

b) If the child dies before attaining age 21, the property is distributed to the minor's estate or appointee (under a general power granted to the minor).

#### 2) Minor's Failure to Exercise General Power

The disposition of the trust property under the terms of the trust to another person upon the minor's death before age 21 in default of the exercise of the required power of appointment is permitted. [Treas. Reg. § 25.2503–4(b)(3)]

#### 3) Income Interest May Qualify Separately

The income interest of a minor trust alone may qualify for the exclusion if it meets the section 2503(c) requirements—i.e., if that income is to be used for the benefit of the minor, and any accumulations are to be distributed to the minor at age 21 (or to the minor's estate or appointee, etc.). [**Commissioner v. Herr,** 303 F.2d 780 (3d Cir. 1962)] Thus, under the rule of the *Herr* case, distribution of the principal may be deferred beyond age 21.

#### 4) Power to Require Distribution of Accumulated Income

The property (or income interest) will also qualify for the annual exclusion under section 2503(c) even though the trust instrument provides for continuation of the trust beyond age 21, ***as long as*** the minor is granted a power to require distribution of the property (or accumulated income) upon attaining age 21 and this power persists until the time specified for mandatory distribution. **[Heidrich v. Commissioner,** 55 T.C. 746 (1971)]

### (b) Outright Gifts to Minors

The IRS ruled in Revenue Ruling 54–400 that an outright gift to a minor, whether it is with or without the appointment of a guardian, is not a future interest and qualifies for the annual exclusion. The gift is of present enjoyment unless the use or enjoyment is restricted in some manner.

### (c) *Crummey* Trusts

#### 1) Demand Rights

In the landmark case of **Crummey v. Commissioner,** 397 F.2d 82 (9th Cir. 1968), grantors created trusts for the benefit of their children. Under the terms of the trusts, income was to be accumulated until the children reached age 21, but the trustee had the discretion to make distributions. In addition, each child had the right to "demand" withdrawals. The court allowed the annual exclusion even though no guardian had been appointed because the children had the "right to enjoy" the payments.

#### 2) Significant Opportunity for Tax Savings

The use of *Crummey* demand rights can result in substantial tax savings. For example, in **Mikel v. Commissioner,** T.C. Memo. 2015–64, the court allowed annual exclusions totaling $1,440,000 for *Crummey* rights given to 60 trust beneficiaries even though the trust contained a mandatory arbitration clause and an *in terrorem* provision that discouraged the beneficiaries from challenging the trustees' discretionary powers.

#### 3) Contingent Beneficiaries

The court in **Cristofani v. Commissioner,** 97 T.C. 74 (1991), allowed annual exclusions for contingent beneficiaries with *Crummey* rights.

### (d) Annual Exclusion for Contributions to 529 Accounts

The annual exclusion is allowed for contributions to a 529 saving plan. Further, the Code permits an account owner to elect to spread the contribution over five years for gift tax purposes. [I.R.C. § 529(c)(2)(B)] For example, assume that the owner transfers $80,000 to the 529 Plan in 2022, and the section 2503(b) annual exclusion is $16,000. The taxpayer can apply the annual exclusion for the next five years to shelter the entire gift from gift taxation. However, if the owner dies within five years, the portion of the transfer allocable to the post-death period will be included in her gross estate. [I.R.C. § 529(c)(4)(C)]

## e. Annual Exclusion Is Disallowed if the Present Interest Is Not Ascertainable

Closely related to the requirement that the gift not be a future interest is the requirement that the value of the present interest be "ascertainable." [Treas. Reg. § 25.2503(c)] Essentially, this means that there must be no ***condition*** or ***power*** that could operate to impair or destroy the gift. [**Geller v. Commissioner,** 9 T.C. 484 (1947)]

### (1) Discretionary Power in Trustee

If a trustee is given ***discretionary power to accumulate or distribute income,*** the income interest is a ***future interest.*** [*See* **Prejean v. Commissioner,** 354 F.2d 995 (5th Cir. 1966)] Likewise, if the trustee is given power to sell assets and apportion proceeds among several beneficiaries, the income interests are future interests. [**Van Den Wymelenberg v. United States,** 272 F. Supp. 571 (E.D. Wis. 1967); Rev. Rul. 55–303,1955–1 C.B. 471] In both cases, the income interests have no ascertainable value because the trustee's power could impair or destroy beneficial enjoyment.

### (2) Conditional Gifts

Even though an interest (on trust or otherwise) is "vested," if it can be divested upon the happening of some condition and the probability of the condition occurring cannot be determined actuarially, the interest has ***no ascertainable value*** and no annual exclusion will be allowed. For example, if property is transferred on trust with income to be paid "to A for life or until A remarries," the income interest will not qualify for the annual exclusion.

### (3) Unproductive Property

Sometimes it is impossible to ascertain the value of a gift because of the nature of the gift itself. For example, if A transfers stock on trust with directions to pay the income to C, the income interest is a present interest. But, if the stock is in a closely held corporation that has never paid dividends and seems unlikely to do so in the future, and if the trustee is directed to retain the shares [i.e., is precluded from making the property "productive"), there is no way of ascertaining the present value of the income interest and, hence, no annual exclusion will be allowed. [*See* **Stark**

**v. United States,** 477 F.2d 131 (8th Cir. 1973)] Similarly, no annual exclusion was allowed for an outright gift of an interest in a limited liability company (LLC) where the operating agreement foreclosed any current economic benefit and foreclosed the right to transfer the ownership. **[Hackl v. Commissioner,** 118 T.C. 279 (2002), *aff'd* 335 F.3d 664 (7th Cir. 2003)]

## 3. Exclusion for Certain Transfers for Educational or Medical Expenses

The 1981 Act amended section 2503 to allow an ***unlimited*** exclusion for payments made to an institution or person furnishing education or medical services to another person. [I.R.C. § 2503(e)] The person receiving the educational or medical services need not be related to the donor.

### a. Limitations—Education

The exclusion is limited to ***tuition*** paid to a ***qualified educational organization*** (described in section 170(b)(1)(A)(ii)) for the ***education or training*** of an individual. [I.R.C. § 2503(e)(2)(A)] According to the Committee Reports, the exclusion is permitted for either full-time or part-time students, but is limited to direct tuition cost (i.e., no exclusion for books, supplies, dormitory fees, etc.).

e.g. **Example:** A grandmother was looking for a way to provide educational benefits to her granddaughter and save on gift tax without utilizing her applicable exclusion amount. The grandmother paid her granddaughter's tuition directly to the school and was able to utilize this education exclusion. She did not need to file a gift tax return to report this gift.

### b. Limitations—Medical Services

The payments must be made directly to the person or institution that provides the medical care. Hence, reimbursements to the patient do not qualify. Moreover, the exclusion is limited to costs or expenses for medical services defined in section 213 (e.g., for diagnosis, care, mitigation, treatment, or prevention of disease). Also, no exclusion is allowed for amounts that are reimbursed by insurance.

# C. Deductions

## 1. Introduction

Once the amount of "gross gifts" has been determined, there are two possible gift tax deductions that may be taken in arriving at "net" or "taxable gifts," within the meaning of section 2503(a): (i) the ***charitable deduction*** [I.R.C. § 2522]; and (ii) the ***marital deduction*** [I.R.C. § 2523].

## 2. The Charitable Deduction

A United States ***citizen or resident*** is allowed an ***unlimited*** deduction for the ***full value*** of all property transferred to a public, religious, charitable, scientific, literary, or educational institution that meets the tests specified in the statute. [I.R.C. § 2522]

### a. Nonresident Aliens

A nonresident alien's right to this deduction is limited. Basically, when the donee is a corporation, a deduction is allowed only if the corporation is ***domestic,*** and, when the donee is a trust, foundation, etc., the gifts must be used ***within the United States*** exclusively for charitable purposes. [I.R.C. § 2522(b)]

### b. Requirements

The requirements for allowance of the gift tax charitable deduction are virtually identical to those of the estate tax charitable deduction.

#### (1) Donee Must Be a "Charitable Object"

Only gifts to certain types of identified organizations for certain identified charitable purposes qualify for the deduction. [I.R.C. § 2522(a); ***and compare*** I.R.C. § 2055(a)] These purposes include an entity operating for religious, charitable, scientific, literary or educational purposes. There are other purposes listed that make a charity "qualified." [I.R.C. § 2522(a)(3)]

#### (2) Limitations on Amount

The amount of the deduction is limited to the value of the property transferred to the charity. [I.R.C. § 2522(a)] Additionally, in determining the amount of the charitable gift, any allowable annual exclusion related to the gift must be taken into account. [I.R.C. §§ 2524, 2503(b)] It is important to note that this is different from charitable deductions for income tax purposes under section 170. In that case, the percentage limitation is based on the adjusted gross income.

e.g. **Example:** If $26,000 was given outright to a charity in 2022, the amount of the gift eligible for the charitable deduction would be $10,000—the value of the gift less the $16,000 annual exclusion; and the amount of the charitable deduction would be limited to $10,000. Otherwise, of course, there would be a "double deduction" with respect to $16,000.

### c. Split-Interest Gifts

Just as in the case of the estate tax, the gift of a remainder to a charity after an intervening (noncharitable) life estate or term of years (a "charitable remainder gift"), or the gift of a term of years to a charity followed by a remainder to a noncharitable object (a "charitable lead gift") must be made in certain specified forms to qualify for the deduction.

#### (1) Specified Forms

Such split-interest gifts must be in the form of an "annuity trust," a "unitrust," or a "pooled income fund." [I.R.C. § 2522(c)(2)]

#### (2) Exceptions

These specific forms are not required in the case of an undivided interest in property, or a remainder interest in a personal residence or a farm. [I.R.C. § 2522(c)(2)]

### d. Partial Versus Outright Gifts

In the case of an outright gift to a charity, the charitable deduction allowed on the property is the value of the entire property. In contrast, if anything less than the full interest in the property is given to charity, then the value of the property transferred (even if that is the partial property) is the value of the charitable deduction allowed.

e.g. **Example:** The donor has a life estate in an item of property. The donor gives a nephew the life estate while giving the remainder to a charity. In this case, the value of the remainder would be deductible under the charitable deduction.

## 4. The Marital Deduction

In computing "net gifts," a deduction is also allowed for the value of any property transferred by the taxpayer to the taxpayer's spouse. [I.R.C. § 2523] It is important to note that following the landmark case of **United States v. Windsor,** 570 U.S. 744 (2013), the marital deduction is allowed for legally married same-sex couples.

### a. Background

As in the case of the estate tax marital deduction, the gift tax marital deduction was enacted in 1948 to give residents of noncommunity property states "tax-splitting" advantages similar to those enjoyed by spouses who reside in community property states. The underlying rationale for the allowance is now to exempt all intraspousal transfers from tax, which is accomplished by allowing a ***100% deduction*** for gifts by one spouse to another. The marital deduction provides large tax savings for spouses through the proper utilization of the deduction.

### b. Requirements

The gift tax marital deduction is governed generally by the same rules and concepts as the estate tax marital deduction. Indeed, the differences that do exist are because of the practical context in which the transfer is made, not because of any underlying theoretical difference (i.e., the gift tax marital deduction applies to transfers made by a living donor, whereas the estate tax marital deduction is applicable to a deceased spouse's estate).

#### (1) Citizenship

The donee must be a citizen of the United States. [I.R.C. § 2523(i)]. The marital deduction is denied in the case where the donee spouse is not a citizen of the United States.

##### (a) Rationale

If the donee spouse is not a citizen of the United States, the property given to the donee spouse may escape estate and gift taxation when it leaves the marital unit.

e.g. **Example:** Taylor made a gift of stock worth $1 million to her husband, Joseph, in 1984. Taylor was a United States citizen and resident at the time of the gift. Joseph resided in the United States but was a French citizen at the time of the gift. Taylor claimed the marital deduction of $1 million with respect to the gift. Several years later, Taylor died, and Joseph returned to France. He died two years later devising the stock to their daughter. Since he was not a U.S. citizen and died in France, the $1 million devise escaped estate taxation. Note that if Taylor had made the gift after July 14,1988, the marital deduction would have been denied.

#### (2) The Interest Must Be a "Deductible Interest"

For purposes of the gift tax, any completed gift to the donor's spouse will be a gift of a deductible interest, unless it is a nondeductible terminable interest. A terminable interest is an interest in property that terminates upon the death of the surviving spouse or upon the occurrence of some other event.

| REQUIREMENTS FOR THE MARITAL DEDUCTION | GILBERT |
|---|---|
| **THE BASIC REQUIREMENTS FOR THE MARITAL DEDUCTION ARE:** | |
| ☑ The ***donee*** must be a ***United States citizen*** at the time the gift is made | |
| ☑ If the donee is ***not*** a United States citizen, the spouse receives a ***$100,000 annual exclusion adjusted for inflation*** ($164,000 for 2022) | |
| ☑ The donee ***must have been married*** at the time of the gift | |
| ☑ The interest ***must be a deductible interest*** | |

#### (a) Community Property

Under prior law, a gift of the donor's interest in community property was not a gift of a deductible interest. This was because the spouses already enjoyed transfer tax relief in relation to community property. With the enactment of the 100% marital deduction, however, community property qualifies as a "deductible interest" to the same extent as separate property.

### (3) The "Nondeductible Terminable Interest Rule" Under the Gift Tax

The basic rules, definitions, and rationale of the nondeductible terminable interest rule under the gift tax are the same as under the estate tax discussed Chapter Two. [I.R.C. § 2523(b)–(f)]

#### (a) Definition of Terminable Interest

As in the case of the estate tax, a terminable interest is defined as one where "on the lapse of time, on the occurrence of an event or contingency, or on the failure of an event or contingency to occur, such interest transferred to the spouse will terminate or fail. . . ." [I.R.C. § 2523(b)]

#### (b) Nondeductible Terminable Interests

In addition to the situation where an interest in the same property was transferred by the donor to a third party (the ownership of which would allow the third party to possess or enjoy the property after the interest of the donee-spouse terminates), a terminable interest is a nondeductible for gift tax purposes where:

1) ***The donor retains*** an interest that would allow the donor to possess or enjoy any part of the property after the donee-spouse's interest terminates [I.R.C. § 2523(b)(1)]; or

2) ***The donor*** immediately after the transfer ***has the power to appoint an interest*** in the property "which he can exercise in such a manner that the appointee may possess or enjoy any part of such property after such termination. . . ." [I.R.C. § 2523(b)(2)] It ***does not*** matter whether this retained power is exercisable by the donor alone or in conjunction with ***any*** person, or that the power cannot be exercised until ***after the lapse*** of some time period, or ***only*** upon the occurrence or nonoccurrence of some event or contingency.

### (c) Joint Interests

Although nondeductible terminable interests generally provide that the donee-spouse cannot possess a concurrent interest in the property, the Code provides that the creation of a transfer of an undivided interest to the donee-spouse as joint tenant with right of survivorship with the donor is a deductible interest, despite the fact that the donor possesses an interest in the property. [I.R.C. § 2523(d)]

#### 1) Rationale

The donee spouse does possess a present one-half undivided interest in the property (analogous to a life estate) and, in the case of a joint tenancy, can sever the joint tenancy, thereby extinguishing the right of survivorship (analogous to a power to appoint the property to herself).

#### 2) Note

Even though a tenant by the entirety may not have a power of severance, this "exception" also applies to tenancies by the entirety. [I.R.C. § 2523(d)]

## (4) Exceptions to the Terminable Interest Rule

### (a) Life Estate with Power of Appointment Exception

The gift tax allows for the same "life estate with the power of appointment" exception that is recognized under the estate tax. [I.R.C. § 2523(e)] Accordingly, an interest transferred to one's spouse will qualify for the gift tax marital deduction if:

1. ***The donee spouse is entitled to all of the income*** (or to a specific portion thereof) ***for life,*** payable at least annually;
2. ***The donee spouse has a power to appoint the interest*** (or a specific portion thereof) ***to the donee spouse, or to the donee spouse's estate*** (during life or by will, or both). It is important to note that the donee-spouse's power to appoint the interest is narrower than the general power of appointment under I.R.C. § 2041;
3. ***The power is exercisable by the donee spouse alone and in all events;*** and
4. ***No other person has a power to appoint*** the interest to ***any person other than the donee spouse.***

### (b) Exception for "QTIP" Interests

The gift tax allows a deduction for "qualified terminable interest property" given to one's spouse. [I.R.C. § 2523(f)] This exception to the nondeductible terminable interest rule likewise tracks the QTIP exception under the estate tax.

#### 1) Requirements

Property transferred to one's spouse will qualify for the gift tax marital deduction if:

**a)** The donee spouse receives a qualifying income interest for life in property transferred from the donor spouse; and

b) The donor spouse makes an election to have the property qualify for the QTIP treatment, thus, taking advantage of the marital deduction. [*See* I.R.C. § 2523(f)(2), (3)]

2) **Election**

The required election is made by the donor spouse on the gift tax return for the calendar year in which the interest is transferred. Once made, the election is irrevocable. [I.R.C. § 2523(f)(4)]

3) **Effect—Property Ultimately Taxed to Donee**

Such QTIP property will be subject to estate taxes in the estate of the donee spouse or, if the life interest is disposed of before death, as a taxable gift made by the donee-spouse. [*See* I.R.C. §§ 2044 and 2519]

#### (c) Exception for Certain Charitable Remainder Trusts

The gift tax now allows a deduction, coordinate with that allowed under the estate tax, for the value of the ***income*** interest given to one's spouse in a qualified charitable remainder annuity trust or unitrust. [I.R.C. § 2523(g)]

#### (d) Exception for Income to Surviving Spouse

The gift tax allows a deduction where all the income goes to the surviving spouse for life and the spouse died within six months of the donor spouse's death.

## c. Maximum Allowed for Marital Deduction

### (1) Present Law

The gift tax marital deduction is allowed for the full value (100%) of the property transferred to the donee spouse, subject to two limitations:

#### (a) Net Value

If the property is subject to an encumbrance, or if the donee incurs some obligation as a condition of receiving the gift, the deduction is limited to the ***net*** value of the property (its value less the amount of the encumbrance or obligation).

#### (b) Annual Exclusion

The marital deduction must be reduced by the amount of any allowable annual exclusion. [I.R.C. § 2524]

### (2) Gifts Made in 1977 Through 1981

Prior to the 1976 Tax Reform Act, the maximum gift tax marital deduction was one-half of the value of the deductible interest given by one spouse to the other (***before*** taking the annual exclusion—then $3,000). The 1976 Tax Reform Act liberalized the gift tax marital deduction to a certain extent. Under this Act, the first $100,000 of cumulative gifts given to a spouse after December 31,1976, was entirely tax-free; the second $100,000 of cumulative gifts was fully taxable (after the annual exclusion); and the former limitation of 50 percent of value applied with respect to cumulative gifts in excess of $200,000. [I.R.C. § 2523(a)]

**Example:** W gave her spouse, H, $150,000 in 1977. The amount of the marital deduction would be $100,000. The first $100,000 of the gift was fully deductible and the excess ($47,000 after application of the annual exclusion) was fully taxable. If W then gave H $100,000 in 1978, W could claim a marital deduction of $23,500: The first $53,000 of the gift was fully taxable; and one-half of the cumulative gifts in excess of $200,000 ($47,000) was deductible.

# Chapter Four

# Miscellaneous Gift Tax Rules

CONTENTS PAGE

# Chapter Approach

This chapter describes the rules related to powers of appointment, disclaimers, and gift splitting and their gift tax implications. With proper planning, spouses can reduce exposure to gift taxation by strategically splitting gifts and disclaiming interests to maximize the basic exclusion amount.

# A. Powers of Appointment

A power of appointment is a power of disposition over property. An owner of property can give a power to a third person (a powerholder) through deed or will. Powers are typically classified as general or nongeneral (limited or special) powers.

Under technical property law, the exercise or nonexercise of a power of appointment is not a "transfer" by the holder of the power to the appointees or takers in default; rather, the property is deemed to pass from the original donor of the power. Thus, just as with the estate tax, a special statute is required to reach property subject to a power of appointment.

## 1. General Powers of Appointment

Only general powers of appointment are subject to the gift tax whether exercised or not. [I.R.C. § 2514(a), (b)] This is consistent with the estate tax rules. If a powerholder possesses a general power of appointment exercisable at death, it is included in the powerholder's gross estate under section 2041.

### a. General Powers of Appointment

The powerholder of a general power of appointment is akin to having full ownership of the property.

(1) Under section 2514(c), a general power is any power that is exercisable in favor of:

  (a) **the powerholder;**

  (b) **the powerholder's creditor;**

  (c) **the powerholder's estate;** or

  (d) **creditors of the powerholder's estate**

(2) The definition of a general power for gift tax purposes is the same as that for estate tax purposes. [*See* I.R.C. § 2041(b)(1)]

### b. Powers Limited by the Ascertainable Standard

Powerholders with the power to consume or invade the property for their own benefit hold a general power of appointment. However, such power is ***not considered "general"*** if it is limited by an ascertainable standard relating to the powerholder's health, education, support, or maintenance. [I.R.C. § 2514(c)(1); Treas. Reg. § 20.2041–1(c)(2)]

### c. Powers Exercisable in Conjunction with Another Person

If a powerholder holds a power created on or before October 21, 1942 that is exercisable in conjunction with any other person, it is not a general power of appointment. [I.R.C. § 2514(c)(2)] If a powerholder holds a power created after October 21, 1942 that is exercisable in conjunction with the creator of the power or someone with a substantial adverse interest, it is not considered a general power of appointment.

**Example:** A creates a trust after October 21, 1942 with B as the income beneficiary and C as the beneficiary of the corpus. Under the terms of the trust, B is given the power to withdraw $20,000 from the corpus annually with C's consent. B does not have a general power of appointment because C has a substantial adverse interest.

#### d. Exercise or Release of General Powers of Appointment

If the powerholder of a general power of appointment exercises or releases the power, the powerholder is subject to gift taxable. [I.R.C. § 2514(a) and (b)] This rule applies only to powers created after October 21, 1942. Powers created on or before October 21, 1942 are taxable to the powerholder only if they are exercised.

#### e. Lapse of General Powers of Appointment

A lapse of a power of appointment created after October 21, 1942 is considered to be a release of the power. This rule is subject to the so-called "5 and 5" power.

##### (1) 5 and 5 Power

The "5 and 5" power provides that a ***lapse*** of a power of appointment during any calendar year is ***considered a release*** subject to the gift tax ***only to the extent that the property that can be appointed exceeds the greater of $5,000 or five percent of the aggregate value of the property*** subject to the power. [*See* I.R.C. § 2514(e) and Treas. Reg. § 25.2514–3(c)(4)] As a result, a settlor/donor should limit the powerholder's withdrawal rights to the greater of $5,000 or five percent for a stated period of time to avoid subjecting the powerholder to the gift tax.

**Example:** A trust has a corpus of $100,000. The beneficiary has the right to withdraw $5,000 of the trust corpus each year. The beneficiary is not subject to gift tax because the withdrawal right is limited to $5,000 and 5% of the aggregate value of the property subject to the power of appointment.

**Example:** A trust has a corpus of $200,000. The beneficiary has the right to withdraw $25,000 of the trust corpus each year. The beneficiary is considered to have made a gift of $15,000 to the corpus beneficiary, the extent to which the withdrawal right exceeds the greater of $5,000 or 5 percent of the aggregate value of the trust corpus. In this example, 5 percent of the corpus is $10,000. To avoid gift taxation, the withdrawal right should have been limited to $10,000.

## 2. Nongeneral Powers of Appointment

Nongeneral powers of appointment escape taxation entirely even if exercised. Nongeneral powers of appointment are often called "special" powers or "limited" powers. Whether the powerholder exercises, releases, or allows the power to lapse, the nongeneral power of appointment will have no gift tax consequences under section 2514 or estate tax consequences under section 2041.

#### a. Tax consequences of Powerholder's Disposition of Corpus on Income Interest

The Internal Revenue Service has maintained that a powerholder's exercise of a nongeneral power of appointment over the trust corpus in which the powerholder has an unqualified income interest is a taxable gift of the balance of the income interest. [Treas. Reg. § 25.2514–1(b)(2)] The Tax Court upheld this position in **Estate of Regester v.**

**Commissioner,** 83 T.C. 1 (1984), which declined to follow a much earlier decision to the contrary in **Self v. United States,** 142 F. Supp. 939 (Ct. Cl. 1956).

### b. State Law over Nongeneral Power of Appointment

Although an instrument, such as a trust or will, may denote that a power of appointment is a nongeneral power of appointment, the court evaluating the power will look to the substance of the power, not the form. Similarly, a state law may denote the power as a nongeneral power but substance over form controls. [*See* **Martin v. United States,** 780 F.2d 1147 (4th Cir. 1986)]

# B. Disclaimers

A disclaimer (or renunciation) is an unqualified refusal to accept a transfer of property. As discussed under the estate tax rules, although other persons may acquire an interest in the property as a result of the disclaimer, an effective disclaimer is ***not a "transfer." Rationale:*** No property interest was ever acquired by the disclaimant and, thus, no interest passes from the disclaimant to another. [Treas. Reg. § 25.2511–1(c)] The interest will be considered to have passed directly from the transferor to the recipient of the interest as a result of the disclaimer.

If the disclaimer does not meet the requirements under section 2518, but it is valid for state law purposes, the disclaimant will be considered to have made a gift to the recipient of the interest.

## 1. Requirements for a Qualified Disclaimer

### a. The Disclaimer Must Be in Writing

For a disclaimer to be qualified, the disclaimer ***must be in writing.*** The writing must "identify" the disclaimed interest, and the disclaimant must sign the disclaimer. [Treas. Reg. § 25.2518–2(b)(2)]

### b. Within Nine Months of the Transfer

The disclaimer must be ***received by the transferor*** (or the transferor's estate) ***within nine months*** of the date of the transfer creating the interest (or within nine months of the date on which the disclaimant reaches age 21). [I.R.C. § 2518(b)(2)] The disclaimant's knowledge is not a factor in determining when the nine-month period.

There is a distinction between testamentary transfers and inter vivos transfers with respect to the nine-month period. For testamentary transfers, the nine-month period begins on the decedent's death. For inter vivos transfers, the period begins when the transfer is complete for gift tax purposes. [Treas. Reg. § 25.2518–2(c)(3)]

### c. Nonacceptance of Any Benefit

***If the disclaimant accepts any benefit from the interest, then a qualified disclaimer cannot occur.*** Acceptance consists of "acts indicative of acceptance" including "using the property or the interest in the property; accepting dividends, interests, or rent from the property." [Treas. Reg. § 25.2518–2(d)(1)]

e.g. **Example:** A is the beneficiary of multiple distributions from B's trust. The first distribution occurs upon B's death. A accepts the first distribution but three months later (still within the nine-month window) writes a disclaimer as to A's interest in the trust. This disclaimer is not a qualified disclaimer under section 2518 because A has already accepted a benefit from the interest in B's trust.

A disclaimer may still be a qualified disclaimer if a portion of the property can qualify even if the beneficiary accepts the other property. [Treas. Reg. § 25.2518–3(1)(ii)] A qualified disclaimer can also be ***separately applied to each interest*** in property. [*See* Rev. Rul. 2005–36, 2005–1 CB 1368 (disclaimant's acceptance of income from required distribution of an IRA did not prevent the disclaimant from disclaiming the balance of the IRA)]

### d. No Control over Disposition of Disclaimed Interest

As a result of the refusal to accept property, the interest must ***pass to a person other than the disclaimant without any direction*** on the part of the disclaimant. [I.R.C. § 2518(b)(4)]

Under the 1978 Act, section 2518 was amended to provide that a disclaimer will be a ***"qualified disclaimer,"*** even though, as a result of the disclaimer, ***an interest passes to the disclaiming spouse*** of the decedent. The purpose of this amendment is to allow a surviving spouse to disclaim (e.g., an absolute bequest, but take a life estate under the nonmarital portion of the will). Disclaimers allow a surviving spouse to adjust the amount of the marital deduction or take advantage of an unused applicable credit amount in the estate of the first spouse to die.

Estate plans frequently include a ***"bypass trust"*** (also known as a "family trust" or "credit shelter trust") to take advantage of the applicable exclusion amount of the first spouse to die. The bypass trust may provide life income and limited principal invasion rights for the surviving spouse without violating section 2518(b)(4).

## 2. Partial Disclaimers

Initially, there was concern that the requirement that a person not accept "the interest or ***any*** of its benefits" might prevent a partial disclaimer for federal tax purposes—even though such a partial disclaimer was valid under the local law. However, the Internal Revenue Service has determined that, subject to certain limitations, partial disclaimers are valid for federal tax purposes. [*See* Treas. Reg. § 2518–3(a); Priv. Ltr. Rul. 7913119] A partial disclaimer, however, must be of an undivided portion of an interest and cannot be of a remainder interest. [**Walshire v. United States,** 288 F.3d 342 (8th Cir. 2002)]

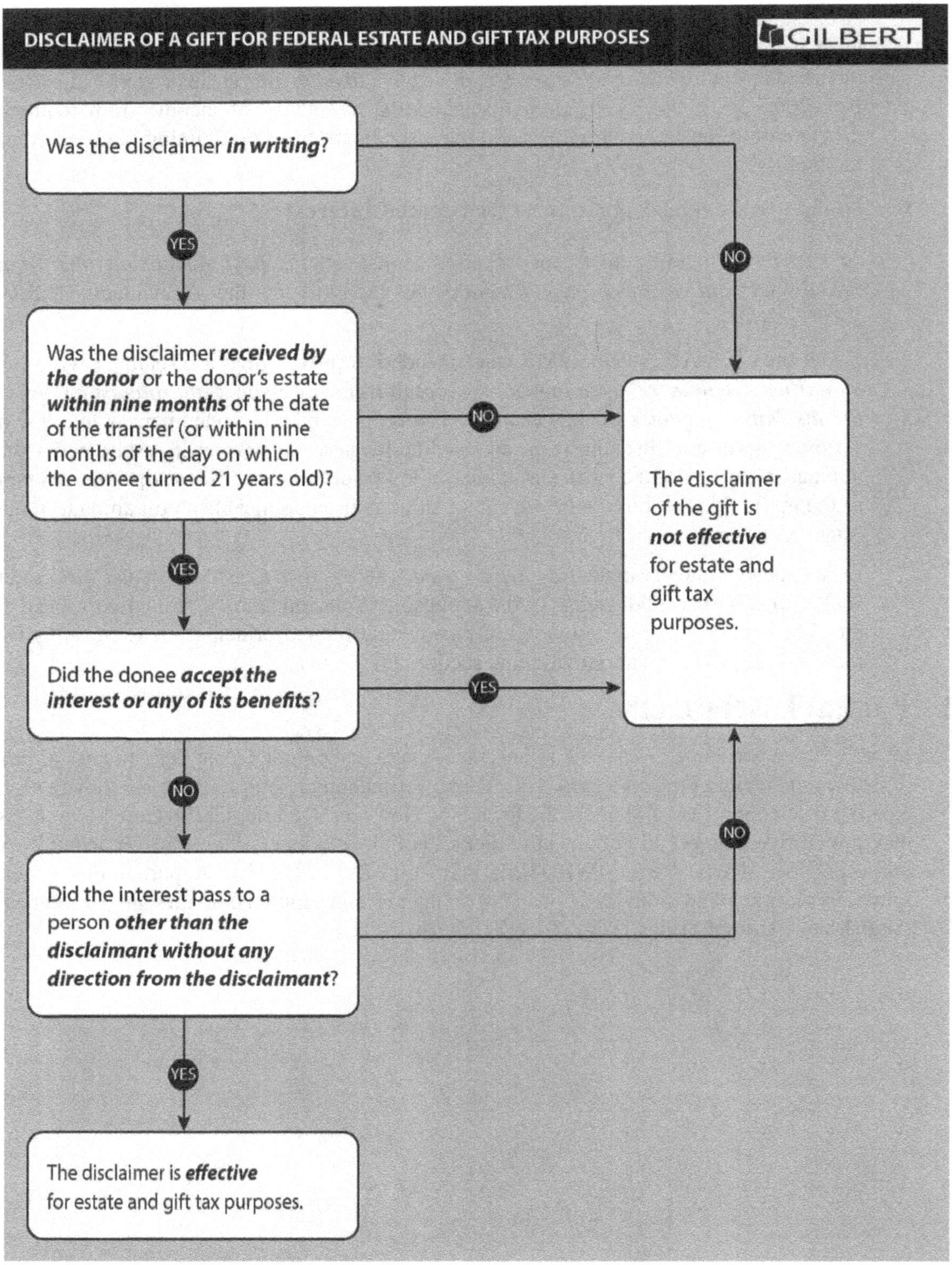


# C. Gift Splitting

## 1. Gift Splitting Between Spouses—General Rule

I.R.C. § 2513 permits spouses by mutual consent to elect to treat gifts as having been made one-half by each spouse. If such consent is elected (on the gift tax return(s) timely filed by the spouse(s)), the donor spouse is able to reduce potential gift tax exposure because all gifts made during the year will be subject to the other spouse's annual exclusion and applicable exclusion amount.

## 2. Automatic for Community Property

Since each spouse in community property states has a vested one-half interest in the community property, a gift of such property is treated as a gift by ***each*** spouse of his or her one-half interest. Thus, the gift is "split," and one-half of the value of the property is exposed to the separate gift taxation for each spouse. Moreover, each spouse is entitled to a separate annual exclusion, thereby enabling the spouses to jointly give a total of $32,000 (inflation-adjusted figure for 2022) tax-free each year to each donee. Section 2513, enacted in 1948, allows for the same tax advantage when the separate property of one spouse is transferred by gift (whether or not the spouse resides in a community property or common law state).

## 3. Requirements for Gift Splitting

For a gift to meet the requirements of gift splitting, the spouses must be married at the time of the gift and if divorced or widowed, the spouse cannot remarry during the balance of the calendar year, both spouses must commit to splitting all gifts for the calendar year, both spouses must be a resident or citizen of the United States at the time of the gift, and the donor spouse cannot give the other spouse a general power of appointment with respect to the property transferred. [*See* I.R.C. § 2513]

e.g. **Example:** If A transfers property on trust for B for life, remainder to C, but grants the spouse, D, a power to appoint the property to whomever the spouse wishes, the gift may not be "split."

### a. No Cherry Picking Permitted

The consent must be applied to ***all*** gifts made by each spouse during the calendar year in question. [Treas. Reg. § 25.2513–1]

### b. Exception for Gifts to Spouse

Gift splitting is allowed only for gifts by a spouse to a ***third party.*** The statute does not reach gifts made between spouses.

### c. Joint and Several Liability

A spouse who consents to gift splitting is subject to joint and several liability for the donor spouse's gift tax liability, if any, in the year that the gifts are split. [I.R.C. § 2513(d)]

### d. Impact upon Estate Tax

For purposes of determining the amount included in the gross estate, the provisions of section 2513 are inapplicable. For example, if A released a power to revoke a revocable trust within three years of death, the full value of that property would be included in A's estate under section 2035 even though A's spouse consented to "split" the gift.

# Chapter Five
# Valuation

| CONTENTS | PAGE |
|---|---|

# Chapter Approach

Although, as a practical matter, valuation problems and controversies absorb a great deal of professional time, you will probably see this issue only peripherally in your estate and gift tax course; the primary emphasis is on the substantive law of the transfer tax system. However, understanding how valuation works is important to fully grasping the determination of estate, gift, and generation-skipping taxes.

# A. Introductory Comments

## 1. Valuation of Estates and Gifts

Both the estate and gift taxes are measured by the "fair market value" of the property transferred. Thus, the valuation questions under each of the transfer taxes are essentially the same. However, certain special rules (e.g., concerning the valuation date and the property subject to tax) apply separately and sometimes differently for estate and gift tax purposes.

The valuation method for generation-skipping taxes is generally the same as the method employed for determination of gift and estate tax.

## 2. Valuation Issues Addressed

As with most estate and gift tax courses, this Summary addresses three categories of valuation issues:

a. ***Rules of law*** relating to valuation under the estate and gift taxes;

b. An introduction to ***valuation methods;*** and

c. A review of the valuation of ***certain specific types of property.***

# B. Rules of Law Relating to Valuation

## 1. Introduction

While valuation is essentially a factual determination, there are certain rules of law that must also be considered.

## 2. Valuation Date

As a general proposition, it is the value of the property ***at the date of the transfer*** that is critical. This value is determined by value of the property passing from donor. [I.R.C. § 2512(a)]

### a. Gift Tax

A taxable gift is valued for gift tax purposes as of the date the gift is made. Thus, the issue is dependent upon the substantive rules relating to when a gratuitous transfer is complete. [I.R.C. § 2512(a); **Goodman v. Commissioner,** 156 F.2d 218 (2d Cir. 1946)] Events that occur after the gift play no role in determination of the value. **Ithaca Trust Co. v. United States,** 279 U.S. 151 (1929).

### b. Estate Tax

The estate tax attaches at the instant of death. Consequently, the value of the assets included in the decedent's estate is their fair market value ***immediately after*** death, not the instant before death. [*See, e.g.,* **Goodman v. Granger,** 243 F.2d 264 (3d Cir. 1957) (finding that executory contracts which had only a speculative value until decedent died, but which acquired a fixed value upon his death, were included in the decedent's estate at the fixed value)]

**EXAM TIP** GILBERT

Be sure to remember this simple detail for your exam: An asset's value for estate tax purposes is its ***fair market value immediately after death,*** not the fair market value immediately prior to death. But, as discussed below, an executor may elect the alternate valuation date.

#### (1) Alternate Valuation Date

Under section 2032 of the Code, the executor of the estate may make an election to value the estate assets either at the date of the decedent's death or at the "alternate valuation date." If the executor elects the alternate date, all assets included in the gross estate are valued as of ***six months after*** the decedent's death, ***except*** that any assets sold, distributed, exchanged or otherwise disposed of during the six months following death are valued as of the date of their sale, distribution, etc. [Treas. Reg. § 20.2032–1(a)]

Property included in the decedent's gross estate (e.g., retained interests under section 2036) may be valued based on the alternate valuation date. The Regulations go into detail as to what property is included or excluded. Income earned or accrued after the date of the decedent's death is generally excluded whereas property interests owned at the date of the decedent's death are includible even if they change during the six months after the decedent's death. [Treas. Reg. § 20.2032–1(d)]

When utilizing the alternate valuation date, dividends on the stockholder's record on or before the date of the decedent's death are excluded. [Priv. Ltr. Rul. 9637006].

##### (a) Purpose

The alternate valuation date is made available for the purpose of minimizing the danger of an unexpected tax burden or even complete confiscation of estates due to a sudden decline in market value of the decedent's assets following death.

The alternate valuation election is particularly useful when the value of assets in the estate has decreased by the time of the alternate valuation date. If the estate would have been subject to the estate tax, then the alternate valuation election would be a favorable option.

##### (b) Limitation—Valuation Changed by Lapse of Time Disregarded

Since the purpose of section 2032 is to protect against sudden declines in value, it does not apply to changes in value (declines) attributable solely to lapse of time.

e.g. **Example:** The value of a patent, an annuity, or a life estate on the life of another, etc., naturally diminishes with lapse of time because its "life" is thereby shortened. However, such changes are disregarded; therefore, even though the decedent's executor has elected the alternate valuation date, these assets are valued as of the date of the decedent's death. [Treas. Reg. § 20.2032–1 (a)(3)]

#### (c) Procedure—Election Made on Estate Tax Return

The executor's election to value the assets at the alternate valuation date must be made on the estate tax return. Moreover, once made, the election is ***irrevocable*** and affects ***all*** assets except as indicated above. Hence, the executor cannot elect on an item by item basis. [Treas. Reg. § 20.2032–1(b)]

**EXAM TIP** GILBERT

For your exam, remember that the election of an alternate valuation date is both ***irrevocable*** and ***"all or nothing,"*** in that the executor cannot pick and choose which assets will be valued with the alternate date.

#### (d) Election Must Decrease Gross Estate and Estate Tax

No election is allowed under section 2032 unless the election will decrease ***both*** the gross estate and the estate tax payable. [I.R.C. § 2032(c)] After the enactment of the unlimited marital deduction in 1982, estates that incurred no estate tax were electing an alternate valuation date when assets had increased in value in order to increase the basis of the assets for income tax purposes. This amendment, effective for decedents dying after July 18,1984, limited section 2032 to its intended purpose.

### (2) Valuation of Assets Transferred Inter Vivos but Included in the Decedent's Estate

Assets included in the decedent's estate under sections 2035 through 2038 (e.g., because of a retained life estate, etc.) are valued on the basis of their value at the ***date of the decedent's death*** (or alternate valuation date)—not their value at the time of transfer.

#### (a) Gifts of Cash or Property

Thus, as a general rule, it is the value of the ***actual property transferred,*** as of the date of the donor's death, that is included in the gross estate. The fact that the donee may have sold, exchanged, replaced, or consumed the donated property is irrelevant.

#### (b) Gifts on Trust

However, if the property was transferred to a trust, the value of the trust ***principal/corpus*** is included in the decedent's estate, even though this may consist of property other than that which was originally transferred.

#### (c) Improvements Made by Donee

If the donee improves the property with the donee's own funds, the value of the improvements is excluded in determining the includible amount.

#### (d) Income from Donated Property

Where property is included in the gross estate under sections 2036 through 2038, income that is ***accumulated*** and added to the principal of the gift ***is*** included in the gross estate, provided the taxable interest or power extends to this accumulated income as well as to the principal. However, income that is ***distributed*** is not included. [**United States v. O'Malley,** 383 U.S. 627 (1966)]

## 3. Fair Market Value

As mentioned above, the "fair market value" of the property measures the gift and estate taxes. This is generally defined as the price that a willing buyer and a willing seller would arrive at after arm's length bargaining where there is no compulsion to buy or to sell and where both parties are aware of all relevant facts. [Treas. Reg. § 20.2031–1(b)]

### a. Determination of Fair Market Value

The taxpayer (donor or estate) has the burden of proof to determine the fair market value of the property. The Service's determination of fair market value is presumed correct unless the taxpayer proves it erroneous.

#### (1) Valuation Statements by IRS

The 1976 Tax Reform Act requires that, on the taxpayer's request, the Service must furnish a written statement explaining any determination or proposed determination of the value of the property. The statement must: (i) explain the basis of the valuation, (ii) set forth any computation, and (iii) include a copy of any expert appraisal. However, the method employed in arriving at the valuation is not binding on the Service. I.R.C. § 7517]

### b. Special Use Valuation for Estate Tax Purposes

Under section 2032A (enacted as part of the 1976 Tax Reform Act), farmland and real property used in connection with other closely held businesses may be valued in the decedent-owner's estate at less than its fair market value.

#### (1) Background

The statute was promulgated out of recognition that it is often unreasonable to tax such land at its fair market value. Basically, the price that farmland can command on the market frequently exceeds the value that would be economically justified on the basis of the income it produces. Accordingly, the estate tax burden imposed upon the land's inflated value might often force the estate to sell the land to pay the taxes, thereby depriving succeeding generations of the opportunity to continue the "family farm." Furthermore, a sale might have the effect of removing the land from agricultural use when it is purchased at its speculative value by developers. Section 2032A was adopted to provide relief for "family farms," when the farmland has been and will remain in agricultural production in which family members of the decedent will be actively engaged.

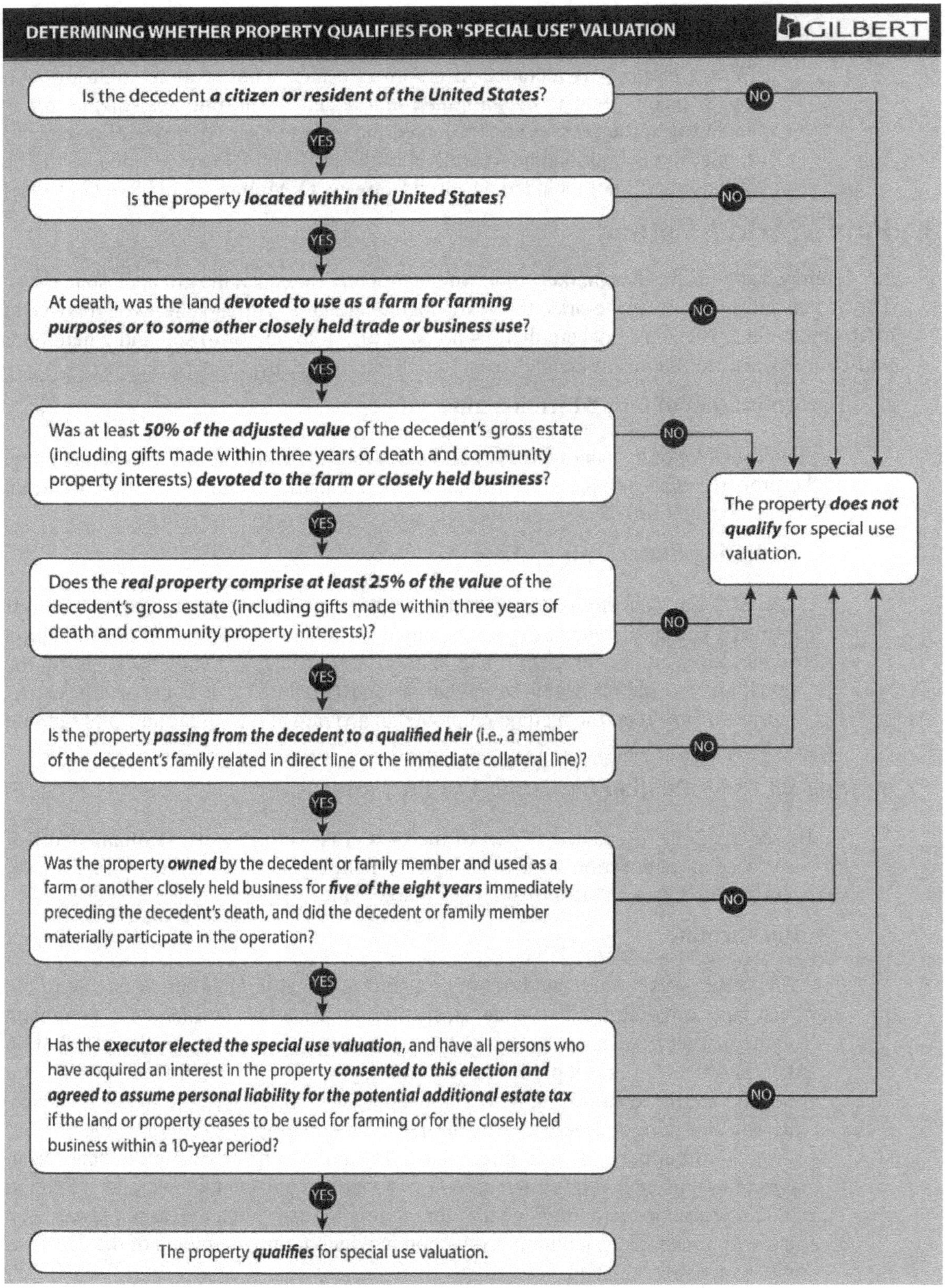


### (a) Expanded to Trade or Business

Although this relief was initially extended to benefit farmland, it was ultimately extended to real property devoted to "use in a trade or business other than . . . [that] of farming." [I.R.C. § 2032A(b)(2)(B)] Such other trade or business must, apparently, be a ***"closely held business,"*** as defined in section 6166(b), since section 2032A(g) directs the Treasury to promulgate Regulations as to the application of section 2032A to "an interest in a closely held business (within the meaning of paragraph (1) of section 6166(b))."

### (2) Special Valuation in Lieu of "Fair Market Value"

If certain requirements are met, special methods of valuation may be used which take into account the earning power of the land, as farmland, rather than its speculative, inflated "market value." [*See* I.R.C. § 2032A(a)]

#### (a) Limitation

The decrease in value for estate tax purposes cannot exceed $750,000 [I.R.C. § 2032A(a)(2)], indexed for inflation in increments of $10,000 [I.R.C. § 2032A(a)(3)]. The section 2032A inflationary amount is $1,230,000 during 2022.

#### (b) Valuation Methods

1) ***Farmland*** may be valued by dividing the net average annual gross cash rental for comparable land (gross cash rental or "net share rental," less real estate taxes) by the average annual effective interest rate for all new federal land bank loans. [I.R.C. § 2032A(e)(7)(A)] The preceding five calendar years are used to obtain the averages. If there is no comparable land from which a gross cash rental can be determined, but there is land from which the average net share rental can be determined, average net share rental can be used instead of average gross cash rental. [I.R.C. § 2032A(e)(7)(B)]

2) ***Real property used in other closely held businesses*** (or farmland, if the special farm method is not applicable) may be valued by various methods which rely principally upon a capitalization of earnings and which may produce a value lower than the land's speculative value. [I.R.C. § 2032A(e)(8)]

### (3) Basic Requirements

Essentially, six requirements must be met in order for the estate to invoke the special use valuation:

#### (a) U.S. Decedent and Property

The decedent must have been a citizen or resident of the United States, and the real property must be located in the United States. [I.R.C. § 2032A(a)(1)(A), (b)(1)]

#### (b) Qualified Use

At the date of the decedent's death, the land must have been devoted to use as a farm for farming purposes (or to some other closely held trade or business use). [I.R.C. § 2032A(b)(1), (2)]

#### (c) Adjusted Value

Fifty percent or more of the adjusted value of the gross estate must consist of the adjusted value of property (real or personal) that was being so used, ***and*** 25% or more of the adjusted value of the gross estate must consist of the adjusted value of ***real property*** that was being so used. [I.R.C. § 2032A(b)(1), (3)]

1) **Gifts Made Within Three Years of Death**

Although outright gifts made within three years of death are no longer included in the donor-decedent's gross estate, they are taken into account for purposes of the 50%/25% tests. [I.R.C. § 2035(c)] The purpose of this provision is to prevent persons from obtaining special valuation for real property by "death bed" gifts of nonqualifying property.

#### (d) "Qualified Heir"

The qualified property must pass from the decedent to a "qualified heir"—a member of the decedent's family related in direct line or the immediate collateral line. [I.R.C. § 2032A(b)(1), (e)(1), (2)]

1) ***Under section 2032A(e)(9),*** property will be deemed to have "passed" to a qualified heir where it is distributed to the heir by bequest, devise, or inheritance or acquired from the estate or a trust that is included in the decedent's gross estate.
2) ***The 1978 Act amended section 2032A(b)*** to make it clear that only such qualifying property as actually passes to a qualified heir may be used in determining the applicability of the 50%/25% tests.

#### (e) Use of Property

The property must have been owned by the decedent or a member of decedent's family and used as a farm (or in another closely held business) for five of the eight years immediately preceding the decedent's death, and the decedent or member of his family must have "materially participated in its operation." [I.R.C. § 2032A(b)(1)(C)] Note that liberalized "material participation" rules applicable to retired or disabled persons and to surviving spouses were added by the 1981 Act. [*See* I.R.C. § 2032A(b)(4), (5)]

#### (f) Election of Special Use Valuation

The executor must elect the special use valuation, and all persons who acquire an interest in the property must consent to this election and assume personal liability for the potential "additional estate tax" discussed below. [I.R.C. § 2032A(a)(1), (d)]

### (4) Additional Tax Imposed upon Termination of Qualified Use

Unless the land continues to be owned by a qualified heir and continues to be used for farming (or other closely held business use) in which a member of the decedent's family materially participates, the estate tax that was saved as a result of electing the special use valuation will become due and payable. [I.R.C. § 2032A(c); *see also* special "material participation" rules for retired or disabled persons and for surviving spouses under I.R.C. § 2032A(b)(4), (5)]

#### (a) Liability

However, liability for the "additional estate tax" is imposed upon the qualified heir; therefore, the decedent's estate does not remain liable for this potential recapture of the estate taxes saved. [I.R.C. § 2032A(c)(5)]

#### (b) And Note

Continued ownership and use is required for a ***10-year period.*** [I.R.C. § 2032A(c)(1)]

## c. Special Valuation Rules

### (1) Chapter 14 Valuation Rules

Congress enacted Chapter 14 to limit a donor's tax-free gift of a substantial share of future appreciation in the value of a business. Previous congressional attempts of preventing "estate tax freeze" devices proved to be unsuccessful. Chapter 14 contains four special gift tax valuations that apply to a variety of intra-family transactions. The three types of situations affected by Chapter 14 are: 1) Transfers of ***interests in corporations or partnerships*** [I.R.C. § 2701]; 2) Transfers of ***interests in trusts*** [I.R.C. § 2702]; 3) Valuation of ***property subject to certain rights and restrictions*** [I.R.C. § 2703]; and 4) Treatment of certain ***lapsing rights and restrictions.*** [I.R.C. § 2704]

#### (a) Transfer of Interests in Corporations or Partnerships

In general, section 2701 applies if a person transfers an interest in a corporation or partnership ***to or for the benefit of a family member*** (defined in section 2701(e)(1) as the transferor's spouse, descendants of the transferor or spouse, and spouses of such descendants), ***and*** the transferor or an "applicable family member" (defined in section 2701(e)(2) as the transferor's spouse, ancestors of the transferor or spouse, and spouses of such ancestors) ***retains an interest*** in the same corporation or partnership. [I.R.C. § 2701(a)(1)]

Transfers include contributions to new or existing entities, restructuring of existing entities, and redemptions. [Treas. Reg. 25.2701–1(b)(2)]

##### 1) General Exceptions to the Application of Section 2701:

a) When ***market quotations*** are readily available for the transferred stock or the retained interest. [I.R.C. § 2701(a)(1), (2)(A)]

b) When there is only ***one class*** of interest or, ***if two classes,*** the classes of interest ***differ only as to voting rights.*** [I.R.C. § 2701(a)(2)(B), (C)]

c) When there is ***a proportionate transfer*** of all classes of interest. [I.R.C. § 2701(a)(2)(C)]

##### 2) Valuation Rules

In general, the value of the interest transferred will be its fair market value, determined under usual valuation rules but subject to the following special rules.

###### a) Zero Value Rule for Retained Interests

The transferred interest is valued by a "subtraction method." The subtraction method takes the value of the retained interest and subtracts it from the fair market value of the entire enterprise. And, if the retained interest is an "applicable retained interest," the value for application of the subtraction method will be ***zero.*** [I.R.C. § 2701(a)(1), (3)(A)] The effect is to expose to the gift tax the entire (proportionate) value of the business with no reduction for the theoretical value of the retained interest.

### i. Applicable Retained Interest

***"Applicable retained interest"*** is defined in section 2701(b)(1) as a ***"distribution right"*** or a ***"liquidation, put, call or conversion right."*** These rights, in turn, are defined as:

a. ***Distribution right*** is any right to ***receive distributions from a corporation*** with respect to its stock or from a partnership with respect to a partnership interest. [I.R.C. § 2701(c)(1)(A)]

b. ***Liquidation, etc., right*** includes such rights or similar rights ***that affect the value of the transferred interest.*** [I.R.C. § 2701(c)(2)(A)]

### ii. Exceptions

Section 2701 contains a number of special exceptions. The most generally applicable are:

#### a. Control

The zero value rule will not apply to a distribution right unless the *transferor* (or applicable family member) ***holds at least 50% of the value or voting power*** of the entity immediately before the transfer. [I.R.C. § 2701(b)(1)(A), (2)]

#### b. Qualified Payments

Nor does the zero value rule generally apply to distribution rights in the form of ***"qualified payments"*** defined as ***a fixed amount (or rate) payable on a periodic basis*** under a cumulative preferred stock or similar partnership interest. [I.R.C. § 2701(a)(3)(A), (c)(3)(A)]

#### c. Junior Equity

Similarly, distribution rights with respect to ***a retained junior equity interest*** are not subject to the zero value rule. [I.R.C. § 2701(c)(1)(B)] For this purpose, "junior equity" means ***common stock or an analogous subordinate interest in a partnership.*** [I.R.C. § 2701(a)(4)(B)]

#### d. Fixed Rights

A liquidation right, etc., that must be exercised at ***a specific time, amount, and manner*** is also excepted. [I.R.C. § 2701(c)(2)(B)]

**EXCEPTIONS TO THE ZERO VALUE RULE FOR RETAINED INTERESTS** GILBERT

**THE MOST COMMON EXCEPTIONS TO THE ZERO VALUE RULE FOR RETAINED INTERESTS ARE:**

- ☑ ***No Control***—When ***50% of the value or voting power*** of the entity is not held by the transferor immediately before the transfer
- ☑ ***Qualified Payments***—When the distribution rights are in the form of ***a fixed amount (or rate) payable on a periodic basis*** under a cumulative preferred stock or similar partnership interest
- ☑ ***Junior Equity***—When the interest is ***a retained junior equity interest*** (i.e., common stock or an analogous subordinate interest in a partnership)
- ☑ ***Fixed Rights***—When a liquidation right, etc., ***must be exercised at a specific time, amount, and manner***

#### b) Minimum Value Rule

If a "junior equity interest" is transferred, the proportionate value of the interest must be determined by valuing all junior equity interests at not less than 10% of the total value of all equity interests in the entity, ***plus*** the total amount of any indebtedness of the entity to the transferor or to an applicable family member. [I.R.C. § 2701(a)(4)(A)] The effect of this is to assure some value for gift tax purposes even where the zero value rule for retained interests is not applicable.

### 3) Valuation of Retained Interest upon Death of Transferor

Section 2701 affects valuation for gift tax purposes. If the retained interest of the transferor was subject to the zero value rule but is valued in the gross estate at its fair market value, some "double taxation" would occur.

#### a) Adjustments to Avoid Double Taxation Mandated by Statute

Section 2701(e)(6) requires the promulgation of regulations to allow "appropriate adjustments" for the estate, gift, and generation-skipping tax "to reflect the increase in the amount of the prior taxable gift made by the transferor. . ."

#### b) Adjustments Allowed by Regulations

The Regulations provide that in computing the estate tax, the retained interest will be included at its fair market value, ***but*** the decedent's "adjusted taxable gifts" are to be reduced by the ***lesser*** of the amounts by which the decedent's taxable gifts were increased by reason of section 2701 or the difference between the value of the retained interest for estate tax purposes and the value assigned to that interest under section 2701 at the time of the initial transfer. [*See* Treas. Reg. § 25.2701–5(b)] e.g. **Example:** A owns all of the stock of M Corp., which is presently valued at $1 million. M Corp. is a prospering business, and it is expected to at least double in value before A dies. A surrenders all of her stock to the corporation and receives, in return, 10,000 shares of voting preferred stock and 1,000 shares of voting common stock. The preferred stock has a par value and liquidation preference of $100 per share (aggregate book value of $1 million); the common stock has a nominal stated value of $.001 per share (aggregate book value of $1). A then gives all the common stock to her children. By these transactions, A intends to give all the residual equity and all future appreciation in value of the business to her children (at a minimal present gift tax cost), retain the present financial worth and voting control of the corporation during her life, and limit the estate tax value of her retained interest (in the form of the preferred stock) to about $1 million. The entire corporation is worth $2 million when A dies.

**i.** If A's "distribution rights" (dividends on preferred stock) are not fixed and cumulative ("qualified payments") or her liquidation right is not a "fixed right," her retained rights (all the preferred stock) will be valued at zero, and the gift of all common stock to her child will be valued at $1 million—the entire present value of the corporation.

**ii.** If the dividends payable on the preferred stock retained ***are*** "qualified payments" and the liquidation provisions are "fixed rights," the zero value rule will not apply, ***but*** the value of the common stock must be assigned a value of at least $100,000 (10% of $1 million). Assuming that the valuation of the common stock, taking into account its junior equity status, minority discount, and lack of marketability, would be $40,000, the "minimum value rule" of section 2701(a)(4) will nevertheless produce a taxable gift of $100,000.

**iii.** Upon A's death the preferred stock will be included in her estate under section 2033. Assuming that its fair market value, taking into account the liquidation preference and a premium for control, is determined to be $1.1 million, it will be included at that value.

However, to avoid "double taxation," adjustments of A's "adjusted taxable gifts" are permitted:

**a.** If the zero value rule applied to the lifetime gift of the common stock, A's adjusted taxable gifts would be reduced by $960,000—the lesser of the value of the includible preferred stock and the amount by which her lifetime gift was increased by virtue of the application of the zero value rule (assuming, as in b), above, that the common stock would have been valued at $40,000 apart from section 2701).

**b.** Assuming that the minimum value rule applied, so that the gift value under the rule was $100,000 when it otherwise would have been $40,000, A's adjusted taxable gifts would be reduced by $60,000.

#### 4) Comment

Note that although section 2701 clearly prevents undervaluation of the lifetime gift (indeed, it may produce overvaluation in some instances), it does not eliminate the opportunity to "freeze" estate tax values nor the opportunity to give away a significant amount of the anticipated appreciation in value.

### (b) Transfers of Interests in Trusts

Retained interest gifts in a trust were also deemed to provide a context for both the tax-free transfer of appreciation in value and for undervaluation of the interest transferred during life.

e.g. **Example:** D transfers real property valued at $100,000 to a trust for the benefit of his children. The property generates a modest income of about $6,000 per year (presently 6% of value). The property is held primarily for appreciation in value. D retains a right to income from the trust for a period of 10 years. Using the then current 10% tables prescribed for the valuation of term interests, the value of D's reserved 10-year term is approximately $62,000, and the taxable gift of the remainder would be valued at $38,000. However, if the actual 6% return was used for valuation, D's retained interest would be valued at approximately $44,000, and the value of the taxable gift would be $56,000. Moreover, if D lives more than 10 years, the remainderman will succeed to the then appreciated property with no further gift tax, and no inclusion in D's gross estate under section 2036.

#### 1) GRITs, GRATs, and GRUTs—Section 2702

Under section 2702, a "grantor retained income trust (GRIT)" is a right to receive ***all income*** at least annually which will be valued at zero for purposes of determining the value of the taxable gift of the remainder. [I.R.C. § 2702(a)(1), (2)(A)]

##### a) Qualified Interests Valued at Greater than Zero

A value will be assigned to the grantor's retained interest only if it is a "qualified interest." [I.R.C. § 2702(a)(2)(B)] There are two general types of qualified interests:

###### i. GRAT

An interest that consists of a right to receive a ***fixed amount,*** payable at least annually, is a "grantor retained annuity trust," or "GRAT." [I.R.C. § 2702(b)(1)]

###### ii. GRUT

An interest that consists of a right to receive a ***fixed percentage*** of the fair market value of the trust property, determined annually, is a "grantor retained unitrust (GRUT)." [I.R.C. § 2702(b)(2)]

#### 2) Applies to Term Interests as Well as Remainders

If one gives a term interest but retains a remainder, the remainder will be valued at zero unless the remainder is "noncontingent," and the term interest is in the form of either a GRAT or GRUT. [I.R.C. § 2702(b)(3)]

#### 3) Exceptions

The section 2702 zero value rule does not apply to:

##### a) Transfers to Nonfamily Members

Section 2702 only applies to the transfer of remainder interests to the transferor's family members if the retained interest is held by the transferor or an applicable family member. [I.R.C. § 2702(a)(1)]

##### b) Incomplete Gifts

The Code logically and specifically excepts gifts that are "incomplete" for gift tax purposes. An incomplete gift consists of any transfer which is not treated as a gift. [I.R.C. § 2702(a)(3)(A)(i), (B)]

##### c) Personal Residence

The zero value rule does not apply to the transfer of an interest in property that is to be used as a personal residence by the persons holding the term interests [I.R.C. § 2702(a)(3)(A)(ii)], although the Service has issued regulations that restrict the availability of this exception. [*See* Treas. Reg. § 25.2502–5]

#### 4) Comment

Again, this section does not prevent gifts of anticipated appreciation in value. But it does prevent undervaluation of the lifetime gift and increases the real cost (present gift tax) of making the gift of anticipated (speculative) appreciation.

#### 5) Interest Rate Used to Value Interests Is Revised Monthly

To avoid abuses brought about by discrepancies between market interest rates and rates used by the Service, I.R.C. § 7520 was enacted to require monthly adjustments to the interest rate used to value annuities, life estates, and terms of years.

### (c) Valuation of Property Subject to Certain Rights and Restrictions

When valuing the entity interests, the value is determined without regard to any restriction on the right to sell or use the property. A right or restriction would be contained in entity documents such as a partnership agreement, articles of incorporation, corporate bylaws, a shareholder's agreement, or various other entity documents. [Treas. Reg. § 25.2703–1(a)(3)]

The requirements apply to any restriction implicit within the appropriate entity documents. [Treas. Reg. § 25.2703–1(a)(3)]

#### 1) Exceptions

Under I.R.C. § 2703, the restrictive agreement will not be disregarded if: the agreement is a bona fide business arrangement, it is not a device to transfer property to the natural objects of the transferor's bounty for less than full and adequate consideration, and its terms are comparable to those of similar arrangements entered into by persons in an arm's-length transaction. I.R.C. § 2703]

### (d) Treatment of Certain Lapsing Rights and Restrictions

Under prior law, tax free transfers of significant economic benefits were possible where a transferor transferred an interest in property by gift, retained valuable rights with respect to the property, and then permitted or caused these rights to lapse, thus effectively shifting the value of these rights to the original donee. In general, property is valued without regard for lapsing restrictions.

**Example—Right to Vote Stock:** Parent owns all the stock of a corporation. Parent transfers 40% of the stock to her child retaining, however, voting control through the 60% stock ownership not given away. Subsequently, Parent causes or permits the voting power of the retained stock to lapse. Following the lapse, child-donee would possess 100% of the voting power, and this shift of control enhances the value of the child's stock while decreasing the value of Parent's.

#### 1) Taxable Transfers Under Section 2704

Unlike the other provisions of Chapter 14, which prescribe special ***valuation*** rules, section 2704 provides that the lapse of any voting or liquidation right in a corporation or partnership shall be treated as a ***transfer by gift*** or as a transfer ***includible in the decedent's gross estate.*** [I.R.C. § 2704(a)(1)]

##### a) Operative Limitation—Control

A lapse of such a right is treated as a transfer (above) only if the individual holding the right immediately before the lapse and members of that individual's family (both before and after the lapse) *control* the corporation or partnership. [I.R.C. § 2704(a)(2)]

Control is defined as ownership of 50% or more of the voting power or value of the stock of a corporation, or 50% or more of the capital or profits interest in a partnership. [I.R.C. §§ 2704(c)(1), 2701(b)(2)]

###### i. Implicit Limitation—Family-Owned Entities

The transfer treatment is limited to the shifting of economic benefits resulting from the lapse within family units (as defined in section 2704(c)(1) and (2)).

##### b) Amount of the Transfer

The taxable amount is the difference between the value of the interest retained immediately prior to the lapse and its value immediately after the lapse. And, for this purpose, the fact that the interest may be subject to lapsing rights is to be disregarded. [I.R.C. § 2704(a)(2), (b)(1), (2)]

##### c) Exception for Certain Restrictions on Liquidation

Commercially reasonable restrictions imposed by an unrelated party in connection with a financing transaction and restrictions imposed by any federal or state law are not considered as restrictions to be disregarded in valuing any transfer. [I.R.C. § 2704(b)(3)]

#### 2) Property Subject to Restrictions

Various types of burdens on property must be taken into account in valuing the property and may reduce its "fair market value." For example, restrictions on the transfer of property, options to buy for less than fair market value, or rights to use property for less than a fair rental value decrease the investment value and fair market value of the burdened property.

#### 3) Gift Tax Avoidance

Congress was apparently concerned that real or colorable restrictions might be used to reduce the fair market value of property for gift tax purposes. Thus, section 2703 mandates that such restrictions are to be ***disregarded*** for purposes of the estate, gift, and generation-skipping taxes. [I.R.C. § 2703(a)]

### d. Estate Tax Value of Land Subject to a Conservation Easement

Section 2031(c) provides that a decedent's executor may elect to ***exclude a portion of the value of land*** located in the United States from the gross estate ***if the land is subject to a "qualified conservation easement."***

#### (1) "Qualified Conservation Easement"

I.R.C. § 2031(c)(8) adopts, as a basic definition, that of section 170(h): a perpetual restriction limiting the use of property exclusively for certain designated conservation purposes (except certain historic preservation purposes) which is granted to a "qualified organization." For purposes of the estate tax exclusion, however, special rules are applicable:

**(a)** ***The land subject to the easement must have been owned by the decedent*** or a family member at all times ***during the three-year period*** ending on the date of the decedent's death.

**(b)** ***The easement can be an existing easement or one granted after the death*** of the decedent (but before the date of the executor's election), but it must be granted ***by the decedent, a family member, the decedent's executor, or a trustee holding the land.***

#### (2) Limitations

##### (a) Debt-Financed Property

The exclusion is not allowed for property that, at decedent's death, is subject to an "acquisition indebtedness." [*See* I.R.C. § 2031(c)(4)]

##### (b) Retained Development Right

The exclusion does not apply to the extent of the value of any retained "development right." A development right, for this purpose, is any right to use the land for any commercial purpose, except commercial purposes that are subordinate to and directly supportive of use of the land for farming. [*See* I.R.C. § 2031(c)(5)(A), (D)] However, the exclusion will be allowed if every person who has an interest in the land files an agreement to permanently extinguish the retained development right. This agreement must be filed by the date the estate tax return is due and must be implemented within two years of the decedent's death. [*See* I.R.C. § 2031(c)(5)(B), (C)]

#### e. Amount of Exclusion

Per section 2031(c)(1), the exclusion is the ***lesser*** of the ***"applicable percentage"*** of the value of the land subject to the qualified conservation easement, less any charitable deduction allowed to the decedent's estate under section 2055(f) with respect to this land or the ***"exclusion limitation"*** of $500,000.

##### (1) Applicable Percentage

The applicable percentage is 40% of the value of the land, reduced by 2% for each percentage point by which the value of the easement is less than 30% of the value of the land. [*See* I.R.C. § 2031(c)(2)]

e.g. **Example:** Assume that land included in D's estate is subject to a qualified conservation easement, that none of the limitations apply, and that the land is valued at $400,000 and the easement is valued at $100,000. D's executor could elect to exclude $120,000: The value of the easement is 25% of the value of the land, reducing the "applicable percentage" by 10 points (2 × (30 – 25)). The computed exclusion is, then, $120,000 (30% × $400,000), and this is less than the $500,000 exclusion limitation. Note that if D's estate was entitled to a charitable deduction for a grant of the easement, the exclusion would be $20,000 (the above applicable percentage less the $100,000 charitable deduction.)

#### f. Carryover Basis in Excluded Land

To the extent of the exclusion allowed by section 2031(c), the basis of the land will be the same as its basis in the hands of the decedent. [*See* I.R.C. § 1014(a)(4)]

#### g. Treatment of Easements Granted After Death

The grant of a qualified conservation easement made by a decedent's executor or trustee will qualify for the estate tax deduction under section 2055(f), but no income tax deduction is allowed with respect to such postmortem conservation easements. [*See* I.R.C. § 2031(c)(9)]

#### h. Relation to Section 2032A

A qualified conservation contribution will not be considered a "disposition" by the qualified heir of land subject to special use valuation. Thus, qualified heirs may transfer a conservation easement or make a qualified contribution of the entire interest without triggering the recapture tax. [*See* I.R.C. § 2032A(c)(8)]

# C. Valuation Methods

## 1. In General

There are, essentially, three general methods of valuation commonly used: (i) appraisal based upon known ***prices paid in the market;*** (ii) ***actuarial valuation;*** and (iii) an estimate of the market or investment value of property based upon ***a capitalization of the earnings*** of the property.

## 2. Market Price Method

### a. Reference to Identical Property

If free market prices of ***identical property are known,*** the price at which that property is sold on the relevant valuation date is the best indication of fair market value. Valuation by reference to known market prices is most common in the case of listed securities regularly traded on an exchange.

### b. Reference to Comparable Sales

If free market prices ***of identical property are not known,*** appraisal may be based upon "comparable sales," (i.e., known market prices of similar property). Valuation using comparable sales is most common in the case of real property appraisals.

## 3. Life Estates, Annuities, Remainders, Reversionary Interests, Etc.

***Annuities*** issued by a company ***regularly selling*** annuity contracts ***are valued by reference to the present cost of purchasing a similar contract*** from the company. [Treas. Reg. §§ 20.2031–8, 25.2512–6] All other annuities, life estates, reversions, and other future interests ***are valued under "present worth tables"*** prescribed by the Regulations, which are based upon standard mortality tables. [*See* Treas. Reg. §§ 20.2031–7, 25.2512–5]

The standard mortality tables are found in IRS Publication 1457. On May 5, 2022, the Treasury Department issued proposed regulations with updated mortality tables. The proposed tables are based on mortality experiences during 2010 (as opposed to mortality experiences during 2000 reflected in the current tables). These tables are available at https://www.irs.gov/retirement-plans/actuarial-tables. The current or proposed tables may be used from January 1, 2021 until the final regulations are adopted. Two of the most important tables are Table S (life table) and Table B (term certain). Note that because Table S contains mortality tables, the proposed regulations have updated Table S to reflect mortality experiences during 2010.

e.g. **Example:** A decedent created a testamentary trust. Under the terms of the trust, the decedent's 25 year old daughter is entitled to all income for life from the $1,000,000 transferred to the trust. Upon the daughter's death, the trust will terminate, and the corpus will be distributed to the decedent's grandson. Assume that the current interest rate is 6%. Under proposed Table S, the income factor is .93513. Hence, the value of the daughter's life estate is $935,130. The remainder factor is .06487, and the present value of the grandson's remainder is $64,870. If the daughter is 50 years old at the time the trust is created, the income factor is .79395. Thus, the life estate is valued at $793,950, and the grandson's remainder is valued at $206,050 (remainder factor is .020605).

e.g. **Example:** A donor creates an inter vivos trust and transfers $1,000,000 to the trust. Under the terms of the trust, all income is payable to the donor's son for 20 years. At the end of the 20-year term, the trust will terminate, and the corpus will be distributed to the donor's grandson. Assume that the current interest rate is 4%. Under Table B, the income factor is .543613, and the son's income interest is valued at $543,613. The remainder factor is .456387, and the grandson's remainder interest is valued at $456.387.

## 4. Unascertainable Values

For property that cannot be valued under the actuarial tables, the taxpayer has the burden of establishing the value of the property. In **Robinette v. Helvering,** 318 U.S. 184 (1943), the taxpayer created an irrevocable trust retaining an income interest for life followed by an income interest for life to her mother and stepfather if they survived her. Upon the death of the last surviving life tenant, the property would go to the taxpayer's issue who reached the age of 21. To the extent that there were no issue, the last surviving life tenant had the power to appoint the remainder by will. The taxpayer retained an implied reversion. The issue in the case was the value of the reversionary interest. Because the taxpayer did not meet her burden of establishing the value of her reversionary interest, it was valued at zero. As a result, the entire property was subject to gift taxation except the retained income interest.

## 5. Capitalization of Earnings Method

The market value of property may also be estimated ***by capitalizing the known earnings derived from the property.*** The economic theory underlying this method is that the value of property (what a person would pay for the property) is a function of the income that can be produced by the property. Although this is a rather sophisticated technique, it may be fairly simply described:

(i) ***The anticipated earnings are determined on the basis of historical earnings.*** Usually, the average earnings over the three to five years immediately preceding the valuation date are used.

(ii) ***An educated guess*** is then made (from the appraiser's experience, reference to comparable businesses, etc.) as to the ***return on investment that a prudent investor would expect*** (or require) for the particular property involved, taking into account the stability of the investment, risks involved, etc.

(iii) ***The estimated earning potential of the property is then capitalized*** using the guesstimated rate of return. The result of this computation is the estimated fair market value.

e.g. **Example:** If it is determined that the income to be derived from the property is $10,000 per year and that a prudent investor would require a 10% return on investment for the type of property involved, the fair market value, under a capitalization of earnings method, would be $100,000 ($10,000 × 10).

# D. Valuation of Some Specific Items

## 1. Real Property

As noted above, the fair market value of real property is usually established by appraisals employing a comparable sales method of valuation. Local assessed valuations cannot be used, except where they are shown to represent fair market value throughout the community. [**Garstin v. United States,** 352 F.2d 537 (Ct. Cl. 1965)]

### a. "Highest and Best Use" Standard

As a general rule, the appraisal must take into account the "highest and best use" of the property (i.e., the most economically productive use possible), even though the property was not being so used by the decedent (e.g., decedent's home was on a lot that was zoned for commercial use which was the highest use). Note that section 2032A discussed earlier was intended to provide some relief from that standard for real property used in a trade or business.

## 2. Stocks and Bonds

### a. Listed Securities

If the security is ***listed on an exchange or is regularly sold "over the counter"*** the fair market value is: (i) the mean between the highest and lowest selling price ***on the valuation date***, or (ii) if there are ***no sales on the valuation date,*** the weighted average of the mean between the highest and lowest selling price on the nearest trading date before the valuation date and the mean between the highest and lowest selling price on the nearest trading date after the valuation date. If there are ***no sales on the valuation date or within a reasonable period before and after the valuation date,*** reference is made to the average of bid and asked prices to ascertain fair market value. [Treas. Reg. § 20.2031–2(b)(1)]

#### (1) Control Premium

Where a person owns stock that represents effective ***control*** of a corporation, it may be valued at an amount ***greater*** than the "market price," on the theory that a purchaser will pay more for a controlling block of stock than for an individual share. [**Estate of Chenoweth v. Commissioner**, 88 T.C. 1577 (1987)]

#### (2) Minority Interest Discounts

Related to the concept of control premium is the converse situation of minority interest discounts. For example, if a person owns a 49% interest in a closely held business while another person owns 51% of the business, the person with the majority interest can control the business. Hence, a "willing buyer" of the minority interest in the business will pay less for the interest because of the lack of control. [*See* **Estate of Bright v. United States,** 658 F. 2d 999 (1981)]

### b. Unlisted Securities—Closely Held Stocks, Family Corporations, Etc.

Unlisted securities are valued by considering all recent sales thereof, corporate net worth, earning capacity, etc. Although capitalization of earnings is frequently used to value such securities, all relevant factors must be considered: book value, earning power, general economic outlook, goodwill, reliance on decedent's services, etc. [Treas. Reg. §§ 20.2031–3, 25.2512–3; **O'Malley v. Ames,** 197 F.2d 256 (8th Cir. 1952); Rev. Rul. 59–60, 1959–1 C.B. 237]

#### (1) Effect of Buy-Sell Agreement

Traditionally, the price established in a buy-sell agreement (whereby the decedent agreed to sell the decedent's interest at death to another) has been accepted as the value of the decedent's interest as long as the agreement was bona fide (negotiated at arm's length) and binding on the decedent both during life and at death. [Treas. Reg. § 20.2031–2(h); **Brodrick v. Gore,** 224 F.2d 892 (10th Cir. 1955)] The "anti-freeze" valuation rules continue to recognize this effect of bona fide business arrangements, but also specify that the agreement must not be ". . . a device to transfer . . . property to members of the decedent's family for less than a full and adequate consideration," and that the terms of the agreement must be ". . . comparable to similar arrangements entered into by persons in an arm's length transaction." [I.R.C. § 2703(b)]

### (2) "Blockage Rule"

Securities that constitute a large block of stock or bonds of a particular corporation may be valued at less than market value on the theory that the sale of such a large block would depress the market price obtainable. [Treas. Reg. § 20.2031–2(e)] However, the Service does not apply this rule for purposes of valuing the transfer of stock by inter vivos gift.

**EXAM TIP** GILBERT

For your exam, be sure to keep these concepts straight: The sale of a ***large block of stock*** may be valued ***at less than the market price*** because the sale of a large block would probably ***depress*** the market price. In addition, a willing buyer may pay less than market price for a ***minority interest*** because of a lack of control. Conversely, when ***the decedent's stock represents control of a company,*** it may be valued at ***greater*** than the market price. In other words, if the amount of stock would be ***big,*** the market price would be ***depressed,*** but if the amount of stock would be ***really, really big*** (a controlling block of stock), the market price would be ***increased*** because it would give the buyer effective control over the corporation.

## c. Mutual Fund Shares

Formerly, the Service maintained that mutual fund shares should be valued at their "asking price"—the price for which they could have been purchased on the valuation date—even though the "asking price" is inflated by a sales commission or "load" and, as a practical matter, such shares can only be sold back to the fund at a determined redemption price which does not include the sales "load" and is, thus, less than the asking price. However, the Supreme Court, in **United States v. Cartwright,** 411 U.S. 546 (1973), rejected this position, holding that such shares should be valued at their "net asset value"—i.e., the asking price less any sales commission or "load."

## d. Bonds, Notes, and Evidence of Indebtedness

Such obligations are valued at their face value (unpaid principal) plus accrued interest, unless evidence is introduced to justify a discount (e.g., an interest rate considerably below that regularly being charged). [Treas. Reg. §§ 20.2031–4, 25.2512–4]

**SUMMARY OF VALUATION OF SPECIFIC ITEMS** GILBERT

| ITEM | METHOD USED TO ESTABLISH VALUE |
|---|---|
| **REAL PROPERTY** | Usually established by using ***comparable sales*** method |
| **LISTED STOCKS AND BONDS** | ***Mean*** between the ***highest*** and ***lowest*** selling price on the valuation date; other valuation methods are used if there are no sales on the valuation date |

| | |
|---|---|
| | • ***Large blocks*** of stock may be valued at ***less than market value*** because the sale of such a large block would depress the market price obtainable<br>• ***Minority discounts*** may be allowed where a person owns a ***minority interest*** in a business because of a ***lack of control***<br>• However, if the stock owned by the decedent represents effective ***control of a corporation***, it may be valued ***at*** an amount ***greater than the market value*** (control premium) |
| **UNLISTED STOCKS** | ***All factors*** (e.g., capitalization of earnings, book value, earning power, etc.) are considered<br>• Price set by ***buy-sell agreement*** will control unless it is not bona fide |
| **MUTUAL FUNDS** | ***Net asset value*** (i.e., asking price minus any sales commission and "load") is used |
| **BONDS, NOTES, AND EVIDENCE OF INDEBTEDNESS** | ***Face value*** plus ***accrued interest*** is used, but evidence justifying discount may be shown |

# Chapter Six
# Computation of Tax

| CONTENTS | PAGE |
|---|---|

# Chapter Approach

A basic familiarity with the manner in which the gift and estate taxes are computed will aid your understanding of the operation of the transfer taxes. Moreover, since the unified gift and estate tax system introduced by the Tax Reform Act of 1976 is, essentially, a computational rather than a substantive unification, familiarity with the tax computations is necessary for an understanding of the unified tax system.

The Tax Cuts and Jobs Act of 2017 greatly reduced federal estate and gift taxes by doubling the basic exclusion amount to $10,000,000 (indexed for inflation). However, the Act sunsets after December 31, 2025, and the basic exemption amount reverts to $5,000,000 (indexed for inflation).

This chapter first considers the procedure and rationale of the ***gift tax*** computation, including application of the applicable credit amount. Then, attention is focused on ***estate tax*** computations, in connection with which the special credits against the estate tax allowed by sections 2012 through 2016 are discussed. The chapter concludes with a discussion of ***portability*** of a deceased spouse's unused exclusion amount.

# A. Gift Tax Computations

## 1. Overview

The first four elements of a taxable gift were previously discussed in connection with the substantive aspects of the gift tax. The remaining elements focus on the computation of the gift tax and encompass application of the rates of tax to taxable gifts and allowance of the applicable credit amount. These elements are specified in sections 2502, 2504, and 2505.

### a. Computational Procedure

The gift tax liability for any calendar year is computed as follows:

(1) ***Determine the amount of gifts*** made during the calendar year.

(2) ***Deduct the annual exclusion*** with respect to present interest gifts made to the donee(s).

(3) ***Deduct any allowable charitable and marital deductions*** to arrive at "taxable" gifts.

(4) ***Add to the total value of the taxable gifts for the current year*** the total amount of all taxable gifts made ***in all prior*** calendar periods from the inception of the gift tax in 1932 (i.e., calendar quarters or years, depending upon the law applicable at the time of the prior gift). [I.R.C. § 2502(a)(1), (b); *see also* I.R.C. § 2504(a), (b)]

(5) ***Apply the rate schedule set out in section 2001(c)*** to the ***sum of total taxable gifts***—current taxable gifts plus all prior taxable gifts. [I.R.C. § 2502(a)(1)]

(6) ***Apply the rate schedule of section 2001(c)*** to the total of taxable gifts for ***prior*** years. [I.R.C. § 2502(a)(2)]

(7) ***Subtract the "tentative tax"*** computed with respect to prior taxable gifts (step 6) from the tentative tax computed with respect to all taxable gifts made by the donor (step 5). [I.R.C. § 2502(a)]

(8) ***From this result*** (which represents the tax upon current taxable gifts based on the rate structure in effect at the time of prior as well as current taxable gifts) ***subtract***

***any allowable gift tax applicable credit amount.*** [I.R.C. § 2505] The balance is the tax liability for the current calendar year. [*See* Treas. Reg. § 25.2502–1(a)]

### b. Brief Elaboration

Some "definitional" aspects of the computational elements should be noted.

#### (1) Prior Taxable Gifts

With one exception, the taxable gifts for prior calendar years are determined in accordance with the law applicable at the time the gift was made. [I.R.C. § 2504] Thus, it is the law in effect ***at the time of the actual transfer,*** not the present law, that governs whether a transfer was a "gift," the amount of any exclusion allowed, and the allowable deductions in determining taxable gifts.

##### (a) Application

###### 1) Marital Deduction

Prior to 1948, no marital deduction was allowed; thus, the full value of property transferred to a spouse prior to 1948 would be taken into account in determining prior taxable gifts. And, before 1982, transfers to a spouse were not fully deductible. Thus, for gifts made between 1948 and 1982, any taxable (nondeductible) portions of the gift would enter into the determination of prior taxable gifts.

###### 2) Annual Exclusion

Furthermore, prior to 1982, the amount of the annual exclusion was $3,000 ($4,000 between 1938 and 1943, and $5,000 between 1932 and 1938); and the amount of the exclusion allowable at the time the transfer was made determines the "taxable gift." [Treas. Reg. § 25.2504–1(a)] The annual exclusion is $16,000 as of 2022.

##### (b) Exception—the Specific Exemption

For purposes of determining prior taxable gifts, the deduction for the specific exemption (allowed for gifts prior to 1977) is limited to $30,000, even though an exemption of $40,000 was allowed between 1936 and 1942 ($50,000 between 1932 and 1935). [I.R.C. § 2504(a)(3); [Treas. Reg. § 25.2504–1(b)]

#### (2) Rate of Tax

The rate of tax to be applied in arriving at the tentative tax upon current gifts ***and*** the tentative tax upon prior taxable gifts is the rate ***currently*** specified in section 2001(c), ***without regard*** to the fact that different rates may actually have been used in computing tax liability with respect to prior taxable gifts. [I.R.C. § 2502(a)]

## 2. Unified Tax Rate Schedule

Prior to 1977, gift taxes were computed in accordance with a special tax rate schedule applicable only to the gift tax. However, with passage of the Tax Reform Act of 1976, effective for transfers made after December 31, 1976, the same rate schedule is now applied to both lifetime and testamentary transfers. As originally enacted in 1976, the unified rate schedule was graduated from 18% (upon gifts up to $10,000) to 70% (upon gifts in excess of $5 million). The 1981 Act phased in a reduction of ***top-bracket*** rates to a maximum of 50% (the final reduction to 50% was periodically postponed and then eliminated, leaving a maximum rate of 55% for taxable gifts and estates in excess of $3 million), and the 2001 Act phased in a reduction of top bracket rates to 45% in 2007. The estate tax (but not the gift tax) ***was repealed*** in 2010, and while the estate tax was repealed, the maximum gift tax rate was 35%. Prior to the 2001 Act, the rates used in computing the tentative tax had to be increased by 5% in the case of estates valued between $10 million and $21.04 million (or $18.34 million after 1992). [I.R.C. § 2001(c)(3)] This latter augmentation of rates for mega-estates was designed to reduce and ultimately eliminate the benefit of the graduated rates and the unified credit for these estates.

In December 2010, Congress passed legislation that unified the estate and gifts tax exemption with a flat rate of 35% for transfers in excess of $5 million. The 2010 Act was set to expire at the end of 2012 but on January 2, 2013, the American Taxpayer Relief Act of 2012 was passed. The American Taxpayer Relief Act of 2012 raised the ***flat rate of the tax to 40%,*** with the basic exclusion amount being $5 million (adjusted for inflation annually). In December 2017, the Tax Cuts and Jobs Act of 2017 was passed, which increased the ***basic exclusion amount to $10 million*** (adjusted for inflation annually). The 2017 Act is set to sunset after December 31, 2025. If Congress does not do anything to repeal the sunset, the basic exclusion amount will revert to $5 million.

## 3. Cumulative Nature of Tax

As noted above, the tax rates applicable to current gifts are determined not only by the amount of gifts made during the calendar year but also with regard to ***all prior gifts*** made by the donor since the enactment of the gift tax in 1932. In other words, the gift tax rates are ***cumulative.***

### a. Cumulation of Pre-1977 Gifts

Again, note that the unified tax rates are applied not only with respect to all gifts made after 1976, but also, for purposes of computing the current tax liability, with respect to gifts made prior to 1977.

### b. Effect of Cumulation

This does not mean that a gift tax is paid over and over again! The tentative tax computed with respect to all taxable gifts is reduced by the tentative tax applicable to prior taxable gifts and, thus, there is no multiple taxation. What the cumulation of taxable gifts does, essentially, is to expose current taxable gifts to ***higher marginal rates*** of tax, because the value of the current gifts is "placed on top of" the amount of all prior taxable gifts.

## 4. Applicable Gift Tax Credit Amount

The 1976 Tax Reform Act introduced a gift tax credit (applied directly against tax liability) in place of the former $30,000 specific exemption (which operated as a deduction). [I.R.C. § 2505] This gift tax credit operates in tandem with the applicable estate tax credit to provide, in effect, a ***single credit against transfer taxes, whether the transfers are made during life or upon death.*** However, during 2004–2011, the credit against the estate tax was greater than the credit against the gift tax. Hence, the gift tax credit and the estate tax credit were not unified during those years. Today, the estate tax credit and the gift tax credit are once again unified.

### a. Amount of Credit

As initially enacted, the applicable credit amount (then called the "unified credit") was phased in over a five-year period (1977 through 1981) from $30,000 (in 1977) to $47,000 (by 1981). The 1981 Act substantially increased the amount of the unified credit; by 1987, a credit in the amount of $192,800 could be claimed. [I.R.C. § 2505] The 1997 legislation defined the applicable exclusion amount, rather than the amount of the credit. The credit is determined by computing the tax on the applicable exclusion amount. Legislation in 1998 increased the amount of the credit in stages to reach $345,800 by 2006. The 2001 Act made the $345,800 amount effective in 2002. The 2010 and 2012 legislation increased the credit to $1,730,800 (adjusted annually for inflation). Under the Tax Cuts and Jobs Act of 2017, the credit increased to $4,417,800 in 2018 (adjusted annually for inflation). During 2022, the applicable credit amount is $4,769,800.

### (1) "Clawback" Provision

The scheduled sunset of the increase in the basic exclusion amount at the end of 2025 could create estate tax exposure if a decedent had made gifts totaling more than $5 million between 2018 and 2025 and died after 2025. Hence, the gifts would have been shielded from tax exposure at the time of the gift but could be subject to estate tax at the time of death after the sunset of the 2017 Act. In order to prevent this tax exposure, Congress enacted I.R.C. § 2001(g)(2) allowing the Treasury Department to issue regulations to prevent this "clawback" effect. Under these regulations, a decedent is entitled to use the greater of the basic exclusion amount that was applicable when the gifts were made between 2018 and 2025 or the exclusion amount on the decedent's date of death. [Treas. Reg. § 20.2010–1]

### (2) Exemption Equivalent

The exemption equivalent of a $4,769,800 credit is $12.06 million. Thus, the applicable credit amount effectively eliminates any transfer taxes upon taxable transfers under the gift tax up to this amount.

### (3) Rate Schedule for 2012–2022

| In the Case of Gifts Made and Decedents Dying, During Years | The Applicable Exclusion Amount | Applicable Credit Amount |
|---|---|---|
| 2012 | $ 5,120,000 | $1,772,800 |
| 2013 | 5,250,000 | 2,045,800 |
| 2014 | 5,340,000 | 2,081,800 |
| 2015 | 5,430,000 | 2,117,800 |
| 2016 | 5,450,000 | 2,125,800 |
| 2017 | 5,490,000 | 2,141,800 |
| 2018 | 11,180,000 | 4,417,800 |
| 2019 | 11,400,000 | 4,505,800 |
| 2020 | 11,580,000 | 4,577,800 |
| 2021 | 11,700,000 | 4,625,800 |
| 2022 | 12,060,000 | 4,769,800 |

### (4) Effect of Pre-1977 Gifts

With one exception, the amount of the applicable gift tax credit is ***not*** affected by the amount of pre-1977 gifts or by the fact that the donor utilized the full $30,000 exemption allowed under prior law. The one exception pertains to gifts made between September 8 and December 31, 1976: If any portion of the $30,000 specific exemption, then allowable, was applied as a deduction against these gifts, the amount of the applicable credit available for post-1976 transfers is reduced by 20% of that portion of the specific exemption that was so utilized. [I.R.C. § 2505(b)]

e.g. **Example:** If a taxpayer made a present interest gift of $15,000 in December 1976 and applied $12,000 of an allowable specific exemption against the $12,000 "gross gift" (after the $3,000 annual exclusion then applicable), the amount of the applicable credit available to the taxpayer after 1976 will be reduced by $2,400 ($12,000 × 20%).

### b. Limitation—Applicable Credit Must Be Claimed or Forfeited

The statute expressly states that the amount of the applicable credit available for current gifts must be reduced by the sum of any amounts allowable as a credit for prior gifts. [I.R.C. § 2505(a)] Thus, unlike the $30,000 specific exemption which would not be reduced or lost merely because it was not claimed as a deduction against prior gifts, the applicable gift tax credit must be applied against the tax liability produced by post-1976 gifts in the order of time in which they are made and, if not so applied, the amount of the credit that could have been claimed for preceding calendar years is forfeited.

### c. Relationship to Estate Tax

Because the applicable gift and estate tax credits are set forth under separate sections of the Code, it may appear that they operate consecutively. However, the computational mechanics of the estate tax assure that only a single, applicable credit will be allowed against lifetime and testamentary transfers.

## 5. Computation of the Gift Tax

Assume that a donor made a present interest gift of $15,015,000 to a donee in 2020. Assume further that the donor made a present interest gift of $5,016,000 to another donee in 2022. The annual exclusion was $15,000 for 2020 and $16,000 for 2022. The donor had not made any gifts prior to 2020 and had never been married. Based upon the above hypothetical facts, the donor's gift tax liability for 2020 and 2022 would be computed as follows:

(1) The donor's 2020 gift tax liability would be $1,368,000:

| | |
|---|---|
| Total Gifts [I.R.C. §§ 2501, 2511] | $ 15,015,000 |
| *Less:* Annual Exclusion [I.R.C. § 2503(b)] | (15,000) |
| Taxable Gifts | 15,000,000 |
| Tentative Tax ($345,800 + [40% x $15,000,000]) [I.R.C. § 2001(c)] | $ 5,945,800 |
| *Less:* Applicable Credit Amount [I.R.C. §§ 2502(a), 2010(c)] | (4,577,800) |
| Gift Tax Liability | $ 1,368,000 |

(2) And the donor's 2022 gift tax liability would be $1,808,000:

| | |
|---|---|
| Total Gifts | $ 5,016,000 |
| *Less:* Annual Exclusion | (16,000) |

| | |
|---|---|
| Taxable Gifts | 5,000,000 |
| *Add:* Prior Taxable Gifts | 15,000,000 |
| Cumulative Taxable Gifts | $20,000,000 |
| Tentative Tax ($345,800 + [40% x $14,000,000]) | 7,945,800 |
| *Less:* Tentative Tax on Cumulative Taxable Gifts | (5,945,800) |
| Tentative Gift Tax | 2,000,000 |
| Current Year Applicable Credit Amount (2022 limit less credit previously allowable: $4,769,800 less $4,577,800) | (192,000) |
| Gift Tax Liability | $ 1,808,000 |

Note that the total liability for 2020 and 2022 equals $3,176,000 ($1,368,000 + $1,808,000). A simplified approach to computing the gift tax is to reduce the total taxable gifts by the applicable exclusion amount and multiply that figure by 40%. Hence, $20,000,000 minus $12,060,000 equals $7,940,000; $7,940,000 times 40% = $3,176,000.

# B. Estate Tax Computations

## 1. Background

Prior to the 1976 Tax Reform Act, the estate tax liability was determined separately, without regard to whether the decedent had made taxable gifts during life. This allowed for substantial aggregate transfer tax savings where a person was willing and able to make completed gifts during life which would not be exposed to the estate tax. The advantages were threefold: (i) the donor would utilize the separate gift tax exclusions and specific exemption, as well as the former $60,000 exemption under the estate tax; (ii) the prior gift tax rates were set at 75% of the estate tax rate within the same brackets; and (iii) property not given away during life received a "new start" through the separate graduated estate tax rates rather than being exposed to marginal rates of tax determined "on top of" previous lifetime gratuitous transfers.

### a. Pre-1977 Estate Tax Computations

From the value of the gross estate, allowable deductions were subtracted to arrive at the taxable estate. The separate estate tax rate schedule was then applied to the taxable estate to arrive at the estate tax. Finally, where applicable, the estate tax could be reduced by certain credits against tax allowed under sections 2011 through 2014. The result was the estate tax liability.

### b. Post-1976 Estate Tax Computations

The 1976 Act retained the same basic procedure but made several important changes designed to equalize the tax treatment of gratuitous transfers, whether testamentary or inter vivos. The 1976 Act undertook to produce essentially the same aggregate tax results whether the property is transferred during life or upon death. While the 2001 Act decoupled the gift tax and estate tax by making the applicable credit amounts unequal, the gift tax and the estate were once again unified after the sunset of the 2001 Act and remain unified under the 2017 Tax Cuts and Jobs Act.

#### (1) Application

A unified rate schedule applies for ***both*** estate and gift taxes, ***and*** the aggregate amount of taxable gifts made by the decedent after 1976 (other than gifts included in the gross estate under sections 2035 through 2038) is ***added*** to the taxable estate to form the relevant estate tax base. Then, as with the cumulative gift tax computation, the tentative tax—computed by applying the unified rate schedule to aggregate gratuitous transfers—is reduced by the gift taxes payable with respect to gifts included in the estate tax base.

#### (2) Remaining Advantages of Lifetime Gifts

Although the unified system reduces the transfer tax savings that can be produced by making lifetime gifts, it does not eliminate the advantages altogether.

e.g. **Example:** The gift tax annual exclusion of $16,000 (as adjusted for inflation) per donee is still allowed. Thus, by making annual gifts to multiple donees (and splitting these gifts with one's spouse), considerable amounts of property can be transferred with no transfer tax exposure.

e.g. **Example:** The gift tax is based upon the value of the property at the date of the gift. Hence, if the gift is complete (not subject to the estate tax), all appreciation in value of the transferred property between the date of gift and date of death "passes" to the donee with no transfer tax exposure.

e.g. **Example:** Gifts made that are not within three years of the donor's death and which incur a gift tax will receive the benefit of the gift tax paid in determining the estate tax (step (5) in the overview section below*)* without the gift tax itself being included in the gross estate. The gift tax is said to be "tax exclusive" and the estate tax "tax inclusive."

## 2. Overview

The "taxable estate" (gross estate less allowable deductions) is determined in accordance with the rules previously discussed in connection with the substantive aspects of the estate tax. The remaining elements of the cumulative estate tax computation are analogous to (but differ somewhat from) the cumulative gift tax computation.

### a. Computational Procedure

The present estate tax computation may be divided into seven steps:

(1) First, determine the value of the gross estate.

(2) ***From the gross estate, any allowable deductions*** are subtracted. The result is the taxable estate.

(3) ***The amount of "adjusted taxable gifts" (discussed below) is then added*** to the amount of the taxable estate. [I.R.C. § 2001(b)(1)] The result is the base for the "tentative estate tax."

(4) ***The "tentative estate tax"*** is then ascertained by applying a unified rate schedule to the estate tax base. [I.R.C. § 2001(b) & (c)]

(5) ***From the tentative estate tax, there is subtracted the aggregate amount of "tax payable"*** under the gift tax with respect to gifts made by the decedent after December 31, 1976. [I.R.C. § 2001(b)(2)] The result is the estate tax.

(6) ***The estate tax thus computed is then reduced by the amount of the estate tax applicable credit amount.*** [I.R.C. § 2010]

(7) ***And finally, any applicable credits*** under sections 2012 through 2014 are subtracted. The result is the estate tax liability.

**CALCULATING THE ESTATE TAX** GILBERT

**TO CALCULATE THE ESTATE TAX, THE FOLLOWING STEPS ARE PERFORMED:**

**Value of the Gross Estate**

− Any Allowable Deductions

---

**Taxable Estate**

\+ Adjusted Taxable Gifts

---

**Base for the Tentative Estate Tax**

× Unified Rate Schedule

---

**Tentative Estate Tax**

− Aggregate Amount of "Tax Payable"

---

**Estate Tax**

− Applicable Estate Tax Credit

− Applicable Credits Under I.R.C. §§ 2012–2014

---

**ESTATE TAX LIABILITY**

## b. Applicable Definitions

Certain definitions and special aspects of the computational mechanics should be noted.

### (1) "Adjusted Taxable Gifts"

This is defined as the total amount of taxable gifts made by the decedent ***after*** December 31,1976, ***except*** gifts that comprise part of the "taxable estate" that are includible in the decedent's gross estate. [I.R.C. § 2001(b)]

e.g. **Example:** In arriving at the total amount of taxable gifts, the annual exclusion is taken into account. For example, if a present interest gift of $25,000 was made in 1990 against which an annual exclusion ($10,000) was applied, $15,000 would be deemed part of "adjusted taxable gifts."

(a) **Note**

"Adjusted taxable gifts" are ***limited*** to gifts made ***after*** the effective date of the Tax Reform Act (after December 31, 1976). Contrast this with the cumulative gift tax computation, which takes into account all taxable gifts made by the taxpayer.

(b) **Split Gifts**

In the case of "split gifts" under section 2513, the estate of each spouse would treat the one-half of each split gift attributed to the spouse as an "adjusted taxable gift" made by that spouse, ***except*** that where the full value of the gift is included in the ***gross estate*** of the ***actual donor*** under section 2035 (transfers within three years of death), ***no portion*** of the gift will be included in the ***consenting spouse's*** estate tax computation as an adjusted taxable gift. [I.R.C. § 2001(e)]

(2) **"Tax Payable"**

The gift "tax payable" which will reduce the tentative tax computed on the entire estate tax base includes those gift taxes payable with respect to ***all*** gifts made ***after December 31, 1976***—i.e., gifts included in the gross estate (and thus the taxable estate), as well as "adjusted taxable gifts." It does not include gift taxes paid or payable with respect to pre-1977 gifts since these gifts do not form any part of the estate tax base. [I.R.C. § 2001(b)(2)]

(3) **Adjustment for Gift Tax Paid by Spouse**

If the decedent's spouse consented to split a gift which is thereafter included in full in the decedent's gross estate (since the decedent was the actual donor), the tentative tax is reduced by the ***entire*** amount of the gift tax payable with respect to the gift—i.e., the gift tax imposed upon the decedent's spouse as well as that imposed upon the decedent. [I.R.C. § 2001(d)]

## 3. Rate of Tax

For purposes of determining the "tentative estate tax" and the "tax payable" (with respect to prior gifts made by the decedent), the tax rate of section 2001(c), ***as in effect at the decedent's death,*** are applied. [I.R.C. § 2001(b)] As noted, the current rate is a flat 40% rate. In determining the gift taxes payable, the applicable credit amount of the gift tax, and not the estate tax, is used.

## 4. Estate Tax Applicable Credit Amount

Since the estate tax and gift tax credit are unified again after the sunset of the 2001 Act, the credit will be used for both the estate tax and gift tax. Under the Tax Cuts and Jobs Act of 2017, the basic exclusion amount was increased from $5 million to $10 million (subject to inflationary adjustments) through 2025. During 2022, the basic exclusion amount is $12.06 million, and the applicable credit amount is $4,769,800. The basic exclusion amount will revert to $5 million after December 31, 2025 unless Congress repeals the sunset.

### a. No Double Credit

Although the applicable gift and estate tax credit amounts are separately applied under two different sections of the Code, the ***computational mechanics of the estate tax assure that the total amount of credit used cannot exceed the applicable estate tax credit amount.*** Because the gift "tax payable" (which serves as a type of credit against the tentative estate tax) will have been reduced by any applicable gift tax credit amount allowed or allowable against gift taxes, the use of the applicable gift tax credit amount is effectively factored out at this point of the estate tax computation and, thus, must be reintroduced by application of the estate tax credit amount against the tentative estate tax liability.

### b. Reduction of Credit for Certain Pre-1977 Gifts

Just as in the case of the applicable gift tax credit amount, the deduction of the former $30,000 gift tax specific exemption against pre-1977 taxable gifts does not generally affect the allowance of the applicable credit amount with respect to post-1976 gift or estate tax liability. However, if the specific exemption was applied against gifts made between September 8, 1976, and December 31, 1976, the amount of the allowable applicable credit amount is reduced by 20% of the amount of the exemption so used. [I.R.C. § 2010(b)]

## 5. Other Credits Allowed Against Estate Tax

In addition to the unified estate tax credit, the Code authorizes four other credits against the estate tax:

### a. Credit for Certain Pre-1977 Gift Taxes Paid

As previously noted, in order to prevent "double" taxes, a credit was allowed for gift taxes paid on gifts that were also included in the donor's gross estate. [I.R.C. § 2012(a)] This credit may still be claimed with respect to pre-1977 gifts. However, the credit is inapplicable to gifts made after 1976 since the reduction of the tentative estate tax by the gift "tax payable" under section 2001(b)(2) accomplishes this same result. [I.R.C. § 2012(e)]

### b. Credit for Taxes Paid on Prior Estate—Property Previously Taxed to Another

Section 2013 authorizes a credit for the estate tax imposed upon other estates with respect to property that passed from such other estates to the decedent which is included in the latter decedent's gross estate. This credit was enacted to relieve against repeated estate taxation, in quick succession, of property passing from one decedent to another. The following rules are applicable:

(1) ***A credit*** is allowed for the federal tax actually paid on any property passing to the decedent during her lifetime from the estate of some prior decedent. The credit is available as to property passing from one spouse to another, but only to the extent that the property did *not* qualify for the marital deduction.

(2) ***It is not required*** that the same property that the present decedent received from the prior decedent be a part of her estate. All that need appear is that some property subject to a prior estate tax was received by the decedent, even if the decedent has consumed, sold or otherwise disposed of that property.

(3) ***The amount of the credit*** depends upon the interval between deaths. If the first decedent died within two years of the death of the present decedent, 100% of the estate tax paid in the first decedent's estate is allowable; 80% if within four years; 60% if within six years; 40% if within eight years; and 20% if within 10 years. [I.R.C. § 2013(a)]

(4) ***One other limitation*** is imposed—the credit cannot be more than the estate tax savings if the previously taxed property were entirely excluded from the decedent's

estate. This is to account for situations where property has fallen steeply in value since the date of the first decedent's death. [I.R.C. § 2013(c)]

### c. Foreign Tax Credit

Both foreign real and personal property may be included in the estate of a United States citizen. Since such property is usually also taxed by the country in which it is located, the decedent's estate may be subject to double taxation. To avoid this, section 2014 allows a credit against the United States estate tax for the amount of any foreign death taxes payable with respect to property situated in a foreign country and included in the decedent's gross estate for federal tax purposes.

#### (1) Executor's Election

Under section 2053(d), the executor may elect to claim certain foreign death taxes as a deduction in computing the decedent's taxable estate in lieu of applying these taxes as a credit.

#### (2) Credit Pursuant to Treaty

In addition to the foreign tax credit, the United States has treaties with several foreign nations providing reciprocal recognition and credits for death duties paid. Where death taxes are paid to a country with which such a treaty is in effect, the estate may claim the larger of the statutory credit or the treaty credit.

## 6. Estate Tax Computation

Assume that D made taxable gifts of $7 million in 2017, had not made any prior gifts, and was unmarried. In addition, assume that D died in 2022, leaving a taxable estate of $10 million. D's gift tax liability for 2017 was $604,000. It is computed as follows: Gift tax = $2,745,800 ($345,800 + [40% times $6 million]); applicable credit amount = $2,141,800; gift tax liability = $604,000. The $604,000 figure is also computed as follows: $7,000,000 (taxable gifts) less $5,490,000 (applicable exclusion amount for 2017) = $1,510,000; $1,510,000 times 40% = $604,000.

### a. Illustrative Computation

D's estate tax liability would be $1,372,000, computed as follows:

| | |
|---|---|
| Taxable estate | $10,000,000 |
| ***Add:*** adjusted taxable gift (post-1976 gifts only) [I.R.C. §2001(b)(1)] | +7,000,000 |
| Base for tentative tax | $17,000,000 |
| Tentative tax ($345,800 + 40% of $16 million) [I.R.C. §2001(c)] ***Less:*** gift taxes payable (post-1976 gifts only): | $ 6,745,800 |
| ($345,800 + [40% of $6 million ***less*** allowable credit]) | ( 604,000) |
| Tax | $ 6,141,800 |
| Less: unified credit [I.R.C. § 2010] | (4,769,800) |

| Estate tax liability | $ 1,372,000 |
|---|---|

The combined 2017 gift tax of $604,000 and estate tax of $1,372,000 is $1,976,800. If D had not made any taxable gifts and died with a taxable estate of $17,000,000, D's estate tax is $1,976,000 ($345,800 + 40% of $16,000,000; $6,745,800 less $4,769,800 applicable credit amount).

# C. Deceased Spousal Unused Exclusion Amount ("Portability")

## 1. Meaning and History

"Portability" was first introduced in the 2010 Act and was set to expire at the end of 2012. However, the American Taxpayer Relief Act of 2012 ***made portability permanent***. Section 2010(c) allows for ***"portability" of the unused exclusion amount*** between spouses ***for gift and estate tax purposes*** (it does not apply to the generation-skipping transfer exemption). This allows a surviving spouse to use the surviving spouse's basic exclusion amount increased by any unused exclusion amount from the deceased spouse. [I.R.C. § 2010(c)(2)(B)] This unused amount is called the "deceased spousal unused exclusion amount" (DSUE) and is the lesser of, the basic exclusion amount, or the excess of the exclusion amount of the last deceased spouse of the surviving spouse minus the tentative tax on the estate of the deceased spouse. [I.R.C. § 2010(c)(4)]

## 2. How to Elect Portability

The ***DSUE is eligible for decedents dying after December 31, 2010.*** [I.R.C. § 2010(c)(4)] The deceased spouse's executor must make an election on the estate tax return to allow the surviving spouse to use the DSUE, and the tax return must not be filed late. [I.R.C. § 2010(c)(5)(A)] The IRS can grant an extension if an estate tax return is not required to be filed. The ***election is irrevocable***. [I.R.C. § 2010(c)(5)]

e.g. **Example:** Julia died in 2022 survived by her husband, Jose. Julia had made taxable gifts worth $2 million during her lifetime and died with a taxable estate of $4.06 million. During 2022, the basic exclusion amount totaled $12.06 million. Because Julia only used $6.06 million of her exclusion amount, the DSUE is $6 million. If the executor of Julia's estate makes the DSUE election on her estate tax return, Jose will be able to use the $6 million along with his own $12.06 million exclusion for an applicable exclusion amount of $18.06 million.

e.g. **Example:** In 2022, Darius passed away survived by his husband, Michael. Darius had not made any taxable gifts during his lifetime but died with a taxable estate of $7 million. On his estate tax return, Darius used $7 million of the exclusion amount, and the executor elected portability. The DSUE was $5.06 million. If Michael made taxable gifts while he was still alive, the $5.06 million DSUE would be applied to these taxable gifts. Michael's $12.06 million exclusion amount will not be reduced until the $5.06 million DSUE is used up. Note that portability is allowed in this example because same-sex marriages are treated the same as heterosexual marriages under the Code as of 2013.

## 3. Use of the "Last Deceased Spouse" Applicable Exclusion Amount

### a. Who Is a Last Deceased Spouse?

It is important to note that ***only the DSUE of the "last" deceased spouse may be used.*** [I.R.C. § 2010(c)(4)(B)(i)] Assume that a deceased spouse's executor elected portability with a DSUE of $10 million. The surviving spouse remarried. The new spouse died with a DSUE of $1 million. Even if the new spouse's executor did not elect portability, the surviving spouse could no longer use the first spouse's DSUE. The surviving spouse could only use the DSUE of the most recent deceased spouse and not the first deceased spouse.

### b. Examination of the Deceased Spouse's Tax Returns

The ***IRS may examine a deceased spouse's return to determine the DSUE.*** The IRS's authority applies with respect to each transfer by the surviving spouse to which a DSUE amount has been applied. [Treas. Reg. § 20.2010–3(d)] The IRS's examination may take place ***even if*** the statute of limitations under section 6501 has expired. [I.R.C. § 2010(c)(5)(B)] However, this authority ***does not permit the IRS to assess a deficiency*** against the deceased spouse's estate ***if the statute of limitations has already expired.*** In **Estate of Sower v. Commissioner,** 149 T.C. 279 (2017), the estate argued that the IRS could not adjust the DSUE because the deceased spouse made the gifts before December 31, 2010, the effective date of section 2010(c)(5)(B). The court rejected the estate's argument and determined that the effective date of section 2010(c)(5)(B) did not preclude the IRS from adjusting the DSUE amount by gifts given before the effective date.

# Chapter Seven

# Tax on Generation-Skipping Transfers

| CONTENTS | PAGE |
|---|---|

# Chapter Approach

As discussed, life estates and other interests that are granted to a decedent and which ***terminate*** on the decedent's death are not subject to the estate tax. And where a person is granted a ***nongeneral (special)*** power of appointment, the exercise or nonexercise of the power is not subject to either the estate or gift taxes, although there is a minor exception to that rule. Furthermore, a person may be a permissible distributee or appointee of property and have access to (and enjoyment of) the property for support, etc., during life without estate tax exposure upon death. These limitations upon the scope of the estate and gift taxes created opportunities for considerable tax avoidance and, in turn, led to the enactment of Chapter 13, the "Generation-Skipping Transfer Tax."

For purposes of analysis of generation-skipping transfer tax provisions, you should determine:

1. ***The transfers to which the tax applies;*** and
2. ***The amount of the transfer*** **(i.e., the tax base).**

Although unlikely to be found in your exam questions, you should also review the sections on computation of the tax and payment of the tax found at the end of this chapter.

# A. Background and Introduction

## 1. Prior Law

Prior to 1976, so-called generation-skipping transfers were a popular estate and tax planning device. By granting successive life estates to succeeding generations—frequently coupled with powers in the trustee to distribute corpus for support, etc., powers to withdraw up to $5,000 or 5% of corpus annually, and nongeneral powers to appoint all or a portion of the property during life or upon death—succeeding generations could be afforded significant enjoyment of the transferred property without transfer tax exposure (i.e., the shifting of enjoyment from one generation to a succeeding generation would not attract the gift or estate taxes).

e.g. **Example:** D conveys property on trust for D's son, S, for life, and upon S's death to S's daughter, D, for her life, and upon D's death to her surviving children. Under prior law, there was no estate tax payable on the death of S or D, because their interests terminated on their deaths.

### a. Note

The only effective legal limitation upon the use of such generation-skipping transfers was the common law Rule Against Perpetuities. But, despite the Rule, it was frequently possible to "skip" two and sometimes three generations before an outright distribution would be required. Further, most states have abolished the common law Rule, thereby putting no limitations on the use of generation-skipping transfers.

### b. Comment

While the use of such generation-skipping transfers was theoretically available to everyone, in practice the device was most valuable to, and was used most often by, the very wealthy because multi-generational trusts are economically feasible only when significant wealth is involved, and thus wealthier families could enjoy the greatest tax savings.

## 2. Overview of the Tax Under the 1976 Act

The generation-skipping transfer tax was promulgated to close this gaping loophole in the federal transfer tax system and to eliminate the special advantage enjoyed by the "super rich." The taxing provisions are contained in Chapter 13 of the Code.

### a. Transfer Tax

Like the estate and the gift taxes, this new tax was a ***transfer*** tax. It applied only when a "generation-skipping" transfer occurred.

### b. Separate Transfer Tax

The tax did not amend or modify the substantive law of the estate and gift tax systems. Rather, it was an entirely separate transfer tax.

### c. Correlation with Estate and Gift Tax

Nevertheless, the tax was closely related, technically and conceptually, to the estate and gift tax.

#### (1) Approximated Same Tax Results

It was designed to achieve the same tax result in the case of generation-skipping transfers as would occur if the property were transmitted outright, by gift or bequest, through succeeding generations.

#### (2) Method

Not only was the unified estate and gift tax schedule applied, but the tax was imposed upon the value of the generation-skipping transfer as if the transfer had been made by an ancestor to a descendant (by gift or bequest); i.e., the value of the transfer was cumulated with the taxable gifts and/or taxable estate of the ancestor.

## 3. Objections to the 1976 Act

As originally enacted, the generation-skipping transfer tax ("GST") embodied a number of complex provisions that were perceived as major defects from the viewpoint of practical administration of the tax. Consequently, Congress continually deferred the effective date for the application of this tax. The principal objections were:

### a. Computational Complexity

Tying the amount of the GST to the gift and estate taxes of the ancestor, including the cumulative taxable gifts and the taxable estate of the ancestor, was unduly complicated.

### b. Gaps in Coverage

The 1976 GST only addressed generation-skipping through the use of successive interests in a trust or trust equivalent. It did not take into account generation-skipping by the super-rich using outright gifts ("direct skips") to multiple successive generations.

## 4. Repeal and Replacement in 1986

As part of the 1986 Tax Reform Act, Congress repealed the 1976 GST, and replaced it with a new generation-skipping transfer tax.

### a. Retroactive Repeal

The 1976 provisions were repealed retroactively. As a result, any generation-skipping transfers that occurred ***prior to the effective date of the 1986 Act's GST are not subject to the GST.***

### b. 1986 GST

The GST of the 1986 Act is essentially the same in all substantive respects to its predecessor, with two notable exceptions:

#### (1) Simplified Computations

The present GST imposes a ***flat rate tax of 40%*** upon generation-skipping transfers. The computational complexities of the 1976 Act, which tied the rate of tax to the ancestor's cumulative gift and estate taxes, are eliminated.

#### (2) Direct Skips Also Taxed

Direct skips are now subject to the GST.

# B. Transfers to Which the Tax Applies

## 1. Introduction

The GST is imposed upon "every generation-skipping transfer." [I.R.C. § 2601] Such transfers include: (i) "taxable distributions," (ii) "taxable terminations," and (iii) "direct skips." [I.R.C. § 2611]

## 2. Basic Definitions

Definitions of the three categories of generation-skipping transfers are contained in I.R.C. § 2612.

### a. "Taxable Distribution"

This is defined as any distribution from a trust to a "skip person," except a distribution that would be considered a "taxable termination" or a "direct skip." [I.R.C. § 2612(b)]

e.g. **Example:** A distribution to a grandchild of the transferor ("skip person") while a child of the transferor ("non-skip person") remains a beneficiary of the trust.

### b. "Taxable Termination"

This means any termination (by death, lapse of time, release of a power, or otherwise) of an interest in property held in a trust, except where a "non-skip person" has an interest in the property immediately after the termination, ***or*** if no distribution may thereafter be made by the trust to a skip person. [I.R.C. § 2612(a)]

e.g. **Example:** Transferor creates a trust for a single child ("non-skip person") and after the child's death, distributes to (or remains in trust for) grandchildren ("skip persons"). The death of the child is a taxable termination because no "non-skip person" has interest in the trust and distribution thereafter may be made to skip persons.

### c. "Direct Skip"

This is a transfer that is subject to the gift or estate tax but which is made to a skip person (e.g., direct bequest for a grandchild). [I.R.C. § 2612(c)]

## 3. Subsidiary Definitions

To understand the basic definitions, one must understand the special meaning of the terms used in these definitions.

### a. "Trust"

For purposes of the GST, a "trust" refers not only to an actual trust but also to "***any arrangement*** (other than an estate) which . . . has substantially the same effect as a trust." [I.R.C. § 2652(b)(1)] Thus, successive legal life estates would be treated in the same manner as successive income interests in a trust.

### b. "Interest in Property"

A person has an interest in the property held by a trust if that person has a right to receive distributions of income or principal from the trust, ***including permissible*** (discretionary) ***distributions,*** but ***excluding*** distributions that cannot be made until sometime in the future. [I.R.C. § 2652(c)]

### c. "Skip Person" and "Non-Skip Person"

A "skip person" is a person assigned to a generation that is two or more generations below that of the transferor. [I.R.C. § 2613(a)(1)] A "non-skip person" is a person who is not a skip person. [I.R.C. § 2613(b)]

#### (1) Skip Person Can Include Trust

A trust will be treated as a skip person if all interests in the trust are held by skip persons, or if no person holds a present interest in the trust but all future distributions from the trust must be made to skip persons (i.e., no non-skip person may receive any future distributions). [I.R.C. § 2613(a)(2)]

#### (2) Generation Assignments

The starting point for assignment of persons to generations is the "transferor."

##### (a) "Transferor"

For purposes of the GST, the "transferor" is the decedent or the donor, depending upon whether the trust or direct skip is initiated by bequest or lifetime gift. [I.R.C. § 2652(a)] After a taxable termination, for purposes of measuring future taxable events, the generation level of the transferor drops to one above the beneficiary having the highest generation assignment left in the trust. [I.R.C. § 2653(a)]

e.g. **Example:** A trust is created for the child and great grandchildren of the transferor. Upon the death of the child, only great grandchildren remain as beneficiaries so that the transferor will now be the grandchildren's generation and great grandchildren will become non-skip persons.

##### (b) Family Generations

Generations are ordinarily determined along family lines. For instance, the transferor and the transferor's siblings would be in the same generation. Any of their children (including adopted children) would be assigned to the first younger generation. Grandchildren would be assigned to the next younger generation, and so forth. [I.R.C. § 2651(b)] Spouses of transferors or of lineal descendants of transferors are assigned to the same generation as the other spouse. [I.R.C. § 2651(c)]

#### (c) Nonfamily Generations

The generation assignment of nonfamily members is determined by comparing their ages to that of the transferor. A person born within 12-$^1/_2$ years of the date of the transferor's birth is assigned to the transferor's generation; persons born more than 12-$^1/_2$ years but less than 37-$^1/_2$ years from the date of the transferor's birth are assigned to the first younger generation; and each succeeding 25 years defines new generations. [I.R.C. § 2651(d)]

#### (d) Entities

If any entity—estate, trust, partnership, or corporation—has an interest in the property, the individuals having a beneficial interest in the entity are treated as having an interest in the property and are assigned to generations according to the above rules. [I.R.C. § 2651(f)(2)]

## 4. General Exceptions

Exceptions are contained in section 2611(b). The two exceptions of general applicability are:

### a. Excluded Under Gift Tax

If the transfer would be excluded under section 2503(e) of the gift tax (transfers for educational or medical expenses), it is not taxable under the GST. [I.R.C. § 2611(b)(1)]

### b. No Tax Avoidance

The GST does not apply to any transfer to the extent that: (i) the property was subject to a prior generation-skipping tax; (ii) the prior taxable transfer was to a transferee assigned to a generation the same as or lower than that of the present transferee; and (iii) the transfer does not have the effect of avoiding the generation-skipping tax. [I.R.C. § 2611(b)(2)]

## 5. Special Exception for Descendant with Deceased Parent

If, at the time when generations are assigned (when a tax is imposed under Chapter 11 (estate tax) or Chapter 12 (gift tax), a lineal descendant of a parent of the transferor has a parent who is also a lineal descendant of a parent of the transferor who is deceased, such individual shall be treated as one generation below the transferor (i.e., a non-skip person). [I.R.C. § 2651(e)] This section shall apply to collateral relatives of the transferor only if the transferor has no lineal descendants.

e.g. **Example—Taxable Distribution:** During life, D created a trust directing the trustee to pay the income of the trust to D's child, C. The trustee is also authorized to pay such amounts of corpus to any of C's children as may be necessary for their health, education, support, and maintenance. This year the trustee pays $ 20,000 to G, a child of C, for support. Under the general rules of the GST, this distribution for G's benefit would be a taxable distribution.

e.g. **Example—Taxable Termination:** Assume the same trust as above. The trust provides that upon the death of C, the trust corpus is to be divided into as many shares as there are surviving children of C and, thereafter, the income of each share is to be distributed to the appropriate child of C. Upon C's death, there will be a taxable termination of C's interest.

e.g. **Example—Direct Skip:** D devises the residue of her estate to her grandchild, G. This is a direct skip. Moreover, it is subject to the GST even though the property is subject to the estate tax in D's estate. It will be subject to the special "deceased parent" exception only if G's parent (D's child) is dead.

# C. Amount Taxable

## 1. Introduction

The amount taxable depends on the type of generation-skipping transfer. [I.R.C. § 2602(1)]

## 2. Taxable Distributions

The base for the GST in the case of a taxable distribution is the value of the property ***received*** by the transferee, ***reduced by*** any expenses incurred by the transferee in connection with the determination or collection of the GST tax. [I.R.C. § 2621(a)]

### a. Payment of GST Tax-Special Rule

If the trust pays the GST tax for the recipient of a taxable distribution, the amount of the GST tax so paid is considered a taxable distribution. [I.R.C. § 2621(b)]

## 3. Taxable Terminations

The taxable amount is the value of all property that was the subject of the taxable termination, ***reduced by*** expenses of a nature that would be allowable as estate tax deductions under section 2053(b). [I.R.C. § 2622]

## 4. Direct Skips

The GST is imposed on the value of the property received by the transferee. [I.R.C. § 2623]

## 5. Valuation Rules

The value of the property is its fair market value ***at the time of the generation-skipping transfer,*** reduced by any consideration provided by the transferee. [I.R.C. § 2624(a), (d)]

### a. Time of Transfer

In the case of a taxable distribution or a direct skip produced by a lifetime gift, the time of the transfer is the date of the distribution or gift. In the case of a direct skip produced by bequest from a decedent, the time of the transfer is the date of the decedent's death. In the case of a taxable termination, the time of the transfer is the date of the termination—the date of death of the holder of the prior interest if death is the cause of the taxable termination. [I.R.C. § 2624(a)]

### b. Alternate Valuation Date

Where a direct skip or a taxable termination occurs as a result of death, special rules allow use of the alternate valuation date. [I.R.C. § 2624(b), (c)]

## 6. GST Exemption

Section 2631 allows a GST exemption equal to the basic exclusion amount [I.R.C. § 2010(c)] which may be allocated by a transferor (or the transferor's executor) to any property transferred by the transferor. [*See* I.R.C. § 2632—special allocation rules] Prior to 2004, the GST exemption was $1 million indexed for inflation from 1997. Under the 2010 Act, generation-skipping transfers had a tax rate of zero during 2010. This meant that there was not a GST tax during that year. The 2010 Act increased the basic exclusion amount to $5 million indexed for inflation, and thus the GST exemption was increased to $5 million indexed for inflation. The 2017 Tax Cuts and Jobs Act did not make any changes to section 2631. However, it increased the basic exclusion amount to $10 million indexed for inflation. As a result, the GST exemption is also $10 million. The ***GST exemption for 2022*** after factoring in the adjustment for inflation is ***$12.06 million***. A surviving spouse is unable to use a deceased spouse's unused GST exemption (portability is inapplicable).

### a. Not an Exclusion

Note that the GST exemption does not operate as an exclusion or deduction. Rather, it is used in the tax computation to determine the effective rate at which a generation-skipping transfer will be taxed.

### b. Reverse QTIP Election

Under section 2652(a)(3), the decedent spouse's estate or the donor spouse may elect to reverse a previous qualified terminable interest property (QTIP) election. If the estate or donor spouse makes the election, it ***will be treated as if the QTIP election has not been made***. Hence, the decedent or donor spouse will be ***entitled to the marital deduction and use the GST exemption for the property subject to the QTIP election.*** [I.R.C. § 2652(a)(3)]. In order to make this special election the decedent or donor spouse must have made a QTIP election for a trust under sections 2056(b)(7) and 2523(f).

#### (1) Significance-Tax Savings

The reverse QTIP election becomes significant when the donor spouse has used up the basic exclusion amount for estate and gift tax purposes but has not used up the GST exemption. If the donor spouse makes the reverse QTIP election, the donor spouse can claim the marital deduction while still being considered as the transferor for GST purposes of the trust property instead of the donee spouse, which will allow the donor spouse's GST exemption to be used to shelter the trust property from the GST tax.

e.g. **Example:** Jacob and Alyssa were married and had one son, Brian. Jacob died, and under his will a trust was created that would pay income to Alyssa for her life with the corpus distributed to their grandchildren upon Alyssa's death. Jacob's executor made a QTIP election for the trust. As a result, the trust property would be included in Alyssa's estate under section 2044 or subject to gift taxation under section 2519. Alyssa would be considered the transferor of the trust property for GST purposes. However, if Jacob had not used his GST exemption for previous transfers, his executor could make a reverse QTIP election, which would make it as if the QTIP election had not been made for GST purposes. This would allow Jacob's GST exemption to be used for the trust property, instead of Alyssa's GST exemption.

# D. Computation of Tax

## 1. Amount of GST

The amount of the GST is the taxable amount multiplied by the "applicable rate." [I.R.C. § 2602]

## 2. Applicable Rate of Tax

This is the ***maximum federal estate tax rate*** in effect on the date of the generation-skipping transfer, multiplied by the **"*inclusion ratio*"** with respect to the transfer. [I.R.C. § 2641]

## 3. Inclusion Ratio

This is a fraction arrived at by subtracting the "applicable fraction" from the number 1. The applicable fraction will have, as its numerator, the amount of the GST exclusion allocated to the trust (or direct skip property) and, as its denominator, the value of all the property transferred to the trust (or transferred in the direct skip) less any federal estate or death taxes actually paid from the property (and any charitable deduction allowed with respect to the property). [I.R.C. § 2642] A trust can be severed into two or more trusts in a qualified severance if the trust is divided on a fractional basis, and the new trusts are the same in regard to the succession of interests to the beneficiaries. [I.R.C. § 2642(a)(3)(B)(i)] In order for a trust with an inclusion ratio greater than zero and less than one to be considered a qualified severance it must be split into two trusts, one with an inclusion ratio of one and one with an inclusion ratio of zero. [I.R.C. § 2642(a)(3)(B)(ii)]

e.g. **Example:** D bequeathed the residue of her estate to a trust, with directions to pay all the income from the trust to her niece N, and upon N's death, to distribute the trust corpus to the children of N. The residue of D's estate was $4 million. The residuary trust's share of D's federal and state death taxes (which it paid from the property it received) was $1 million. D's executor allocated the $1 million GST exemption to this residuary trust. Upon N's death in 2022, the value of the property held by the trust was $5 million.

**a.** ***The value*** of the property that is subject to the taxable termination occurring at N's death is $5 million—the fair market value at the time of the termination.

**b.** ***The inclusion ratio*** is 1 minus $ 1 million (allocable GST exemption) over $ 3 million ($4 million transferred to the trust less the $ 1 million death taxes paid by the trust); i.e., 1 – 1/3 = 2/3.

**c.** ***The applicable rate*** of .40 (federal estate tax rate in 2022) is then multiplied by 2/3, or .27.

**d.** ***And the GST tax is*** .27 multiplied by $5 million (the taxable amount), or $1.35 million.

# E. Payment of Tax

## 1. Introduction

The person liable for the GST tax depends upon the type of generation-skipping transfer.

## 2. Taxable Distributions

The transferee, i.e., the person who receives the distribution, is liable to pay the tax. [I.R.C. § 2603(a)(1)]

## 3. Taxable Terminations

The trustee is liable for the tax. [I.R.C. § 2603(a)(2)] For arrangements that are not formal trusts, "trustee" means the person in actual or constructive possession of the property that is the subject of the arrangement. [I.R.C. § 2652(b)(2)]

## 4. Direct Skips

The transferor pays the tax. [I.R.C. § 2603(a)(3)]

# Chapter Eight

# Returns and Payment of Tax

| CONTENTS | PAGE |
|---|---|

# Chapter Approach

This chapter considers some of the basic rules relating to the filing of returns and the payment of transfer taxes and also introduces some special provisions relating to installment payment of estate taxes. Although this material comprises only a very minor portion of most estate and gift tax courses, a review of the basic rules is appropriate for you to have a systematic understanding of the transfer tax schemes.

# A. Gift Tax

## 1. Returns

A gift tax return must be filed for any calendar year in which a gift is made. [I.R.C. § 6019]

### a. Exceptions

A gift tax return need not be filed if the only transfers made during the year are fully exempt from tax or are nontaxable because of the 100% marital deduction. [I.R.C. § 6019] Specifically that would be:

(1) If no gift exceeds the ***$16,000 annual exclusion*** for present interest gifts under section 2503(b). [I.R.C. § 6019(1)]

(2) Gifts for ***certain educational or medical expenses*** that are exempt under section 2503(e). [I.R.C. § 6019(1)]

(3) Gifts that qualify for the gift tax ***marital deduction*** under section 2523. [I.R.C. § 6019(2)]

(4) Gifts that qualify for the ***charitable deduction*** under section 2522 if the entire interest given is charitable (i.e., the exception would not apply to split-interest gifts. [I.R.C. § 6019(3)]

| EXCEPTIONS TO THE FILING REQUIREMENTS FOR GIFT TAX RETURNS | GILBERT |
|---|---|
| **A GIFT TAX RETURN NEED NOT BE FILED UNDER THE FOLLOWING CIRCUMSTANCES:** | |
| ☑ No gift exceeds the ***$16,000 annual exclusion*** for present interest gifts under § 2503(b); | |
| ☑ The gift is exempt as an ***educational or medical expense*** under § 2503(e); | |
| ☑ The gift qualifies under the gift tax ***marital deduction*** under § 2523; or | |
| ☑ The gift qualifies as a ***charitable deduction*** under § 2522. | |

### b. Time for Filing

Gift tax returns must be filed on or before the fifteenth day of April following the close of the calendar year in which a gift is made. [I.R.C. § 6075(b)]

(1) **Extensions of Time**

However, extensions of up to six months may be granted upon application. [I.R.C. § 6081(a)]

(2) **Special Rules**

If a donor is granted an extension of time to file an income tax return for the calendar year in which a gift was made, this extension will also apply to any gift tax return to be filed. [I.R.C. § 6075(b)(2)] Also, if a donor dies within the calendar year in which a gift was made, the gift tax return may be filed (by the executor) on or before the time required for the filing of the donor-decedent's estate tax return. [I.R.C. § 6075(b)(3)]

c. **Responsibility for Filing**

The donor is required to file the gift tax return. [I.R.C. § 6019] If the donor is deceased, the donor's executor files the return. [Treas. Reg. § 25.6019–1(g)] If the donor becomes legally incompetent before filing the gift tax return, the donor's guardian is responsible for filing it. [Treas. Reg. § 25.6019–1(g)]

## 2. Payment of Tax

The donor is primarily liable for payment of the gift tax. [I.R.C. § 2502(c)]

a. **Transferee Liability**

If the donor fails to pay the tax, the government has a lien on the donated property to the extent of the tax due, and also has the right to hold the donee liable (transferee liability) for the unpaid gift tax, to the extent of the value of the property received by the donee. [I.R.C. § 6324(b)]

b. **Reimbursement Where "QTIP" Property Transferred**

If a donee-spouse incurs gift tax liability on account of a transfer of the donee-spouse's life interest in "qualified terminable interest property" ("QTIP") the donee-spouse is entitled to be reimbursed by the recipient of the property for the gift taxes attributable to this transfer. [I.R.C. § 2207A(b)]

c. **Time for Payment**

Payment of the tax is due at the same time that the return must be filed (above) and should accompany the return. [I.R.C. § 6151(a)]

(1) **Extensions of Time**

Extensions of time for payment may be granted for up to six months upon application. [I.R.C. § 6161] However, the grant of such an extension does not waive the government's right to interest upon the unpaid tax from the due date.

## 3. Special Rules for Split Gifts

a. **Filing Requirement**

If the gift of a future interest is split, both spouses must file a return reporting one-half of the value of the property. In the case of a present interest gift, the actual donor must file a return if the gift exceeds $16,000 (the current annual exclusion); the consenting spouse need not file a return unless the one-half of the value of the gift that is attributed to that spouse itself exceeds $16,000.

(1) **Note**

If the consenting spouse is not obliged to file a return, the consenting spouse's consent to split the gift will be indicated on the return filed by the actual donor. [I.R.C. § 2513(b)] Otherwise, the consent is indicated on the consenting spouse's return (although apparently it is sufficient if the consent is indicated on the return filed by the actual donor).

There is no reason for spouses to "split" a gift under section 2513 unless the value of the gift will require a return to be filed (i.e., if the gift is of a future interest to which the annual exclusion does not apply, or the value of a present interest gift exceeds $16,000).

b. **Liability for Tax**

Both spouses are jointly and severally liable for payment of the gift tax on split gifts. [I.R.C. § 2513(d)] Note, however, that if the actual donor pays the entire tax (or the consenting spouse pays the entire tax), this payment of the other spouse's "share" is not a taxable gift to the other spouse. [Treas. Reg. § 25.2511–1(d)]

# B. Estate Tax

## 1. Returns

The executor of the decedent's estate is responsible for filing the estate tax return. [I.R.C. § 6018(a)]

a. **"Executor"**

For estate tax purposes, the term "executor" means "the executor or administrator of the decedent, or, if there is no executor or administrator appointed, qualified, and acting within the United States, then any person in actual or constructive possession of any property of the decedent." [I.R.C. § 2203]

b. **Returns by Beneficiaries**

If the executor is unable to file a complete return with respect to some portion of the gross estate, the executor must identify that portion of the estate and provide the name of the persons holding legal title or a beneficial interest in the property. The government may then require those persons to file a return as to that part of the estate. [I.R.C. § 6018(b)]

c. **Limitation—Filing Amount**

A return is required only if the amount of the gross estate exceeds the applicable exclusion amount reduced by certain taxable gifts made by the decedent. [I.R.C. § 6018(a)(1) & (3)]

d. **Nonresident Aliens**

A return is required for estates of nonresident aliens if that part of the gross estate that is situated in the United States exceeds $60,000. [I.R.C. § 6018(a)(2)]

### e. Time for Filing

The return must be filed no later than nine months after the date of the decedent's death. [I.R.C. § 6075(a)]

#### (1) Extensions of Time

However, extensions of time for up to six months may be granted upon application. [I.R.C. § 6081(a)]

## 2. Payment of Estate Tax

The executor is also primarily responsible for payment of the estate tax. [I.R.C. § 6151(a)]

### a. Personal Liability

An executor may become personally liable for payment of the estate tax. In **Estate of Lee v. Commissioner,** T.C. Memo. 2021–92, 122 T.C.M. (CCH) 91 (2021), the executor of the estate was found to be personally liable for unpaid federal estate taxes. The court noted that an executor would become personally liable for unpaid estate taxes if the executor made a distribution when the estate was insolvent or if the distribution caused the estate to become insolvent and the executor had actual knowledge or notice of the tax liability. In this case, the distribution caused the estate to become insolvent. The court determined that the executor had notice of the unpaid tax liability because the executor had received a notice of deficiency and had actual knowledge of the claim because the executor was named as a party in the Tax Court petition.

**EXAM TIP** GILBERT

It may seem odd but remember on your exam that an executor is ***personally*** liable for the decedent's estate tax until the executor has been discharged from liability.

### b. Estate's Right to Reimbursement in Certain Instances

Sections 2206 and 2207 entitle the executor to recover from the beneficiary of life insurance proceeds and from a person who takes property in which the decedent had a taxable power of appointment the proportionate share of the estate tax that was payable because of inclusion of the life insurance proceeds or property subject to the power in the decedent's gross estate, unless the decedent directs otherwise in his will. Section 2207B entitles the executor to recover from receiving property after the expiration of a retained life estate taxable in the decedent's estate under section 2036 the proportionate share of which was payable because of the inclusion of the property in which the decedent retained the life estate, unless the decedent, in his will, specifically indicates an intent to waive such right.

### c. Reimbursement Where Estate Includes "QTIP" Property

If a decedent's estate includes "qualified terminable interest property" per section 2044, the executor (unless otherwise directed by the decedent's will) is entitled to recover from the recipient of the property the amount by which estate taxes are increased by reason of the inclusion of the QTIP property in the decedent's estate. [I.R.C. § 2207A(a)]

### d. Lien for Taxes; Transferee Liability

If the estate tax is not paid when due, those persons who hold legal or beneficial interests in property that was included in the gross estate are liable for the payment of the estate tax to the extent of the value of the property. [I.R.C. § 6324(a)(2)] In addition, the government has a lien on all the estate assets to secure payment of the tax and may institute proceedings to foreclose the lien. [I.R.C. § 6324(a)(1)]

### e. Time for Payment

Payment of the estate tax is due at the same time that the estate tax return must be filed—nine months after the decedent's death. [I.R.C. § 6151(a)]

#### (1) Extensions of Time for Payment

##### (a) Upon Showing of Cause

Extensions of time for payment may be granted, upon a showing of reasonable cause, for periods of up to 10 years from the date upon which the payment is otherwise due. [I.R.C. § 6161(a)(2)] However, as with gift tax payments, the granting of such an extension does not preclude the running of interest.

##### (b) Extensions of Time for Reversionary or Remainder Interests

Further, if the estate of the decedent includes a reversionary interest or a remainder interest in property, the executor may elect to postpone the payment of tax with respect to such interests until six months after the termination of the precedent interest or interests in the property. [I.R.C. § 6163(a)]

##### (c) Installment Payments Allowed in Certain Situations

When an estate is substantially composed of an interest in a "closely held business" (which might have to be liquidated to pay the estate tax at the due date), the Code authorizes payment of the estate tax liability related to the closely held business interest in installments. [I.R.C. § 6166]

###### 1) Five-Year Deferral; Ten Yearly Installment Payments

Under section 6166, the executor may elect to defer payment of the estate tax attributable to a closely held business interest for up to five years, and then pay the tax in up to 10 equal annual installments. [I.R.C. § 6166(a)]

###### 2) Requirements

There are essentially two requirements for this relief:

a) The interest must be an interest in a "closely held business," which is defined for this purpose as a sole proprietorship or a 20% or greater interest in a partnership or corporation (or a lesser interest if the partnership had 45 or fewer partners, or the corporation had 45 or fewer shareholders). [I.R.C. § 6166(b)(1)]

b) The value of the closely held business interest must exceed 35% of the adjusted gross estate. [I.R.C. § 6166(a)(1)]

###### 3) Disqualification—Acceleration

However, provision is made for acceleration of installments upon default or the disposition or withdrawal of more than 50% in value of the business interest. [I.R.C. § 6166(g)]

## f. Apportionment of Tax

The estate tax is imposed upon the estate as a whole, not upon any particular property or asset therein. In the absence of a contrary direction in the decedent's will or in local statutes, the burden of the estate tax follows the general order of abatement prescribed by the state statute; typically, this would require payment of tax first from property that passes by intestacy, then from the residuary estate, then general legacies, and, finally, specific bequests.

| ORDER OF ABATEMENT FOR THE PAYMENT OF ESTATE TAX | GILBERT |
|---|---|
| IN THE ABSENCE OF A CONTRARY DIRECTION IN THE DECEDENT'S WILL OR LOCAL STATUTES, THE GENERAL ORDER OF ABATEMENT IS AS FOLLOWS: | |
| ***FIRST:*** | Intestacy Property |
| ***SECOND:*** | Residuary Property |
| ***THIRD:*** | General Legacies |
| ***FOURTH:*** | Specific Bequests |

# Review Questions and Answers

# Review Questions

**FILL IN ANSWER**

1. Clare, a U.S. citizen, owns a villa on the French Riviera. If France imposes an estate tax upon this property, it would not be included in Clare's gross estate. True or false? ______

2. Harper devises Blackacre to her son Hunter for life, remainder to Hunter's children. Upon Hunter's death, the value of his interest in Blackacre is includible in his gross estate. True or false? ______

3. Prior to his death, Paul instituted an action for personal injuries against Dan. Paul died while the action was still pending. Is the tort claim includible in Paul's gross estate? ______

4. Owen is the owner of an insurance policy on the life of Ted. If Owen predeceases Ted, are the proceeds of the policy includible in Owen's gross estate? ______

5. For a number of years, Tim served as trustee of a trust established by his father for the benefit of various other family members. Upon Tim's death, should the corpus of the trust be included in Tim's gross estate? ______

6. A judgment by the highest state court on the nature or extent of a decedent's interest in property is binding for federal estate tax purposes. True or false? ______

7. At the time of his death, Liam owned corporate stock worth $200,000. Under applicable state law, Liam's spouse, Olivia, has dower rights in the stock. The value of the stock in Liam's gross estate is therefore less than $200,000. True or false? ______

   a. Would the result be different if Olivia had a community property interest in the stock? ______

8. Wanda transferred $100,000 in cash by gift in December 2020 and died in July 2022. Is the value of this property includible in Wanda's gross estate? ______

9. Same facts as in Question 8, above, except that Wanda transferred a life insurance policy on her own life. Assuming that the face amount of the policy was $100,000 but the replacement value was only $35,000, Wanda's executor should include $35,000 in Darlene's gross estate on account of this gift. True or false? ______

10. Mary gave her daughter a painting worth $500,000 in February 2020 and paid a gift tax of $155,800. Mary died in July 2022. With respect to this gift, Mary's executor should include $155,800 in Mary's gross estate. True or false? ______

11. In 2000, Mia transferred certain property to a trust but reserved the power to revoke the trust. In 2017, Mia released the power to revoke the trust. Mia died in February 2019. Assuming that the value of the property transferred by Mia in 2000 was $200,000, that it was worth $800,000 when Mia released the power in 2017, and that it was worth $850,000 when Mia died in 2019, $800,000 should be included in Debbie's gross estate. True or false? __________

    a. Same facts as above. However, assume that the $850,000 corpus of the trust at Mia's death included $150,000 of ***income*** which the trustee had accumulated and added to corpus. For estate tax purposes, this accumulated income should ***not*** be included in Mia's gross estate since Mia never "transferred" the income. True or false? __________

12. Jose established a trust to pay the income to his brother, Ozzie, for life, remainder to Ozzie's children. Ozzie established a similar trust to pay the income to Jose for life, remainder to Jose's children. Is the corpus of the trust established by Ozzie includible in Jose's gross estate? __________

    a. Would the result be the same if Ozzie's trust was to pay the income to Antonio for life, remainder to Antonio's children? __________

13. Fred transfers the residence he owns to his wife, Isabella, but continues to occupy the residence with Isabella until his death. Is this sufficient to show a transfer with retained interest under section 2036? __________

14. Sofia establishes a trust for the support of her minor child. If Sofia dies before the child reaches the age of majority, is the trust corpus includible in Sofia's estate? __________

15. The trustee of a trust created by Ben is empowered to apply the income or corpus of the trust as needed for Ben's support during his life. None of the income or corpus is ever paid to Ben. Is the trust corpus includible in Ben's estate at his death? __________

16. Bruno transfers property to a trust, with all trust income to be paid to Peter for life. Bruno retains the power to designate a new income beneficiary in the event of Peter's death. If Bruno predeceases Peter, is the trust corpus includible in Bruno's estate? __________

17. Emma established a trust, retaining the power to direct that the trust income be accumulated rather than distributed to a life beneficiary. Should the trust corpus be included in Emma's gross estate? __________

    a. Would the result be different if Emma never exercised her power under the trust? __________

18. If Maria names herself as trustee of a trust under which all trust income must be paid to Irving during his life, the trust corpus is includible in Maria's gross estate. True or false? __________

19. Sam transfers certain property to Quincy in trust, retaining a right to income from the trust "except such income as may accrue during the last year of my life." Is the trust corpus includible in Sam's gross estate? __________

20. Lois grants a life estate in certain property to Clark, retaining a secondary life estate in the same property. Is the full value of the property includible in Lois's gross estate? __________

21. A person may always avoid taxation by transferring or releasing any retained, taxable power or interest. Is this correct? __________

22. Larry transfers property "to Cary for life, remainder to Mary unless I am alive at the time of Cary's death." If the reversionary interest retained by Larry is worth more than 5% of the value of the property at the time of Larry's death, is any part of the property includible in his gross estate? __________

23. Assume the same transfer of property described in Question 22, above. If Larry also granted Harry the power to appoint the property free of trust to Cary, would the property be includible in Larry's gross estate under section 2037? __________

24. Ryan transfers property "to Lucy for life, remainder to Ron if Ron is alive at Lucy's death, but otherwise the property is to revert to me." Is the value of the property includible in Ryan's gross estate? __________

25. A retained power to direct the trustee to pay income to the transferor does not fall within the scope of section 2037. True or false? __________

26. Perry transfers property "to Quinn for life, remainder to Ralph unless I am alive when Quinn dies." Only the value of the remainder interest is taxable to Perry's estate under section 2037. True or false? __________

27. Ron transfers certain property to Alyssa, retaining a power to terminate the transfer in the event of Mike's death. If Ron predeceases Mike, is the property taxable to Ron's estate under section 2038? __________

28. Terri transfers certain property to Peter, retaining a power to revoke the transfer; however, such power must be exercised jointly by Terri and Sam. If Sam has a beneficial interest in the property adverse to that of Terri, is the transfer subject to tax under section 2038? __________

29. Nick transfers property to a trust, appointing Frieda as trustee with the power to change the named beneficiaries of the trust income. Nick retains the right to call for Frieda's resignation and appoint a successor trustee. Will the trust property be included in Nick's gross estate? __________

30. Xavier created a trust in 2014 which empowered the trustee to distribute income among a number of beneficiaries. Xavier retained no power with respect to the trust but was subsequently appointed trustee. Will the trust corpus be included in Xavier's estate under section 2038? __________

31. For a tax to attach under section 2038, must the transferor have some beneficial interest in the transferred property? __________

32. Millie transfers property to a trust in which income is to be paid to Harold for 20 years and then to distribute the entire corpus to Harold. If Millie retains the power to terminate the trust and cause __________

the corpus to go to Harold prior to the end of the 20-year term, is the trust corpus includible in Millie's gross estate?

33. A straight life annuity is not includible in the annuitant's gross estate at death. True or false? ______

34. To be taxable under section 2039, the benefit to the surviving beneficiary must be the same basic type of annuity as that paid to the decedent-annuitant. True or false? ______

35. Lee has only a contingent right to receive payments under an annuity contract purchased by his employer. The contingency is not within Lee's control, nor does it occur prior to his death. Are the annuity payments payable to another person after Lee's death includible in Lee's gross estate? ______

36. The interest of a joint tenant in jointly held property may be includible in the tenant's gross estate. True or false? ______

37. Bailey and Collin hold property in equal shares as tenants in common. If Collin dies, is it permissible to include only one-half the value of the property in his gross estate? ______

38. Kyrie and his brother, Julius, acquire property in joint tenancy with a right of survivorship. Kyrie pays $60,000 of the $100,000 purchase price, and Julius pays the remaining $40,000. Upon Kyrie's death, his estate should include the full value of the joint property, less $40,000. True or false? ______

    a. Would the answer be different if Kyrie and Julius were married? ______

39. Al devises property to Kelly and Bryant as joint tenants with a right of survivorship. Should the full value of the joint tenancy property be included in Kelly's gross estate if she predeceases Bryant? ______

40. Marge gives her son, Bart, $50,000. Bart subsequently contributes this money as his part of the purchase price for property acquired by Marge and Bart as joint tenants. If Marge predeceases Bart, is the full value of the joint tenancy property includible in Marge's gross estate? ______

    a. Would the answer be different if Marge and Bart were husband and wife? ______

    b. Would the result be the same if Marge gave Bart a $50,000 certificate of deposit, and Bart contributed the income earned thereon as his share of the purchase price? ______

41. The assumption of a purchase money mortgage by both joint tenants is treated as an original contribution by each joint tenant of one-half the amount of the mortgage. True or false? ______

42. Dirk pays the full purchase price for property acquired by Dirk and his sister, Liz, as joint tenants. Dirk then gives his interest in the property to Cindy, an unrelated friend. If Dirk dies two years later, the full value of the property is includible in his estate. True or false? ______

43. A beneficiary's power to withdraw principal from a trust makes the trust corpus includible in her gross estate. True or false? __________

44. Tomas creates a trust naming Brittney as trustee and giving her a life interest in the income therefrom. The trustee is given the power to invade principal for the benefit of the life beneficiary. Is the trust corpus includible in Brittney's estate under section 2041? __________

45. Sergio transfers certain property to a trust, reserving a general power to change the beneficiaries and trustee thereunder. Does section 2041 require that the trust corpus be included in Sergio's gross estate? __________

46. William is the trustee of a trust giving him a power to appoint the beneficiaries. If William completely exercises this power inter vivos, is the property that comprised the trust corpus includible in his estate under section 2041? __________

47. Post-1942 powers that must be exercised jointly with another person may still be considered general powers under section 2041. True or false? __________

48. Dale carries a medical policy which pays $10,000 if Dale should die from any of several specified ailments. Are such benefits includible in Dale's gross estate? __________

49. Bianca is an employee of Zilch Corporation. Zilch carries a policy on Bianca's life, with benefits payable to Bianca's executor. Bianca pays no premiums on the policy and has no other incidents of ownership. Are the policy benefits includible in her gross estate? __________

    a. Would the result be the same if Bianca's sister, Briana, were the named beneficiary of the policy? __________

50. Tim is insured under his employer's group life insurance policy. If Tim can cancel the insurance by quitting his job, should the benefits thereunder be included in his estate? __________

51. A reversionary interest in a life insurance policy or its proceeds makes the proceeds taxable to the holder's gross estate. True or false? __________

52. Under the terms of her life insurance policy, Ivy (the insured) may change the beneficiaries only by written endorsement on the policy. Ivy never changes the beneficiaries and is not in actual possession of the policy for several years prior to her death. Will Ivy be deemed to have had an incident of ownership in the policy at the time of her death? __________

53. Imani, the insured under a life insurance policy, transfers all interests and rights under the policy to her brother, Ronald, in 2020. If Imani dies in 2022, are the policy proceeds includible in her estate? __________

    a. Would the result be the same if the policy had been purchased by Imani with community property funds? __________

54. A professor tells the class, "A transfer will not be included in the decedent's estate if it was made for consideration that would support an enforceable contract." Is this an accurate statement? ____________

55. Mary bequeathed a substantial sum of money outright to John, an infant. At the request of John's guardian, Mary's executor and the attorney for Mary's estate arrange for the creation of a trust to hold and manage the bequest until John attains majority. Are the fees charged by the executor and the attorney for this service deductible from Mary's gross estate? ____________

56. Prior to their marriage, Henry and Meghan entered into a valid antenuptial agreement under which, in consideration of marriage and Meghan's release of any marital inheritance rights in Henry's estate, Henry agreed to leave Meghan $100,000 in his will. After Henry's death, his executor paid $100,000 to Meghan. Can this amount be deducted as a claim against the estate for federal estate tax purposes? ____________

57. At the time of his death Felipe, a cash basis proprietor, owed salaries to certain of his employees and rent on his business property. After Felipe's death, his executor paid these claims. The payments are deductible against the gross estate and against the estate's taxable income. True or false? ____________

58. An executor may elect to deduct a casualty or theft loss incurred during the administration of the estate from the estate's income tax return. True or false? ____________

59. In his will, Lincoln bequeaths $20,000 to Acme Company for the sole purpose of establishing a scholarship fund for the children of Acme employees. Is the bequest deductible from Lincoln's estate as a charitable contribution? ____________

60. Generally, the gift of a remainder interest to a charity is not deductible unless made in the form of a special, qualifying interest. True or false? ____________

61. The maximum estate tax marital deduction is 50% of the decedent's adjusted gross estate. True or false? ____________

62. Two weeks before his death in April 2017, Hector gave 20% of his cash assets to his spouse, Juanita, as an inter vivos gift. Does this property "pass" to Juanita for estate tax marital deduction purposes? ____________

63. During his life, Abdullah purchases a straight life annuity for his spouse, Alisha, payments on which are to begin upon Abdullah's death. If the annuity is included in Abdullah's gross estate, is its value deductible as a section 2056 marital deduction? ____________

64. Shortly after Howard's death, Margo petitions the local probate court for an allowance for her support during probate. The court reviews Margo's petition and determines that an award of $500 per month from Howard's estate is appropriate. Do these monies qualify for the marital deduction? ____________

65. In his will, Tony bequeaths his rights in an exclusive patent to his spouse, Jane. Will this be considered a terminable interest not deductible under section 2056? ______________

    a. Would the result be different if the bequest is also conditioned upon Jane's surviving Tony by three months? ______________

66. Pam bequeaths certain property to a trust with directions to pay the income to Jim, her surviving spouse, for life, and upon his death to pay the corpus to Jim's estate. Is Pam's bequest deductible under section 2056? ______________

67. Holly devised the entire residue of her estate to Dwight, as trustee, with directions to pay annually all the income from the trust to Michael (Holly's husband) for his life and, upon Michael's death to pay over the entire corpus of the trust to their children in such proportions as Michael might designate in his will or, if Michael did not exercise this power, to their children equally. Will the marital deduction be allowed for this bequest? ______________

68. No marital deduction is allowed for federal estate tax purposes if the surviving spouse is a nonresident alien. True or false? ______________

69. Abe makes a gift of $50,000 to Bryant, on the condition that Bryant give $20,000 to Charlie. Will this be treated as a single taxable gift from Abe to Bryant? ______________

70. Travis places certain property on trust, income and principal to be given to "my first nephew, upon the date of his fifteenth birthday." Is this a taxable gift? ______________

71. Margaret and Bob, an elderly married couple, are both independently wealthy. Harry Bond, a "financial consultant," advises them to leave all their property to each other in the form of a "QTIP" interest. He says that this will avoid all estate taxes in the estate of the first to die (because of the 100% estate tax marital deduction) and eliminate most transfer taxes to the survivor since the survivor can give his or her interest in the "QTIP" away and only be taxed on the value of the life estate that is transferred. Is Harry right? ______________

72. An attorney gratuitously prepares a will for Yasmine. Has the attorney made a taxable gift? ______________

73. Tatianna exercises a special power of appointment under a trust in favor of Titus. Will this be treated as a taxable gift to Titus? ______________

74. Leonard transfers certain property to a trust, naming Peggy as the trust beneficiary. If Leonard can redesignate the trust beneficiary, has he made a taxable gift? ______________

    a. Would the result be different if the power to change beneficiaries was held by Catherine as trustee? ______________

75. If a transfer involves partial consideration but is otherwise a taxable gift, the value of the transfer for gift tax purposes is the fair market value of the property in question. True or false? ______________

76. Hector agrees to pay his spouse, Winona, $50,000 in exchange for Winona's agreement to release her marital rights. Will the $50,000 transfer be treated as a taxable gift? ______

77. Sally, a traveling salesperson, gives a number of her best customers wristwatches as Christmas gifts. Are these transfers subject to the federal gift tax? ______

78. Elton purchases certain securities and has them registered in the names of Elton and John as joint tenants with right of survivorship. Has Elton made a gift of any interest in the securities? ______

79. Archie purchases Blackacre with his own funds but takes title to the property in joint tenancy with his wife, Elizabeth. Has Archie made a taxable gift to Elizabeth? ______

    a. Should Archie file a gift tax return? ______

80. During 2022, Han made gifts of $5,000 to Leia and $20,000 to Luke. Are these gifts fully excludible from gift tax? ______

81. The 1976 Tax Reform Act and subsequent amendments to the Code have eliminated all incentives to make inter vivos (as opposed to testamentary) gifts. True or false? ______

82. Moe transfers certain property to a trust with the income to Larry for life, then to Curly for life, remainder to Sarah. Is the annual exclusion available for the life estate gifts to Larry and Curly? ______

83. Jay creates a trust in which the trustee has discretion to distribute income to John for life according to his needs, and the remainder to Kevin. Would the transfers to both John and Kevin be denied the annual exclusion? ______

84. The "nondeductible terminable interest rule" of the gift tax marital deduction is substantially the same as that under the estate tax. True or false? ______

85. The alternate valuation date for assessing the assets of the gross estate is available only where the assets have declined in value less than 50% since the date of death. True or false? ______

86. Mickey dies, leaving as part of his gross estate a life estate based upon the life of Minnie, his surviving spouse. Will election of the alternate valuation date produce a lower includible value for this asset? ______

87. A farmer's estate includes a farm which is located near a developing "industrial park." The farmer bequeathed the farm to his son, Rick. Assuming that all the requirements of section 2032A (special farm use valuation) are met, the value of the farm in its possible use as an industrial site may be disregarded. True or false? ______

88. Moe owns Stooge Corp. equally with Larry and Curly. If Moe attempts to give away the anticipated appreciation in value free of gift or estate tax liability while retaining the voting power of his one-third interest, will the "zero value rule" come into play? ______

89. In 2018, George opens a part of his large estate as a preserve for endangered monkeys. Although he properly sets aside an easement ______

for such use of his property, the easement also allows him or his heirs to develop the area for commercial purposes. In 2020, George dies, leaving Jane as his sole heir. May the executor of George's estate exclude the value of the easement from George's gross estate?

90. All gifts made by a decedent must be added to his taxable estate to determine the appropriate tax base. True or false? ______________

91. The 1976 Act provided a separate "unified" gift tax credit (applicable credit amount) for gifts made after 1976. True or false? ______________

92. There is a credit allowed against federal estate taxes for state death taxes paid. True or false? ______________

93. The donor is primarily responsible for payment of the gift tax on donative transfers. True or false? ______________

94. Bill is the beneficiary of certain life insurance proceeds that are includible in Hannah's gross estate. Once the proceeds are paid to Bill, is he primarily responsible for paying the federal estate taxes attributable thereto? ______________

95. In Question 94, can Hannah's executor recover payment of the pro rata estate tax from Bill? ______________

96. Greg creates a trust for his brother, Peter, for life, then to Greg's nephew, Oliver, for life, and upon his death to Oliver's son, Bobby. Is this trust subject to the tax on generation-skipping transfers? ______________

97. Blair conveys property on trust to her son, George, for life, then to George's daughter, Jenna, for life, remainder to Jenna's issue. Is there a generation-skipping termination upon George's death? ______________

98. Brandon conveys stock to Molly, his daughter-in-law, as custodian for Jack and Jill, the children of Molly and Brandon's deceased son, Hunter. Is this a generation-skipping transfer? ______________

99. Matthew conveys certain property in trust to his nephew, John, for life, then to John's children, Mark and Luke, for life, remainder to the issue of Mark and Luke. Upon John's death, the value of the life estates of Mark and Luke is subject to the tax on generation-skipping transfers. True or false? ______________

100. Same facts as above. Mark and Luke are personally liable for any tax due on the trust property at John's death. True or false? ______________

# Answers to Review Questions

1. **FALSE** The property would be included in Clare's gross estate, since she is a U.S. citizen. However, the French tax could be credited against the federal estate tax payable.

2. **FALSE** An interest in property that is extinguished by the death of the holder, such as a life estate, is not transferable at death and hence is not taxable under section 2033.

3. **YES** Claims in litigation are property rights includible regardless of their contingent nature (although their value may be minimal, or even zero, depending upon how speculative the potential amount of recovery may be).

4. **NO** Only the value of the policy (i.e., its replacement cost) is includible in the policy owner's estate when he dies before the insured.

5. **NO** When title to property is held solely as trustee for others, there is no beneficial interest in the property; hence, it is not included in the trustee's gross estate.

6. **TRUE** Except when the property or interest is based on federal law, an opinion by the highest state court is determinative.

7. **FALSE** Section 2034 requires that the ***full value*** of decedent's property be included in the gross estate, regardless of the spouse's marital interests therein.

   a. **YES** In this case, Olivia ***owned*** a present one-half interest in the stock at Liam's death, and this would ***not*** be includible in Liam's gross estate.

8. **NO** By virtue of the 1981 Act amendment of section 2035, the estate tax does not attach to outright gifts made within three years of death, with limited exceptions (*see* next question).

9. **FALSE** Although section 2035 does not tax outright gifts made within three years of the donor's death, it continues to interact with other specific taxing provisions, including section 2042, which deals with life insurance. Under section 2042, it is the proceeds (face amount) of the life insurance that is included in the insured's estate if the insured possesses "incidents of ownership" in the policy at death. Also, the interaction of section 2035 with section 2042 will produce the same result where incidents of ownership are transferred within three years of death. Thus, $100,000 is includible.

10. **TRUE** The value of the property given by Mary to her daughter (within three years of her death) is not included in Mary's estate. (*See* Answer 8, above.) However, the gift tax paid with respect to gifts made within three years of death continues to be includible under the section 2035(b) "gross-up" rule.

| | |
|---|---|
| 11. **FALSE** | Section 2035 interacts with section 2038 ("revocable transfers") to produce the same estate tax result that would be obtained if a power to revoke was exercisable by the decedent at the time of her death. Property included in a decedent's gross estate is valued as of the date of the decedent's death (or at the alternate valuation date—six months after death). This rule is applicable to transfers included under section 2038 (and section 2035). Thus, it is not the value of the property at the time of the transfer ($200,000 in 2000), or its value when Mia released the power to revoke ($800,000 in 2017), but its value at Mia's death ($850,000) that is the includible amount. Also, note that section 2035 was amended in 1997 to provide that transfers from a revocable trust within three years of death, which are treated as a "Grantor Trust" under I.R.C. § 676, are not subject to section 2035 [I.R.C. § 2035(e)]. |
| a. **FALSE** | When the taxable power (here, a power to revoke under section 2038) extends to post-gift accumulated income, the accumulated income as well as the original corpus (and its appreciation in value) is includible. |
| 12. **YES** | This is a typical reciprocal trust situation; Jose and Ozzie will each be deemed to have retained a life estate in the trust established by the other (making it taxable to their respective estates). If Jose and Ozzie have not contributed the same amount, only the lesser of the amounts will be considered reciprocal. |
| a. **NO** | In order to be "reciprocal," cross-trusts must have equivalent economic effect. Here, however, Jose has ***no*** life estate interest in either trust; therefore, Ozzie's trust is not includible in Jose's gross estate. |
| 13. **NO** | ***Joint*** occupancy of a residence by husband and wife subsequent to a transfer is not enough to show the implied retention of an interest subject to section 2036. |
| 14. **YES** | There is a retained right to income where the transferred property (or income therefrom) is used to discharge the transferor's legal obligations, such as child support. Furthermore, if decedent-transferor dies before her child attains majority, there is a retention of the right for a period that does not in fact end before her death. |
| 15. **YES** | Ben is deemed to have retained a sufficient right to income, since the trustee's discretion was governed by an ascertainable standard (support) enforceable by Ben. |
| 16. **YES** | The fact that a retained power is contingent (and never exercised) does not prevent the transfer from being taxable under section 2036. *See* Treas. Reg. § 20.2036–1(b)(3). |
| 17. **YES** | This makes the trust taxable under section 2036(a)(2), since the power can be exercised to increase the size of the remainder interest (i.e., trust corpus). |
| a. **NO** | The mere ***retention of*** the power makes the corpus taxable under section 2036(a)(2). |

| | | |
|---|---|---|
| 18. | **FALSE** | To result in a taxable transfer, the power retained must be ***discretionary.*** Here, Maria is required to pay all income to Irving, so the trust would not be taxable in Maria's estate. |
| 19. | **YES** | The retained right to income for a period ascertainable only with reference to the transferor's death brings the property within section 2036. |
| 20. | **NO** | Although the retained secondary life estate causes the property to be included in Lois's estate, it will be included at its full value ***less*** the value of Clark's prior life estate. |
| 21. | **NO** | Although taxation is avoided if the transfer or relinquishment is made more than three years before death, certain transfers ***within*** three years of death would be taxable under section 2035. |
| 22. | **YES** | This is a typical example of a taxable transfer under section 2037. |
| 23. | **PROBABLY NOT** | The power granted to Harry would probably preclude a valuation of the reversionary interest retained by Larry. If so, it will be assigned a value of zero, which is less than the 5% necessary for a taxable transfer under section 2037. |
| 24. | **NO** | Ron need not survive the transferor, Ryan. Rather, he needs to merely survive the life tenant, Lucy. Hence, the survivorship requirement of section 2037 is not satisfied, and the transfer is not taxable. However, if both Lucy and Ron are alive at Ryan's death, the value of the contingent remainder will be taxable in Ryan's estate under section 2033. |
| 25. | **TRUE** | Such a right to income is not a "reversionary interest" subject to section 2037. However, it may well be taxable under section 2036. |
| 26. | **TRUE** | Quinn's life estate is not affected by whether Perry lives or dies. |
| 27. | **NO** | The transfer is not taxable under section 2038 when a retained power to terminate is subject to a contingency beyond the transferor's control ***and*** it does not occur prior to the transferor's death. *See* Treas. Reg. § 20.2038–1(b). |
| 28. | **YES** | If the retained power is otherwise taxable, the fact that it can be exercised only with the consent of a person having an adverse interest will not affect taxability under section 2038. |
| 29. | **YES** | Retention of the power to substitute the trustee with anyone Nick appoints is sufficient access to the taxable power (to change beneficiaries) and therefore results in inclusion in Nick's gross estate. |
| 30. | **YES** | To be a taxable transfer under section 2038, the power need not be retained. It is sufficient that the transferor possessed it at the time of death—whatever the source. |
| 31. | **NO** | It is sufficient if the transferor retains a power to affect the beneficial enjoyment of others. |

| | | |
|---|---|---|
| 32. | **YES** | The power to accelerate the remainder (by terminating the trust) is sufficient for taxation under section 2038, even though Harold is the sole beneficiary under the trust. *See* Treas. Reg. § 20.2038–1(a). |
| 33. | **TRUE** | Section 2039 applies to annuity benefits payable on account of the decedent's death (i.e., survivorship annuities). Since all benefits under a straight life annuity terminate at the annuitant's death, there is no inclusion in the annuitant's gross estate. |
| 34. | **FALSE** | There is no requirement that the payment to the beneficiary correspond in form or amount to that payable to decedent. |
| 35. | **YES** | Since the annuity was purchased by his employer, it is considered a contribution by Lee and is therefore includible in its entirety. The fact that the decedent's right to payment did not mature during his lifetime, or that Lee had no control over the contingency in question, is immaterial. |
| 36. | **TRUE** | Although the interest terminates at death and thus is not taxable under section 2033, it may still be included in the deceased tenant's gross estate under section 2040. |
| 37. | **YES** | "Full value" taxation under section 2040 applies only to those forms of joint ownership having rights of survivorship. It does not apply to tenancies in common. |
| 38. | **FALSE** | The amount included in Kyrie's estate is the value of the property ***proportionate*** to the amount of his original contribution—here, 60% of the present value. |
| | a. **YES** | In the case of interspousal joint tenancies ("qualified joint interests"), the relative consideration furnished is irrelevant. In any case, one-half of the value of the property is included in the estate of the first to die. |
| 39. | **NO** | When the joint tenancy is created by a third party, only the one-half undivided interest of the joint tenant who dies first is included in that tenant's gross estate. |
| 40. | **YES** | Property that originates with the decedent joint tenant cannot be claimed as a "contribution" by the survivor. |
| | a. **YES** | The amount and source of any consideration furnished by the spouses is irrelevant in the case of "qualified joint interests." One-half is included in the gross estate of the first to die in all cases. |
| | b. **NO** | ***Income*** derived from donated property is treated as having originated with the contributor. Hence, only the proportionate share of the property attributable to Marge's contribution would be included in her estate. |
| 41. | **TRUE** | One-half of the mortgage is attributed to each as an original contribution. |
| 42. | **FALSE** | Dirk's gift of his interest to Liz severed the joint tenancy. Section 2040 does not apply if the joint tenancy is severed prior to death—even if the transfer severing the tenancy is made within three years of death. Moreover, given that section 2035 no longer taxes |

outright gifts made within three years of death, ***nothing*** will be included in Dirk's estate on account of this property; neither section 2040 nor section 2035 operates here.

43. **TRUE** This is considered a "general power of appointment" under section 2041.

44. **MAYBE** Brittney's power to invade principal would be a general power of appointment ***unless*** limited by an "ascertainable standard" relating to decedent's health, support, etc. Thus, if Brittney's power were limited to her "maintenance and support," for example, the corpus would not be taxable in Brittney's estate under section 2041.

45. **NO** Section 2041 applies only to powers granted to the decedent by a ***third party.*** It does not cover reserved powers (although these may be taxable under sections 2036 or 2038).

46. **POSSIBLY** If William's exercise of the power was such that it would have been a taxable transfer under sections 2035 through 2038, it falls within section 2041.

47. **TRUE** A general power exists unless the co-holder is either the donor of the power or a person who has a substantial interest in the property (i.e., an "adverse party").

48. **YES** This type of death benefit is also considered "life insurance" under section 2042.

49. **YES** As long as the benefits are payable to Bianca's executor or estate, they are includible in her gross estate regardless of whether Bianca had any incidents of ownership in the policy.

a. **NO** When the beneficiary is someone other than decedent's estate, executor, etc., policy benefits are includible only if decedent had some incident of ownership in the policy.

50. **NO** This "power" is not considered an incident of ownership in the policy.

51. **MAYBE** The value of the reversionary interest must exceed 5% of the value of the policy before it is a sufficient "incident of ownership" to come within section 2042.

52. **YES** The ***right*** to change beneficiaries is an incident of ownership under section 2042, even if the right is not, and as a practical matter could not, be exercised by the insured.

53. **YES** Section 2035 interacts with section 2042. Thus, the transfer of incidents of ownership within three years of death is ineffective to prevent inclusion in the gross estate.

a. **NO** Here, Imani's spouse owns an undivided one-half interest in the policy. Thus, assuming Imani predeceases her spouse, only 50% of the proceeds would be taxable to her estate (assuming all premiums were paid with community funds).

54. **NO** The consideration must be measurable in ***money or money's worth.*** Thus, certain noneconomic consideration that would

support a contract (promise to marry, etc.) would ***not*** prevent estate tax exposure.

55. **NO** Deductibility of expenses depends upon their ***purpose***. When, as here, the purpose is to protect a beneficiary, the expenses are nondeductible.

56. **NO** A claim founded upon a promise or agreement must be supported by "full and adequate consideration in money or money's worth" to be deductible, and section 2053(e) specifically provides that the release of marital rights is not adequate consideration for this purpose.

57. **TRUE** These are items of "deductions in respect of a decedent" that may be deducted both from the gross estate ***and*** estate income.

58. **TRUE** Certain casualty losses may be deductible against the estate's income tax return under section 165 or against the gross estate under section 2054. However, the executor must elect one or the other—double deductions are disallowed.

59. **NO** To qualify under section 2055, the bequest must be made to an organization operated exclusively for a recognized charitable purpose.

60. **TRUE** Under the Tax Reform Act of 1969, charitable remainders are deductible only if the trust involved qualifies as an "annuity trust," "unitrust," or "pooled income fund" (or where the income beneficiary is also a charity).

61. **FALSE** The 1981 Act abolished all "quantitative" limitations on the marital deduction. The full value of qualifying property which passes to the surviving spouse is now 100% deductible.

62. **NO** Inter vivos transfers to a spouse which are includible in the decedent's gross estate under sections 2035 through 2038 are deemed to "pass" to the surviving spouse for marital deduction purposes. However, because outright gifts are no longer includible, even when made within three years of death, no estate tax marital deduction is allowable here.

63. **YES** The annuity was not purchased by Abdullah's executor but by Abdullah himself; and because no interest therein passes to a third person, it comes within section 2056.

64. **NO** The facts indicate that Margo's right to this award is not vested under local law but is discretionary with the court. It is therefore deemed a terminable interest not deductible under section 2056.

65. **NO** The value of the patent is deductible, provided no interest has passed from Tony to a third person which would allow that person to possess the patent after termination of Jane's interest therein.

a. **NO** Although a survivorship condition would otherwise make the bequest a nondeductible terminable interest, there is a statutory exception where the period of survivorship is not more than six months.

| | | |
|---|---|---|
| 66. | **YES** | Jim and his estate are considered the same person. Hence, no interest in the trust passes to one other than the surviving spouse and the bequest is properly part of the marital deduction. |
| 67. | **POSSIBLY** | Since Michael's power is not a "general power," the bequest cannot qualify under the life estate with power of appointment exception. However, it appears to meet the requirements for the "QTIP" exception. Thus, if Holly's executor elects to have the interest qualify, the marital deduction is allowable. |
| 68. | **FALSE** | The marital deduction may be allowed for a bequest to a noncitizen spouse (whether a resident or nonresident alien) if the decedent is a U.S. citizen and the otherwise qualifying bequest is to a "qualified domestic trust." |
| 69. | **NO** | Charlie is a "third-party beneficiary"; the transfer is treated as a direct gift of $30,000 to Bryant and an indirect gift of $20,000 from Abe to Charlie, both of which are taxable. |
| 70. | **YES** | The donee need not be identified (or ascertained) at the time of transfer in order to create a taxable gift. |
| 71. | **PARTLY** | The 100% marital deduction will eliminate taxes to the estate of the first to die. But the gift of the life interest in the "QTIP" property is treated as a gift of the entire property, not just the life interest. |
| 72. | **NO** | A gift of personal services is not taxable, because the services would not otherwise be includible in the attorney's estate. |
| 73. | **POSSIBLY** | Only the exercise of a ***general*** power of appointment is a taxable gift under section 2514. However, if the trust provides that Tatianna must receive all of the income, there may be a gift of the balance of Tatianna's life estate. *See* Treas. Reg. § 25.2514–1(b). *But see* Self v. United States, 142 F. Supp. 939 (Ct. Cl. 1956). |
| 74. | **NO** | The settlor's power to change beneficiaries is sufficient to make the transfer incomplete and hence nontaxable. |
| a. | **YES** | This would be treated as a complete transfer and a taxable gift. |
| 75. | **FALSE** | The value is computed as the fair market value ***less*** the amount of consideration received by the transferor. |
| 76. | **YES** | Winona's release of rights is insufficient consideration for Horatio's payment. |
| 77. | **PROBABLY NOT** | Sally's gifts should come within the "business transaction exception." |
| 78. | **YES** | In creating a joint tenancy and supplying all the consideration therefor, Elton has made a gift of one-half the value of the securities to John. |
| 79. | **YES, BUT** | The creation of the joint tenancy constitutes a gift of an undivided one-half interest from Archie to Elizabeth. However, there will be no tax liability since the 100% marital deduction completely offsets the value of the gift. |

| | | |
|---|---|---|
| | a. **NO** | A gift tax return is not required when the marital deduction eliminates any tax liability. |
| 80. | **NO** | The $5,000 gift to Leia is excludible; but only $16,000 of the gift to Luke is excluded. Note that the $10,000 annual exclusion under section 2503(b) is adjusted for inflation and is $16,000 if the gift is made in 2022. Hence, the taxable gift to Luke is $4,000. |
| 81. | **FALSE** | Although most incentives were removed by requiring that inter vivos gifts be included in decedent's estate tax base and instituting identical gift and estate tax rates and credits, the annual exclusion for inter vivos gifts ($16,000 in 2022) remains in effect. Furthermore, if the gift is made more than three years before death and a gift tax incurred, the donor will not be taxed on the tax itself, which would be the case if the donor died with the property in his or her estate (or within three years of the making of the gift). |
| 82. | **NO** | The exclusion is available for the gift to Larry, since it is a present interest. However, the gift to Curly is a future interest that does not qualify for the exclusion. |
| 83. | **YES** | John's present interest is not "ascertainable," given that the trustee has ***discretion*** to distribute to John according to his needs. Kevin's gift is a future interest and thus not excludible. |
| 84. | **TRUE** | The basic rules, definitions, and rationale of the nondeductible terminable interest rule under the gift tax are the same as under the estate tax. However, although the rules (and their exceptions) are essentially the same in substance and purpose under both transfer taxes, specific applications are not identical because of the different context in which the rules operate—i.e., the estate tax rules operate in the case of property passing from a decedent to a surviving spouse, whereas the gift tax rules operate in the case of lifetime gifts. |
| 85. | **FALSE** | The alternate valuation date may be elected in any case, as long as both the estate and the amount of tax payable will decrease because of the election. |
| 86. | **NO** | Any decrease in value in the life estate after Mickey's death would probably be attributable solely to lapse of time, and such decreases must be ***disregarded.*** |
| 87. | **FALSE** | Given that the special use value allowed by section 2032A may not reduce the "actual" value by more than $750,000 (indexed for inflation), the actual fair market value, which must take into account the "highest and best use" of the land, is still relevant. For 2022, the indexed amount for the reduction is $1,230,000. |
| 88. | **NO** | For the zero value rule to apply, the transferor must hold at least 50% of the value or voting power of the entity immediately before the transfer. |
| 89. | **MAYBE** | The executor may exclude the value of the easement, so long as Jane agrees to extinguish the developmental right in the easement. If Jane does not do so, the value of the easement must be included in George's gross estate. |

| | | |
|---|---|---|
| 90. | **FALSE** | Only "adjusted taxable gifts"—i.e., taxable gifts ***made after*** 1976 ***other than*** those includible in the decedent's gross estate—are added. |
| 91. | **TRUE** | However, this credit can effectively be used only once. |
| 92. | **FALSE** | I.R.C. § 2011, which allowed a credit for state death taxes paid, was repealed in 2014. This means that there is no longer a credit for state death taxes paid against federal estate taxes. However, section 2058 allows a deduction for state estate or inheritance taxes paid. |
| 93. | **TRUE** | However, the donee can be held liable if the donor fails to pay (to the extent of the value of the property the donee receives). |
| 94. | **NO** | The executor of the estate remains primarily responsible for paying all federal estate taxes on Hannah's estate. |
| 95. | **YES** | This is one of the four situations in which the executor may enforce payment of part of the estate tax from outside the estate. |
| 96. | **YES** | Bobby is a "skip person." He is assigned to a generation two generations below that of Greg, the transferor. Upon the death of the survivor of Peter and Oliver, there is a taxable termination. |
| 97. | **YES** | This is a generation-skipping trust. George's death constitutes a "taxable termination" under this trust. |
| 98. | **NO** | The deceased parent exception applies. There is not a generation-skipping transfer to Brandon's grandchildren because Brandon's son, Hunter, is dead at the time of the transfer. The grandchildren are treated as if they are members of Hunter's generation; hence, they are nonskip persons. |
| 99. | **TRUE** | The value of the life estates to Mark and Luke is subject to generation-skipping transfer tax because there is a taxable termination upon John's death. However, the remainder to the issue of Mark and Luke is also subject to the tax. Hence, the entire trust property (not merely the succeeding life estates) is subject to the generation-skipping transfer tax. |
| 100. | **FALSE** | Since John's death results in a taxable termination rather than a taxable distribution, the ***trustee*** is liable for the tax. |

# Exam Questions and Answers

## QUESTION I

Baron purchased Blackacre, taking title in his name and that of Kelvin, his brother, as joint tenants. If Kelvin predeceases Baron, will anything be included in Kelvin's gross estate under the federal estate tax because of his interest in Blackacre?

## QUESTION II

In 1972, Dylan purchased vacant land for $50,000. He took title in the names of "Dylan and Wendy [his wife] as joint tenants with right of survivorship." Early in 2022 Dylan learned that he had a terminal illness. He consulted with his attorney regarding his will and estate plan. Assuming the following transactions are undertaken upon the advice of counsel and that Dylan died in September 2022, what are the federal gift and estate tax consequences to Dylan and Dylan's estate?

(a) Dylan and Wendy deeded one-half of the land "to Dylan" and one-half "to Wendy" as tenants in common.

(b) Dylan and Wendy deeded the entire vacant land "to Wendy."

## QUESTION III

Darren created a trust and transferred income-producing property to it. Under the terms of the trust, income was payable to Arthur for life. Upon Arthur's death, the trust was to terminate, and the corpus would be distributed to "Xavier and his heirs." Under the trust, Darren had the power to revoke the trust if he outlived Arthur. Darren died, survived by Arthur and Xavier. Is the trust property included in Darren's gross estate for federal estate purposes?

## QUESTION IV

Ten years ago, Darla transferred $1 million in stocks and bonds to a trust naming her three children, Andy, Bob, and Charlotte, as beneficiaries. Darla retained no interest or power with respect to the trust but provided that her husband, Harry, should have the power to alter or amend the trust in any way he saw fit, except that he could not make himself beneficiary of the trust, directly or indirectly. Harry was in Europe when Darla created the trust. Upon his return, Darla told Harry about the trust. She informed him that she had given him power to alter or amend the trust so that if any one of their children entered into an unfortunate marriage, they could protect the trust property against the child's undesirable spouse. She further explained to Harry that she had given him the power instead of reserving it for herself so that she could keep the property out of her estate for federal estate tax purposes. Harry was so much impressed by Darla's explanation of the trust that he promptly created a similar trust and transferred $1 million in stocks and bonds to the trust for the children. Under this trust, Harry gave Darla the power to alter or amend the trust in any way she saw fit, except that she could not make herself beneficiary of the trust. Darla and Harry were both killed in an automobile accident in 2022. Will either trust be taxed to Darla's estate under the federal estate tax? Will either trust be taxed to Harry's estate under the federal estate tax?

## QUESTION V

In 2005, Dan took out a $500,000 insurance policy on his life. In 2015, Dan irrevocably assigned the policy to his daughter, completely divesting himself of all incidents of ownership in the policy. However, Dan paid all the premiums on the policy until his death in 2022. Are the insurance proceeds included in Dan's gross estate for estate tax purposes?

## QUESTION VI

During her life, Daniela gratuitously deeded Whiteacre to her son, Samuel, in fee, reserving a term for 20 years. Daniela died. Under her will she left the reserved interest to her husband, Warren.

(a) Does the reserved interest in Whiteacre that Daniela devised to Warren qualify for the marital deduction?

(b) How would the answer be affected if instead of giving an interest in Whiteacre to Samuel, Daniela sold it to him for $300,000, its fair market value?

## QUESTION VII

Under Dave's will, stocks worth $500,000 were added to a testamentary trust. Dave's wife, Wanda, was the beneficiary of the trust, and Troy was named as the trustee. Troy had the right to accumulate the income from the stocks during Wanda's life or to distribute the income to her as Troy in his discretion saw fit. At Wanda's death, Troy was required to pay over the principal of the trust and any accumulated income to Wanda's estate. Does this bequest qualify for the marital deduction?

## QUESTION VIII

In 2012, Andy transferred $1 million in trust for Bennett during the life of Andy, remainder to Olive if Olive survived Andy, and if Olive did not survive Andy, then to Andy or his estate. Andy died this year survived by Olive. Andy's reversionary interest was worth more than five percent of the value of the trust property. To what extent, if at all, is the transfer subject to:

(a) The gift tax?

(b) The estate tax?

## QUESTION IX

Alex transferred $1,000,000 to a trust in which all income was to be paid to Peyton for life, remainder to Brooke. Alex retained the power to change the beneficiaries under this trust with the consent of Brooke. This year, Peyton received $25,000 income from the trust. What are the gift tax consequences upon the creation of the trust and the distribution of $25,000 income from the trust to Peyton? Is the trust property included in Alex's gross estate if he dies when the trust is still in existence?

## QUESTION X

During 2020, Dominic created an inter vivos trust and transferred $8,000,000 to the trust. Dominic named an independent third party as the trustee. Under the terms of the trust, all income was payable annually to Dominic's wife, Laila, for life. The trust granted Laila the power to appoint the remainder to anyone, including her estate. In 2020, Dominic also made gifts of $1,215,000 to each of his two children, Anthony and Aaliyah. Dominic had not made any gifts prior to 2020. During 2022, Dominic passed away with an estate of $15,600,000. Under his will, the $15,600,000 to added to a testamentary trust in which the trustee had discretion to accumulate income or distribute it to Laila annually. Upon Laila's death, the trust would terminate, and the corpus and any accumulated income would be paid equally to Anthony and Aaliyah.

What is Dominic's estate and gift tax liabilities, if any? The annual exclusion for 2020 was $15,000. The basic exclusion amount was $11,580,000 and $12,060,000 during 2020 and 2022, respectively.

## QUESTION XI

Jacob dies in 2022. He makes taxable transfers of $4 million during his life and dies with a taxable estate of $2 million. Assume that for all relevant years, the basic exclusion amount is $12,060,000. If Jacob's executor makes an election on Jacob's estate tax return permitting his surviving spouse, Alyssa, to use the deceased spousal unused exclusion amount, what is Alyssa's applicable exclusion amount based on the circumstances below?

(a) Alyssa does not remarry and has not made any taxable transfers.

(b) Alyssa remarries Zeke. Zeke does not make any taxable transfers during life. He predeceases Alyssa with a taxable estate of $10 million. Zeke's executor elects to allow Alyssa to use Zeke's deceased spousal unused exclusion amount.

## ANSWER TO QUESTION I

Nothing will be included in Kelvin's gross estate. This problem raises the question of the relation between section 2033 and other taxing provisions of the estate tax. Under section 2040, which deals explicitly with joint estates, Kelvin's interest in Blackacre is not taxable to his estate because the surviving joint tenant, Baron, contributed the entire consideration for Blackacre. Kelvin's interest in Blackacre will not be included in his gross estate section 2033 because his interest terminated at his death under the joint tenancy survivorship rule. Since section 2040 is a specific section covering the taxation of joint estates, joint estates are excluded from the tax imposed by section 2033.

## ANSWER TO QUESTION II

(a) Dylan would be treated as having made a gift of one-half of the value of the land to Wendy in 2022, but the 100% marital deduction would preclude any gift tax liability and eliminate any requirement to file a gift tax return. For estate tax purposes, one-half of the land's value is includible in Dylan's gross estate under section 2033.

(b) Dylan would be treated as having made a gift of 100% of the land to Wendy, but the 100% marital deduction would preclude tax liability and any reporting requirement. For estate tax purposes, no part of the value of the land is includible in Dylan's gross estate because he did not own an interest in the land at death.

Prior to 1982, transfers made within three years of death were included in the transferor's gross estate. Although the 1981 Act eliminated estate tax exposure in the case of "outright gifts," it preserved the interaction of section 2035 with sections 2036, 2037, 2038, and 2042. However, under prior law, section 2035 was held ***not*** to interact with section 2040, and this ***lack*** of interaction is preserved since section 2035(a)(2) fails to identify section 2040 as a provision with which section 2035 will interact. Thus:

In part (a), the transfer of the one-half undivided interest in the land to Wendy is not subject to the estate tax under section 2035 (or section 2040), but the one-half interest in the land that Dylan owned at death is includible in his gross estate under section 2033. Note, however, that this transfer did not really change the estate tax result since Dylan died in 2022, at which time the rules relating to "qualified joint interests" under section 2040(b) would require inclusion of only one-half of the value of the property anyway.

In part (b), the transfer of the entire interest to Wendy precludes any inclusion in Dylan's estate. Under the rationale of prior cases, section 2040 is inoperative since a joint tenancy did not exist at Dylan's death. And, since this was an outright gift, section 2035 is inoperative. Finally, since Dylan did not own any interest in the land at death, nothing can be included in his gross estate under section 2033.

## ANSWER TO QUESTION III

The property is included in Darren's gross estate less the value of Arthur's life estate.

There are two possible theories under which the trust property might be exposed to the estate tax upon Darren's death: (1) as a revocable transfer under section 2038; and (2) as a transfer taking effect at death under section 2037. Section 2038 is inapplicable because it does ***not*** apply where, as here, the transferor's power to revoke is contingent upon an event beyond the transferor's control and the contingency has not occurred at the time of the transferor's death. Conversely, the property will be included in Darren's gross estate under section 2037, assuming that Darren's reversionary interest exceeds five percent of the value of the property. As required under section 2037(a)(2), Darren retained a reversionary interest because the trust corpus will revert to Darren if he revokes the trust. In addition, the survivorship requirement under section 2037(a)(1) is satisfied because Xavier's possession or enjoyment of the remainder in the property is dependent upon surviving Darren. However, since Arthur's life estate is vested and not dependent upon Darren's life or death, its value is not included in the gross estate. Note that section 2036(a)(2) is inapplicable because Darren's power does not affect Arthur's beneficial enjoyment of the property.

## ANSWER TO QUESTION IV

The issue raised here is that of the "reciprocal trust doctrine" and its application under these facts to produce a tax under section 2036. Prior to the Supreme Court's decision in United States v. Estate of Grace, 395 U.S. 316 (1969), it is unlikely that either trust would have been taxed in Darla's or Harry's estate. At that time, courts insisted that technical, common law consideration was the touchstone for determining the "actual" transferor. Quite typically, the courts were unable to find such consideration in connection with husband-wife reciprocal trusts. Even where the trusts were created at the same time and pursuant to an apparently integrated plan, the authorities were inclined to view the transaction as merely a division of marital property and not a bargained-for agreement supported by consideration.

In *Grace,* the Supreme Court swept aside the requirement of "consideration," holding that application of the reciprocal trust doctrine requires only that the trusts be ***interrelated*** and that the arrangement, to the extent of mutual value, leave the settlors in approximately the ***same economic position*** as they would have been in had they created the trusts naming themselves as life beneficiaries. However, the Court failed to delineate the scope of its holding, and thus *Grace* presents some problems of interpretation.

If *Grace* adopted a strict "net effect" approach, the trusts here will be subject to the reciprocal trust doctrine. Harry will be deemed the actual transferor of the Darla trust, and Darla will be deemed the actual transferor of the Harry trust. However, if the trusts must be "interrelated" in the sense that they are established pursuant to a mutual plan or understanding between the parties, then reciprocal trusts might not be found. As presented, the facts actually fall somewhere in between mere parallelism and a mutual, prearranged plan. Although there was no prearranged plan, there was a parallel disposition of property undertaken for purposes of avoiding the estate tax but at the same time achieving an economic position identical to the position each transferor would have been in had he or she made a taxable transfer. With this in mind, it would certainly be reasonable to conclude that the reciprocal trust doctrine could and should be applied in this case.

## ANSWER TO QUESTION V

The proceeds of the policy are not includible in Dan's estate under section 2042. Nor will premiums paid by Dan within three years of his death be taxed under section 2035.

Section 2042 does not include insurance proceeds in the gross estate that are payable to beneficiaries other than the estate of the insured unless the insured possessed incidents of ownership in the insurance at the insured's death. Consequently, the insurance is not included in Dan's estate under section 2042. Nor could the insurance be included under section 2035 because the transfer from Dan to the daughter took place more than three years prior to Dan's death. (Note that section 2035 would continue to interact with section 2042 ***if*** incidents of ownership are transferred within three years of death.)

In 1967, the Service undertook to use section 2035 to reach a portion of the proceeds of a life insurance policy, even though the insurance had been irrevocably assigned more than three years before death, where the decedent continued to pay premiums up to (and including the three years before) death. The Service's theory was that since the continued payment of premiums kept the insurance in force, and since payments within three years of the decedent's death were "in contemplation of death," section 2035 would reach not only the three years' premiums but also a portion of the policy proceeds proportionate to the ratio of premiums paid during the last three years to total premiums paid. This position, however, was rejected by the courts as an improper attempt to reintroduce into the 1954 Code the "premium payment test" which Congress had specifically repealed in 1954. The Service, in a 1971 ruling, conceded this point and announced that it would not tax a portion of the policy proceeds under this theory, but it would undertake to tax the last three years' premiums under section 2035. Prior to 1982, the taxation of the actual amount of the last three years' premiums was appropriate since these payments ***were*** gifts (albeit indirect) to the owner of the insurance policy. However, the 1981 Act amendments, which limit the scope of section 2035, prevent inclusion of such "outright" (albeit indirect) gifts.

## ANSWER TO QUESTION VI

(a) The interest does not qualify for the marital deduction because Warren receives a nondeductible terminable interest. A nondeductible terminable interest is an interest in the same property in which the terminable interest passes to a surviving spouse (Warren) also passes for less than adequate consideration to a third person (Samuel) who can possess and enjoy the property only after the surviving spouse's interest terminates. The fact that Samuel acquired his interest under a different instrument and at a different time than Warren acquired his is immaterial.

(b) Under these facts, the term for years which passes to Warren will no longer be a nondeductible terminable interest, and it will qualify for the marital deduction.

The fact that Samuel acquires his interest in the property from Daniela for adequate and full consideration in money or money's worth prevents Warren's interest from being a nondeductible terminable interest per I.R.C. § 2056(b)(1)(A) & (B). Therefore, the marital deduction is available even though Warren took an interest in the property that will terminate or fail and an interest in the same property passes to another (by virtue of which he may enjoy the property after the termination of Warren's interest).

## ANSWER TO QUESTION VII

This bequest qualifies for the marital deduction. Wanda's interest is not a nondeductible terminable interest since no one other than the surviving spouse or her estate acquires any interest in the property. This is a so-called marital deduction estate trust. Unlike the power of appointment trust, it does not have to meet the requirements for the life estate power of appointment exception to the terminable interest rule. It qualifies for the marital deduction, not as an exception to the terminable interest rule, but as an interest that is not a nondeductible terminable interest. This type of trust may be used as an alternative to the marital deduction power of appointment trust (or a "QTIP") and may be preferred where it is not desirable to pay all the income out annually to the surviving spouse, as is required in the case of a marital deduction power of appointment or QTIP trust.

## ANSWER TO QUESTION VIII

(a) A made a taxable gift of the entire trust property less the value of his reversionary interest.

(b) At Andy's death, the trust property—to the extent of Olive's remainder—is taxable to his estate under section 2037 as a transfer taking effect at death.

When Andy created the trust, he clearly made a complete transfer and a taxable gift of Bennett's estate pur autre vie. He also made a taxable gift of Olive's remainder, since he retained no power to revoke the transfer.

Although the remainder is subject to divestment because the property will revert to Andy if he outlives Olive, this does not make the transfer of the remainder incomplete for gift tax purposes. Nor does Andy's reversionary interest coupled with the fact that Olive must survive Andy in order to possess or enjoy the property make Olive's remainder nontaxable under the gift tax.

Since Andy retained his reversionary interest in the trust property, instead of giving it away, the value of this interest (based on actuarial valuation) will be subtracted from the amount of Andy's taxable gift.

The estate tax exposure under section 2037 is clear: Olive's possession and enjoyment is contingent upon surviving Andy, and Andy retained a reversionary interest, the value of which exceeded five percent of the trust property, as required under section 2037.

## ANSWER TO QUESTION IX

When Alex created the trust, he made a completed, and hence taxable, gift of the remainder. The gift was complete because Alex could only revoke the remainder with Brooke's consent, a person possessing a substantial adverse interest in that part of the trust. However, the annual exclusion is not available because the gift to Brooke is a future interest.

Alex did not make a taxable gift of the life estate to Peyton when he created the trust. The gift of the income interest was incomplete for gift tax purposes upon creation because Alex retained the power to revoke the life estate without the consent of a person possessing a substantial adverse interest in that part of the trust. On the other hand, there was a completed taxable gift from Alex to Peyton when Peyton was distributed income of $25,000 from the trust. Alex can claim the annual exclusion against the tax since the gift was a present interest.

For estate tax purposes, the trust property is included in Alex's gross estate under sections 2036(a)(2) and 2038. Section 2036(a)(2) is applicable because Alex retained control of Peyton's beneficial enjoyment of the income by retaining the power to change the income beneficiary. Note that section 2036(a)(2) does not apply to Alex's retained power to change the remainderperson because it does not affect beneficial enjoyment of the trust property. Section 2038 is applicable because Alex had the power to modify the trust by changing beneficiaries. The substantial adverse interest rule is inapplicable to both sections.

## ANSWER TO QUESTION X

Based on the facts, Dominic does not have a gift tax liability. However, he has an estate tax liability of $2,376,000.

The $8,000,000 transferred to the inter vivos trust meets the requirements for the marital deduction. While Laila received a terminable interest, the trust qualifies as a life estate with a power of appointment under section 2523(e). Laila is entitled to all income payable annually, and she can appoint the remainder to anyone, including her estate. The gifts totaling $2,430,000 to Anthony and Aaliyah are eligible for the annual exclusion because the children received present interests. Hence, the taxable gifts for 2020 are $2,400,000, well below the $11,580,000 basic exclusion amount for 2020.

With respect to the estate tax, the $15,600,000 placed in the trust does not qualify for the marital deduction because Laila received a terminable interest, and the trust does not meet any of the exceptions. Because the trustee has the discretion to accumulate or distribute the income to Laila, it is ineligible for the QTIP election (all income ***must*** be paid to Laila at least annually). In order to compute the estate tax, you must add the adjusted taxable gifts ($2,400,000) and the gross estate ($15,600,000). As a result, the total estate tax base is $18,000,000. Because the basic exclusion amount is $12,060,000 during 2022, $5,940,000 is subject to the estate tax ($18,000,000 less $12,060,000). The estate tax on that amount is $2,376,000 ($5,940,000 times .40).

## ANSWER TO QUESTION XI

(a) If Alyssa does not remarry, her applicable exclusion amount is $18,120,000. Since Jacob only used $6 million of his exclusion amount ($4 million taxable gifts plus $2 million taxable estate), he died with a deceased spousal unused amount of $6,060,000 ($12,060,000 less $6 million). Because the executor elected "portability" on Jacob's estate tax return, Alyssa's applicable exclusion amount is $18,120,000 ($12,060,000 + $6,060,000).

(b) If Alyssa remarries Zeke, her applicable exclusion amount is reduced to $14,060,000 after Zeke dies. His taxable estate is $10 million; therefore, the deceased spousal unused exclusion amount is $2,060,000 ($12,060,000 – $10 million). Under I.R.C. § 2010(b)(4), a surviving spouse is entitled to use only the deceased spousal unused exclusion amount of "the last such deceased spouse." Therefore, Alyssa can no longer use Jacob's deceased spousal unused exclusion amount, and her applicable exclusion amount is reduced by $4 million based on these facts. If Zeke had used his entire exclusion amount before he had died, Alyssa would not be entitled to take advantage of portability even though Jacob died with a deceased spousal unused amount of $6,060,000.

# Table of Cases

# Table of Internal Revenue Code Sections

# Index